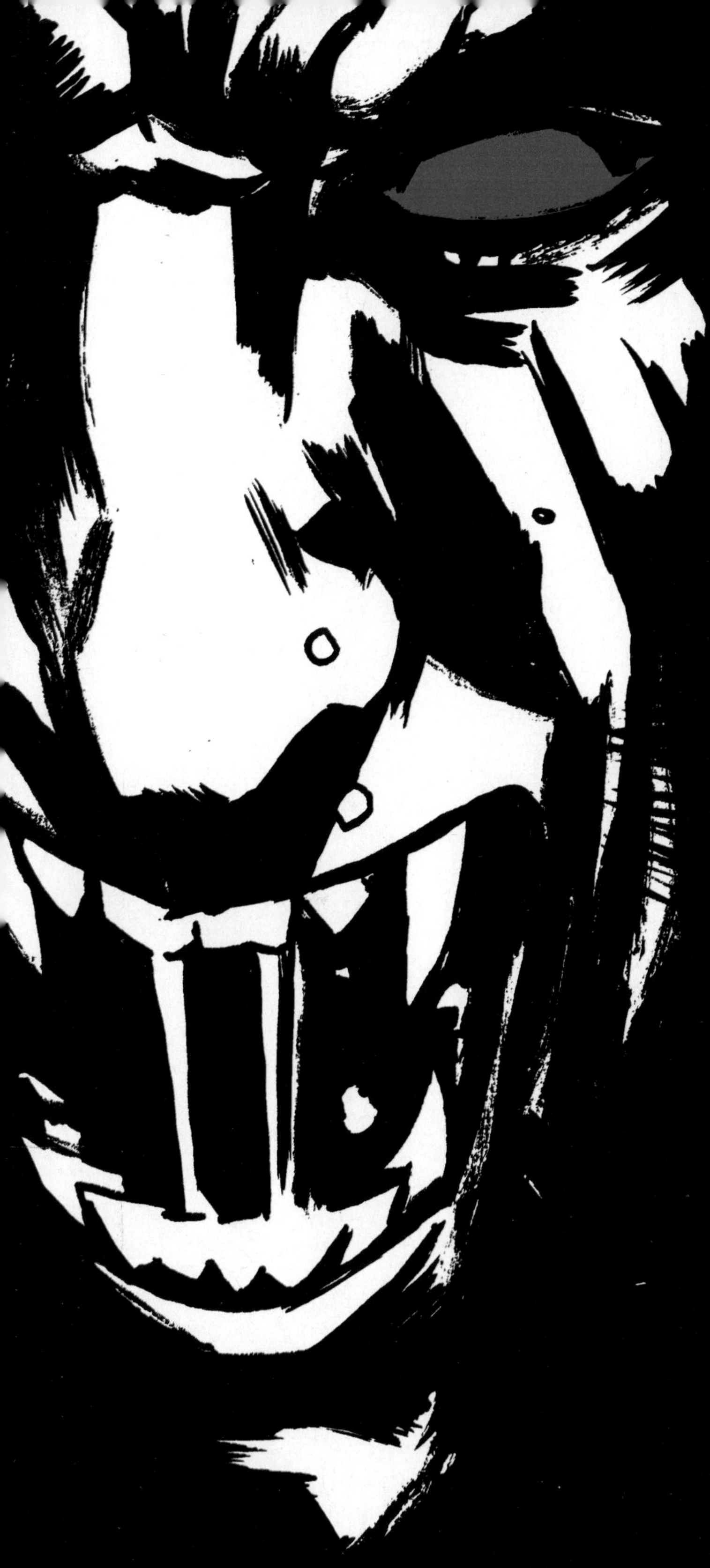

BATMAN
CREATURE OF THE NIGHT

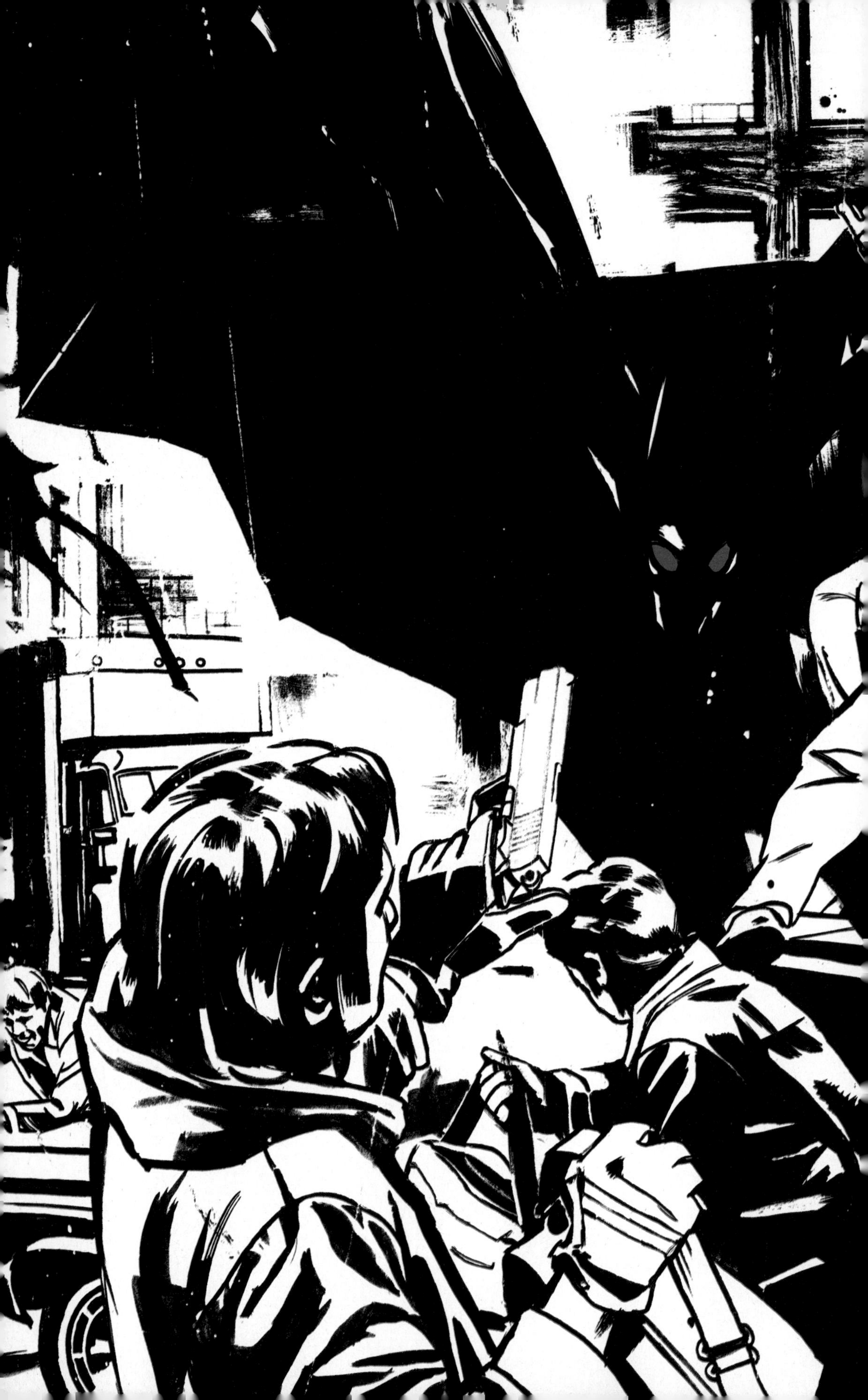

OF THE NIGHT

KURT BUSIEK
writer

JOHN PAUL LEON
artist, colorist, and cover artist

TODD KLEIN
letterer

BATMAN created by
BOB KANE with BILL FINGER

PEFC Certified
This product is from sustainably managed forests and controlled sources
PEFC
PEFC/29-31-337
www.pefc.org

DC Comics, 2900 West Alameda Ave., Burbank, CA 91505
Printed by LSC Communications, Owensville, MO, USA. 3/12/21. First Printing.
ISBN: 978-1-77950-628-3

Library of Congress Cataloging-in-Publication Data is available.

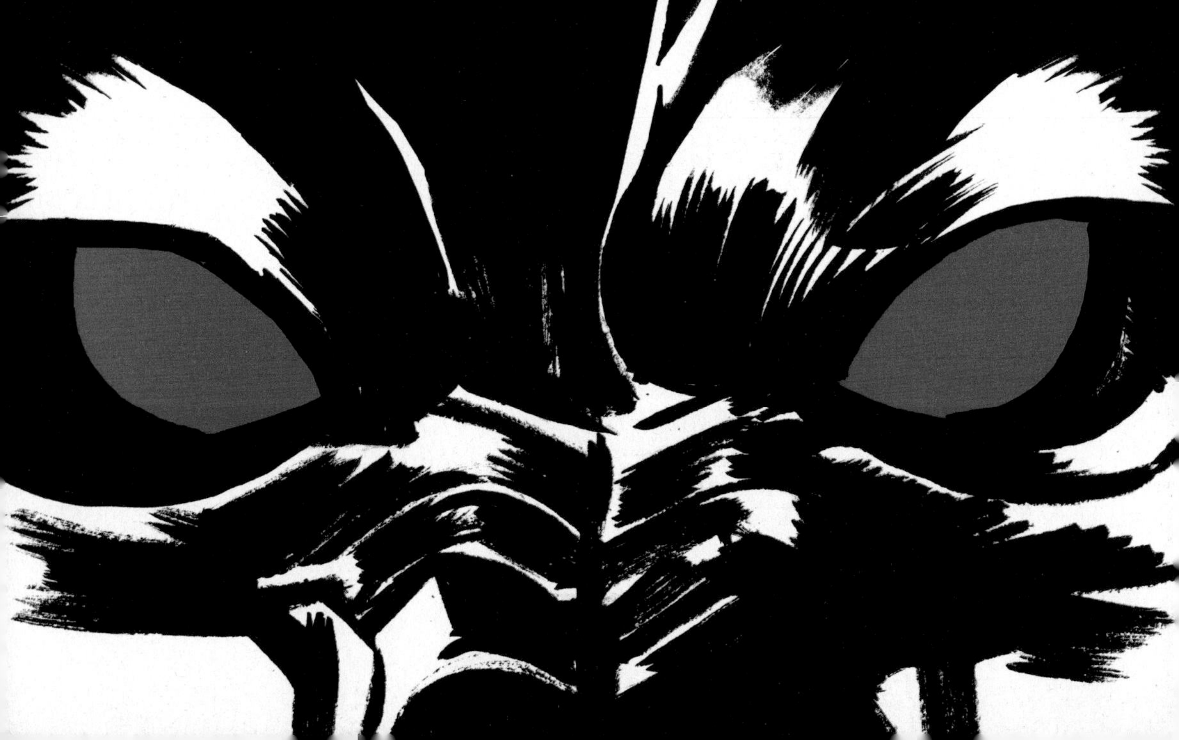

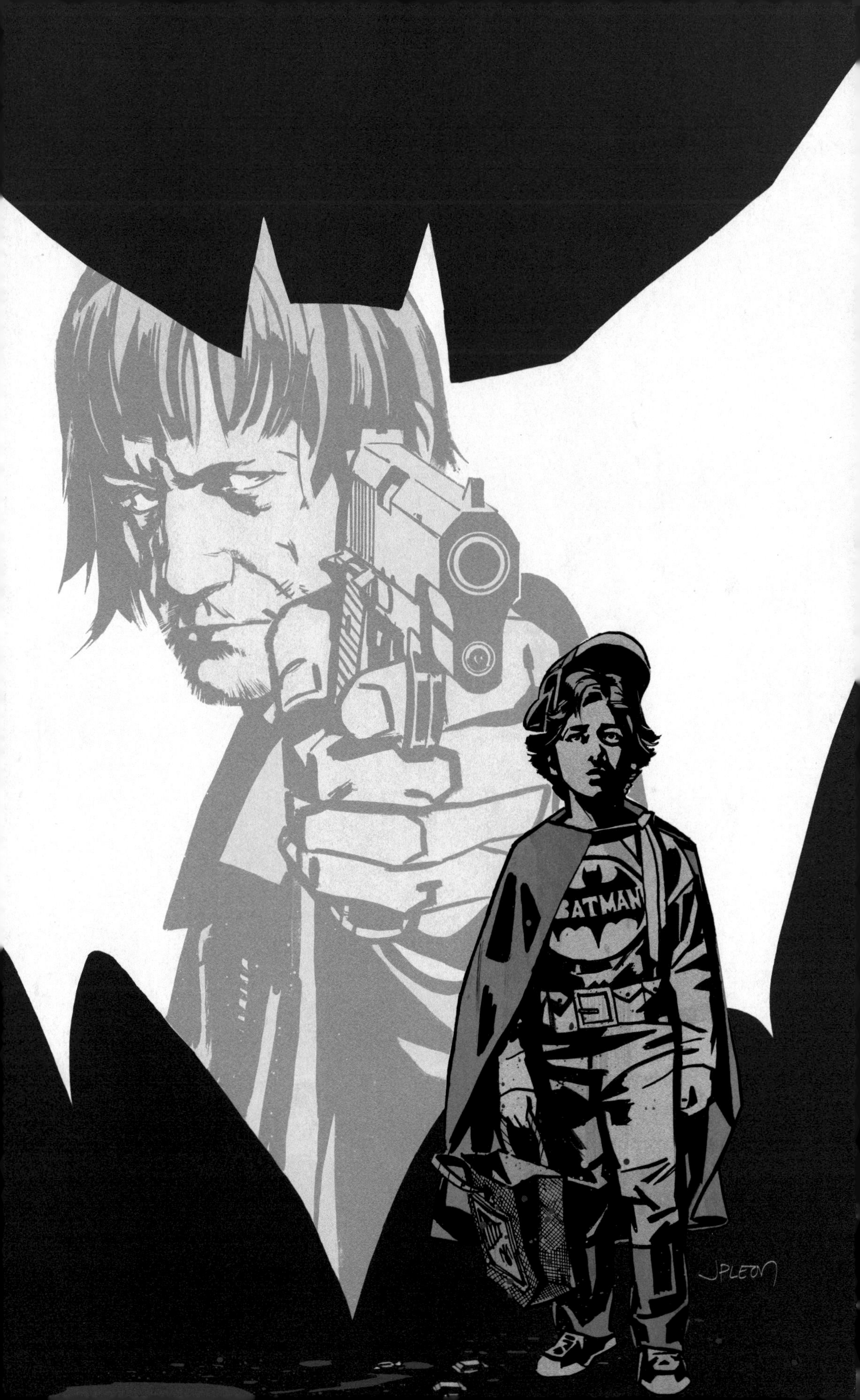
BATMAN
JPLEON

BOOK ONE: **I SHALL BECOME...**

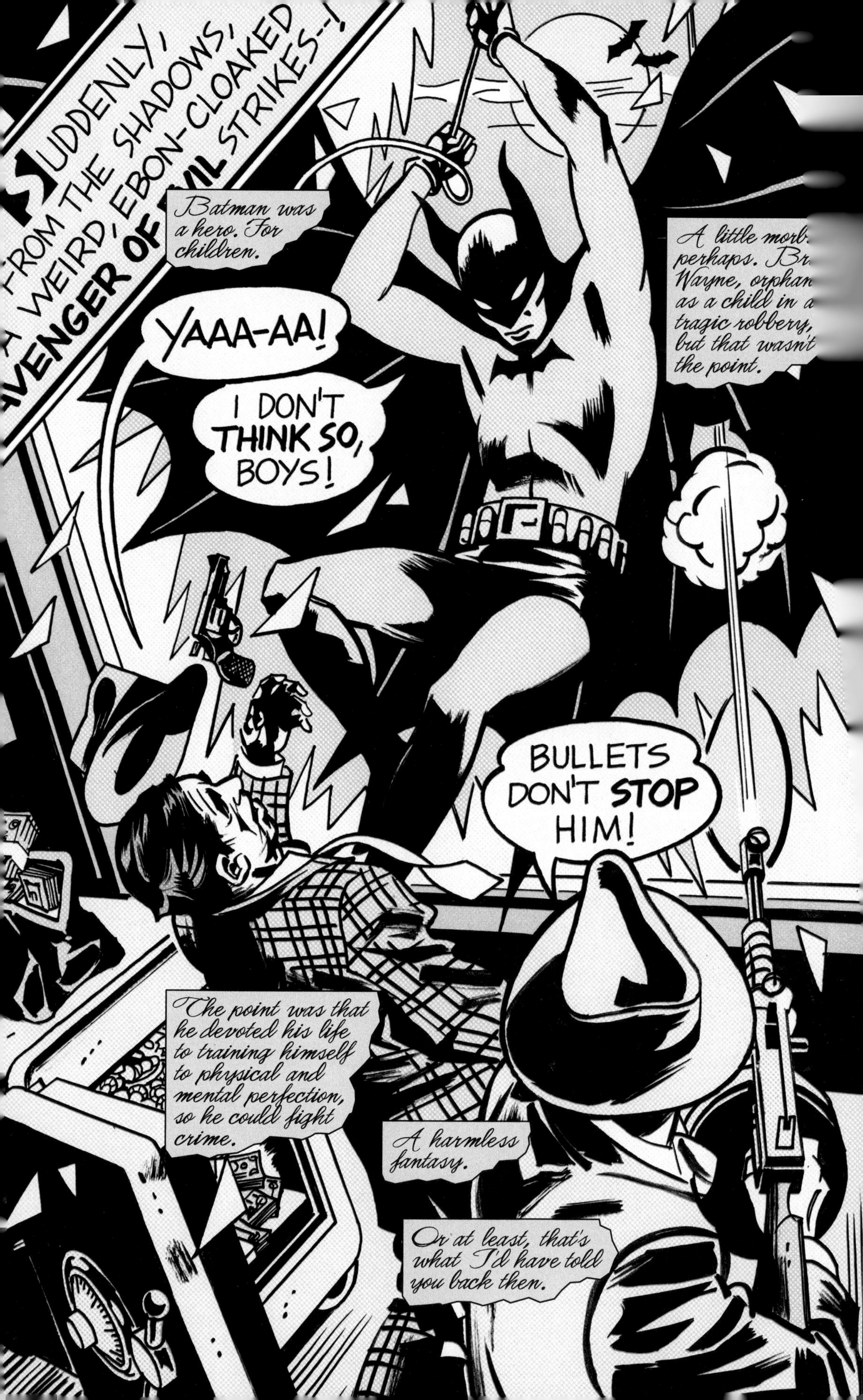

SUDDENLY, FROM THE SHADOWS, A WEIRD, EBON-CLOAKED VENGER OF VIL STRIKES--!
Batman was a hero. For children.
YAAA-AA!
I DON'T THINK SO, BOYS!
A little morb perhaps. Br Wayne, orphan as a child in a tragic robbery, but that wasn't the point.
BULLETS DON'T STOP HIM!
The point was that he devoted his life to training himself to physical and mental perfection, so he could fight crime.
A harmless fantasy.
Or at least, that's what I'd have told you back then.

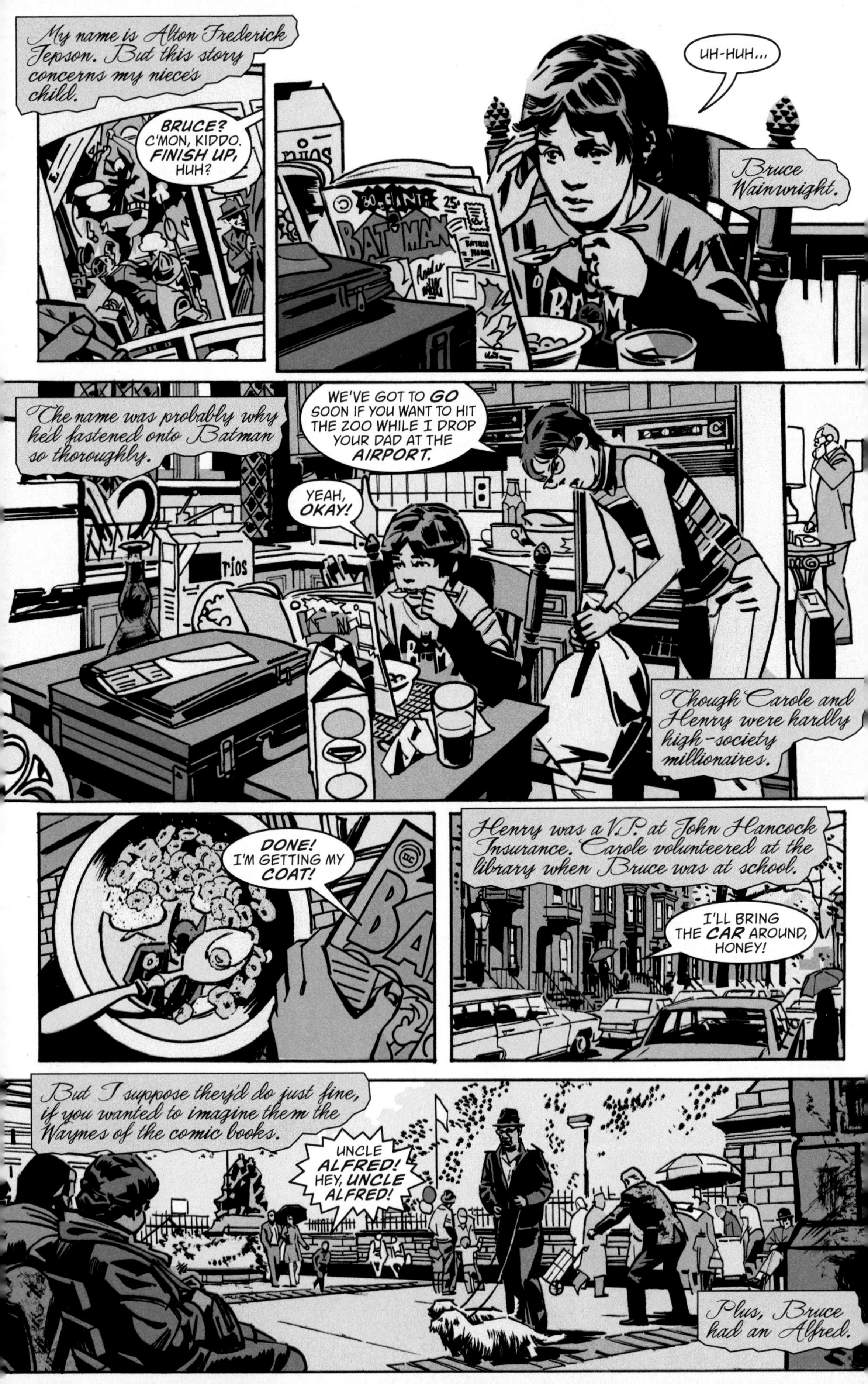

My name is Alton Frederick Jepson. But this story concerns my niece's child.
BRUCE? C'MON, KIDDO. FINISH UP, HUH?
UH-HUH...
Bruce Wainwright.
The name was probably why he'd fastened onto Batman so thoroughly.
WE'VE GOT TO GO SOON IF YOU WANT TO HIT THE ZOO WHILE I DROP YOUR DAD AT THE AIRPORT.
YEAH, OKAY!
Though Carole and Henry were hardly high-society millionaires.
DONE! I'M GETTING MY COAT!
Henry was a V.P. at John Hancock Insurance. Carole volunteered at the library when Bruce was at school.
I'LL BRING THE CAR AROUND, HONEY!
But I suppose they'd do just fine, if you wanted to imagine them the Waynes of the comic books.
UNCLE ALFRED! HEY, UNCLE ALFRED!
Plus, Bruce had an Alfred.

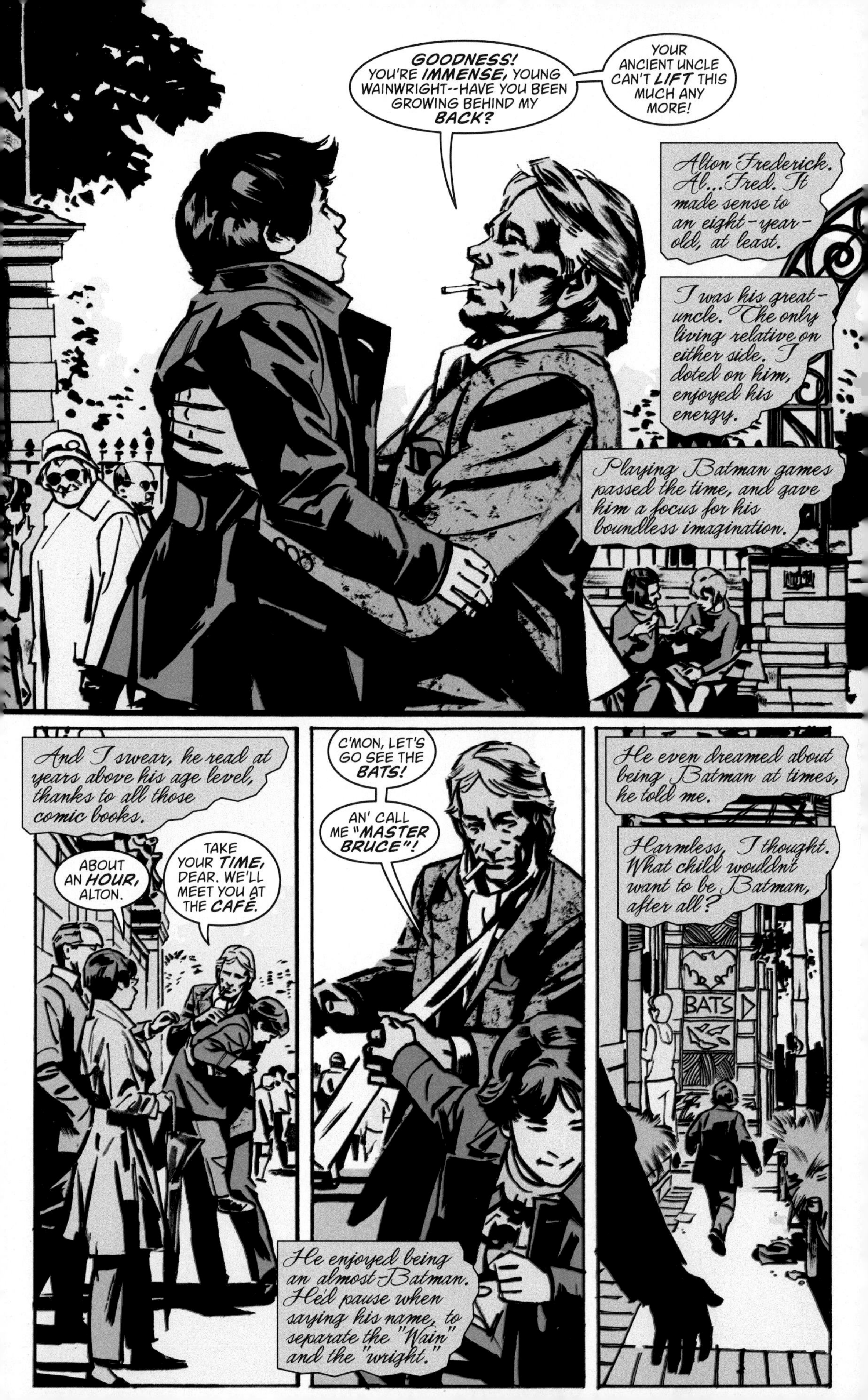
GOODNESS! YOU'RE IMMENSE, YOUNG WAINWRIGHT--HAVE YOU BEEN GROWING BEHIND MY BACK?
YOUR ANCIENT UNCLE CAN'T LIFT THIS MUCH ANY MORE!
Alton Frederick. Al...Fred. It made sense to an eight-year-old, at least.
I was his great-uncle. The only living relative on either side. I doted on him, enjoyed his energy.
Playing Batman games passed the time, and gave him a focus for his boundless imagination.
And I swear, he read at years above his age level, thanks to all those comic books.
ABOUT AN HOUR, ALTON.
TAKE YOUR TIME, DEAR. WE'LL MEET YOU AT THE CAFÉ.
C'MON, LET'S GO SEE THE BATS!
AN' CALL ME "MASTER BRUCE"!
He enjoyed being an almost-Batman. He'd pause when saying his name, to separate the "Wain" and the "wright."
He even dreamed about being Batman at times, he told me.
Harmless, I thought. What child wouldn't want to be Batman, after all?
BATS

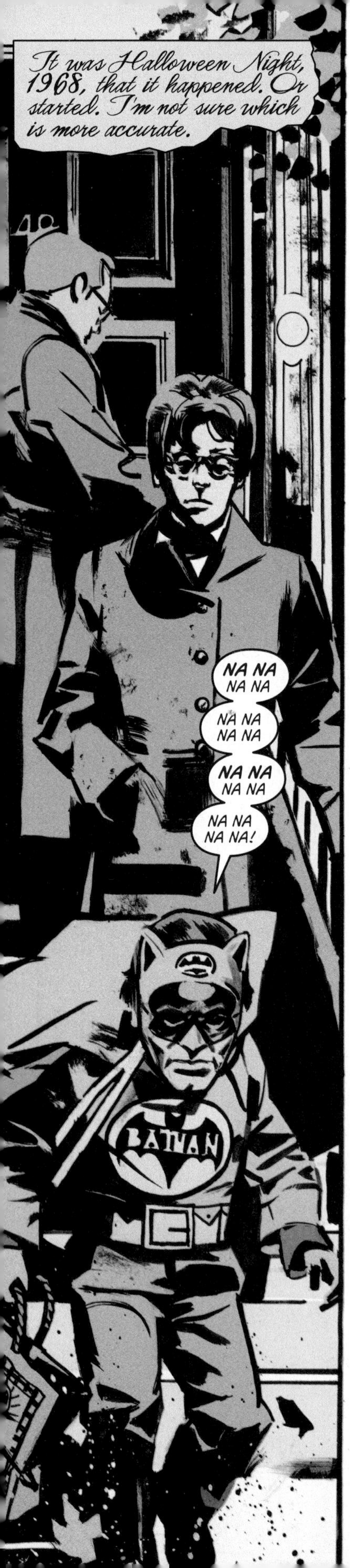
It was Halloween Night, 1968, that it happened. Or started. I'm not sure which is more accurate.
NA NA NA NA
NA NA NA NA
NA NA NA NA
NA NA NA NA!
BATMAN

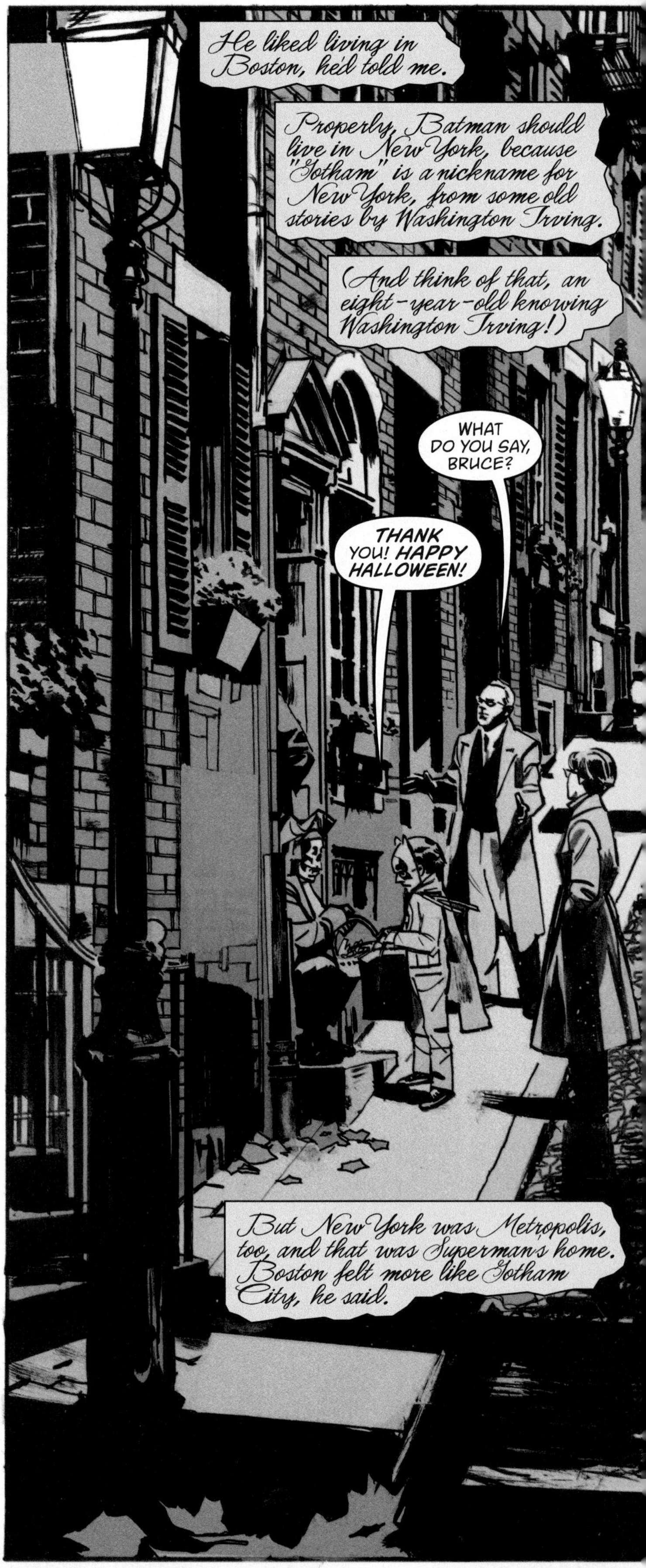
He liked living in Boston, he'd told me.
Properly, Batman should live in New York, because "Gotham" is a nickname for New York, from some old stories by Washington Irving.
(And think of that, an eight-year-old knowing Washington Irving!)
WHAT DO YOU SAY, BRUCE?
THANK YOU! HAPPY HALLOWEEN!
But New York was Metropolis, too, and that was Superman's home. Boston felt more like Gotham City, he said.

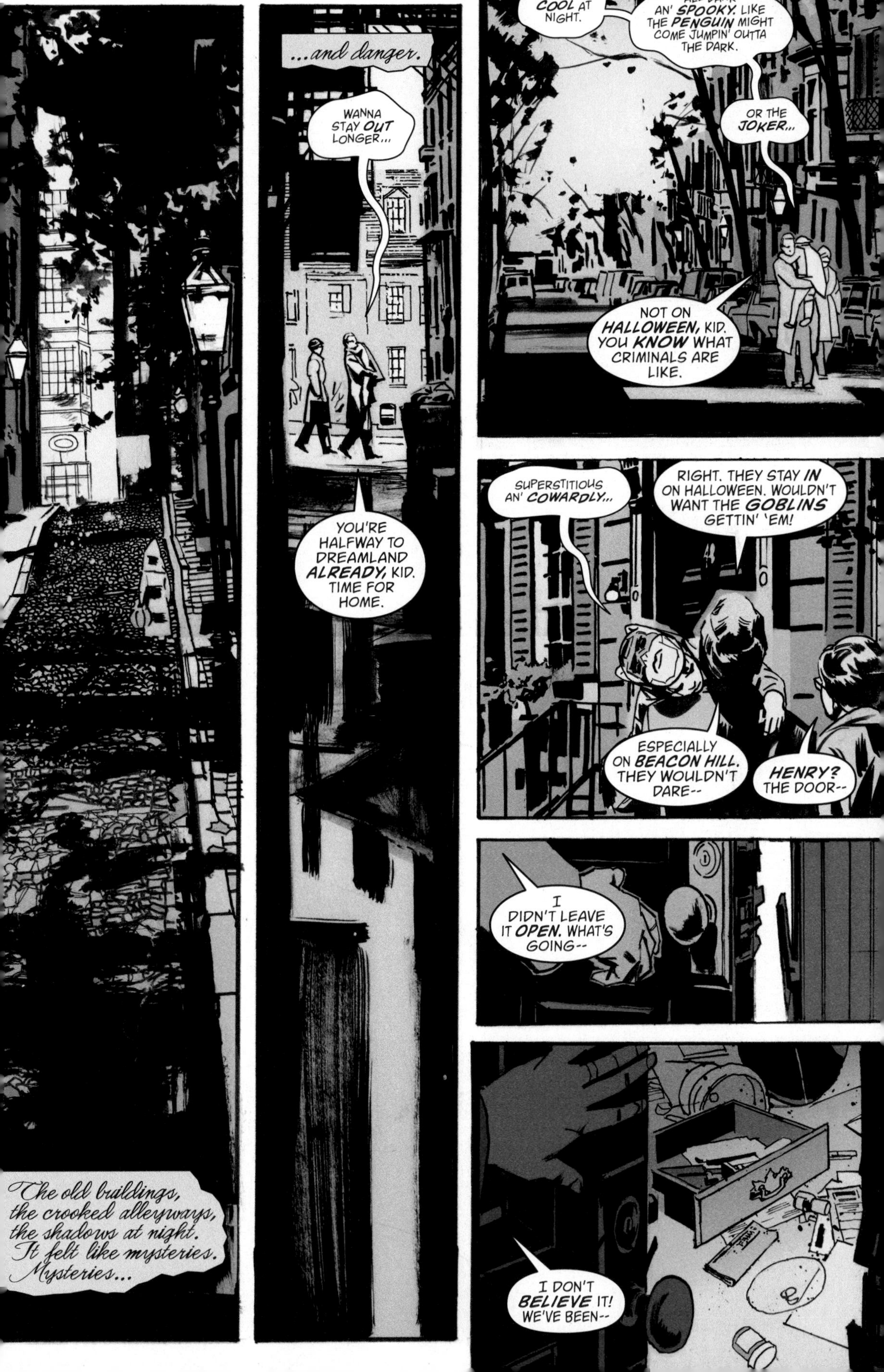
The old buildings, the crooked alleyways, the shadows at night. It felt like mysteries. Mysteries...
...and danger.
WANNA STAY OUT LONGER...
YOU'RE HALFWAY TO DREAMLAND ALREADY, KID. TIME FOR HOME.
IT'S COOL AT NIGHT.
ALL DARK AN' SPOOKY. LIKE THE PENGUIN MIGHT COME JUMPIN' OUTTA THE DARK.
OR THE JOKER...
NOT ON HALLOWEEN, KID. YOU KNOW WHAT CRIMINALS ARE LIKE.
SUPERSTITIOUS AN' COWARDLY...
RIGHT. THEY STAY IN ON HALLOWEEN. WOULDN'T WANT THE GOBLINS GETTIN' 'EM!
ESPECIALLY ON BEACON HILL. THEY WOULDN'T DARE--
HENRY? THE DOOR--
I DIDN'T LEAVE IT OPEN. WHAT'S GOING--
I DON'T BELIEVE IT! WE'VE BEEN--

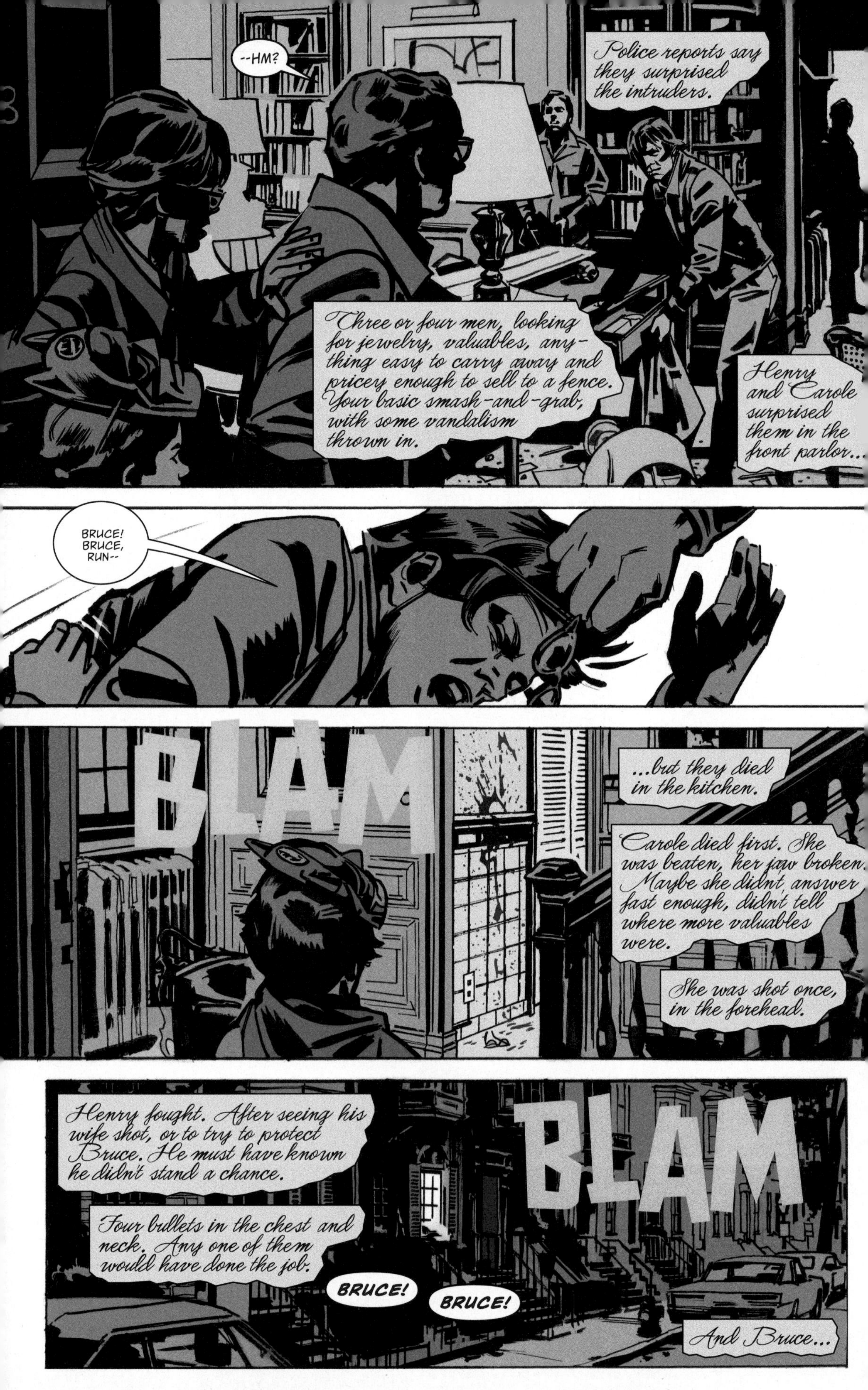
--HM?
Police reports say they surprised the intruders.
Three or four men, looking for jewelry, valuables, anything easy to carry away and pricey enough to sell to a fence. Your basic smash-and-grab, with some vandalism thrown in.
Henry and Carole surprised them in the front parlor...
BRUCE! BRUCE, RUN--
BLAM
...but they died in the kitchen.
Carole died first. She was beaten, her jaw broken. Maybe she didn't answer fast enough, didn't tell where more valuables were.
She was shot once, in the forehead.
Henry fought. After seeing his wife shot, or to try to protect Bruce. He must have known he didn't stand a chance.
BLAM
Four bullets in the chest and neck. Any one of them would have done the job.
BRUCE!
BRUCE!
And Bruce...

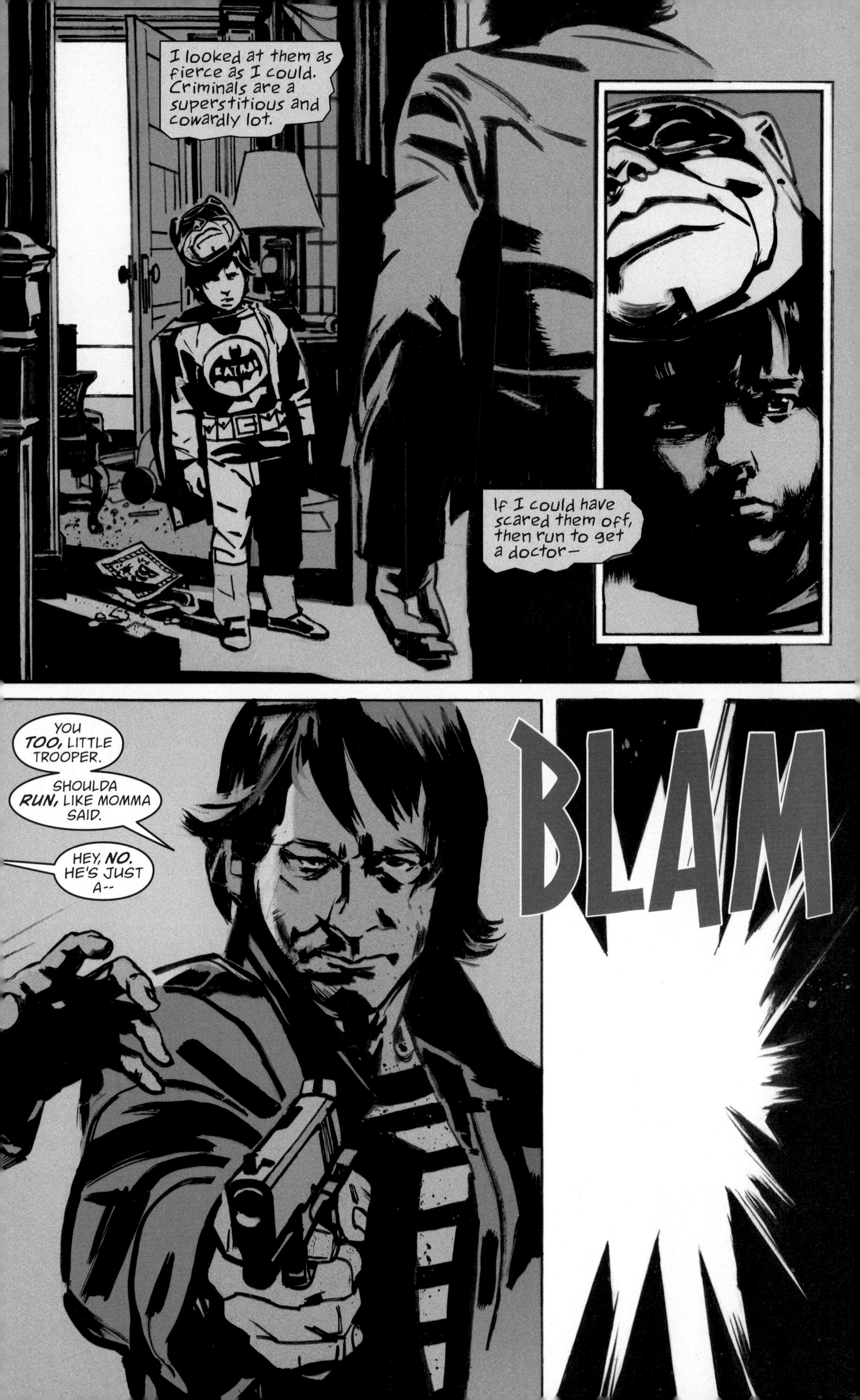
I looked at them as fierce as I could. Criminals are a superstitious and cowardly lot.
If I could have scared them off, then run to get a doctor—
YOU TOO, LITTLE TROOPER.
SHOULDA RUN, LIKE MOMMA SAID.
HEY, NO. HE'S JUST A--
BLAM

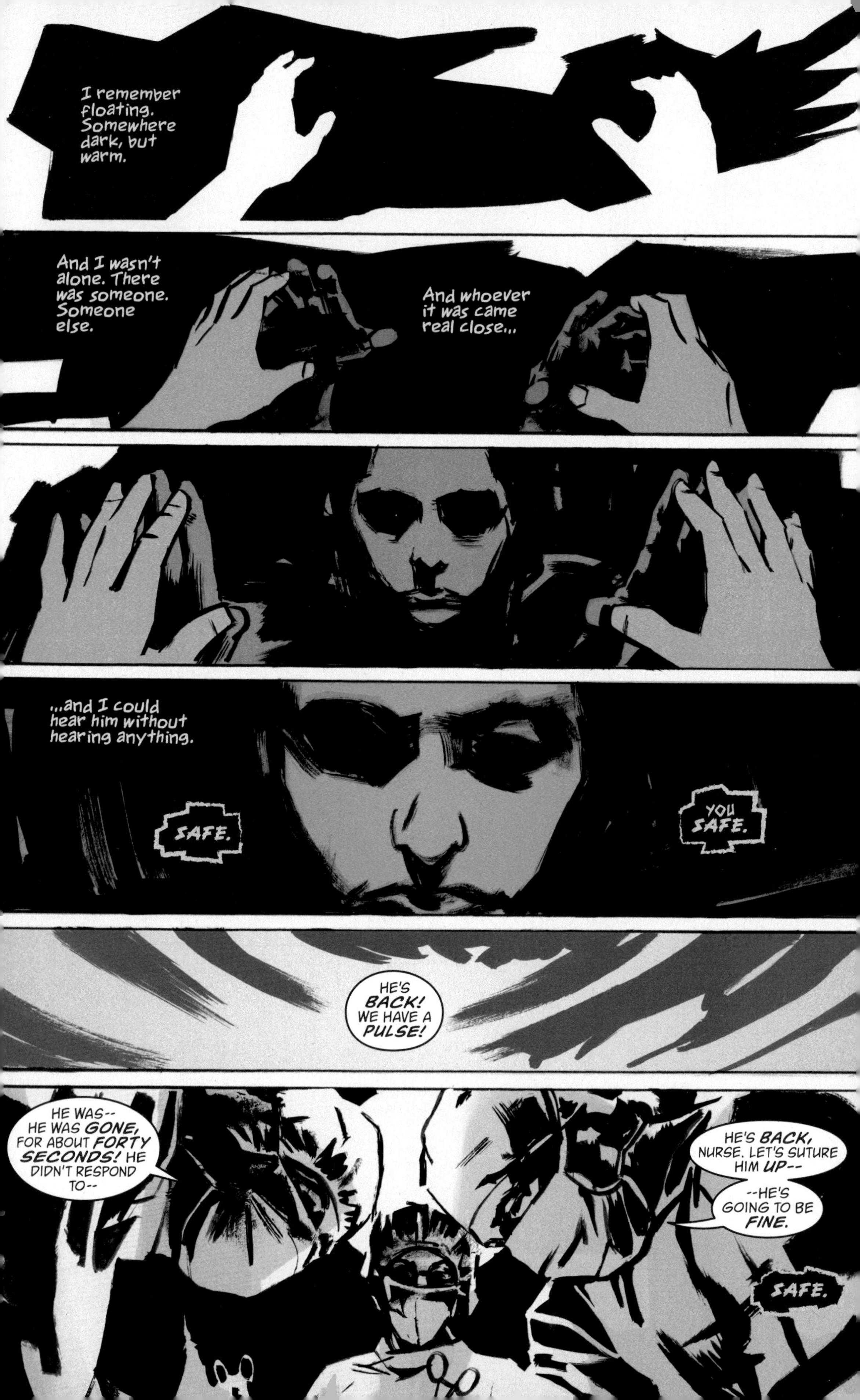
I remember floating. Somewhere dark, but warm.
And I wasn't alone. There was someone. Someone else.
And whoever it was came real close...
...and I could hear him without hearing anything.
SAFE.
YOU SAFE.
HE'S BACK! WE HAVE A PULSE!
HE WAS-- HE WAS GONE, FOR ABOUT FORTY SECONDS! HE DIDN'T RESPOND TO--
HE'S BACK, NURSE. LET'S SUTURE HIM UP--
--HE'S GOING TO BE FINE.
SAFE.

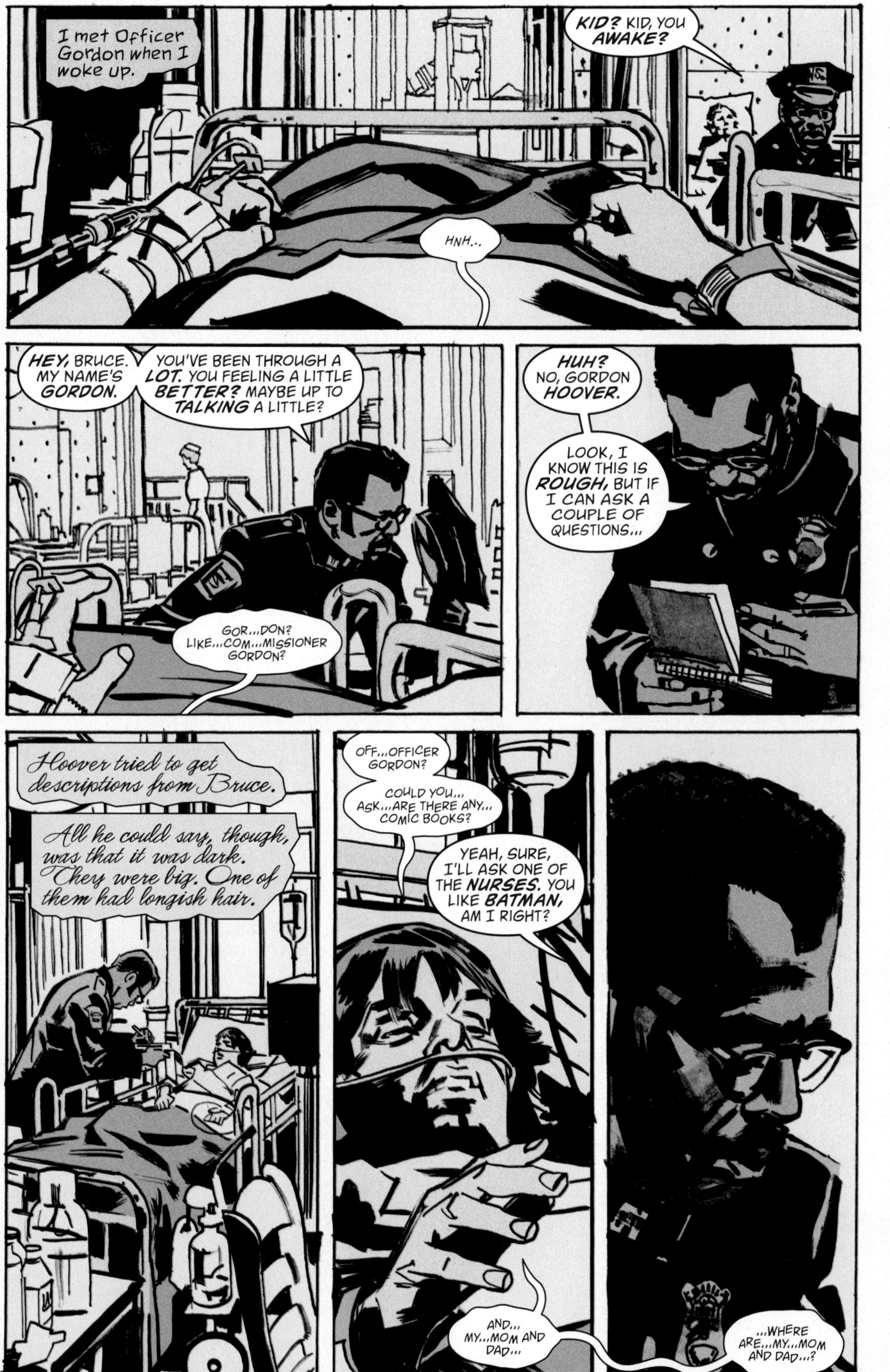
I met Officer Gordon when I woke up.
KID? KID, YOU AWAKE?
HNH...
HEY, BRUCE. MY NAME'S GORDON.
YOU'VE BEEN THROUGH A LOT. YOU FEELING A LITTLE BETTER? MAYBE UP TO TALKING A LITTLE?
GOR...DON? LIKE...COM...MISSIONER GORDON?
HUH? NO, GORDON HOOVER.
LOOK, I KNOW THIS IS ROUGH, BUT IF I CAN ASK A COUPLE OF QUESTIONS...
Hoover tried to get descriptions from Bruce.
All he could say, though, was that it was dark. They were big. One of them had longish hair.
OFF...OFFICER GORDON?
COULD YOU... ASK...ARE THERE ANY... COMIC BOOKS?
YEAH, SURE, I'LL ASK ONE OF THE NURSES. YOU LIKE BATMAN, AM I RIGHT?
AND... MY...MOM AND DAD...
...WHERE ARE...MY...MOM AND DAD...?

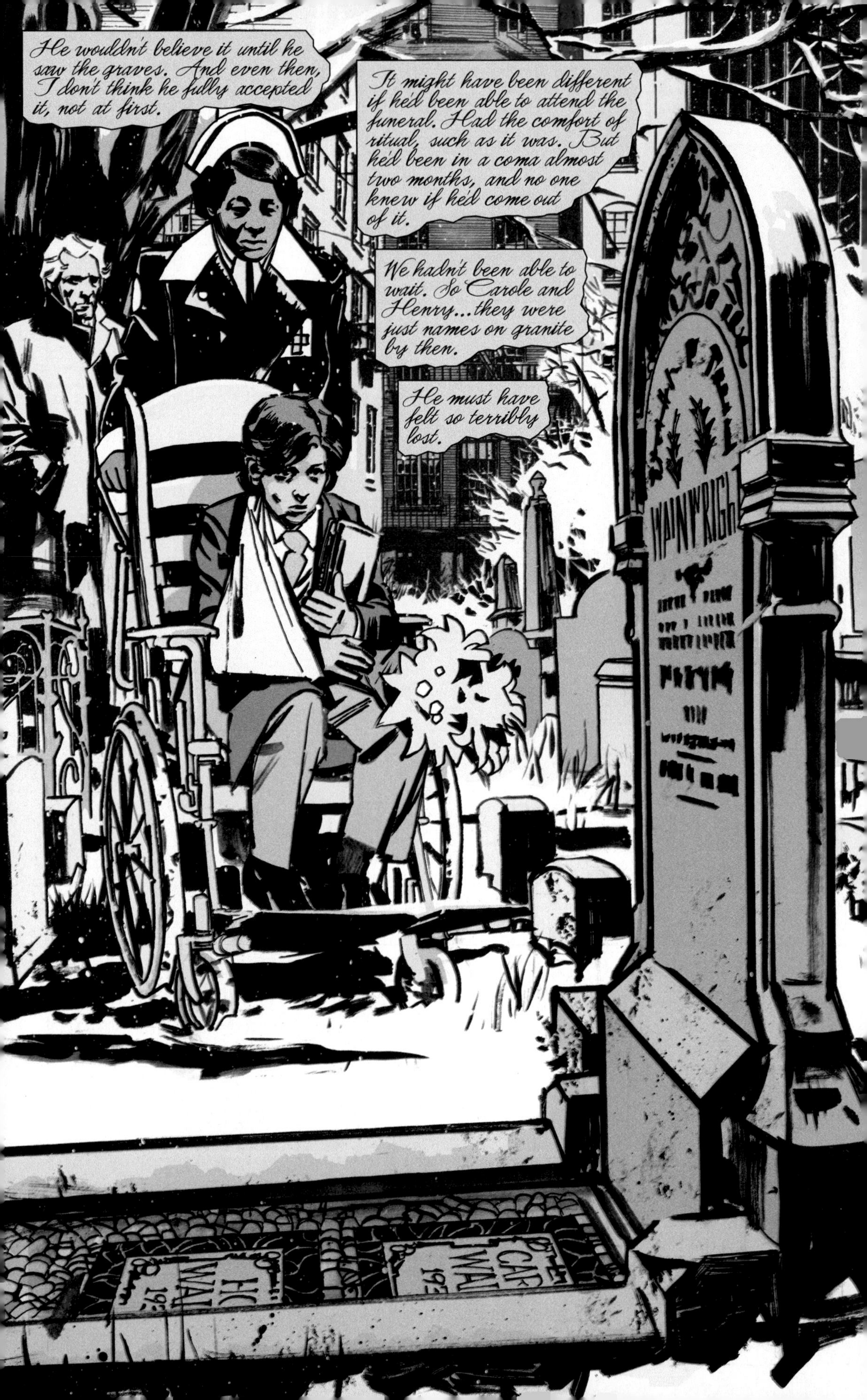
He wouldn't believe it until he saw the graves. And even then, I don't think he fully accepted it, not at first.
It might have been different if he'd been able to attend the funeral. Had the comfort of ritual, such as it was. But he'd been in a coma almost two months, and no one knew if he'd come out of it.
We hadn't been able to wait. So Carole and Henry...they were just names on granite by then.
He must have felt so terribly lost.

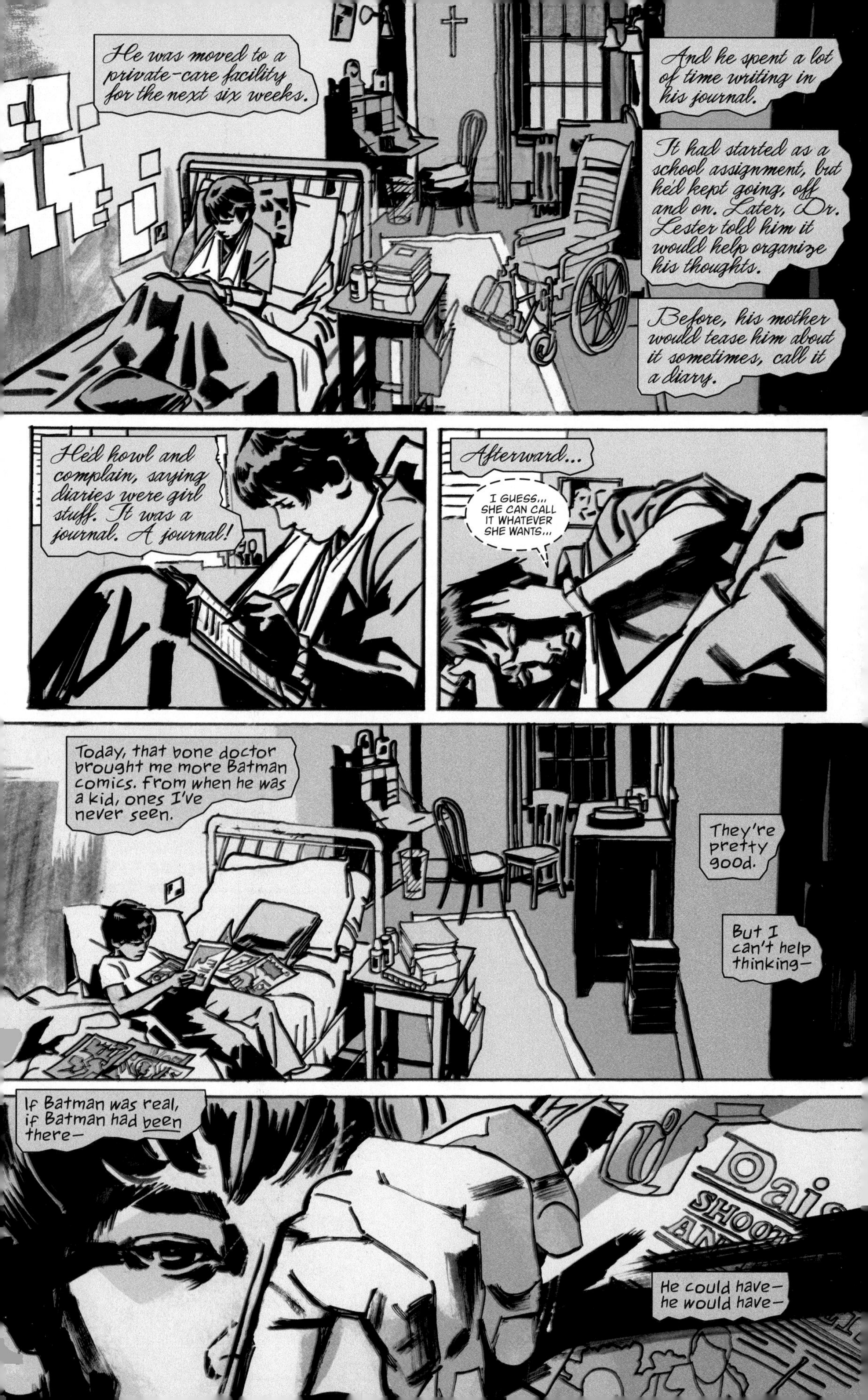
He was moved to a private-care facility for the next six weeks.
And he spent a lot of time writing in his journal.
It had started as a school assignment, but he'd kept going, off and on. Later, Dr. Lester told him it would help organize his thoughts.
Before, his mother would tease him about it sometimes, call it a diary.
He'd howl and complain, saying diaries were girl stuff. It was a journal. A journal!
Afterward...
I GUESS... SHE CAN CALL IT WHATEVER SHE WANTS...
Today, that bone doctor brought me more Batman comics. From when he was a kid, ones I've never seen.
They're pretty good.
But I can't help thinking—
If Batman was real, if Batman had been there—
He could have—
he would have—

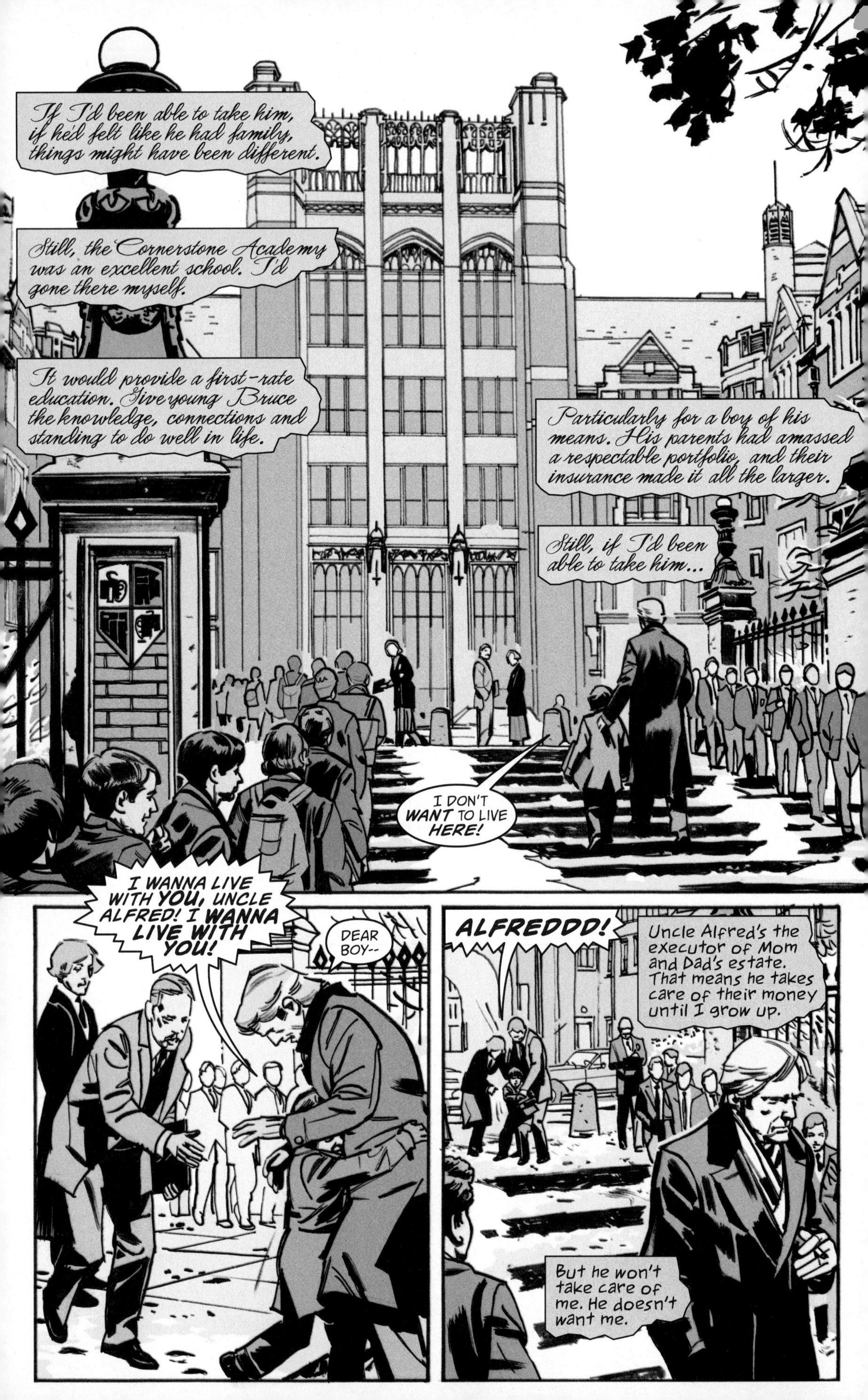

If I'd been able to take him, if he'd felt like he had family, things might have been different.
Still, the Cornerstone Academy was an excellent school. I'd gone there myself.
It would provide a first-rate education. Give young Bruce the knowledge, connections and standing to do well in life.
Particularly for a boy of his means. His parents had amassed a respectable portfolio, and their insurance made it all the larger.
Still, if I'd been able to take him...
I DON'T WANT TO LIVE HERE!
I WANNA LIVE WITH YOU, UNCLE ALFRED! I WANNA LIVE WITH YOU!
DEAR BOY--
ALFREDDD!
Uncle Alfred's the executor of Mom and Dad's estate. That means he takes care of their money until I grow up.
But he won't take care of me. He doesn't want me.

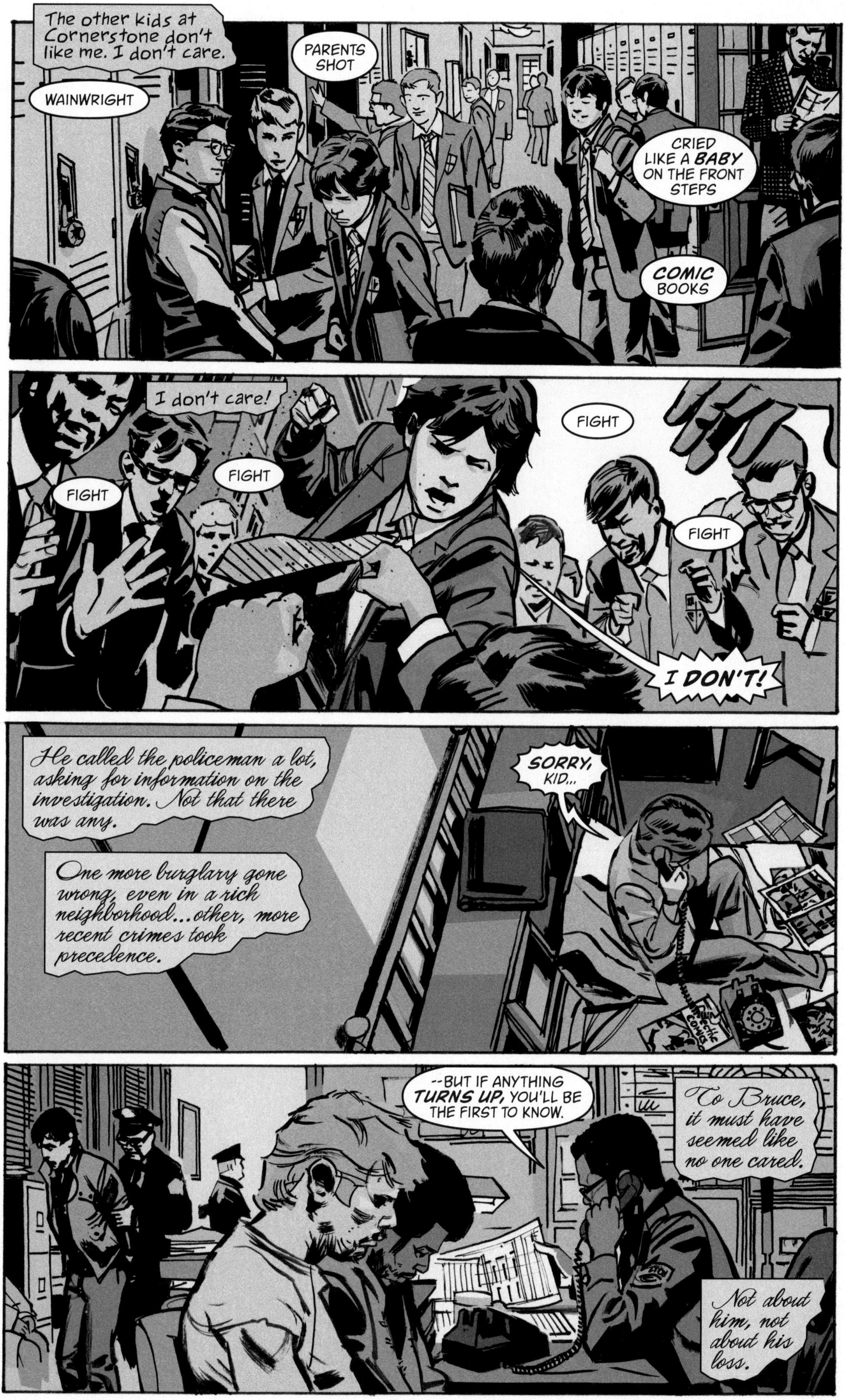
The other kids at Cornerstone don't like me. I don't care.
WAINWRIGHT
PARENTS SHOT
CRIED LIKE A BABY ON THE FRONT STEPS
COMIC BOOKS
I don't care!
FIGHT
FIGHT
FIGHT
FIGHT
I DON'T!
He called the policeman a lot, asking for information on the investigation. Not that there was any.
One more burglary gone wrong, even in a rich neighborhood...other, more recent crimes took precedence.
SORRY, KID...
--BUT IF ANYTHING TURNS UP, YOU'LL BE THE FIRST TO KNOW.
To Bruce, it must have seemed like no one cared.
Not about him, not about his loss.

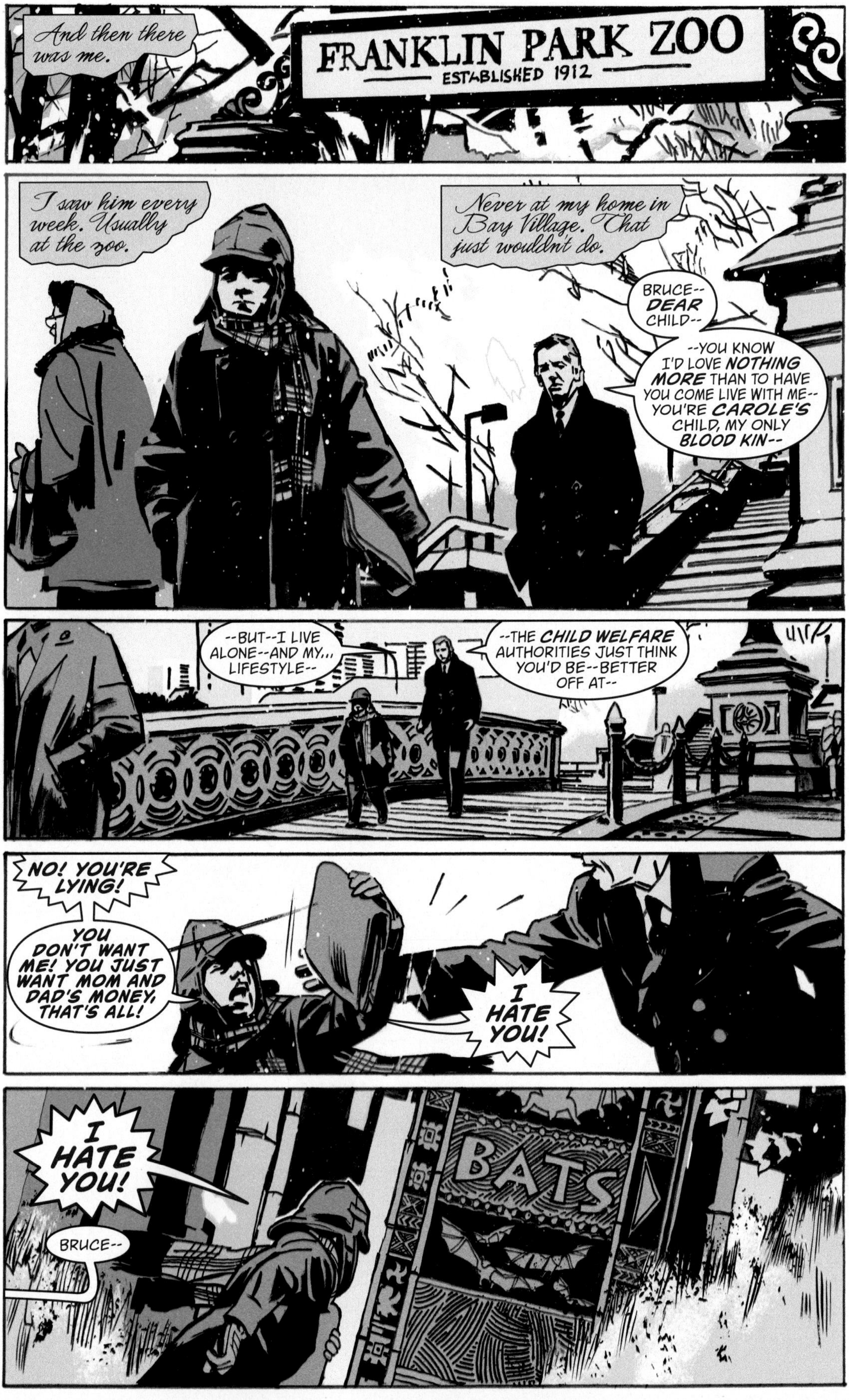
And then there was me.
FRANKLIN PARK ZOO
ESTABLISHED 1912
I saw him every week. Usually at the zoo.
Never at my home in Bay Village. That just wouldn't do.
BRUCE-- DEAR CHILD--
--YOU KNOW I'D LOVE NOTHING MORE THAN TO HAVE YOU COME LIVE WITH ME-- YOU'RE CAROLE'S CHILD, MY ONLY BLOOD KIN--
--BUT--I LIVE ALONE--AND MY... LIFESTYLE--
--THE CHILD WELFARE AUTHORITIES JUST THINK YOU'D BE--BETTER OFF AT--
NO! YOU'RE LYING!
YOU DON'T WANT ME! YOU JUST WANT MOM AND DAD'S MONEY, THAT'S ALL!
I HATE YOU!
I HATE YOU!
BATS
BRUCE--

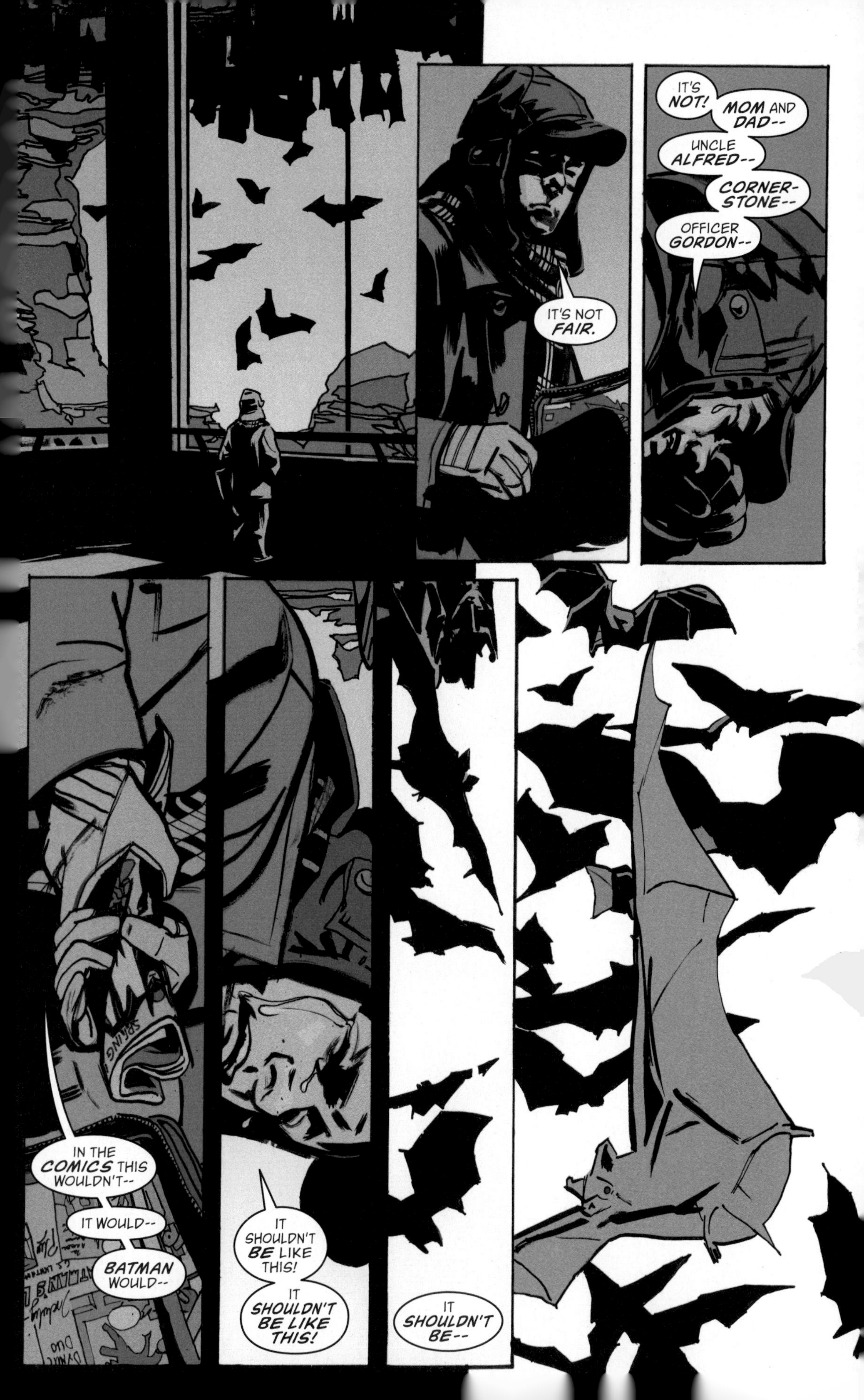
IT'S NOT FAIR.
IT'S NOT!
MOM AND DAD--
UNCLE ALFRED--
CORNER-STONE--
OFFICER GORDON--
IN THE COMICS THIS WOULDN'T--
IT WOULD--
BATMAN WOULD--
IT SHOULDN'T BE LIKE THIS!
IT SHOULDN'T BE LIKE THIS!
IT SHOULDN'T BE--

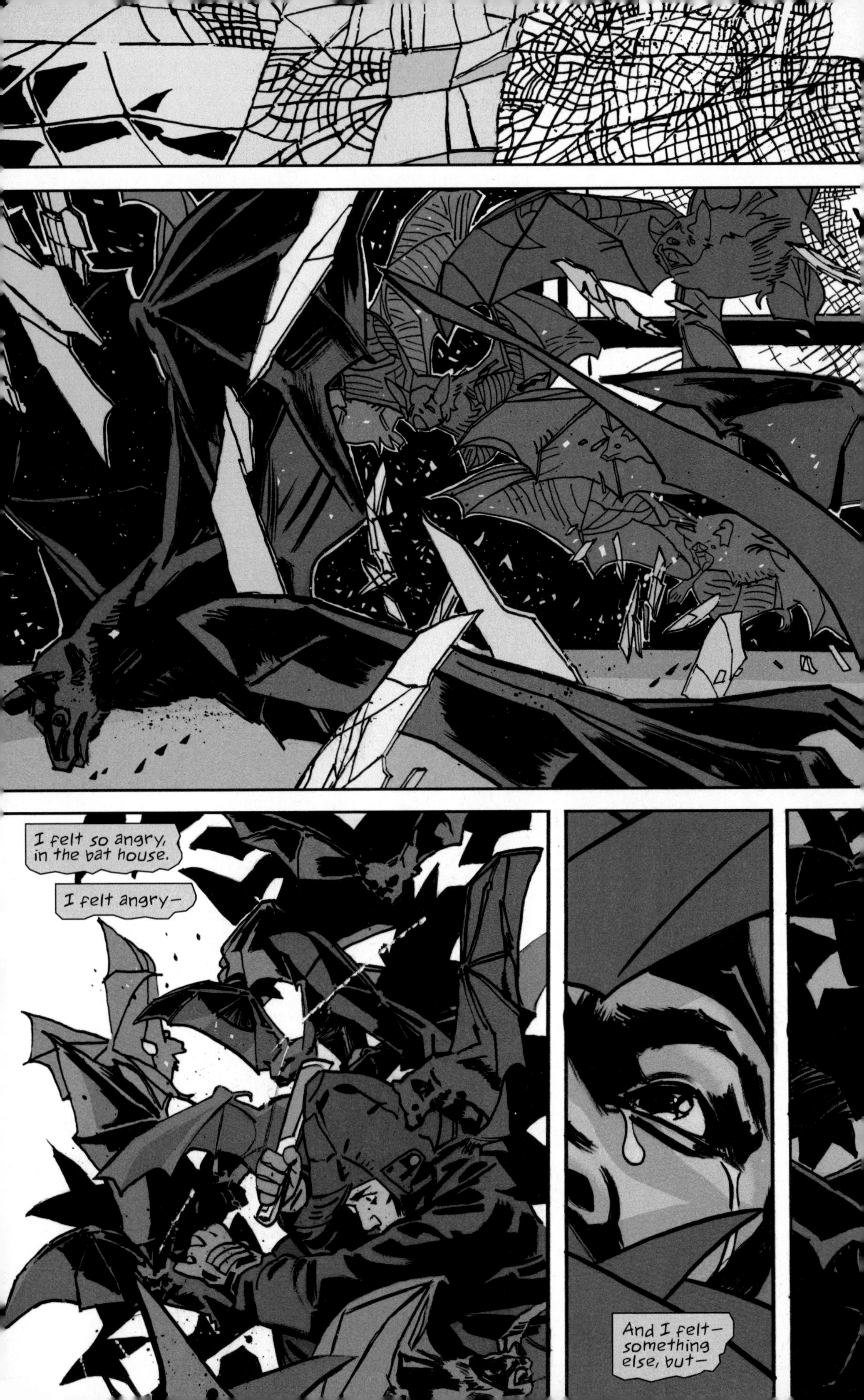

I felt so angry, in the bat house.
I felt angry—
And I felt— something else, but—

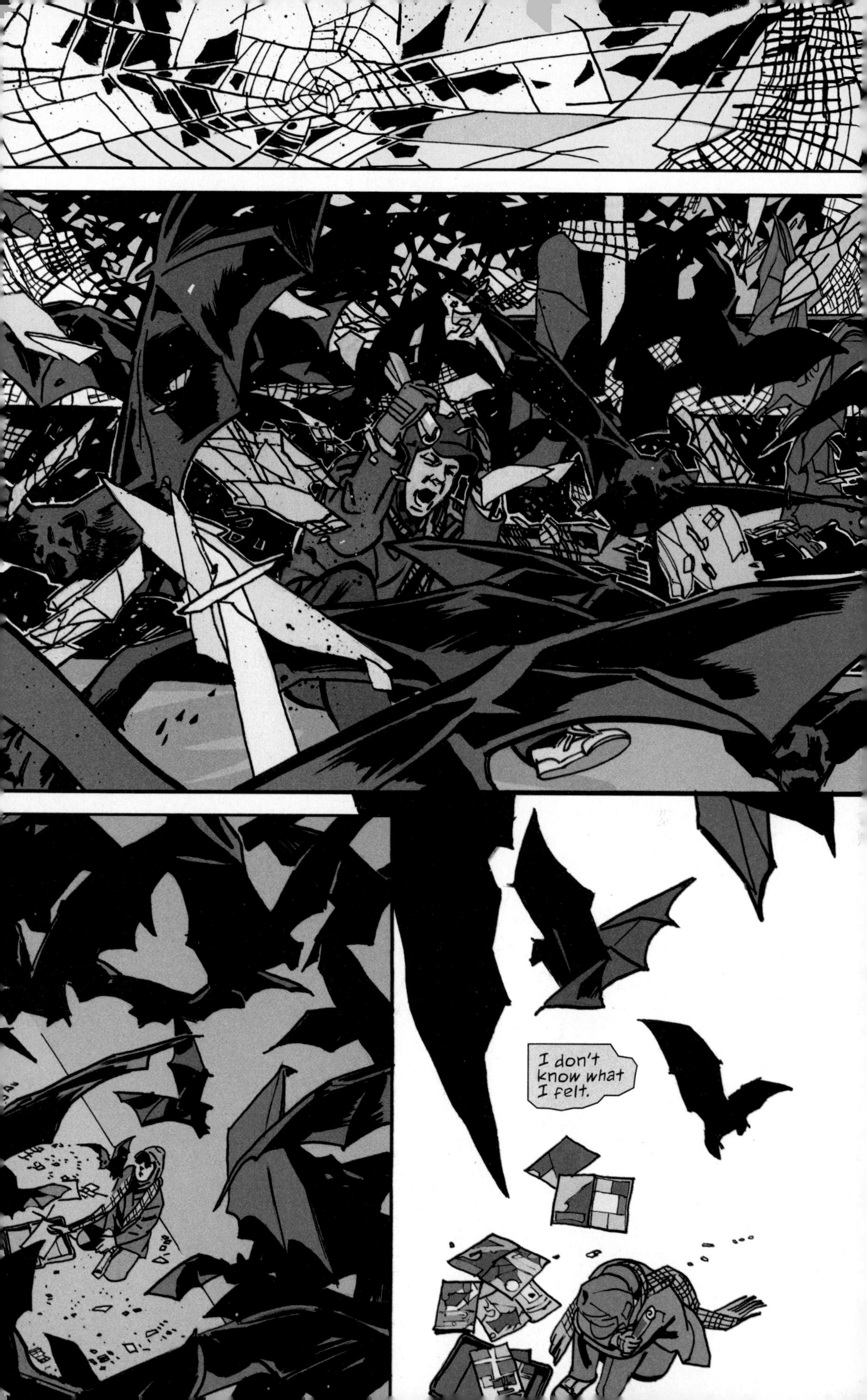
I don't know what I felt.

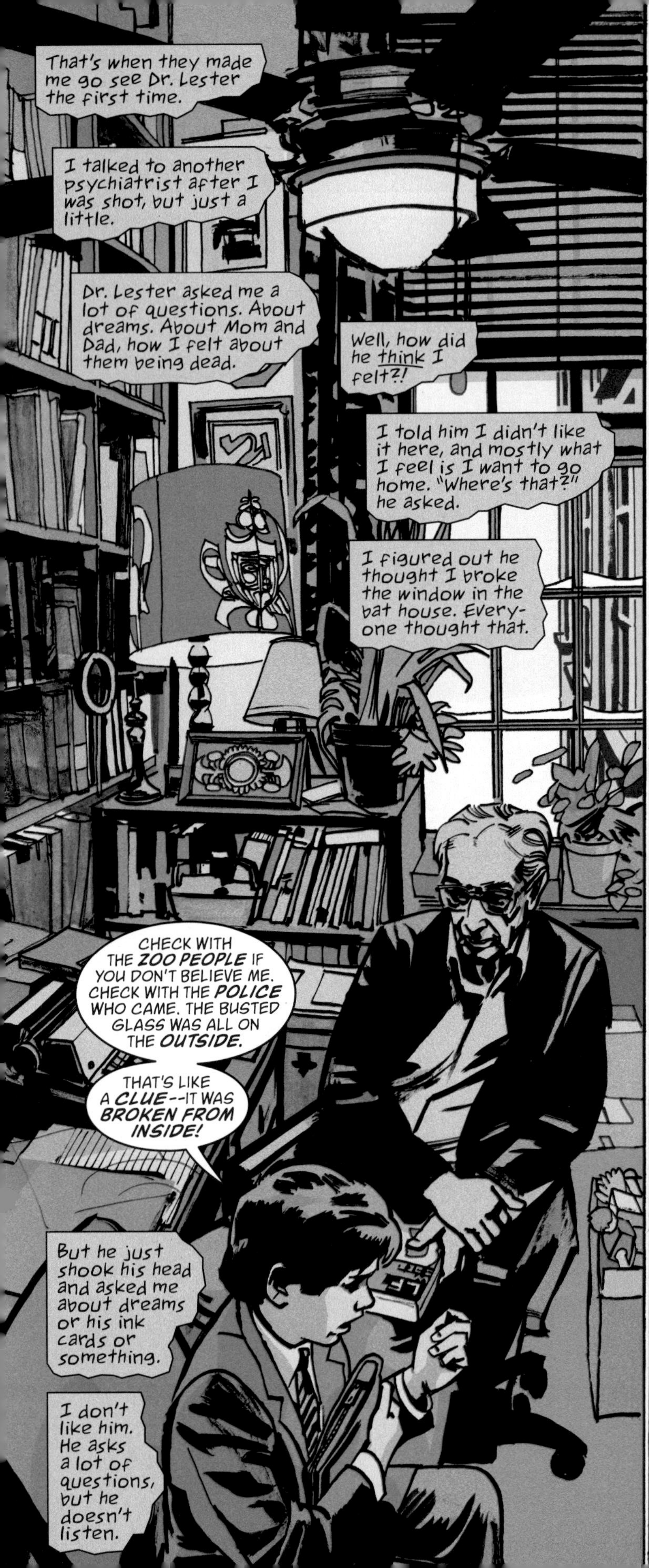
That's when they made me go see Dr. Lester the first time.
I talked to another psychiatrist after I was shot, but just a little.
Dr. Lester asked me a lot of questions. About dreams. About Mom and Dad, how I felt about them being dead.
Well, how did he think I felt?!
I told him I didn't like it here, and mostly what I feel is I want to go home. "Where's that?" he asked.
I figured out he thought I broke the window in the bat house. Everyone thought that.
CHECK WITH THE ZOO PEOPLE IF YOU DON'T BELIEVE ME. CHECK WITH THE POLICE WHO CAME. THE BUSTED GLASS WAS ALL ON THE OUTSIDE.
THAT'S LIKE A CLUE--IT WAS BROKEN FROM INSIDE!
But he just shook his head and asked me about dreams or his ink cards or something.
I don't like him. He asks a lot of questions, but he doesn't listen.

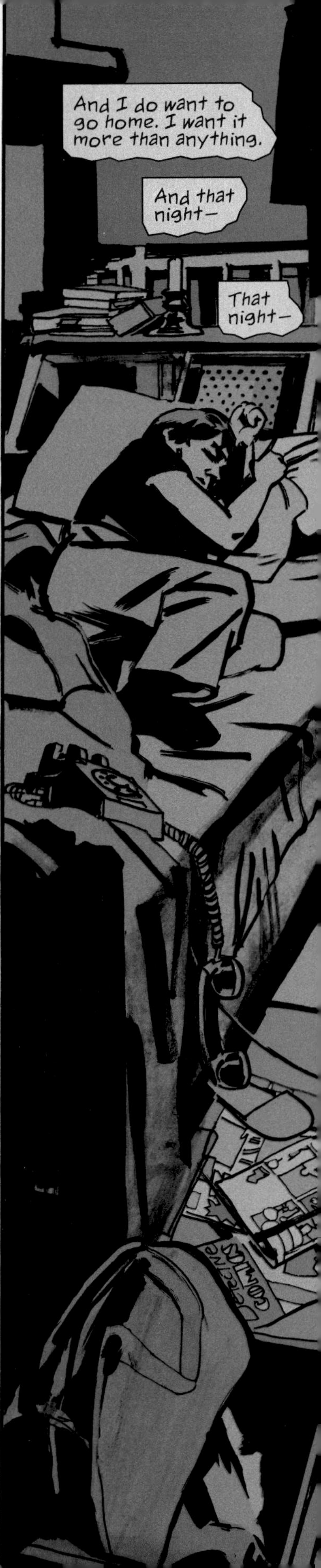
And I do want to go home. I want it more than anything.
And that night—
That night—

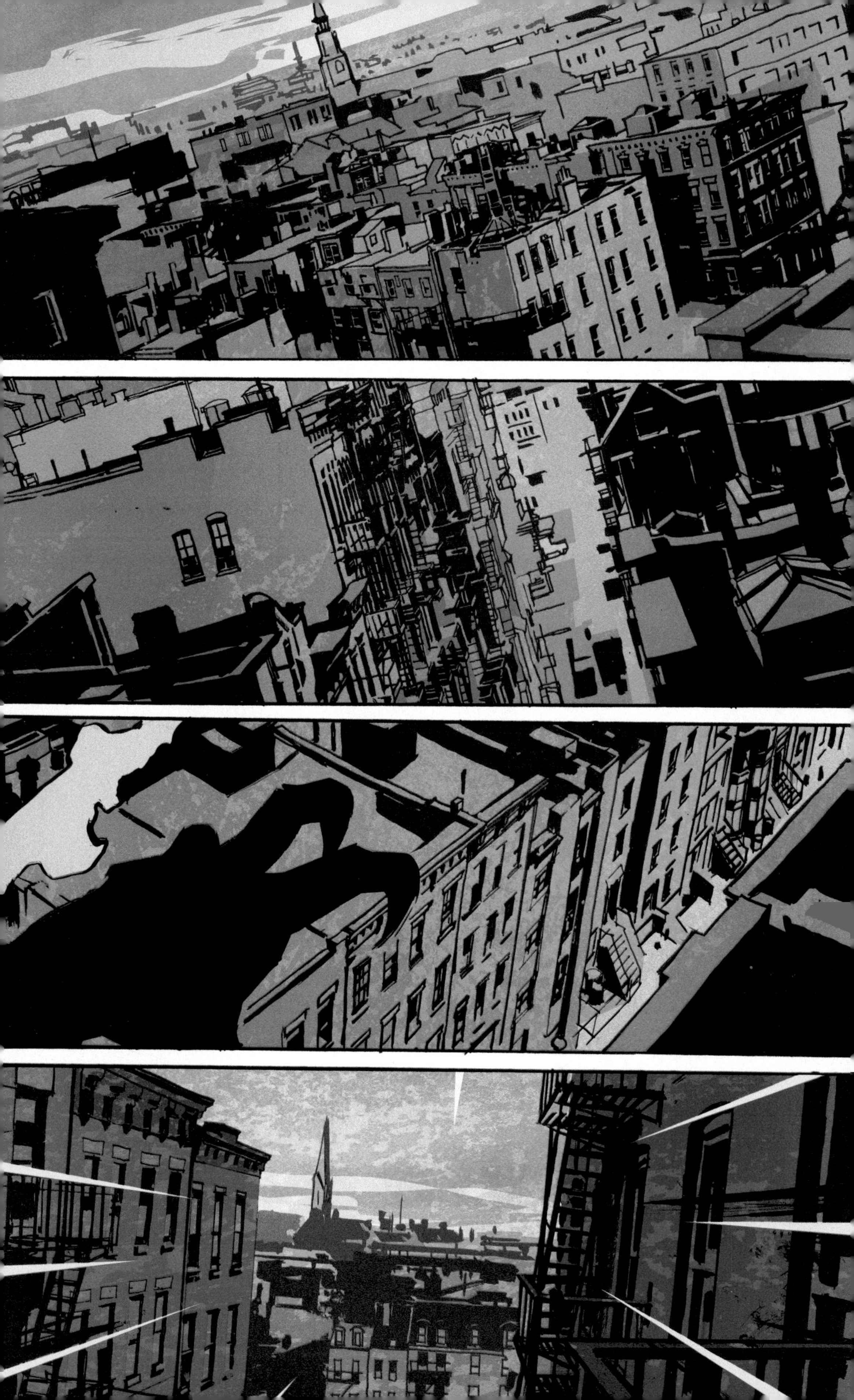

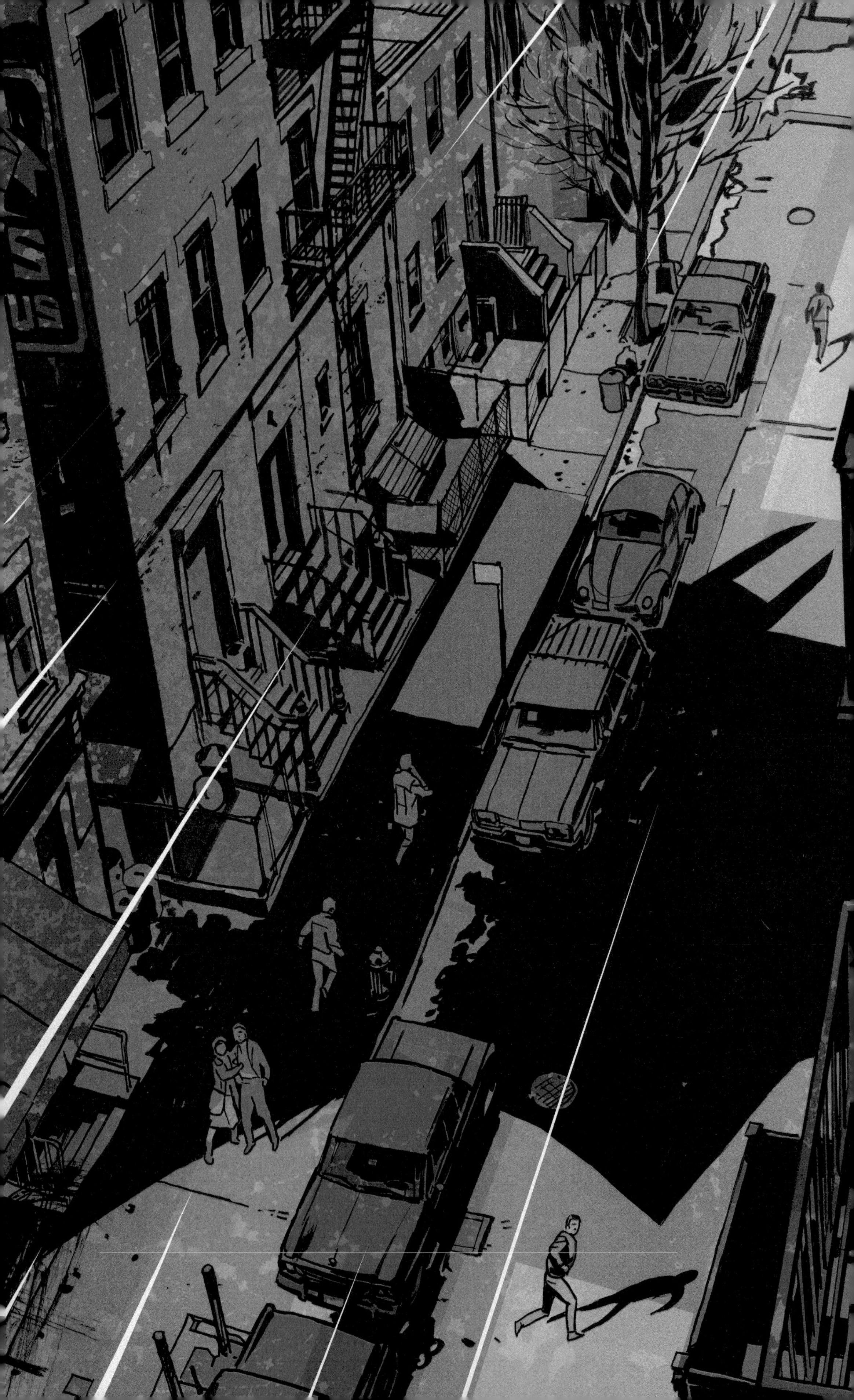

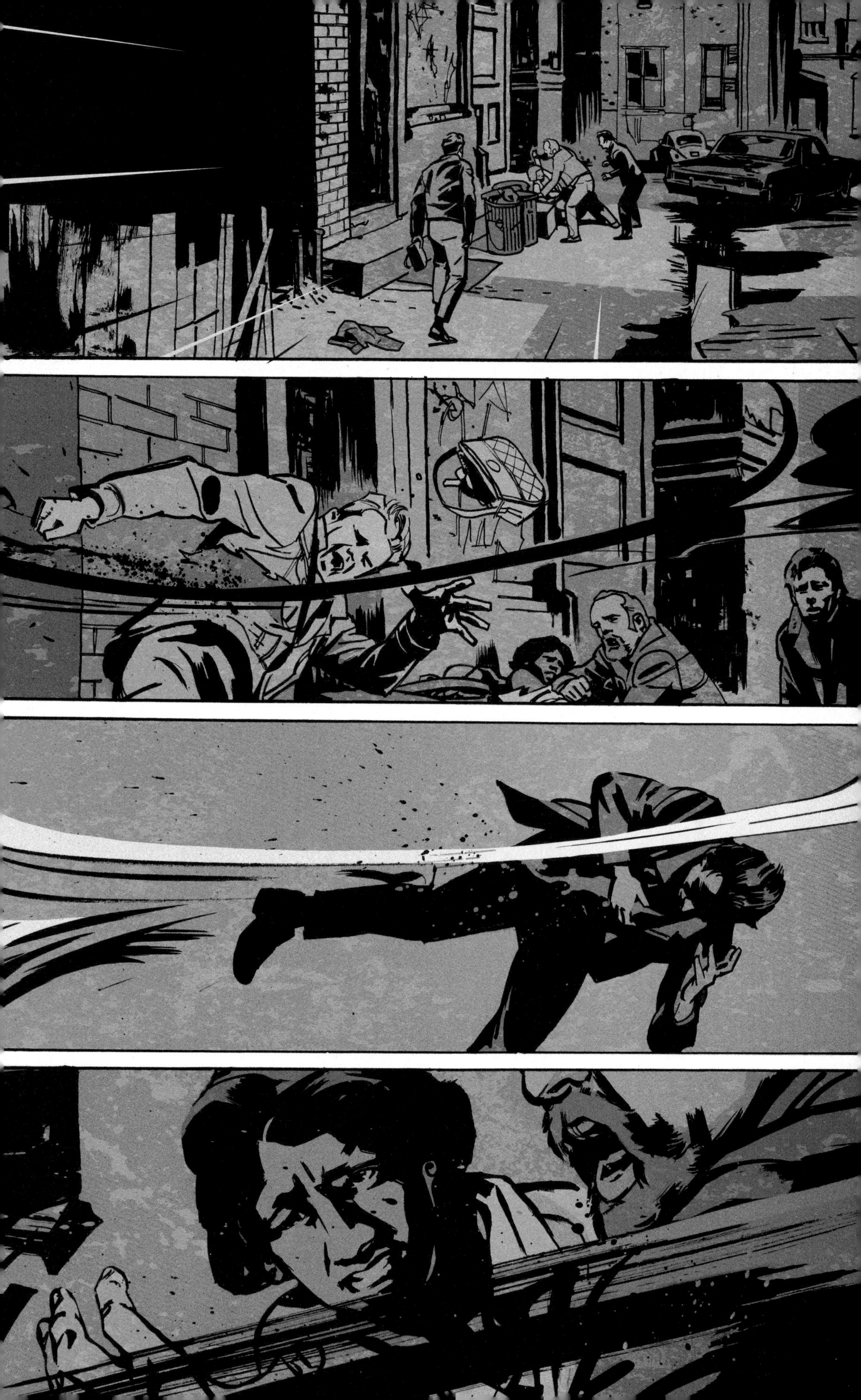

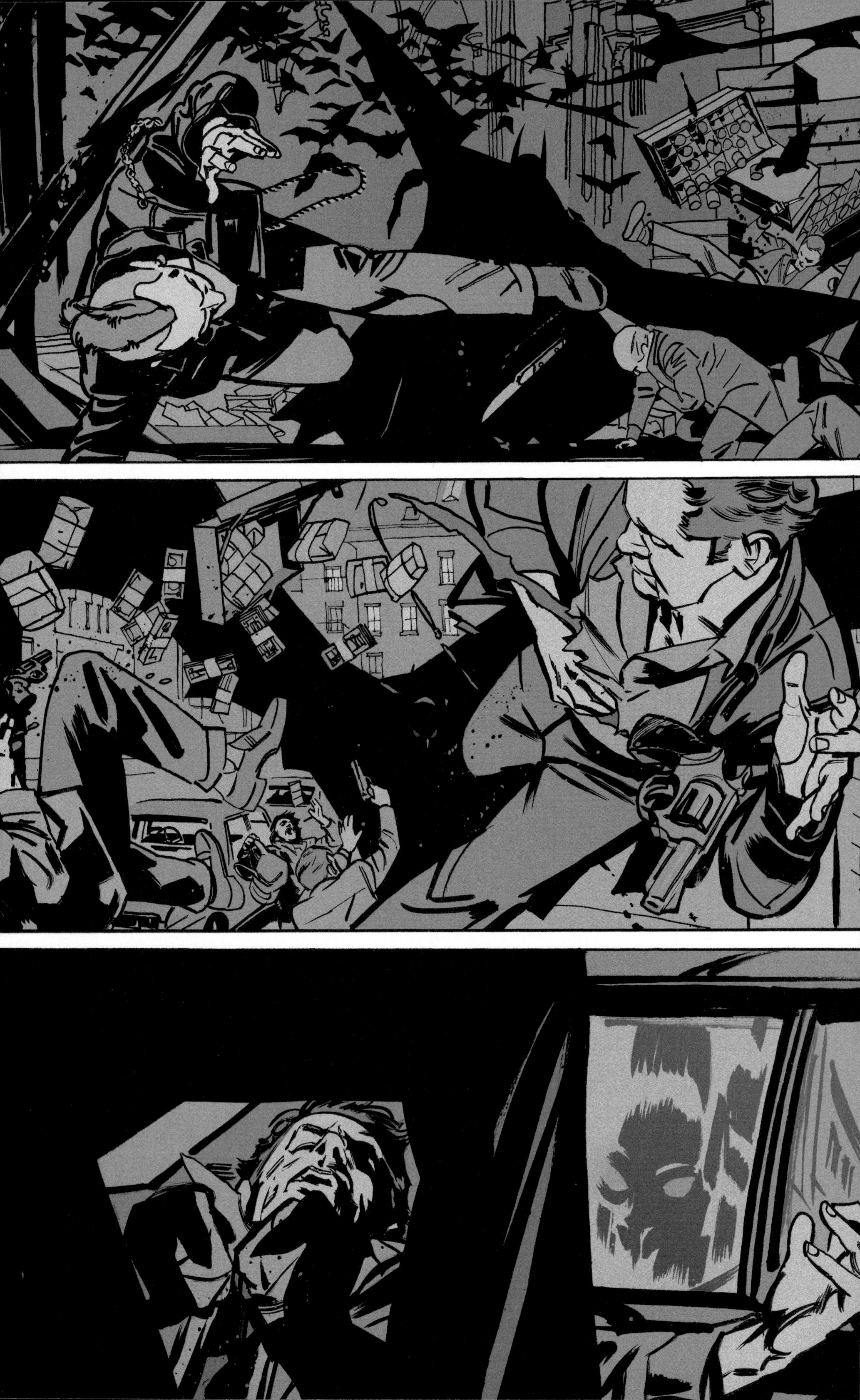

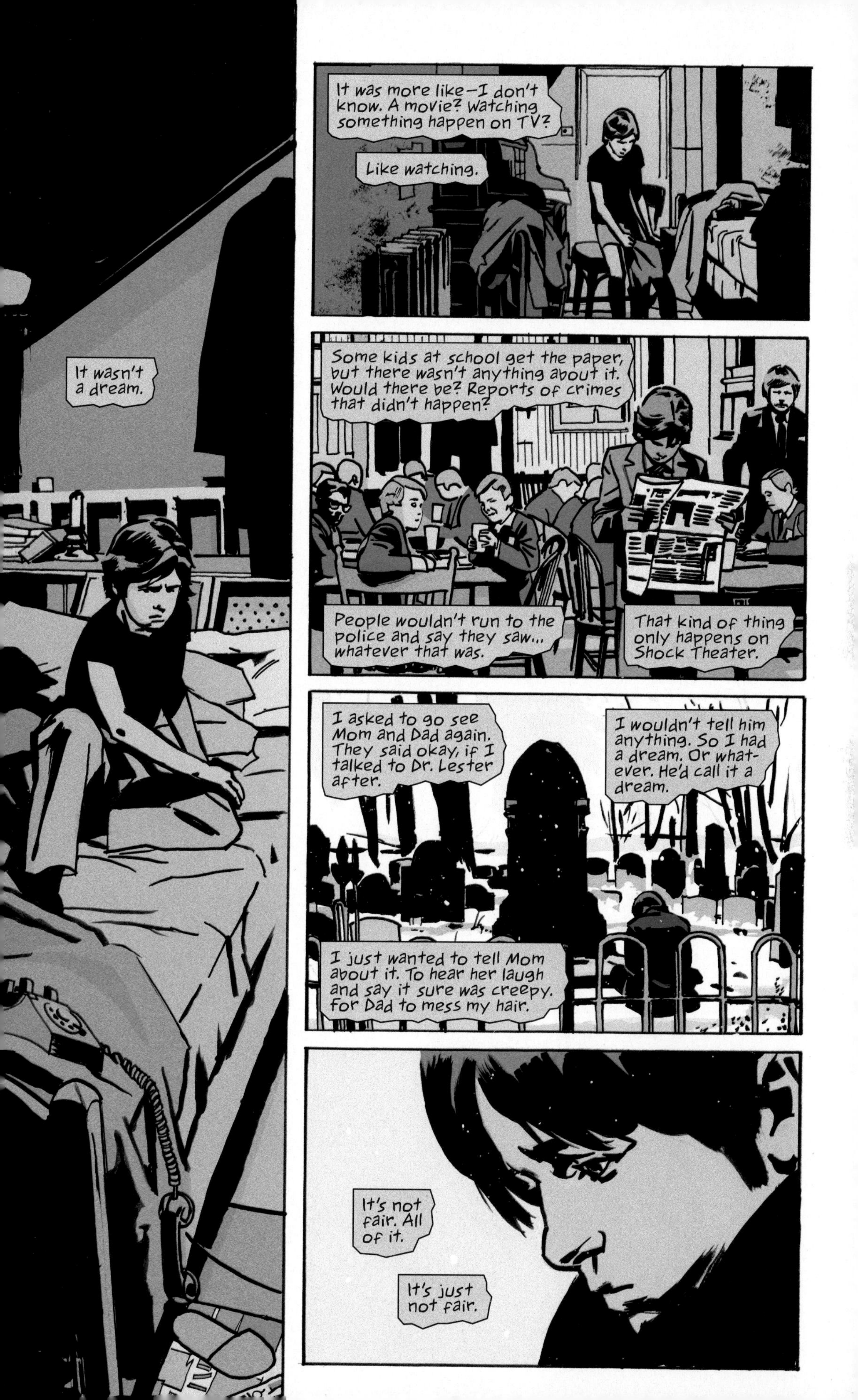
It wasn't a dream.
It was more like—I don't know. A movie? Watching something happen on TV?
Like watching.
Some kids at school get the paper, but there wasn't anything about it. Would there be? Reports of crimes that didn't happen?
People wouldn't run to the police and say they saw... whatever that was.
That kind of thing only happens on Shock Theater.
I asked to go see Mom and Dad again. They said okay, if I talked to Dr. Lester after.
I wouldn't tell him anything. So I had a dream. Or whatever. He'd call it a dream.
I just wanted to tell Mom about it. To hear her laugh and say it sure was creepy. For Dad to mess my hair.
It's not fair. All of it.
It's just not fair.

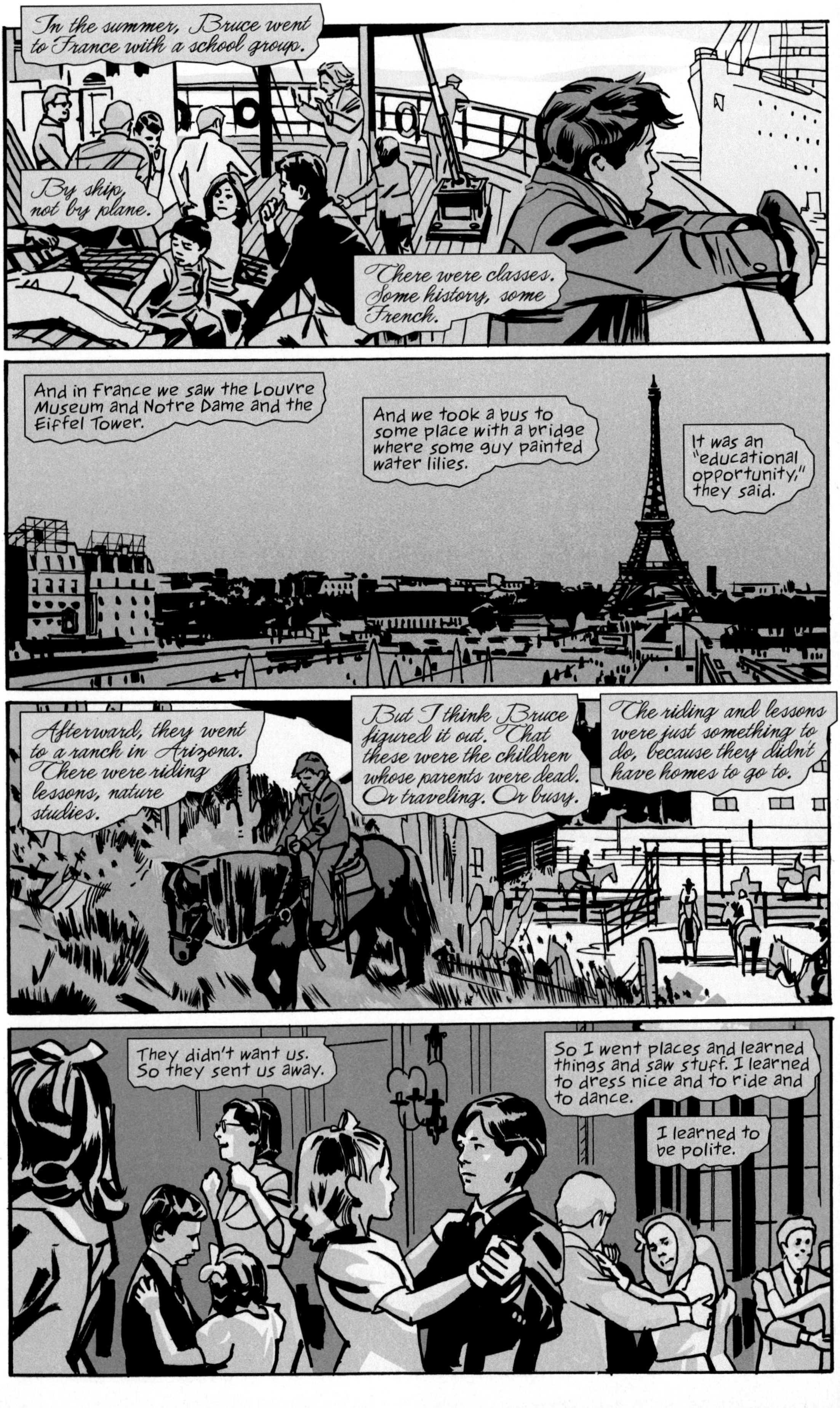
In the summer, Bruce went to France with a school group.
By ship, not by plane.
There were classes. Some history, some French.
And in France we saw the Louvre Museum and Notre Dame and the Eiffel Tower.
And we took a bus to some place with a bridge where some guy painted water lilies.
It was an "educational opportunity," they said.
Afterward, they went to a ranch in Arizona. There were riding lessons, nature studies.
But I think Bruce figured it out. That these were the children whose parents were dead. Or traveling. Or busy.
The riding and lessons were just something to do, because they didn't have homes to go to.
They didn't want us. So they sent us away.
So I went places and learned things and saw stuff. I learned to dress nice and to ride and to dance.
I learned to be polite.

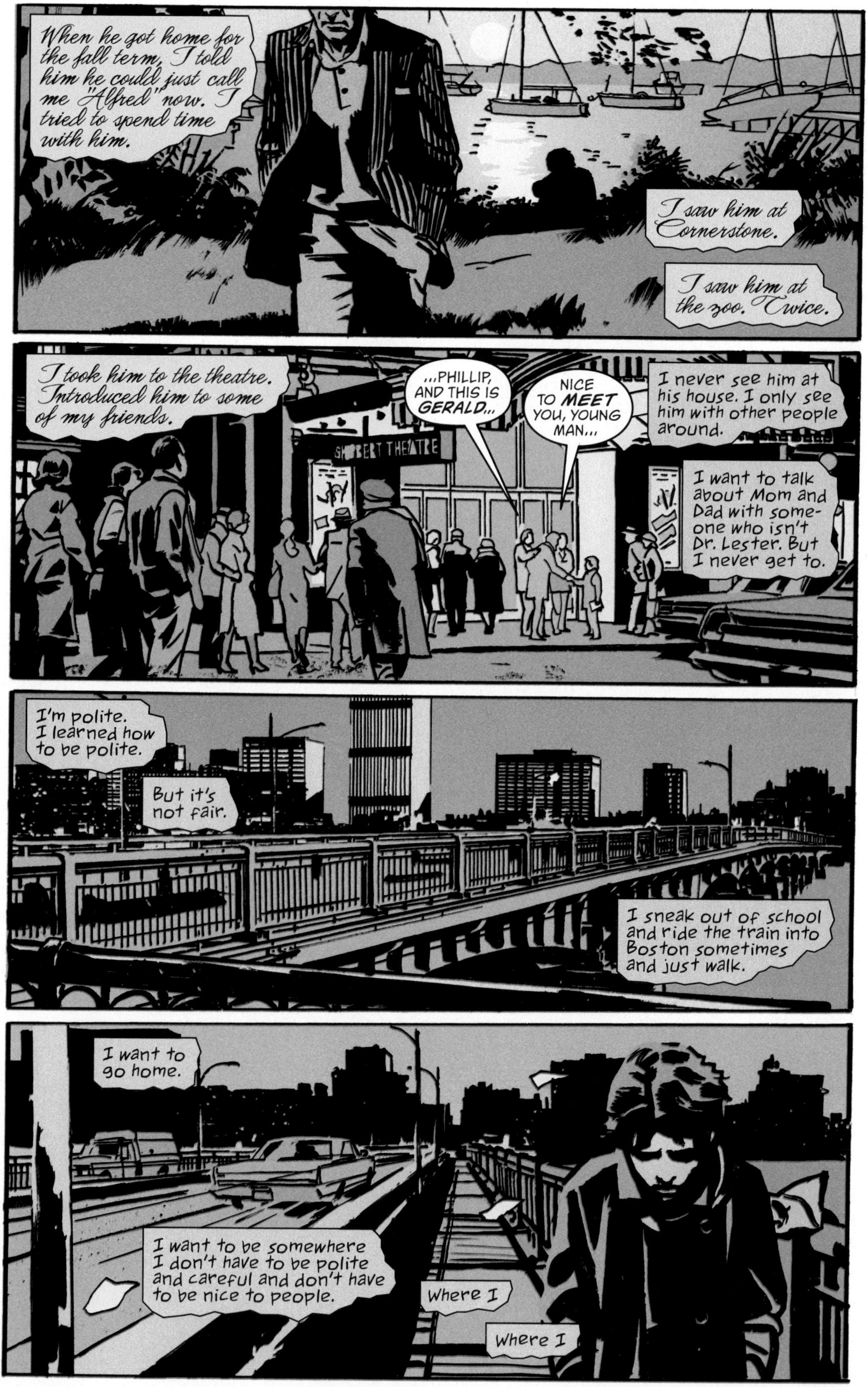
When he got home for the fall term, I told him he could just call me "Alfred" now. I tried to spend time with him.
I saw him at Cornerstone.
I saw him at the zoo. Twice.
I took him to the theatre. Introduced him to some of my friends.
...PHILLIP, AND THIS IS GERALD...
NICE TO MEET YOU, YOUNG MAN...
I never see him at his house. I only see him with other people around.
I want to talk about Mom and Dad with someone who isn't Dr. Lester. But I never get to.
I'm polite. I learned how to be polite.
But it's not fair.
I sneak out of school and ride the train into Boston sometimes and just walk.
I want to go home.
I want to be somewhere I don't have to be polite and careful and don't have to be nice to people.
Where I
Where I

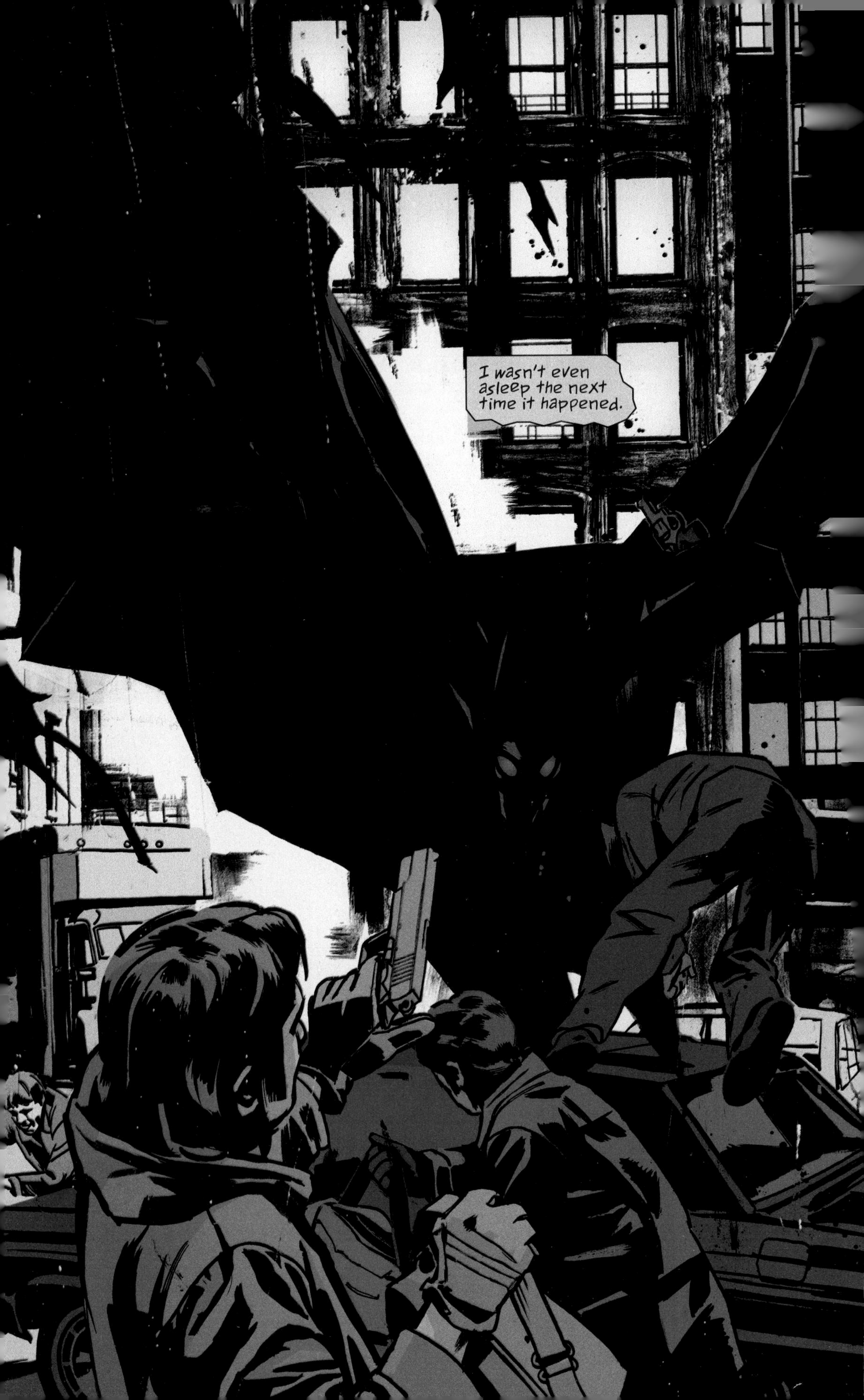
I wasn't even asleep the next time it happened.

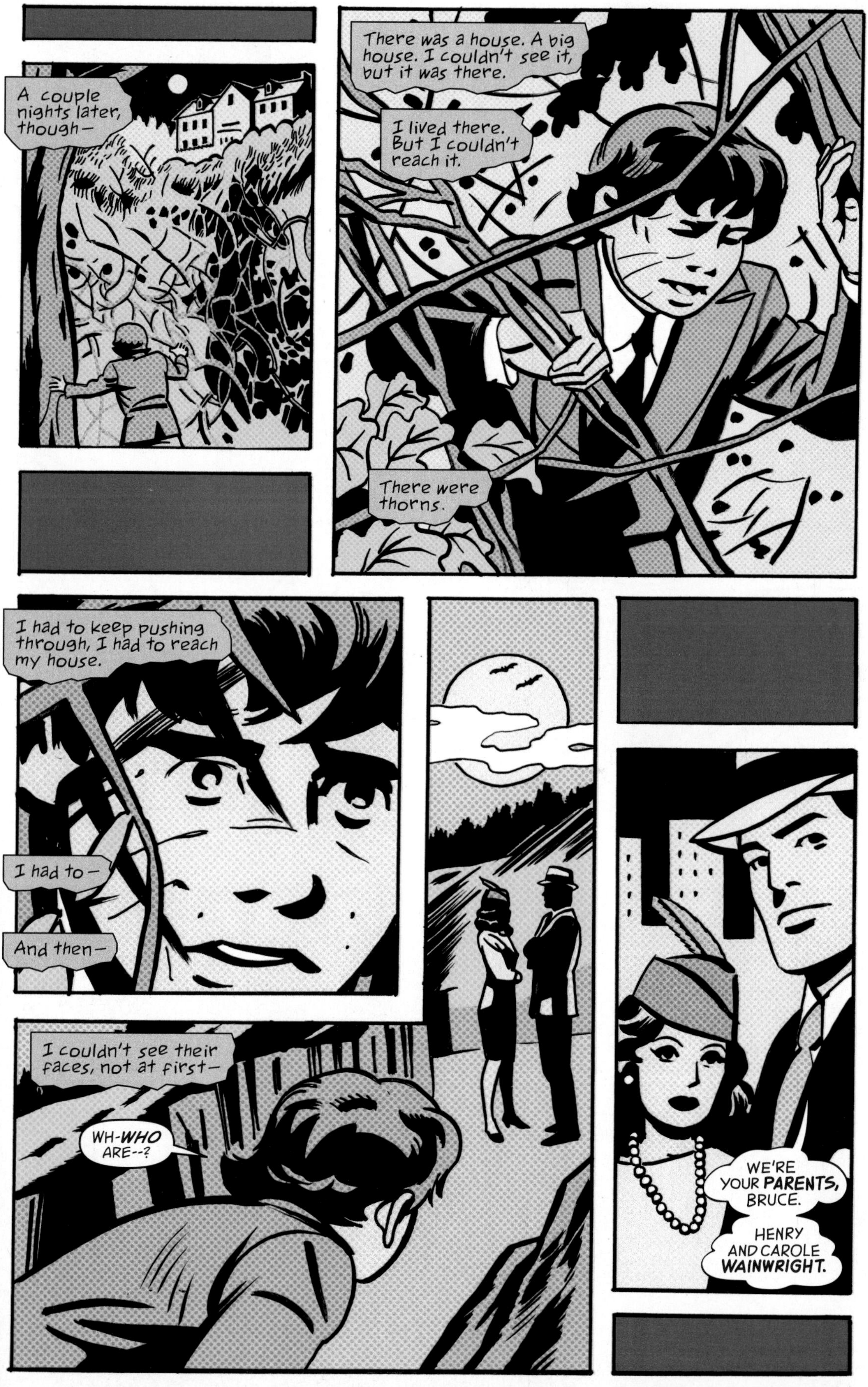
A couple nights later, though—
There was a house. A big house. I couldn't see it, but it was there.
I lived there. But I couldn't reach it.
There were thorns.
I had to keep pushing through, I had to reach my house.
I had to—
And then—
I couldn't see their faces, not at first—
WH-WHO ARE--?
WE'RE YOUR PARENTS, BRUCE.
HENRY AND CAROLE WAINWRIGHT.

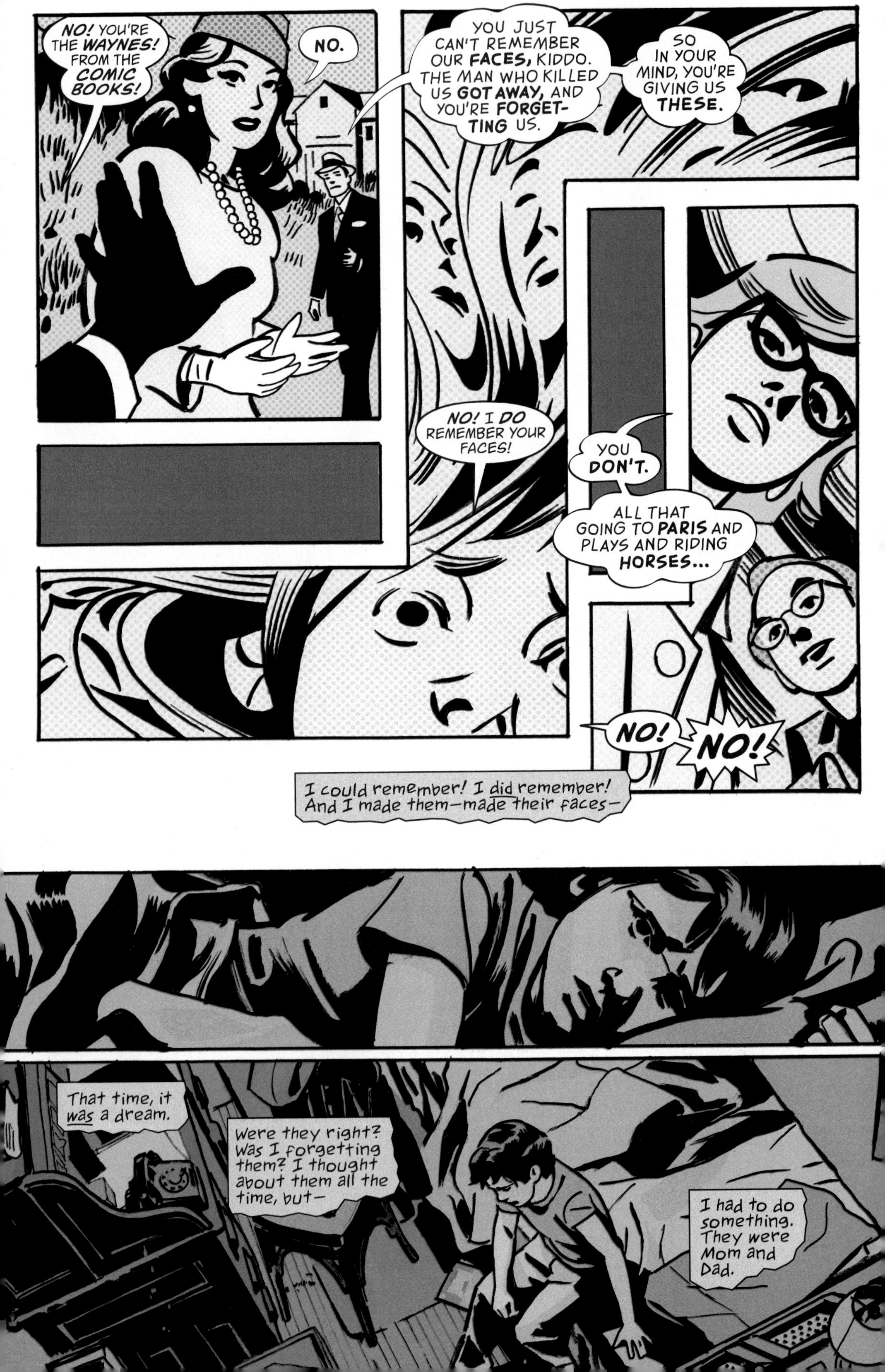

NO! YOU'RE THE WAYNES! FROM THE COMIC BOOKS!
NO.
YOU JUST CAN'T REMEMBER OUR FACES, KIDDO. THE MAN WHO KILLED US GOT AWAY, AND YOU'RE FORGETTING US.
SO IN YOUR MIND, YOU'RE GIVING US THESE.
NO! I DO REMEMBER YOUR FACES!
YOU DON'T.
ALL THAT GOING TO PARIS AND PLAYS AND RIDING HORSES...
NO!
NO!
I could remember! I did remember! And I made them—made their faces—
That time, it was a dream.
Were they right? Was I forgetting them? I thought about them all the time, but—
I had to do something. They were Mom and Dad.

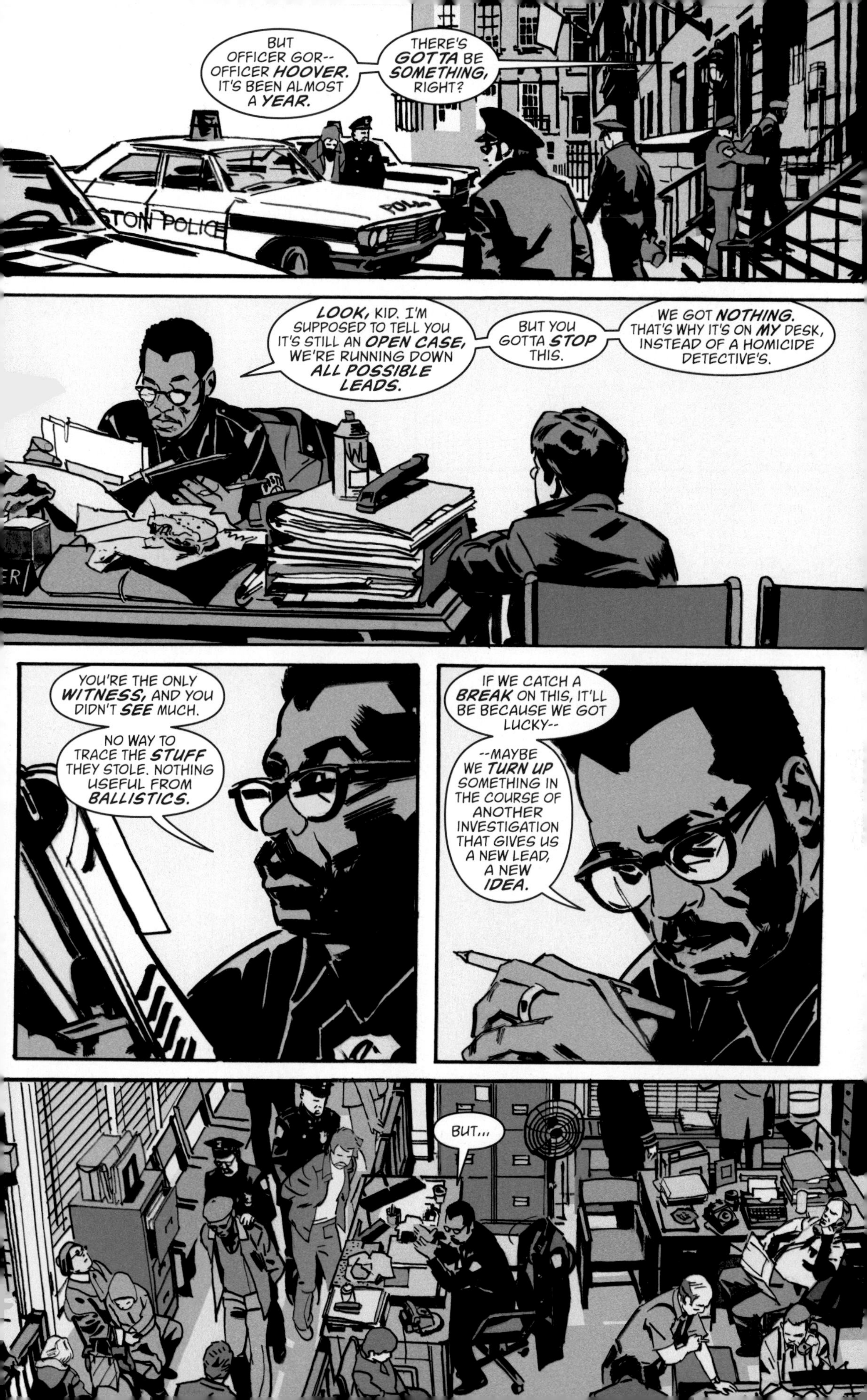

BUT OFFICER GOR-- OFFICER HOOVER. IT'S BEEN ALMOST A YEAR.
THERE'S GOTTA BE SOMETHING, RIGHT?
STON POLICE
LOOK, KID. I'M SUPPOSED TO TELL YOU IT'S STILL AN OPEN CASE, WE'RE RUNNING DOWN ALL POSSIBLE LEADS.
BUT YOU GOTTA STOP THIS.
WE GOT NOTHING. THAT'S WHY IT'S ON MY DESK, INSTEAD OF A HOMICIDE DETECTIVE'S.
YOU'RE THE ONLY WITNESS, AND YOU DIDN'T SEE MUCH.
NO WAY TO TRACE THE STUFF THEY STOLE. NOTHING USEFUL FROM BALLISTICS.
IF WE CATCH A BREAK ON THIS, IT'LL BE BECAUSE WE GOT LUCKY--
--MAYBE WE TURN UP SOMETHING IN THE COURSE OF ANOTHER INVESTIGATION THAT GIVES US A NEW LEAD, A NEW IDEA.
BUT...

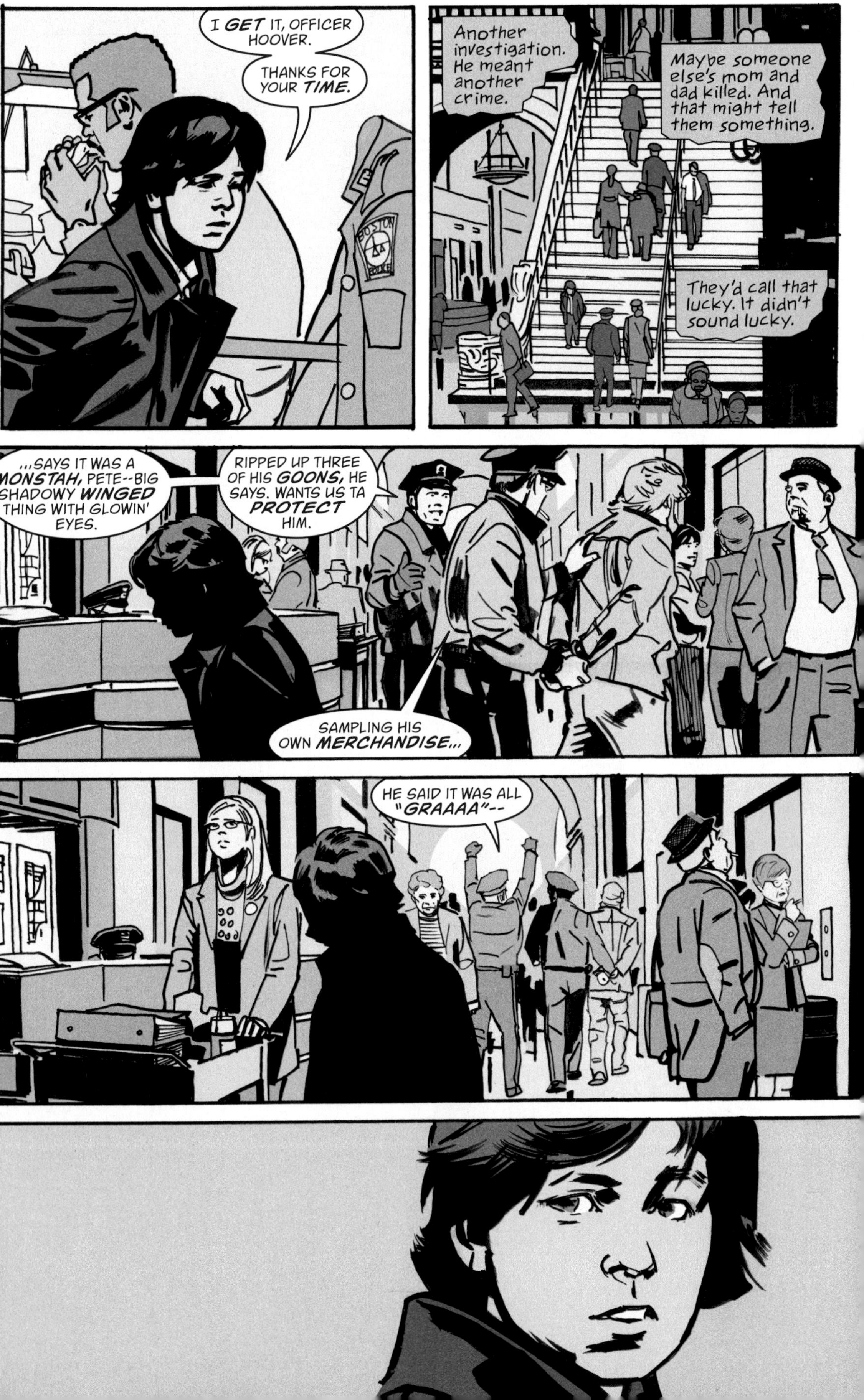
I GET IT, OFFICER HOOVER.
THANKS FOR YOUR TIME.
Another investigation. He meant another crime.
Maybe someone else's mom and dad killed. And that might tell them something.
They'd call that lucky. It didn't sound lucky.
...SAYS IT WAS A MONSTAH, PETE--BIG SHADOWY WINGED THING WITH GLOWIN' EYES.
RIPPED UP THREE OF HIS GOONS, HE SAYS. WANTS US TA PROTECT HIM.
SAMPLING HIS OWN MERCHANDISE...
HE SAID IT WAS ALL "GRAAAA"--

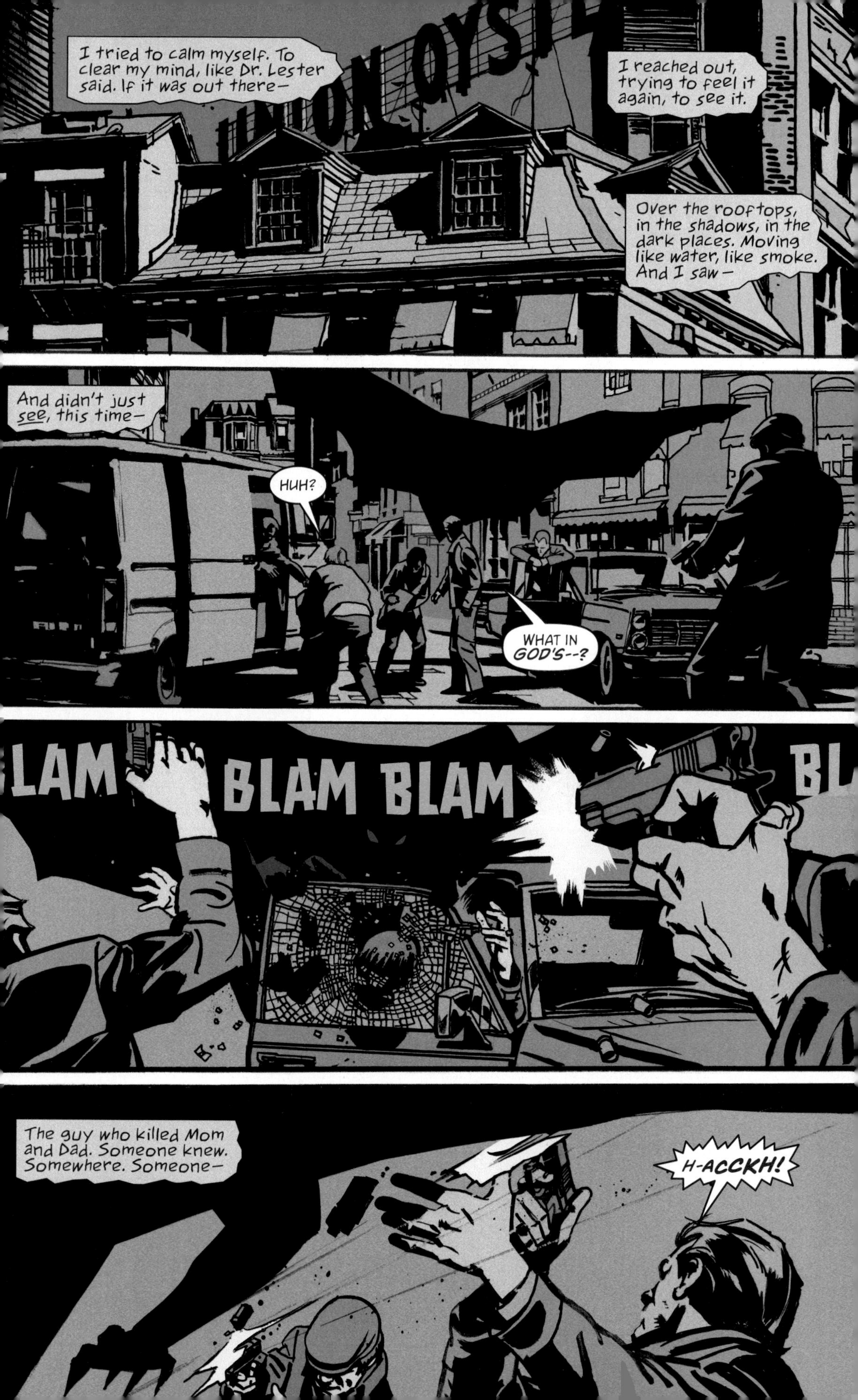

UNION OYST
I tried to calm myself. To clear my mind, like Dr. Lester said. If it was out there—
I reached out, trying to feel it again, to see it.
Over the rooftops, in the shadows, in the dark places. Moving like water, like smoke. And I saw—
And didn't just see, this time—
HUH?
WHAT IN GOD'S--?
LAM
BLAM BLAM
BL
The guy who killed Mom and Dad. Someone knew. Somewhere. Someone—
H-ACCKH!

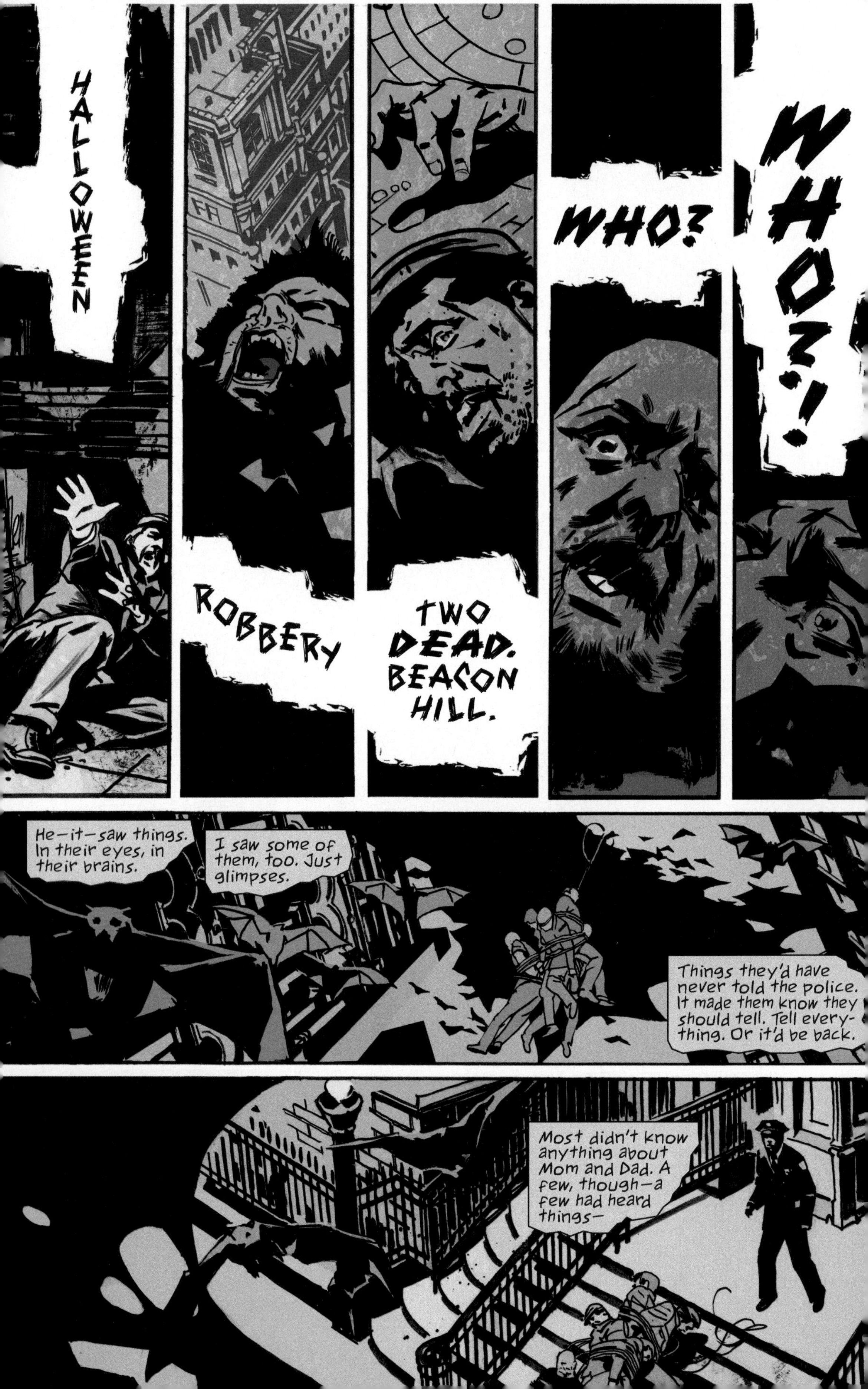
HALLOWEEN
ROBBERY
TWO DEAD. BEACON HILL.
WHO?
WHO?!
He—it—saw things. In their eyes, in their brains.
I saw some of them, too. Just glimpses.
Things they'd have never told the police. It made them know they should tell. Tell every-thing. Or it'd be back.
Most didn't know anything about Mom and Dad. A few, though—a few had heard things—

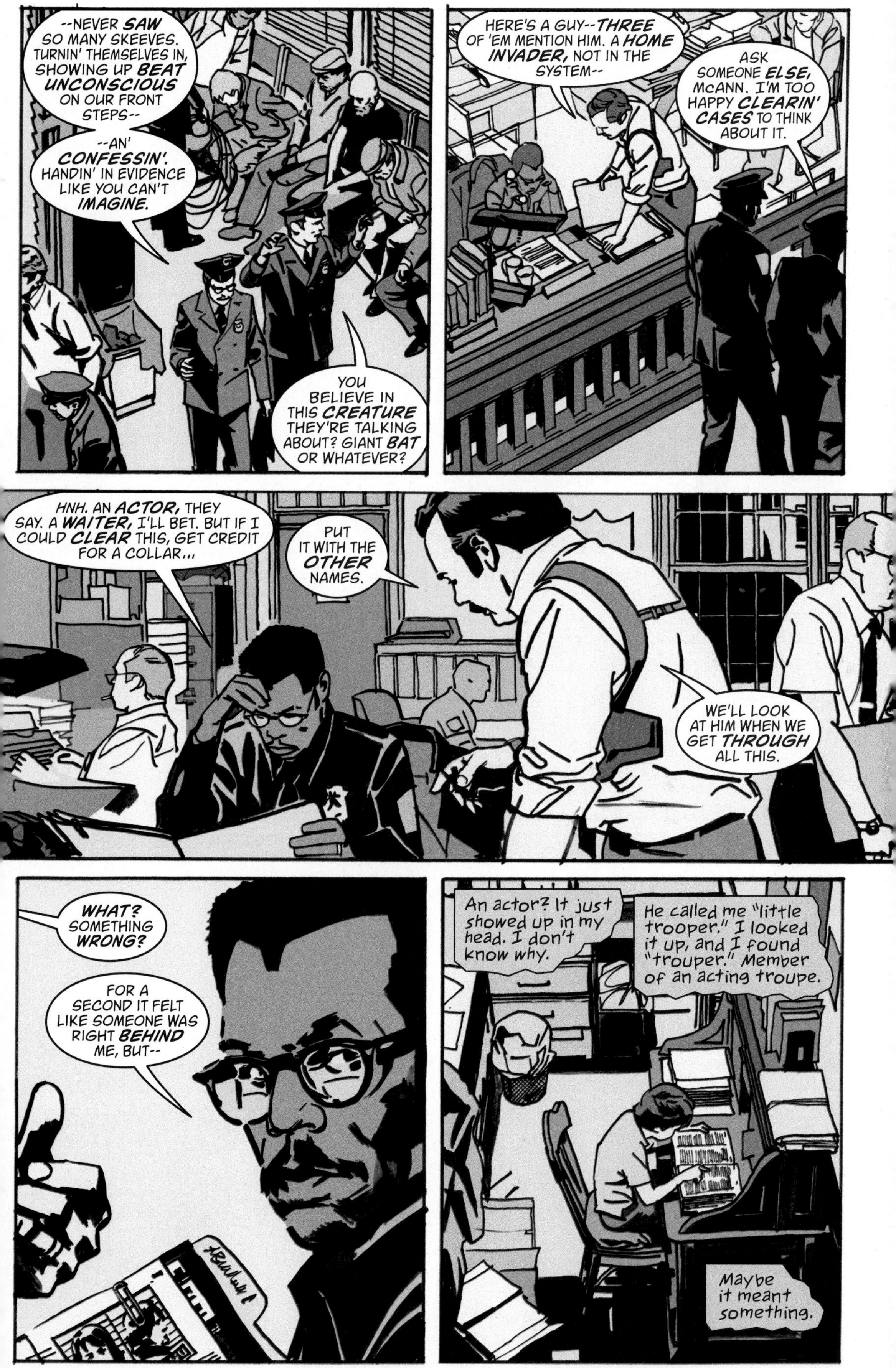
--NEVER SAW SO MANY SKEEVES. TURNIN' THEMSELVES IN, SHOWING UP BEAT UNCONSCIOUS ON OUR FRONT STEPS--
--AN' CONFESSIN'. HANDIN' IN EVIDENCE LIKE YOU CAN'T IMAGINE.
YOU BELIEVE IN THIS CREATURE THEY'RE TALKING ABOUT? GIANT BAT OR WHATEVER?
HERE'S A GUY--THREE OF 'EM MENTION HIM. A HOME INVADER, NOT IN THE SYSTEM--
ASK SOMEONE ELSE, McANN. I'M TOO HAPPY CLEARIN' CASES TO THINK ABOUT IT.
HNH. AN ACTOR, THEY SAY. A WAITER, I'LL BET. BUT IF I COULD CLEAR THIS, GET CREDIT FOR A COLLAR...
PUT IT WITH THE OTHER NAMES.
WE'LL LOOK AT HIM WHEN WE GET THROUGH ALL THIS.
WHAT? SOMETHING WRONG?
FOR A SECOND IT FELT LIKE SOMEONE WAS RIGHT BEHIND ME, BUT--
An actor? It just showed up in my head. I don't know why.
He called me "little trooper." I looked it up, and I found "trouper." Member of an acting troupe.
Maybe it meant something.

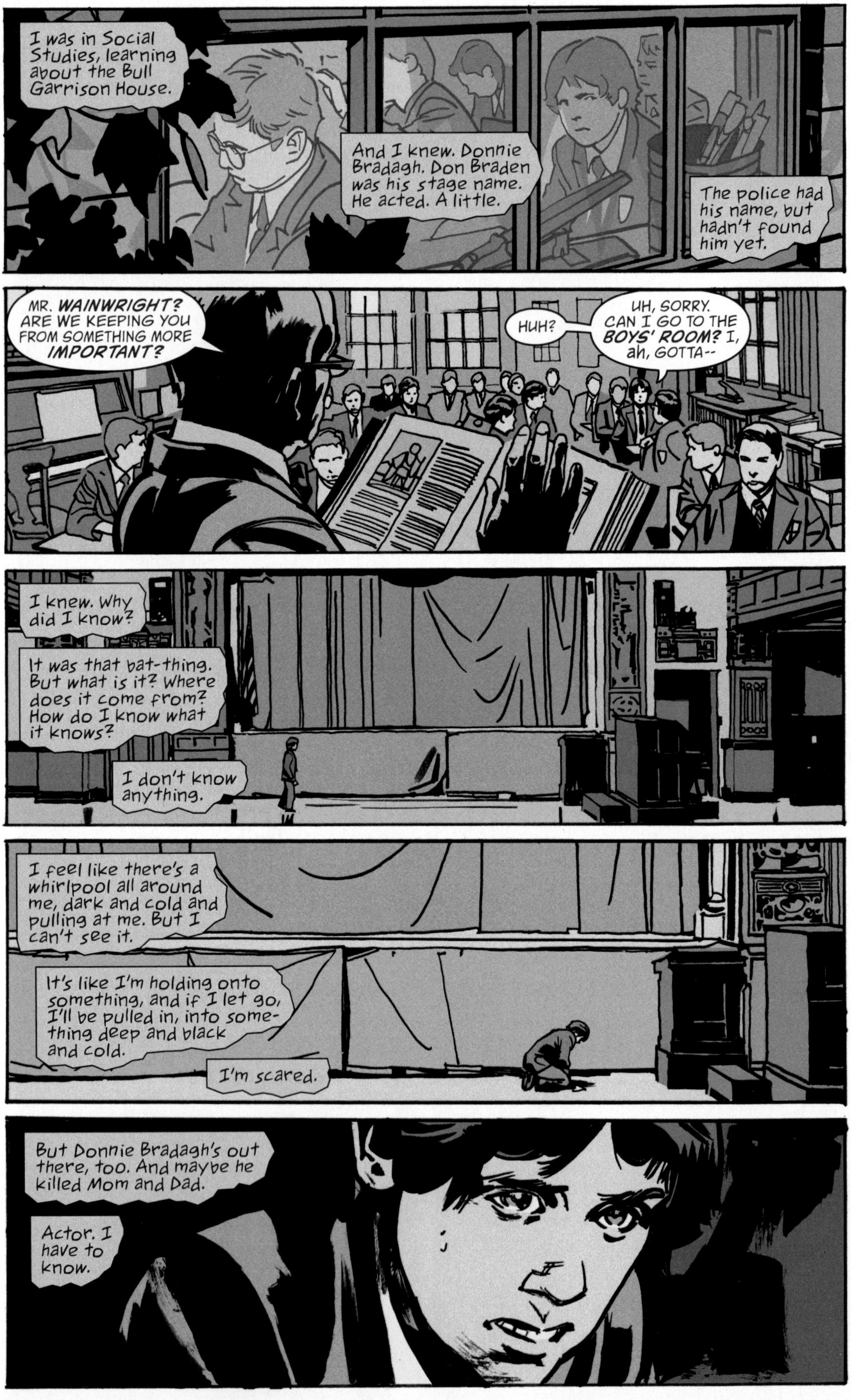
I was in Social Studies, learning about the Bull Garrison House.
And I knew. Donnie Bradagh. Don Braden was his stage name. He acted. A little.
The police had his name, but hadn't found him yet.
MR. WAINWRIGHT? ARE WE KEEPING YOU FROM SOMETHING MORE IMPORTANT?
HUH?
UH, SORRY. CAN I GO TO THE BOYS' ROOM? I, ah, GOTTA--
I knew. Why did I know?
It was that bat-thing. But what is it? Where does it come from? How do I know what it knows?
I don't know anything.
I feel like there's a whirlpool all around me, dark and cold and pulling at me. But I can't see it.
It's like I'm holding onto something, and if I let go, I'll be pulled in, into something deep and black and cold.
I'm scared.
But Donnie Bradagh's out there, too. And maybe he killed Mom and Dad.
Actor. I have to know.

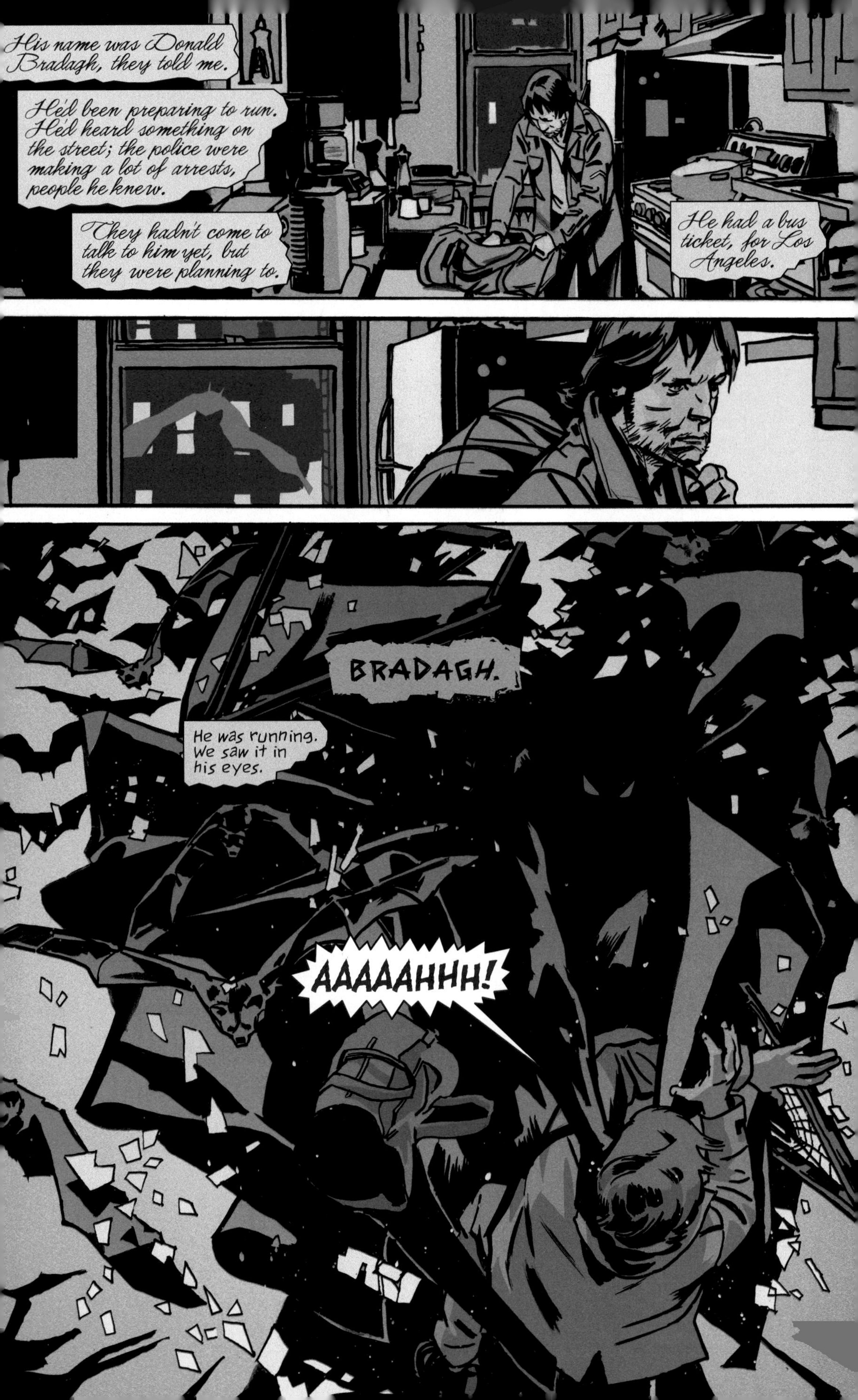
His name was Donald Bradagh, they told me.
He'd been preparing to run. He'd heard something on the street; the police were making a lot of arrests, people he knew.
They hadn't come to talk to him yet, but they were planning to.
He had a bus ticket, for Los Angeles.
BRADAGH.
He was running. We saw it in his eyes.
AAAAAHHH!

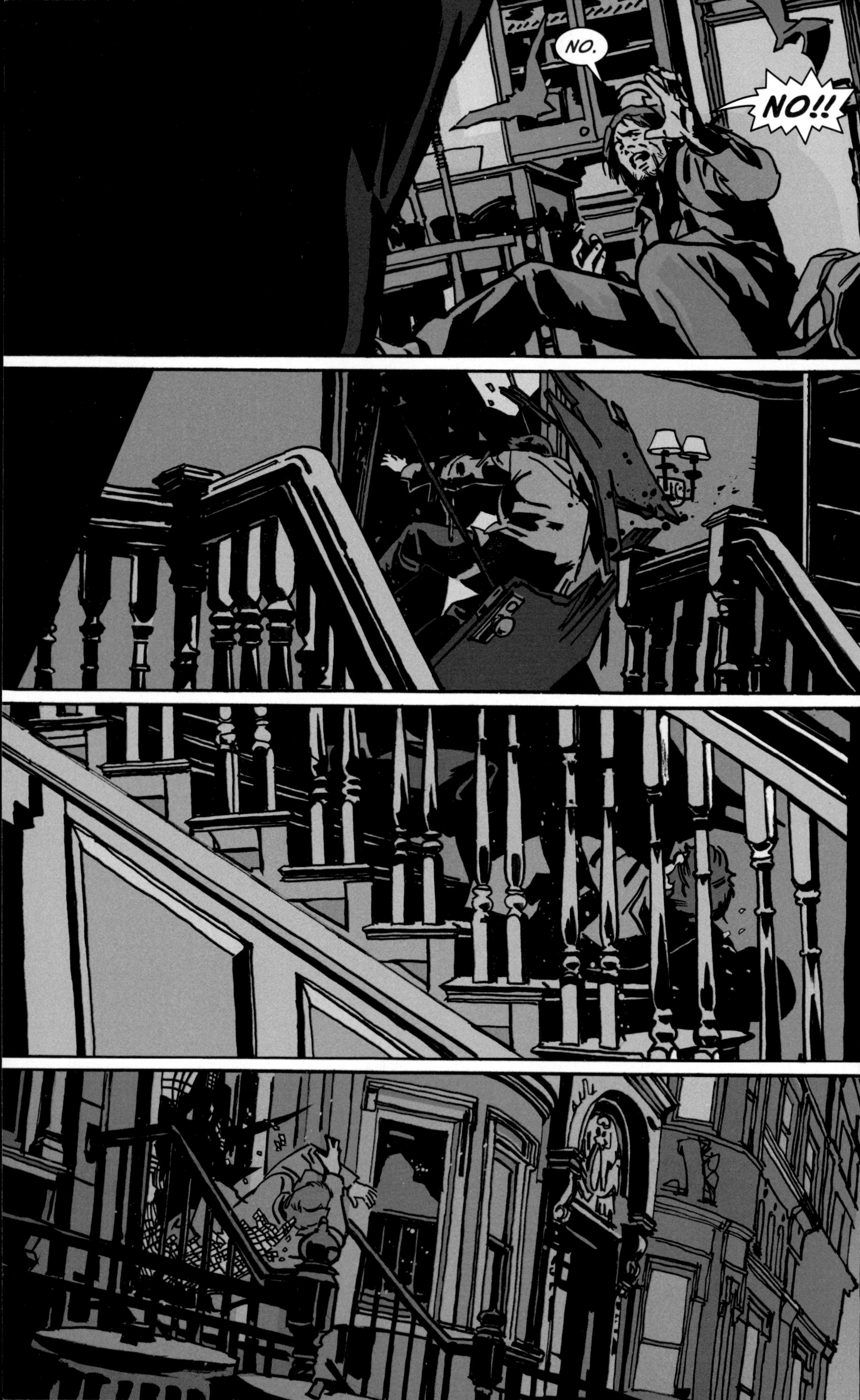
NO.
NO!!

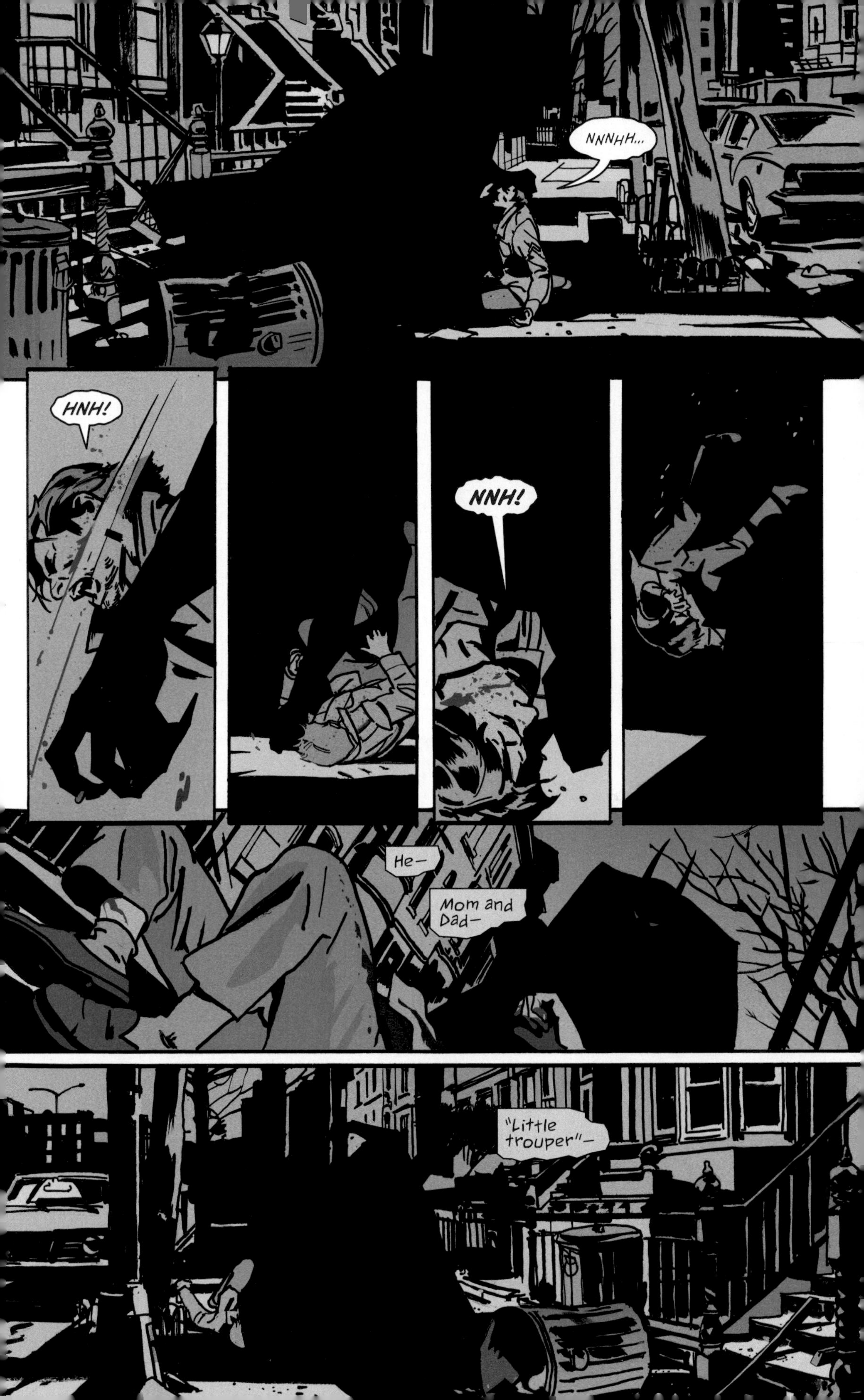
NNNHH...
HNH!
NNH!
He—
Mom and Dad—
"Little trouper"—

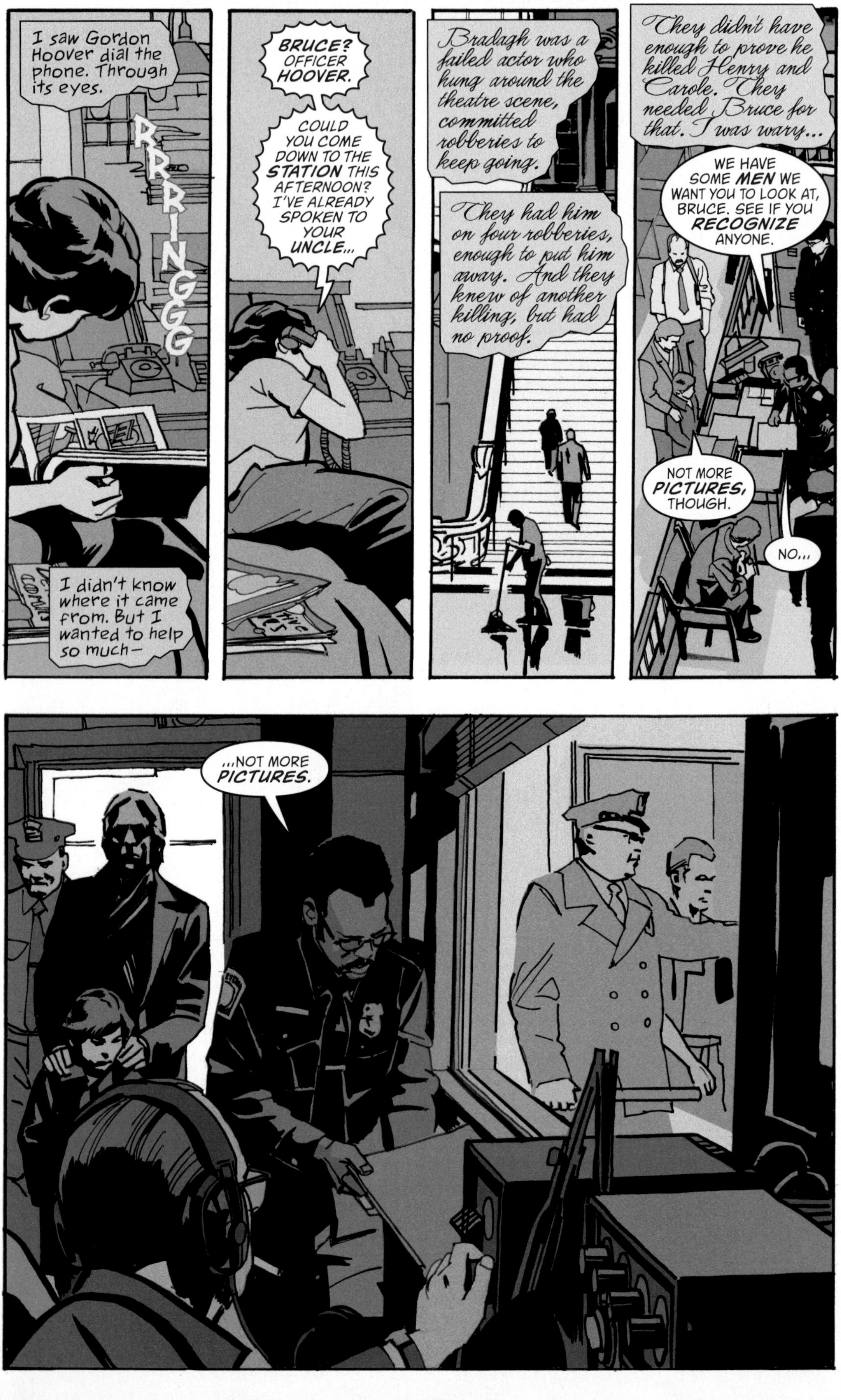
I saw Gordon Hoover dial the phone. Through its eyes.
RRRINGGG
I didn't know where it came from. But I wanted to help so much–
BRUCE? OFFICER HOOVER.
COULD YOU COME DOWN TO THE STATION THIS AFTERNOON? I'VE ALREADY SPOKEN TO YOUR UNCLE...
Bradagh was a failed actor who hung around the theatre scene, committed robberies to keep going.
They had him on four robberies, enough to put him away. And they knew of another killing, but had no proof.
They didn't have enough to prove he killed Henry and Carole. They needed Bruce for that. I was wary...
WE HAVE SOME MEN WE WANT YOU TO LOOK AT, BRUCE. SEE IF YOU RECOGNIZE ANYONE.
NOT MORE PICTURES, THOUGH.
NO...
...NOT MORE PICTURES.

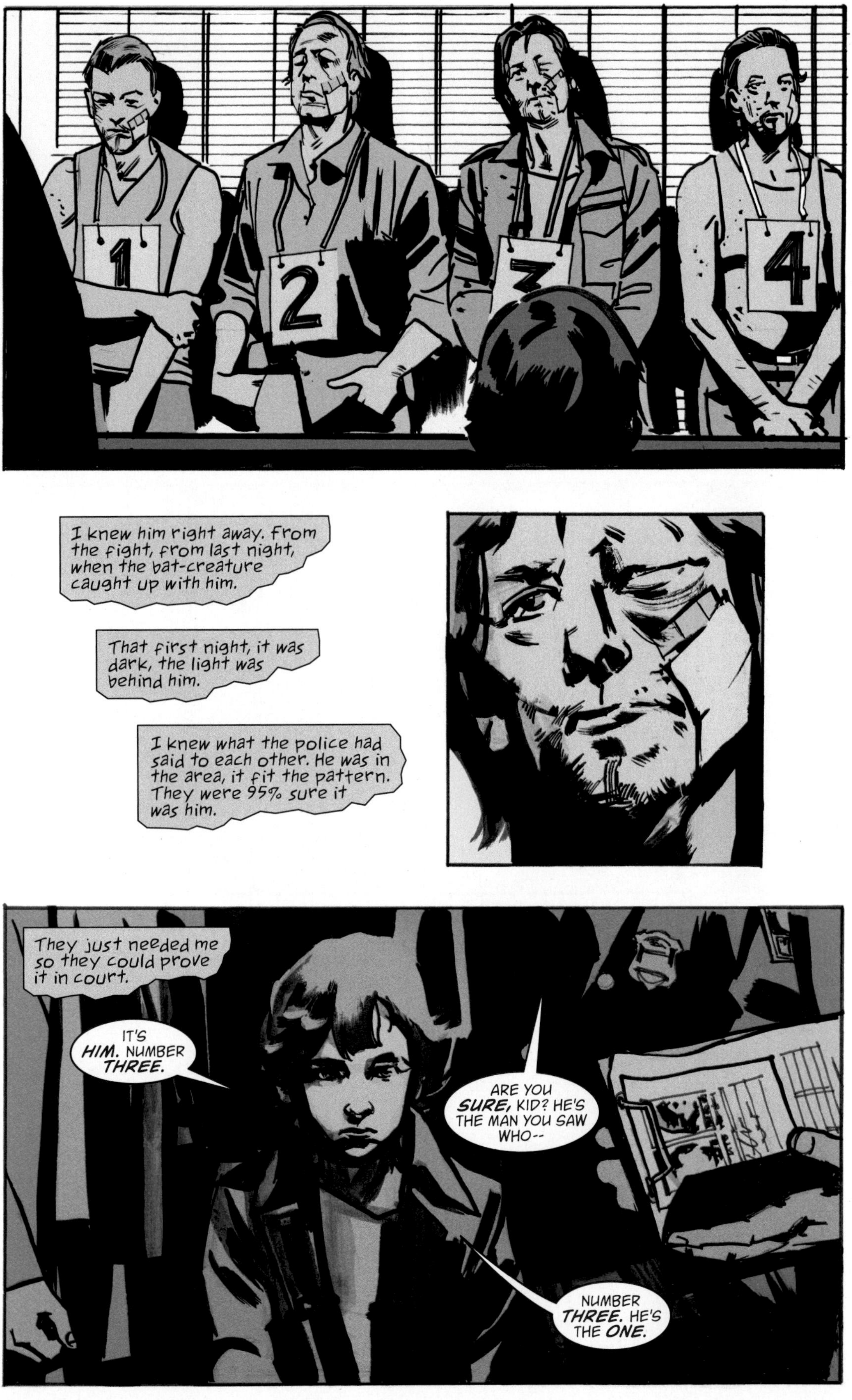
1
2
3
4
I knew him right away. From the fight, from last night, when the bat-creature caught up with him.
That first night, it was dark, the light was behind him.
I knew what the police had said to each other. He was in the area, it fit the pattern. They were 95% sure it was him.
They just needed me so they could prove it in court.
IT'S HIM. NUMBER THREE.
ARE YOU SURE, KID? HE'S THE MAN YOU SAW WHO--
NUMBER THREE. HE'S THE ONE.

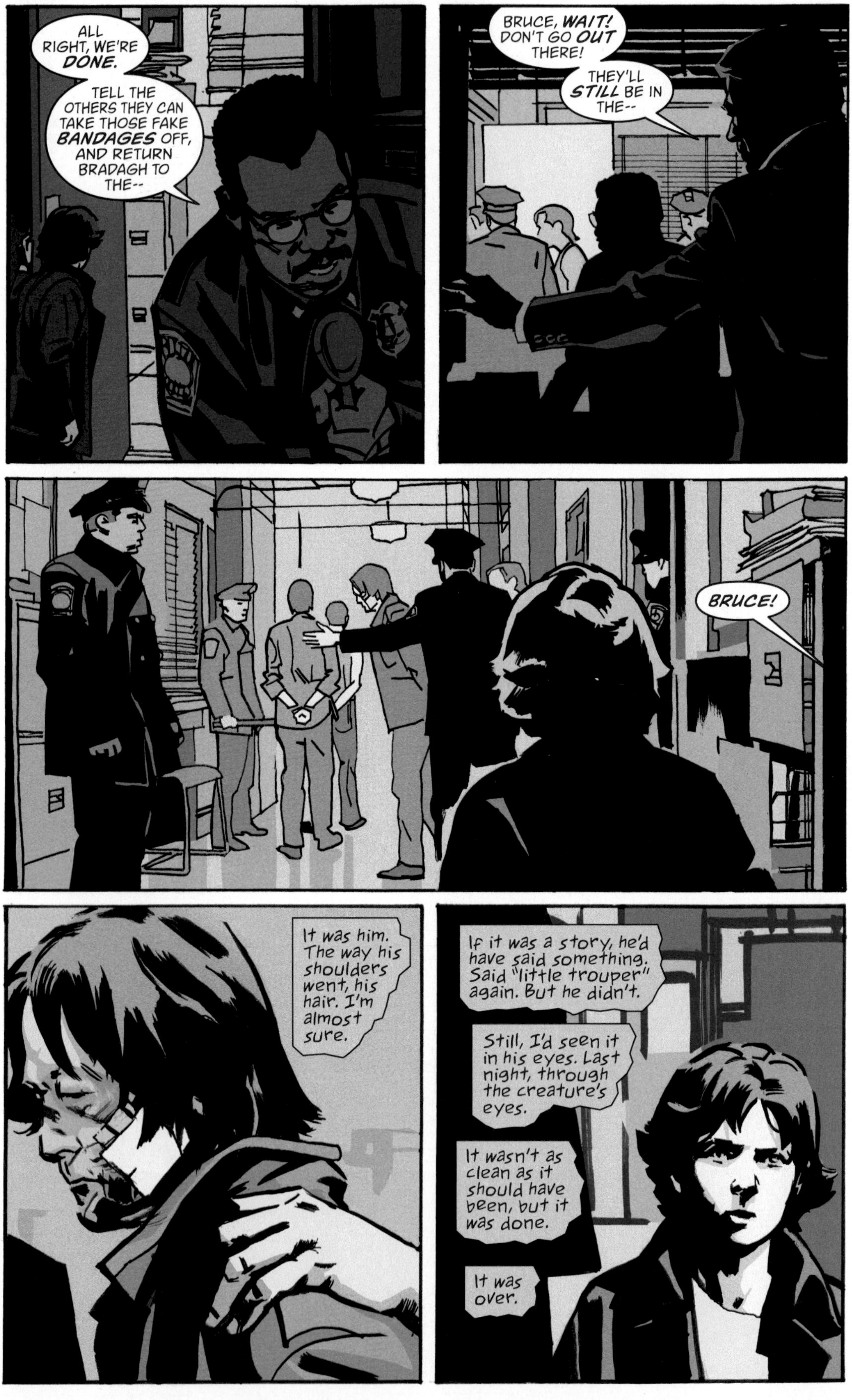
ALL RIGHT, WE'RE DONE.
TELL THE OTHERS THEY CAN TAKE THOSE FAKE BANDAGES OFF, AND RETURN BRADAGH TO THE--
BRUCE, WAIT! DON'T GO OUT THERE!
THEY'LL STILL BE IN THE--
BRUCE!
It was him. The way his shoulders went, his hair. I'm almost sure.
If it was a story, he'd have said something. Said "little trouper" again. But he didn't.
Still, I'd seen it in his eyes. Last night, through the creature's eyes.
It wasn't as clean as it should have been, but it was done.
It was over.

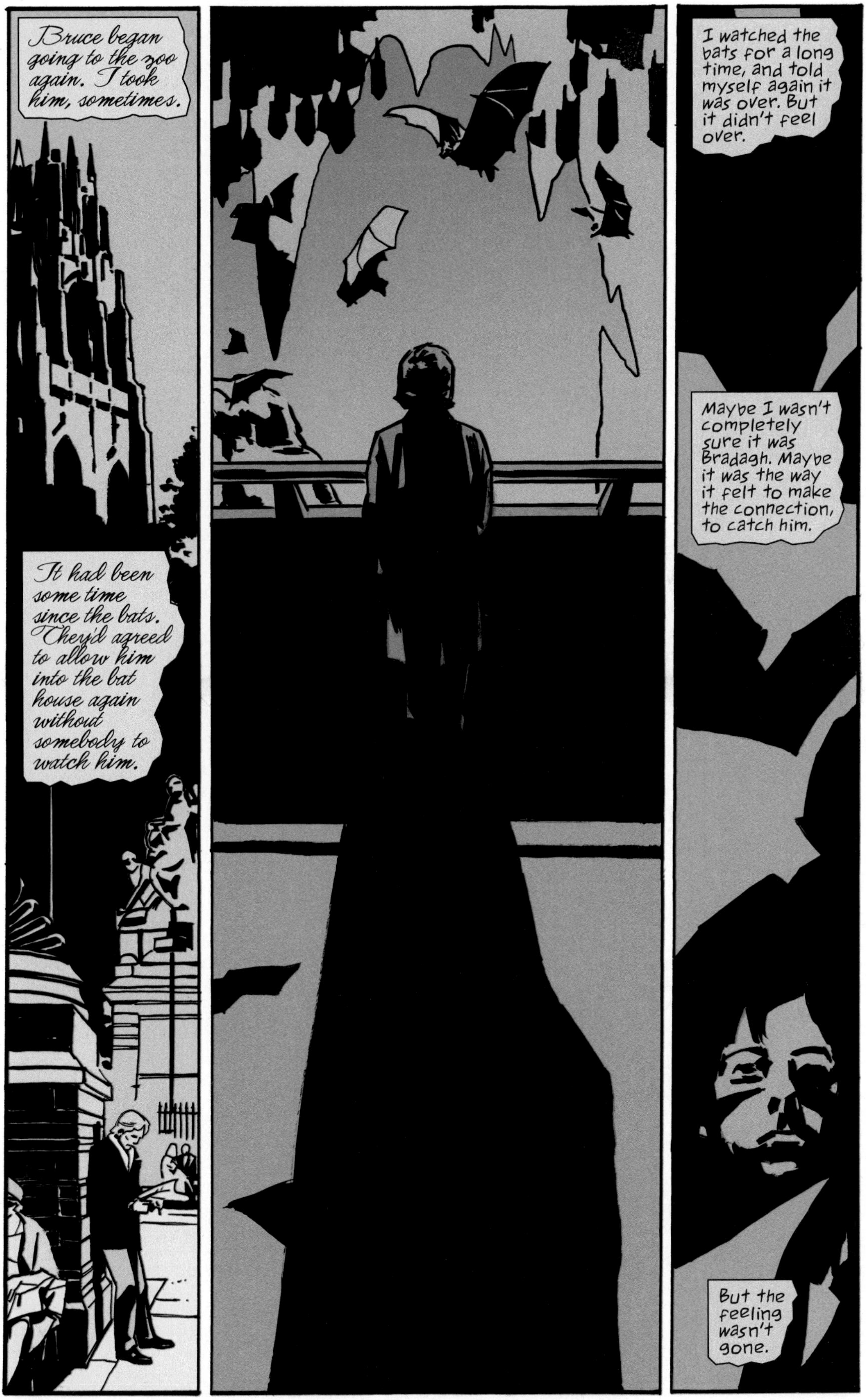

Bruce began going to the zoo again. I took him, sometimes.
It had been some time since the bats. They'd agreed to allow him into the bat house again without somebody to watch him.
I watched the bats for a long time, and told myself again it was over. But it didn't feel over.
Maybe I wasn't completely sure it was Bradagh. Maybe it was the way it felt to make the connection, to catch him.
But the feeling wasn't gone.

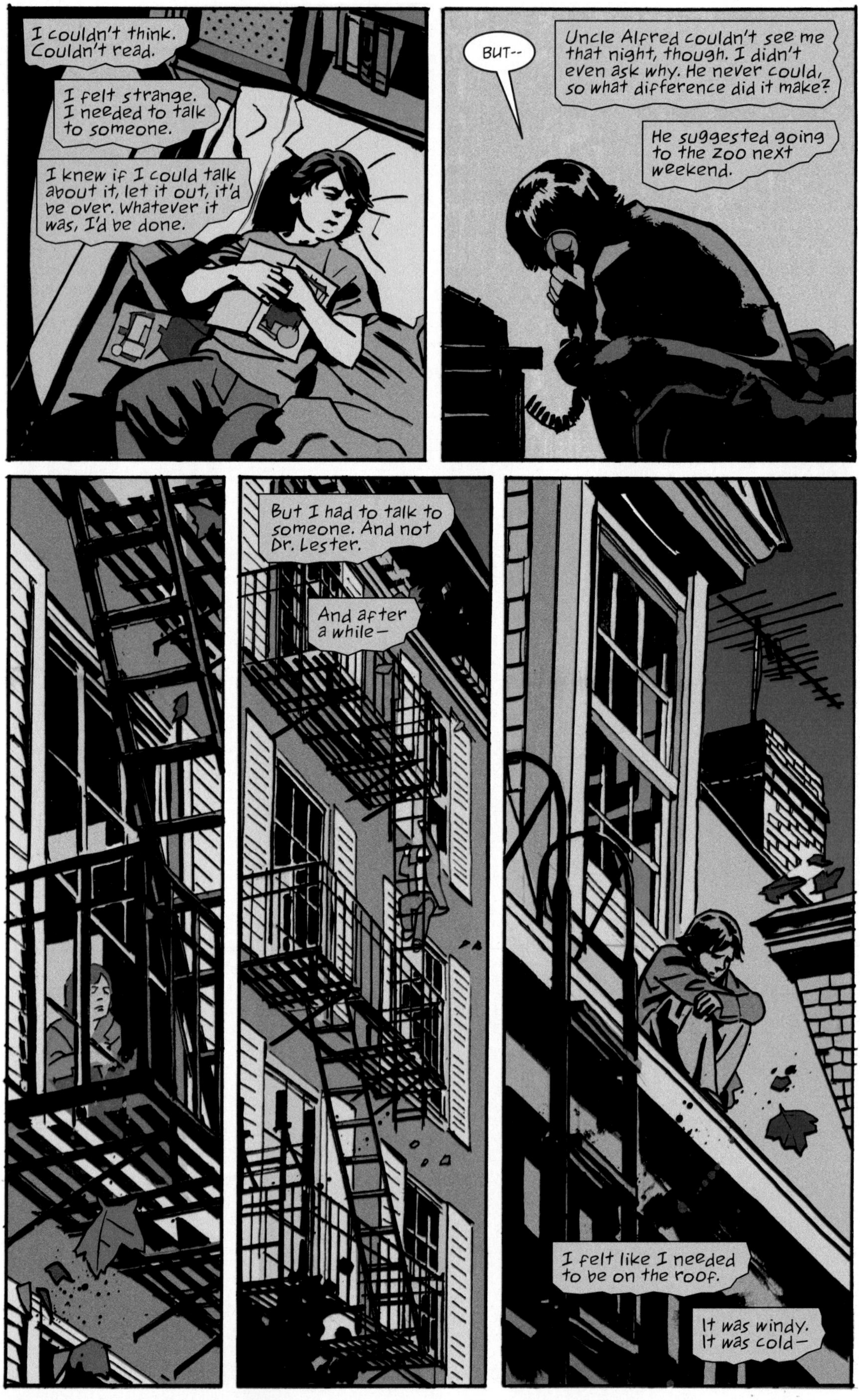
I couldn't think. Couldn't read.
I felt strange. I needed to talk to someone.
I knew if I could talk about it, let it out, it'd be over. Whatever it was, I'd be done.
BUT--
Uncle Alfred couldn't see me that night, though. I didn't even ask why. He never could, so what difference did it make?
He suggested going to the zoo next weekend.
But I had to talk to someone. And not Dr. Lester.
And after a while—
I felt like I needed to be on the roof.
It was windy. It was cold—

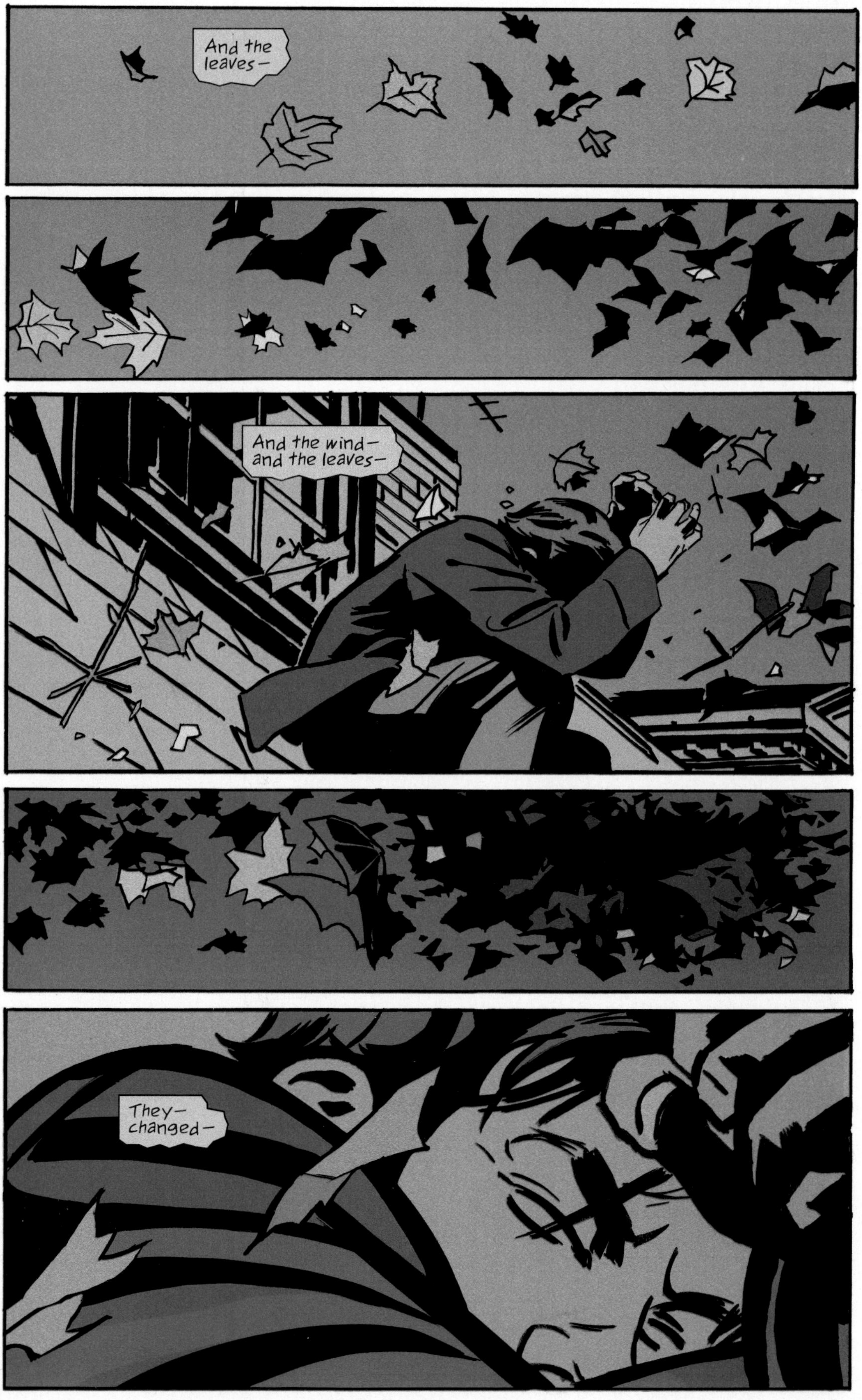

And the leaves—
And the wind—and the leaves—
They—changed—

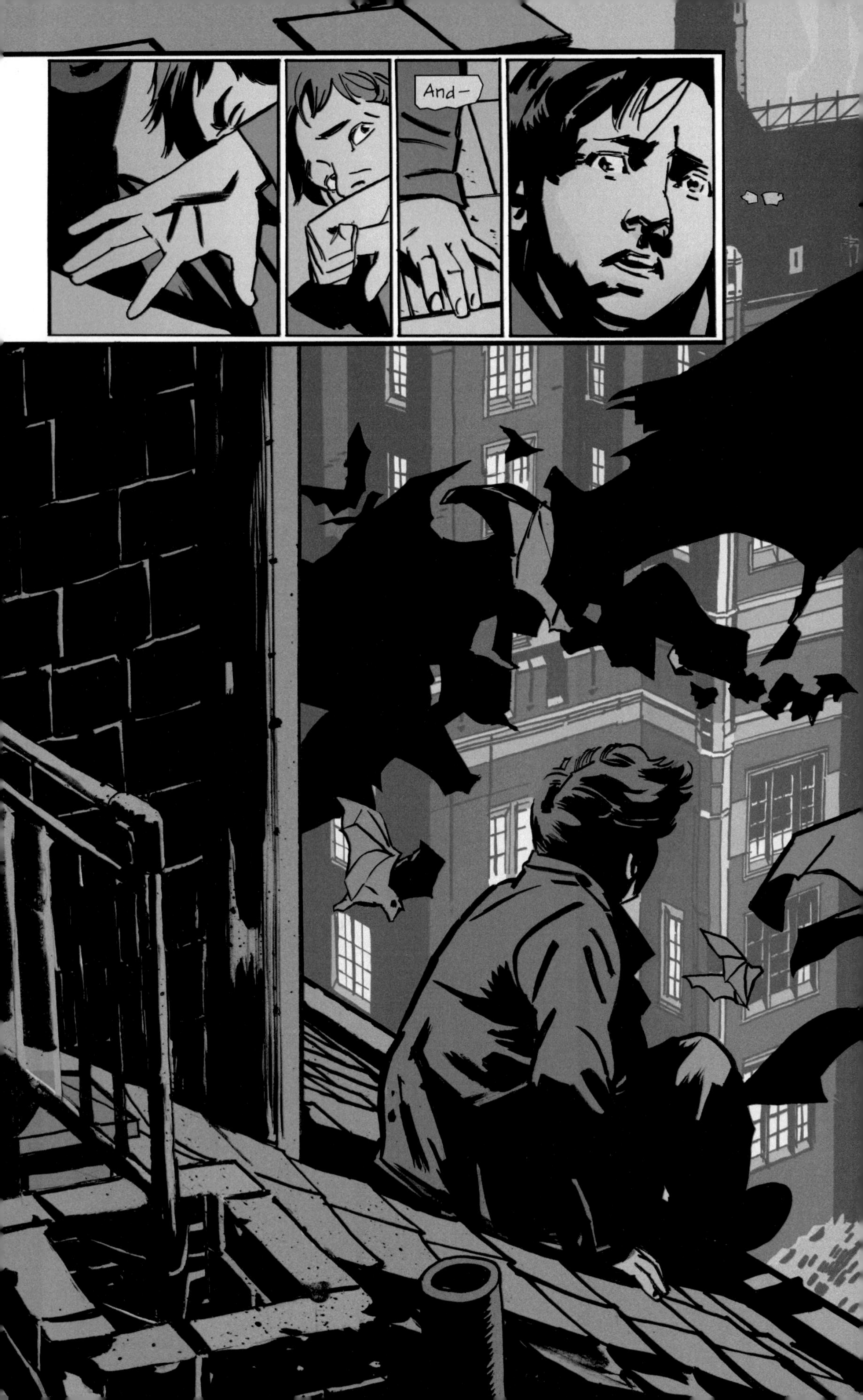
And—

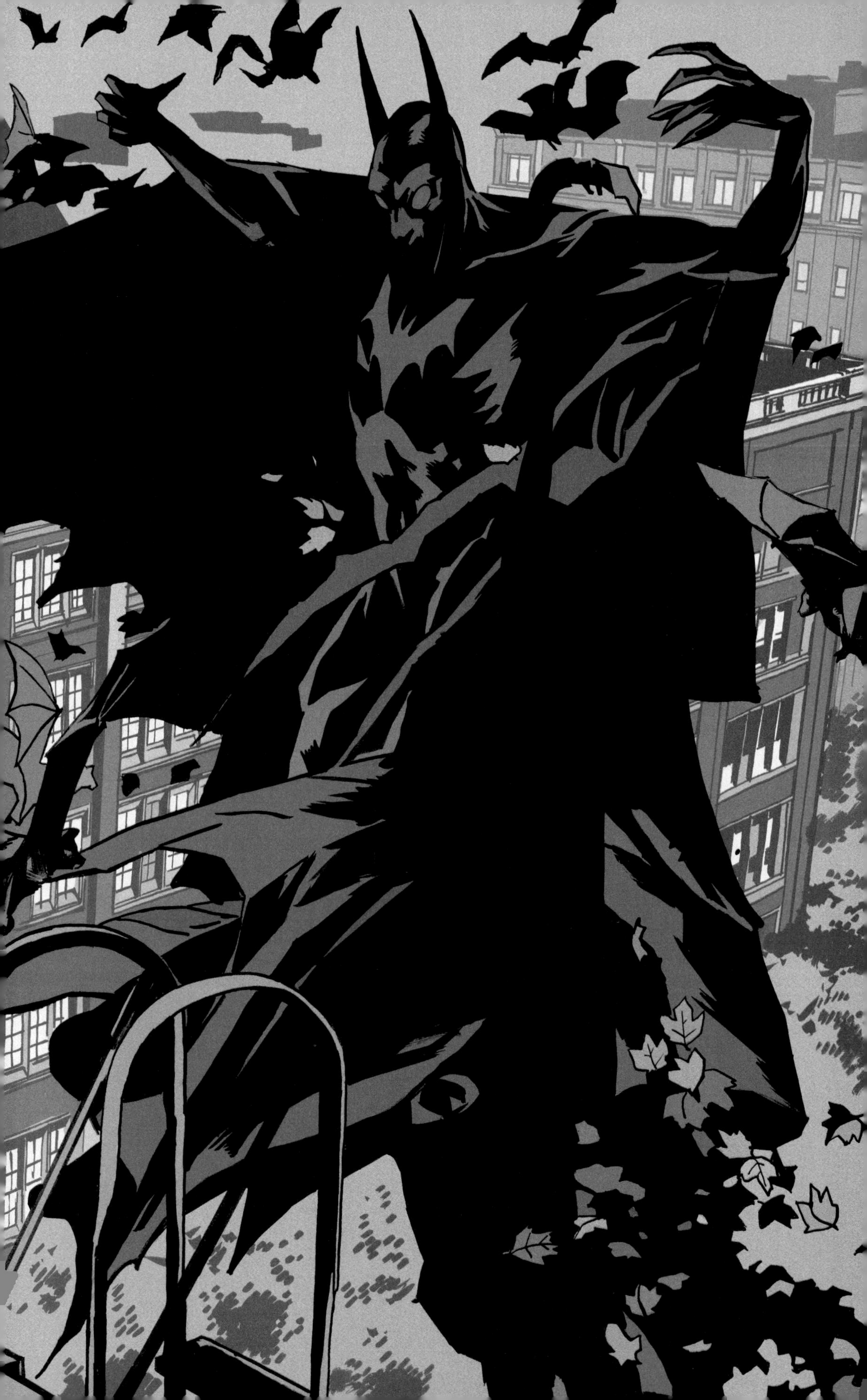

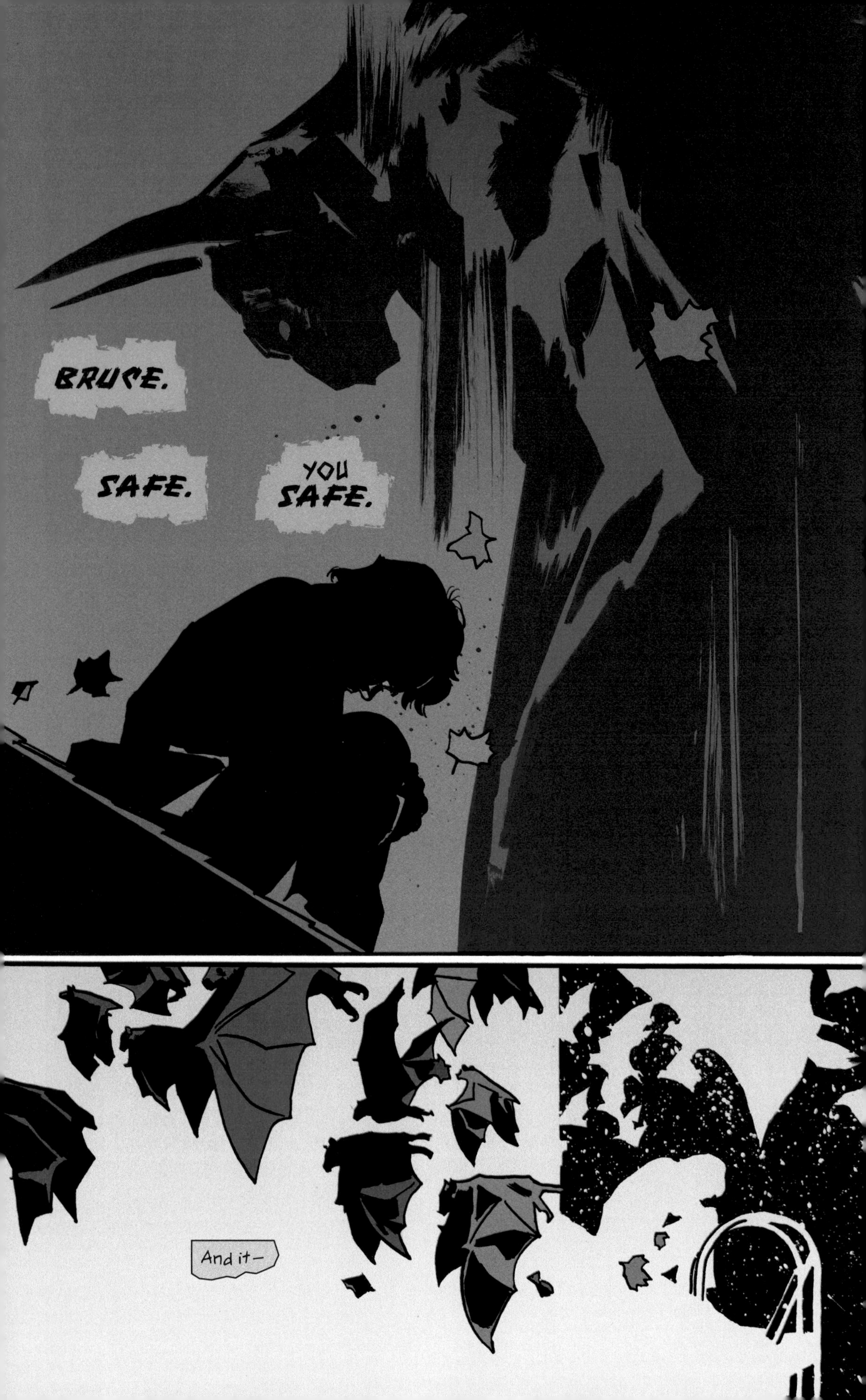
BRUCE.
SAFE.
YOU SAFE.
And it—

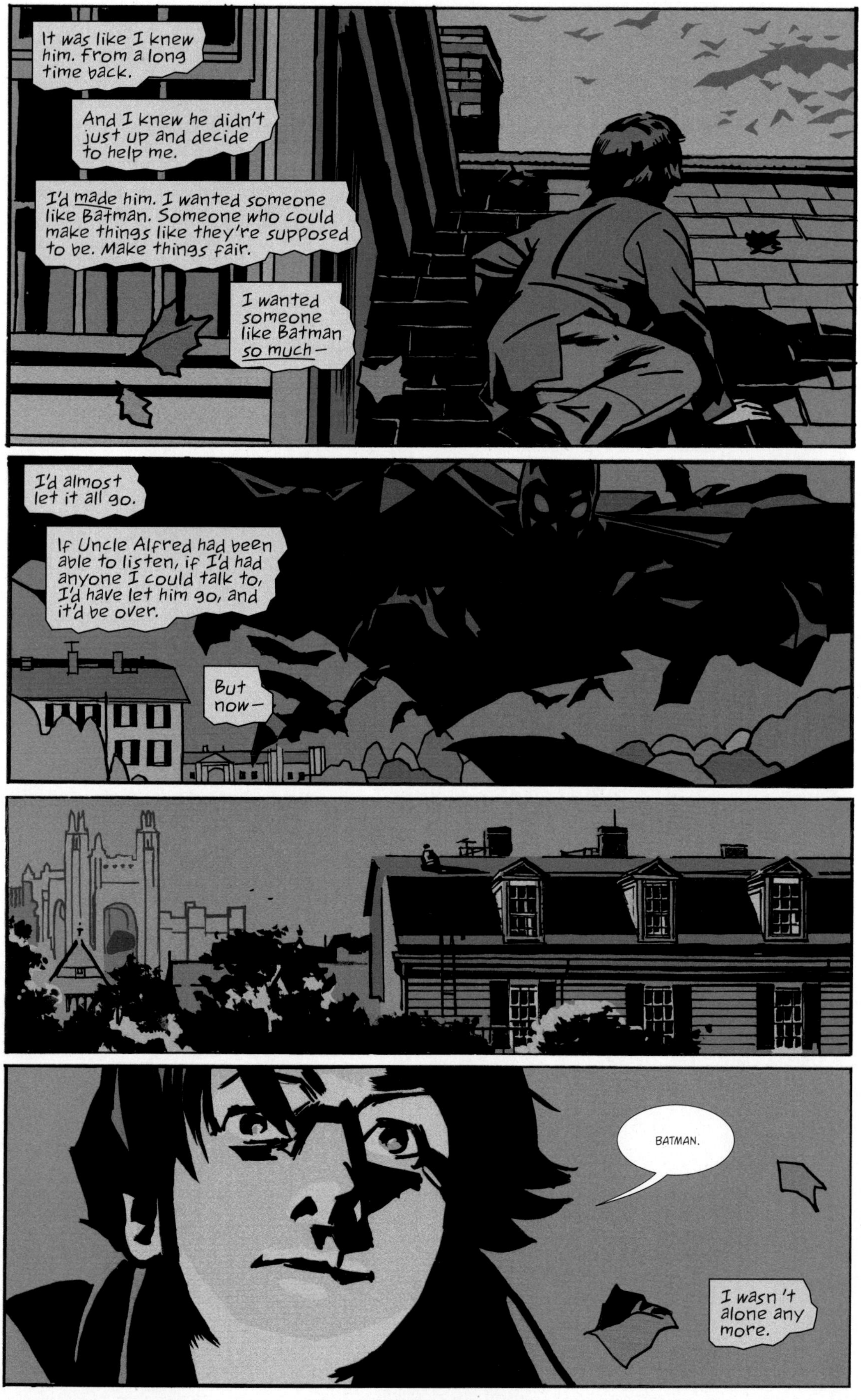
It was like I knew him. From a long time back.
And I knew he didn't just up and decide to help me.
I'd made him. I wanted someone like Batman. Someone who could make things like they're supposed to be. Make things fair.
I wanted someone like Batman so much—
I'd almost let it all go.
If Uncle Alfred had been able to listen, if I'd had anyone I could talk to, I'd have let him go, and it'd be over.
But now—
BATMAN.
I wasn't alone any more.

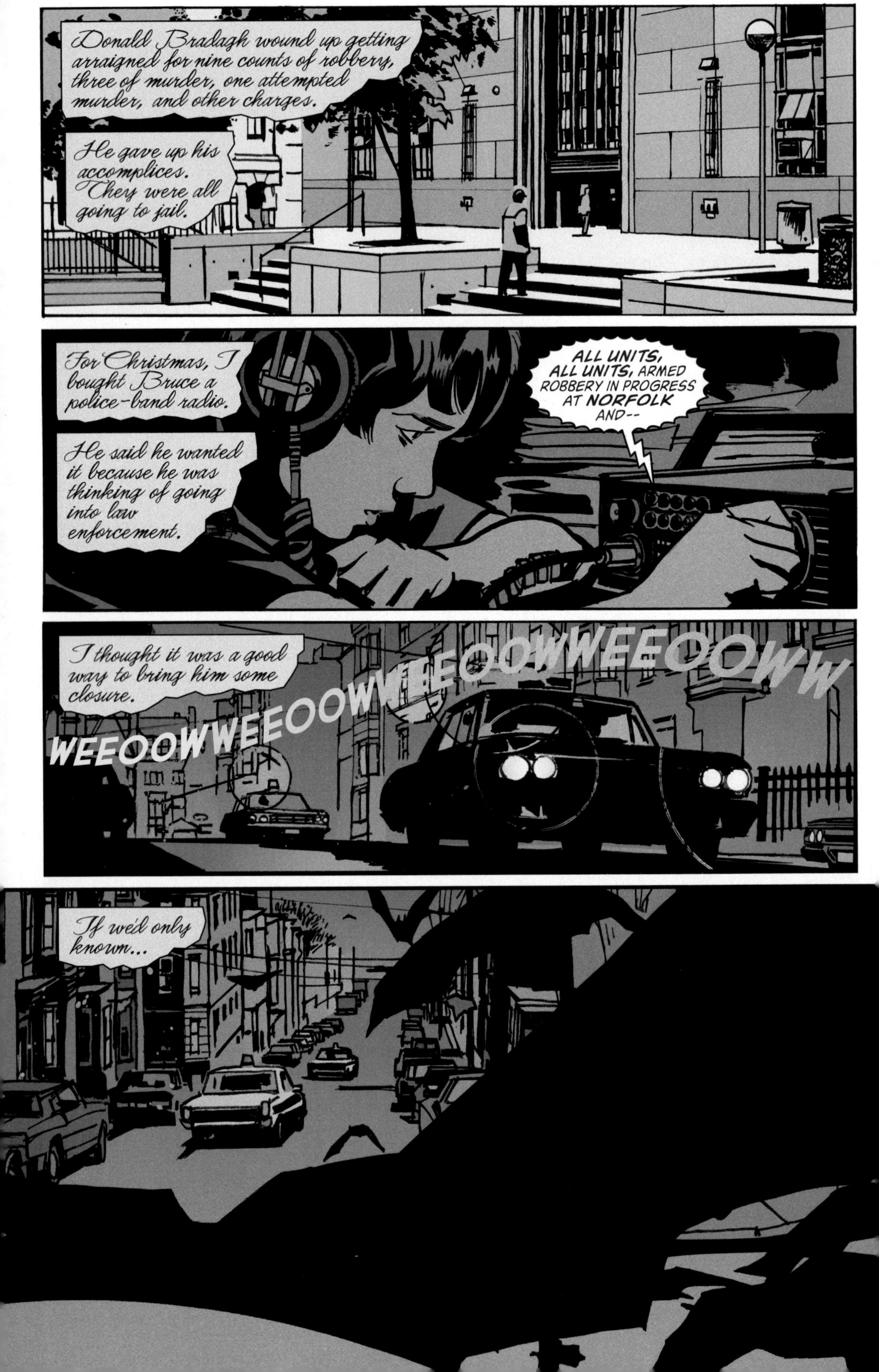
Donald Bradagh wound up getting arraigned for nine counts of robbery, three of murder, one attempted murder, and other charges.
He gave up his accomplices. They were all going to jail.
For Christmas, I bought Bruce a police-band radio.
He said he wanted it because he was thinking of going into law enforcement.
ALL UNITS, ALL UNITS, ARMED ROBBERY IN PROGRESS AT NORFOLK AND--
I thought it was a good way to bring him some closure.
WEEOOWWEEOOWWEEOOWWEEOOWW
If we'd only known...

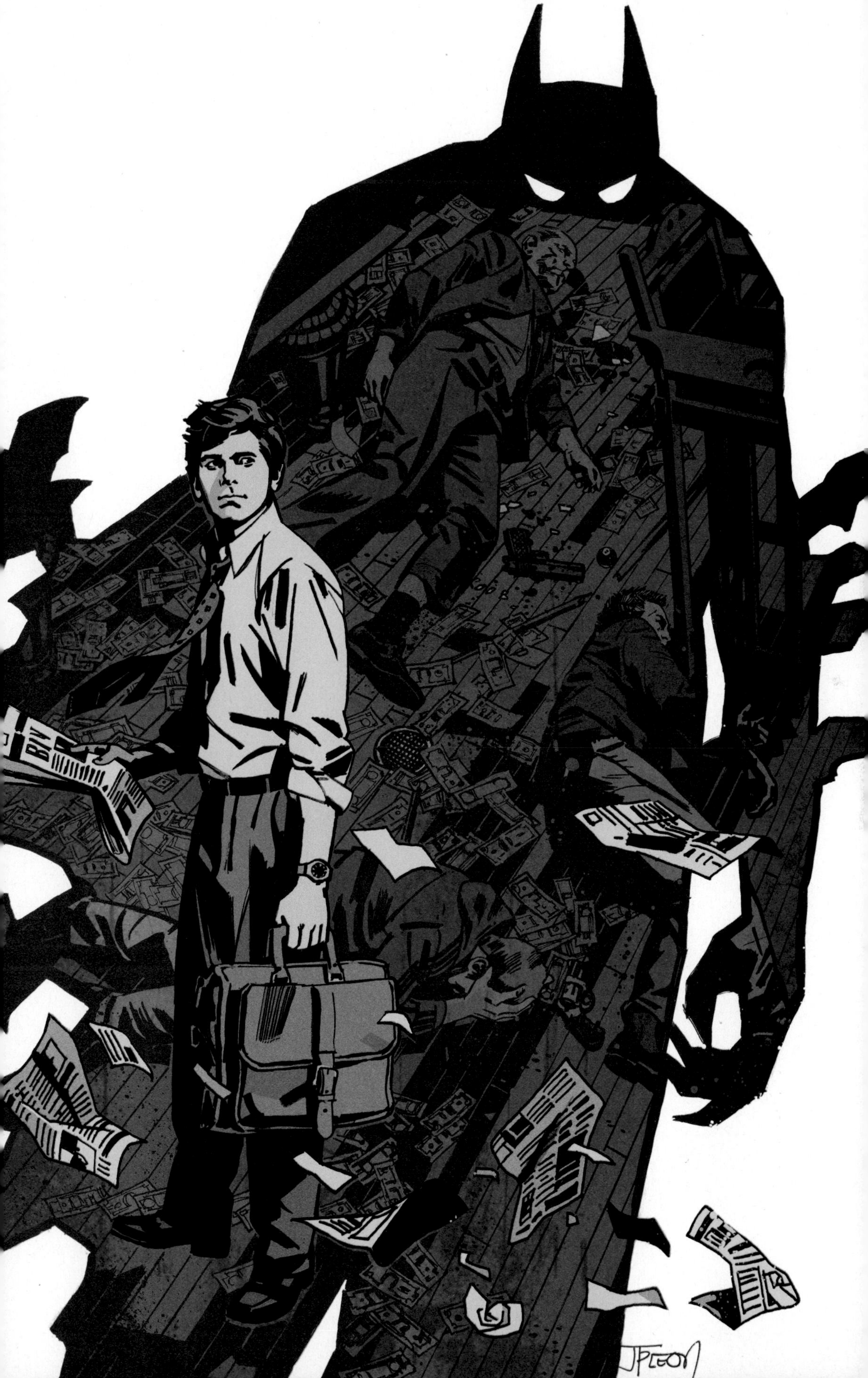

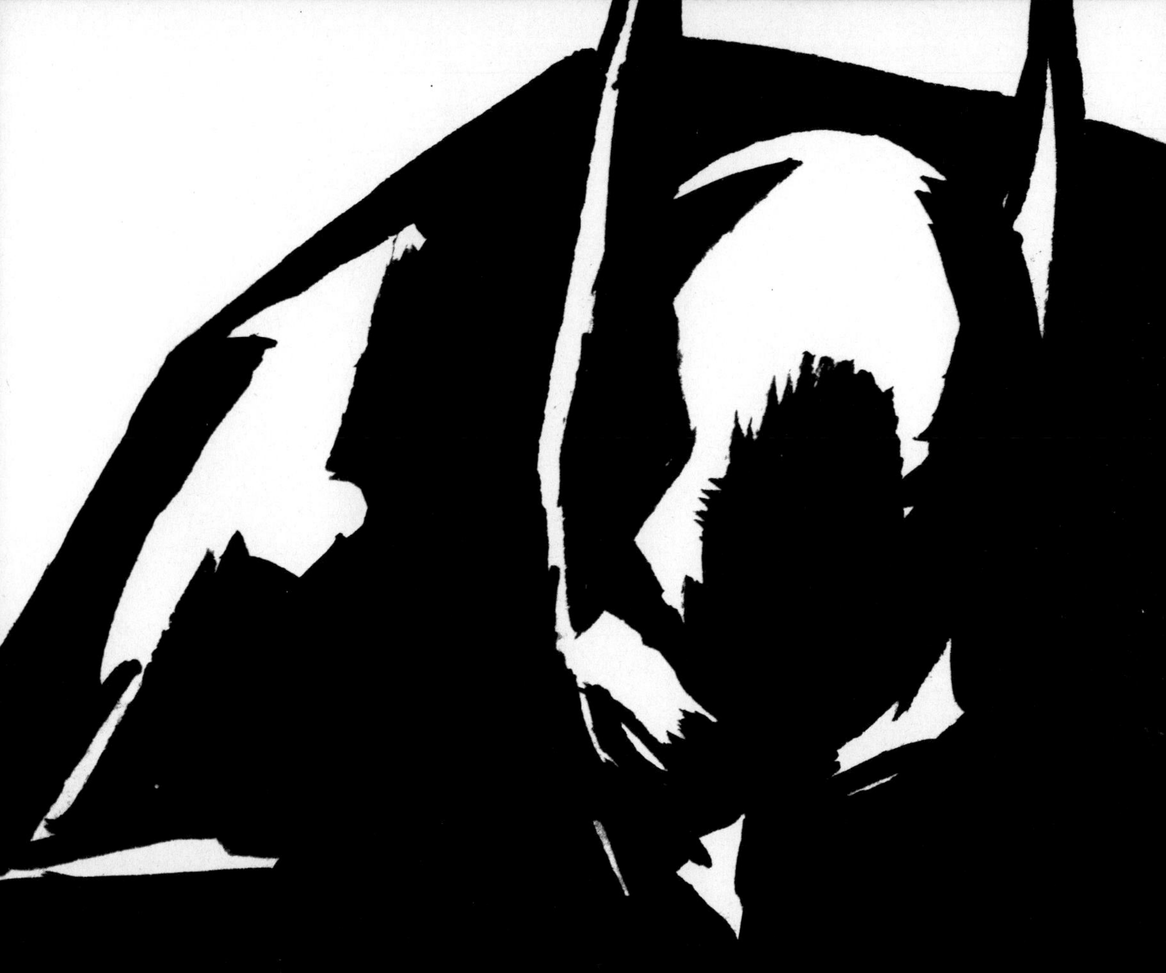

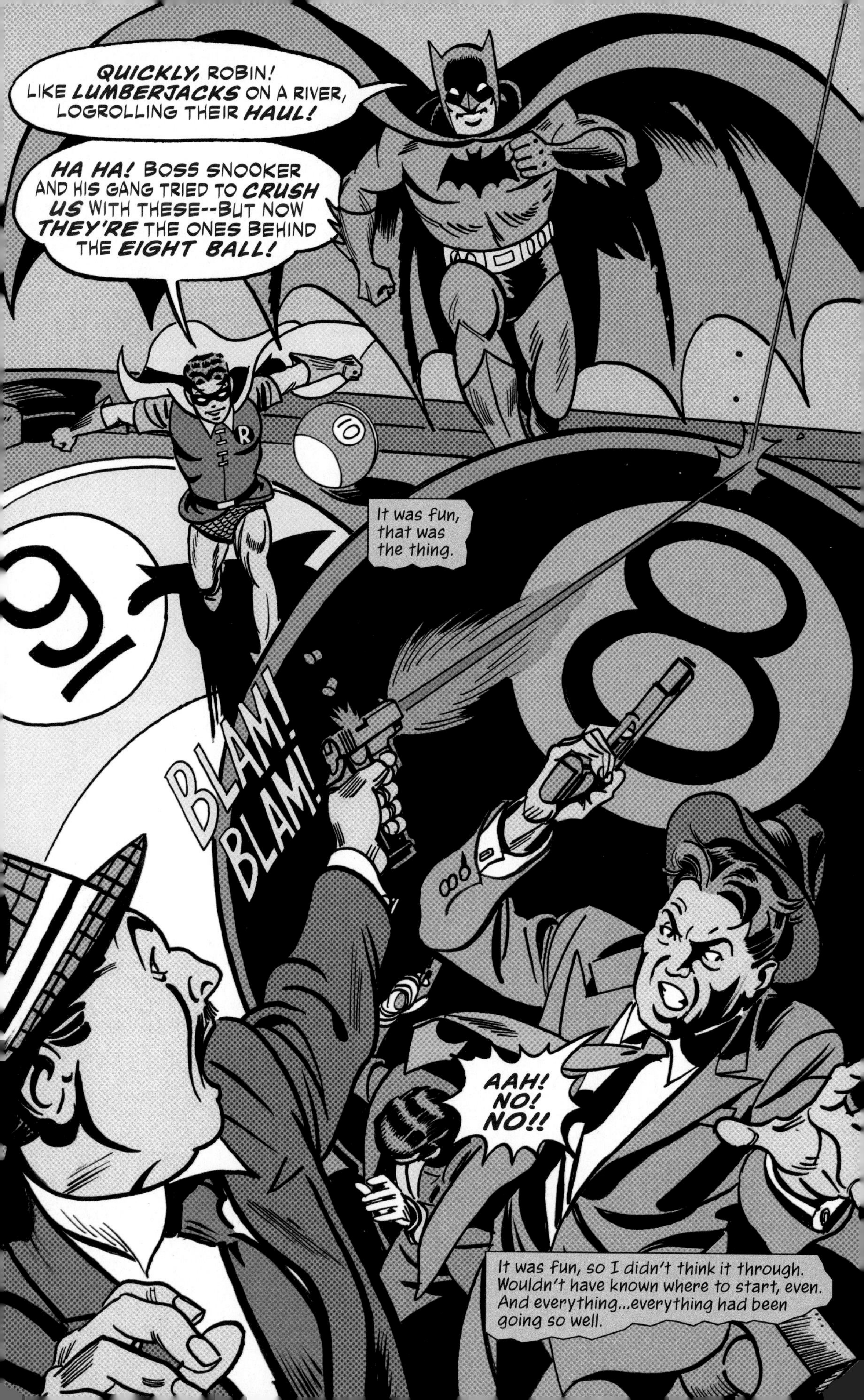

QUICKLY, ROBIN! LIKE LUMBERJACKS ON A RIVER, LOGROLLING THEIR HAUL!
HA HA! BOSS SNOOKER AND HIS GANG TRIED TO CRUSH US WITH THESE--BUT NOW THEY'RE THE ONES BEHIND THE EIGHT BALL!
It was fun, that was the thing.
BLAM! BLAM!
AAH! NO! NO!!
It was fun, so I didn't think it through. Wouldn't have known where to start, even. And everything...everything had been going so well.

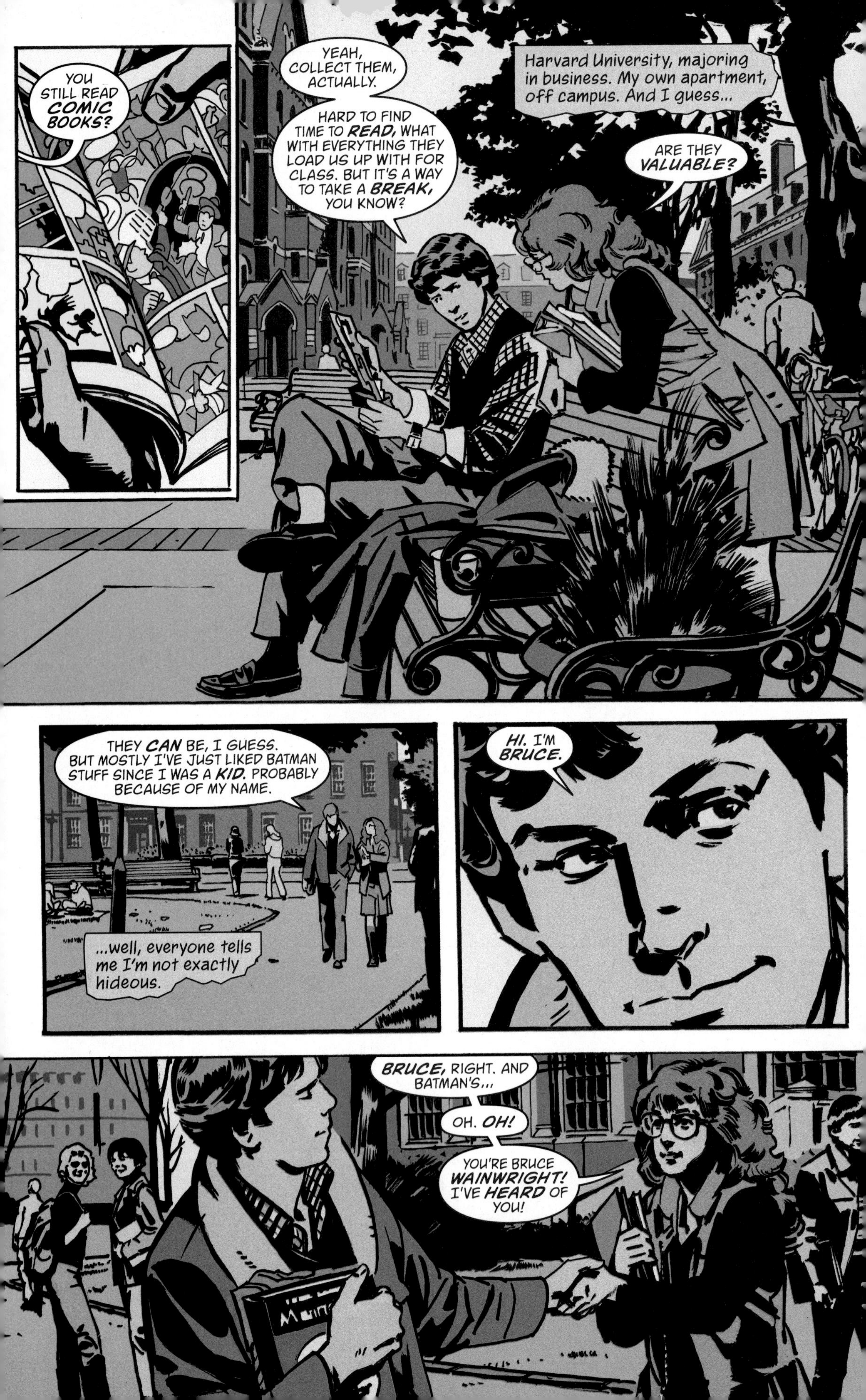
YOU STILL READ COMIC BOOKS?
YEAH, COLLECT THEM, ACTUALLY.
HARD TO FIND TIME TO READ, WHAT WITH EVERYTHING THEY LOAD US UP WITH FOR CLASS. BUT IT'S A WAY TO TAKE A BREAK, YOU KNOW?
Harvard University, majoring in business. My own apartment, off campus. And I guess...
ARE THEY VALUABLE?
THEY CAN BE, I GUESS. BUT MOSTLY I'VE JUST LIKED BATMAN STUFF SINCE I WAS A KID. PROBABLY BECAUSE OF MY NAME.
...well, everyone tells me I'm not exactly hideous.
HI. I'M BRUCE.
BRUCE, RIGHT. AND BATMAN'S...
OH. OH!
YOU'RE BRUCE WAINWRIGHT! I'VE HEARD OF YOU!

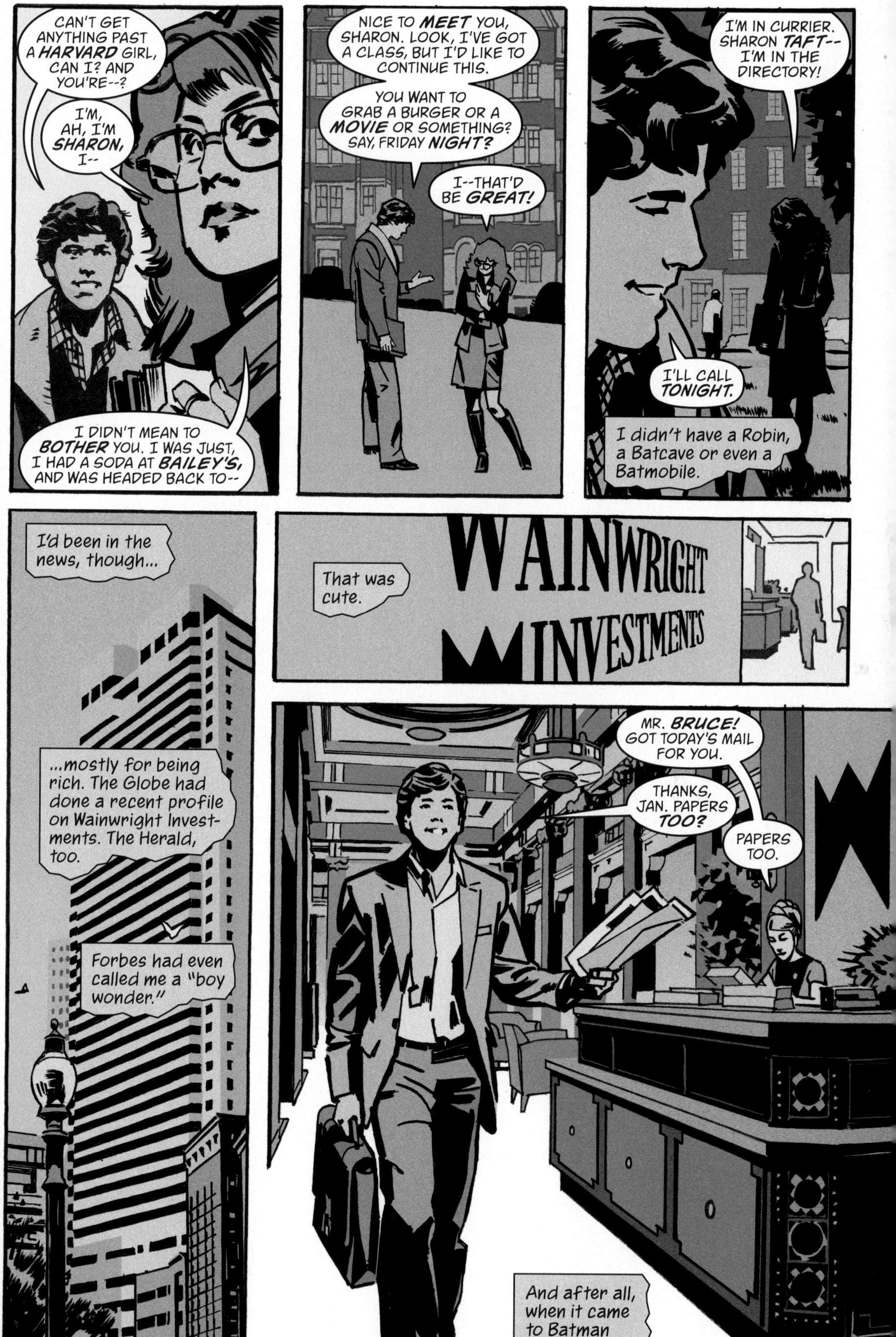
CAN'T GET ANYTHING PAST A HARVARD GIRL, CAN I? AND YOU'RE--?
I'M, AH, I'M SHARON, I--
I DIDN'T MEAN TO BOTHER YOU. I WAS JUST, I HAD A SODA AT BAILEY'S, AND WAS HEADED BACK TO--
NICE TO MEET YOU, SHARON. LOOK, I'VE GOT A CLASS, BUT I'D LIKE TO CONTINUE THIS.
YOU WANT TO GRAB A BURGER OR A MOVIE OR SOMETHING? SAY, FRIDAY NIGHT?
I--THAT'D BE GREAT!
I'M IN CURRIER. SHARON TAFT-- I'M IN THE DIRECTORY!
I'LL CALL TONIGHT.
I didn't have a Robin, a Batcave or even a Batmobile.
I'd been in the news, though...
...mostly for being rich. The Globe had done a recent profile on Wainwright Investments. The Herald, too.
Forbes had even called me a "boy wonder."
That was cute.
WAINWRIGHT
INVESTMENTS
MR. BRUCE! GOT TODAY'S MAIL FOR YOU.
THANKS, JAN. PAPERS TOO?
PAPERS TOO.
And after all, when it came to Batman connections...

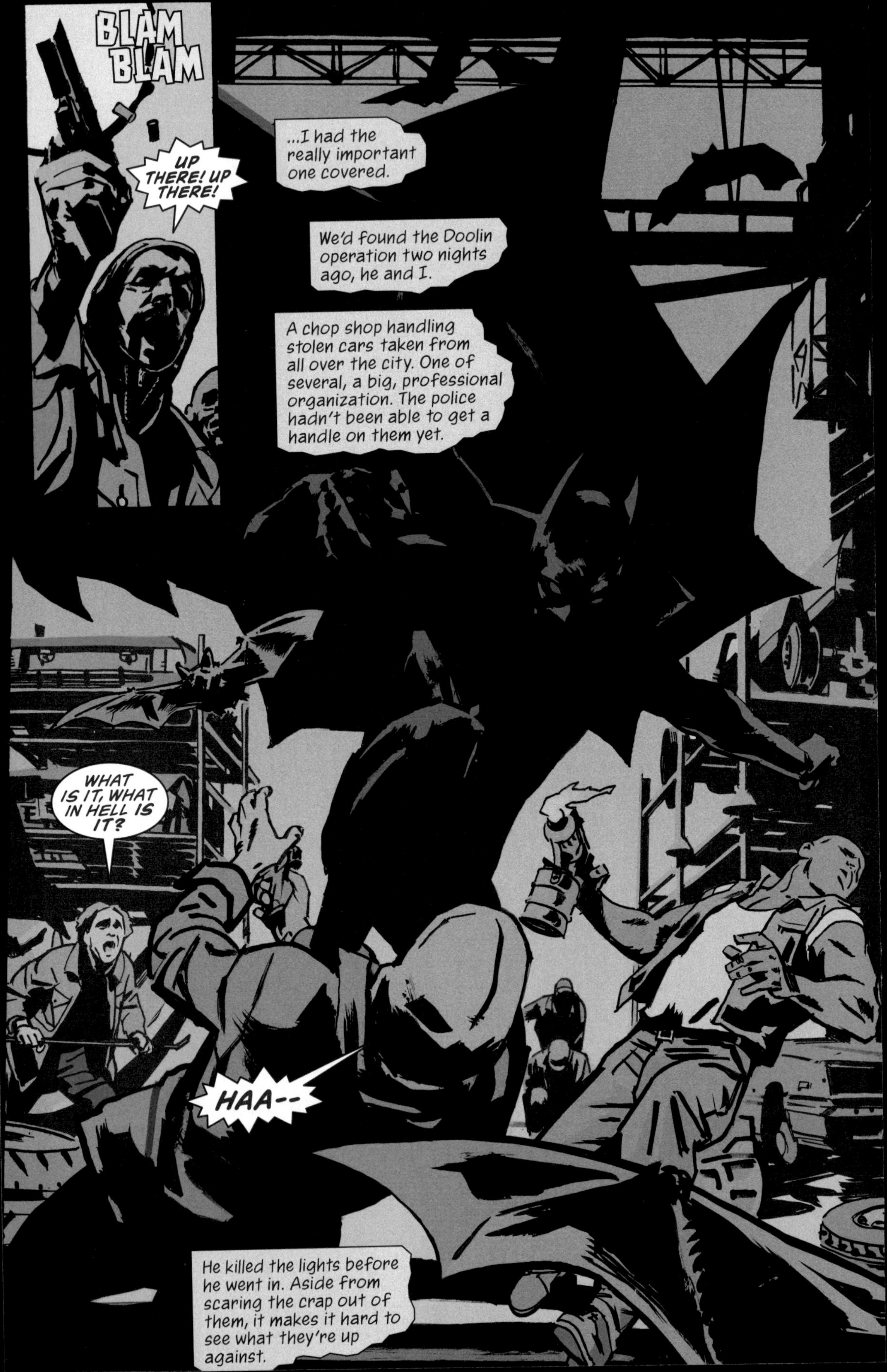
BLAM BLAM
UP THERE! UP THERE!
...I had the really important one covered.
We'd found the Doolin operation two nights ago, he and I.
A chop shop handling stolen cars taken from all over the city. One of several, a big, professional organization. The police hadn't been able to get a handle on them yet.
WHAT IS IT, WHAT IN HELL IS IT?
HAA--
He killed the lights before he went in. Aside from scaring the crap out of them, it makes it hard to see what they're up against.

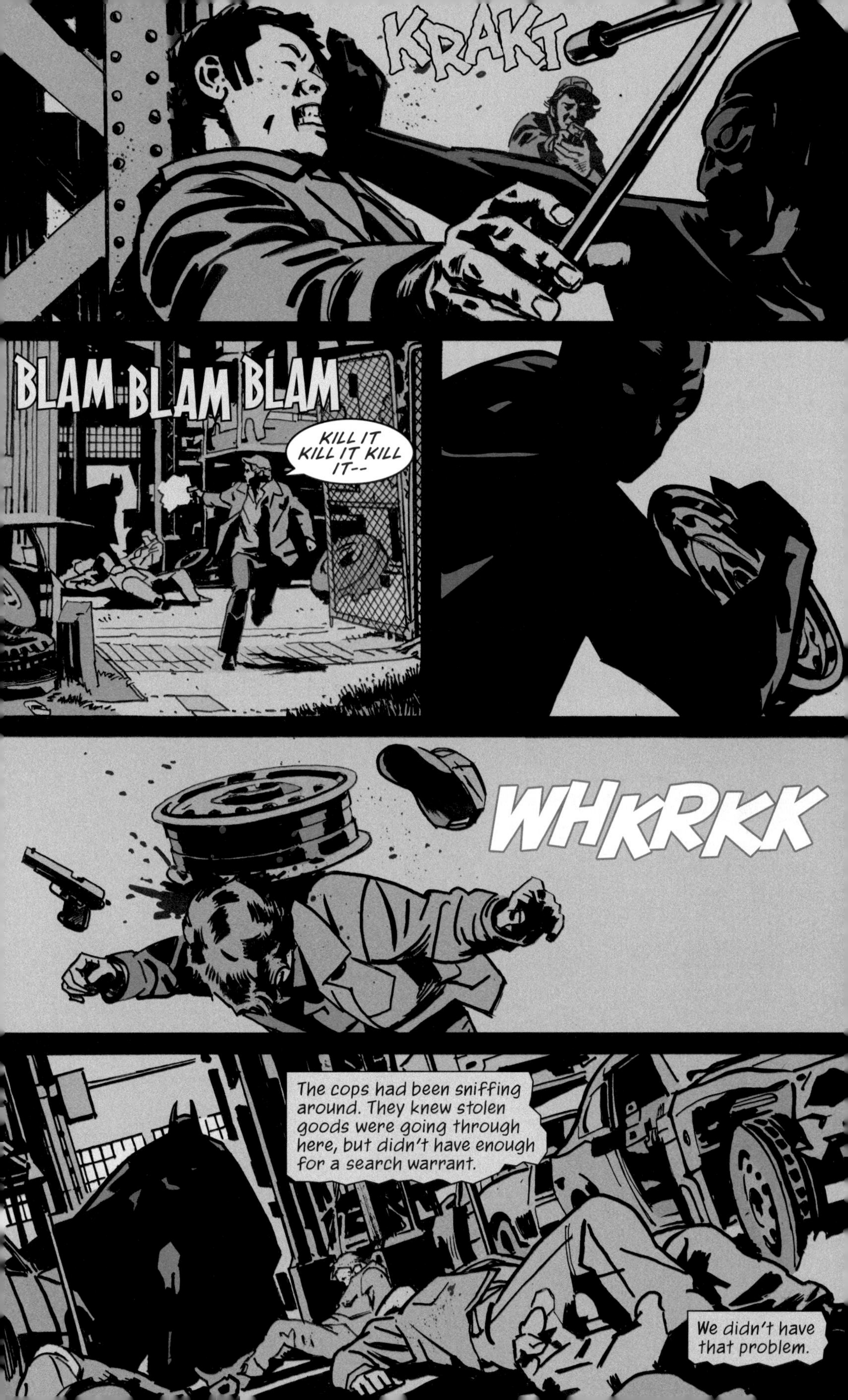
KRAKT
BLAM BLAM BLAM
KILL IT KILL IT KILL IT--
WHKRKK
The cops had been sniffing around. They knew stolen goods were going through here, but didn't have enough for a search warrant.
We didn't have that problem.

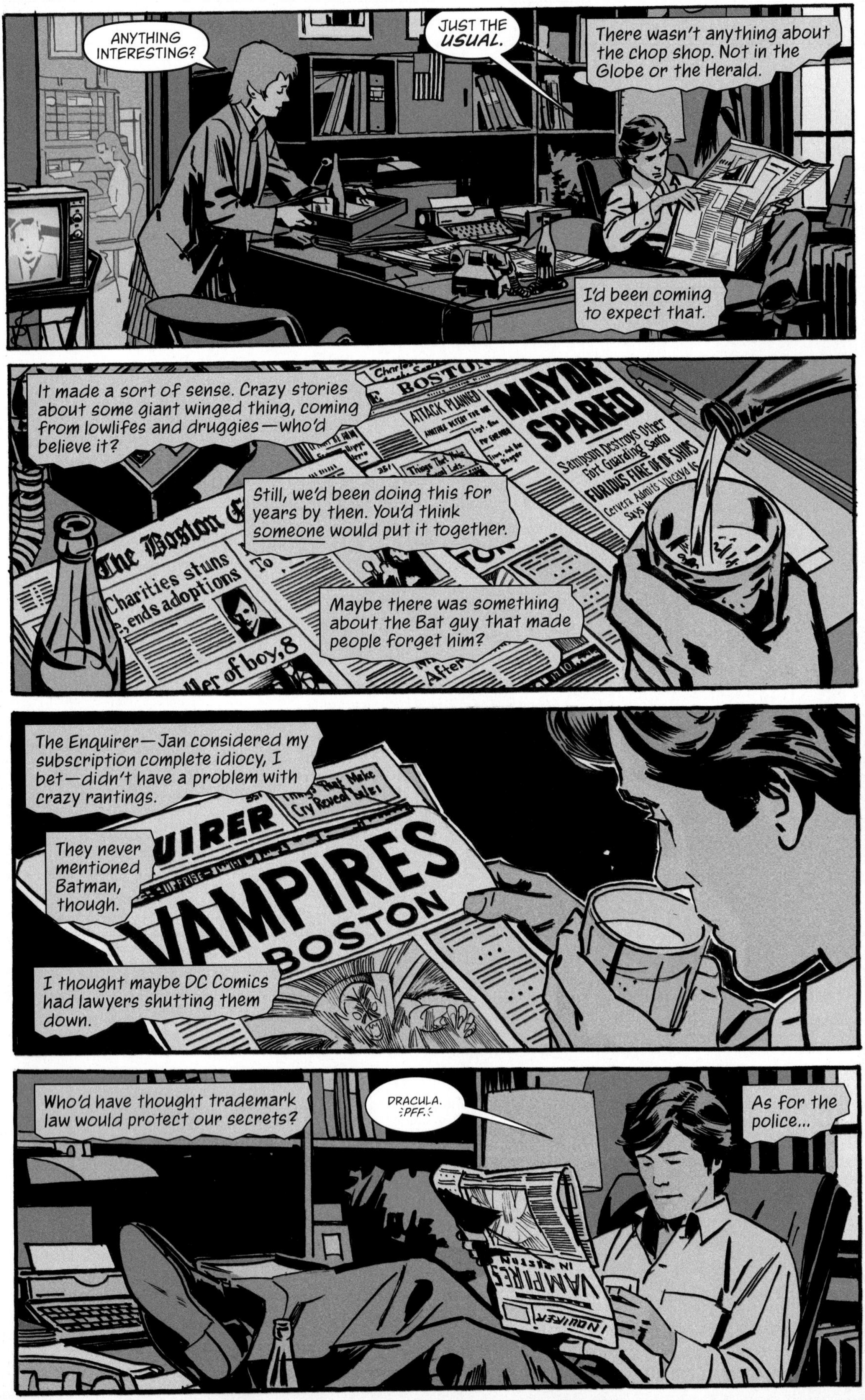
ANYTHING INTERESTING?
JUST THE *USUAL.*
There wasn't anything about the chop shop. Not in the Globe or the Herald.
I'd been coming to expect that.
It made a sort of sense. Crazy stories about some giant winged thing, coming from lowlifes and druggies—who'd believe it?
MAYOR SPARED
Still, we'd been doing this for years by then. You'd think someone would put it together.
The Boston Globe
Charities stuns, ends adoptions
Maybe there was something about the Bat guy that made people forget him?
The Enquirer—Jan considered my subscription complete idiocy, I bet—didn't have a problem with crazy rantings.
They never mentioned Batman, though.
VAMPIRES BOSTON
I thought maybe DC Comics had lawyers shutting them down.
Who'd have thought trademark law would protect our secrets?
DRACULA. PFF.
As for the police...

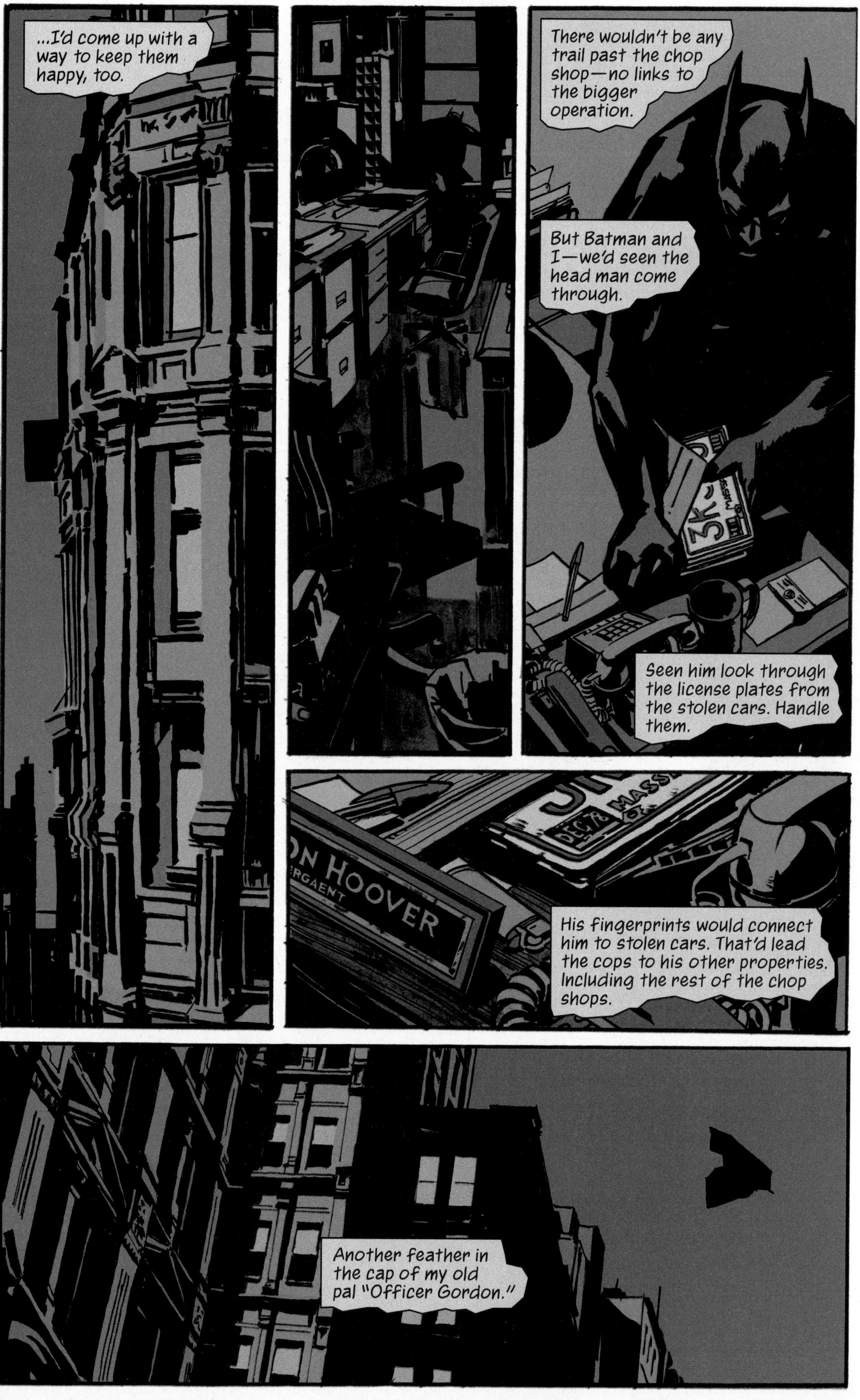
...I'd come up with a way to keep them happy, too.
There wouldn't be any trail past the chop shop—no links to the bigger operation.
But Batman and I—we'd seen the head man come through.
Seen him look through the license plates from the stolen cars. Handle them.
His fingerprints would connect him to stolen cars. That'd lead the cops to his other properties. Including the rest of the chop shops.
Another feather in the cap of my old pal "Officer Gordon."

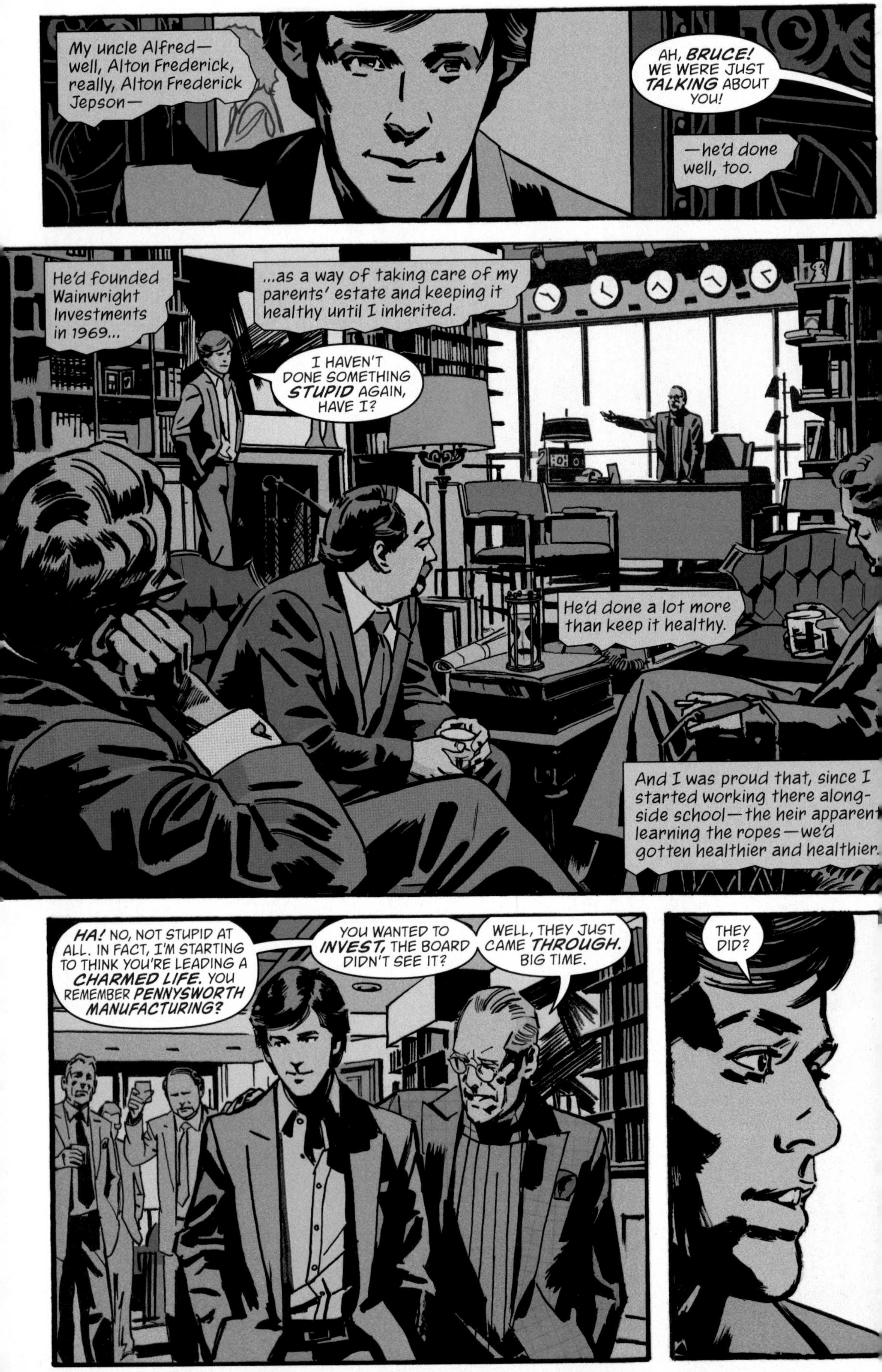
My uncle Alfred—well, Alton Frederick, really, Alton Frederick Jepson—
AH, BRUCE! WE WERE JUST TALKING ABOUT YOU!
—he'd done well, too.
He'd founded Wainwright Investments in 1969...
...as a way of taking care of my parents' estate and keeping it healthy until I inherited.
I HAVEN'T DONE SOMETHING STUPID AGAIN, HAVE I?
He'd done a lot more than keep it healthy.
And I was proud that, since I started working there along-side school—the heir apparent learning the ropes—we'd gotten healthier and healthier.
HA! NO, NOT STUPID AT ALL. IN FACT, I'M STARTING TO THINK YOU'RE LEADING A CHARMED LIFE. YOU REMEMBER PENNYSWORTH MANUFACTURING?
YOU WANTED TO INVEST, THE BOARD DIDN'T SEE IT?
WELL, THEY JUST CAME THROUGH. BIG TIME.
THEY DID?

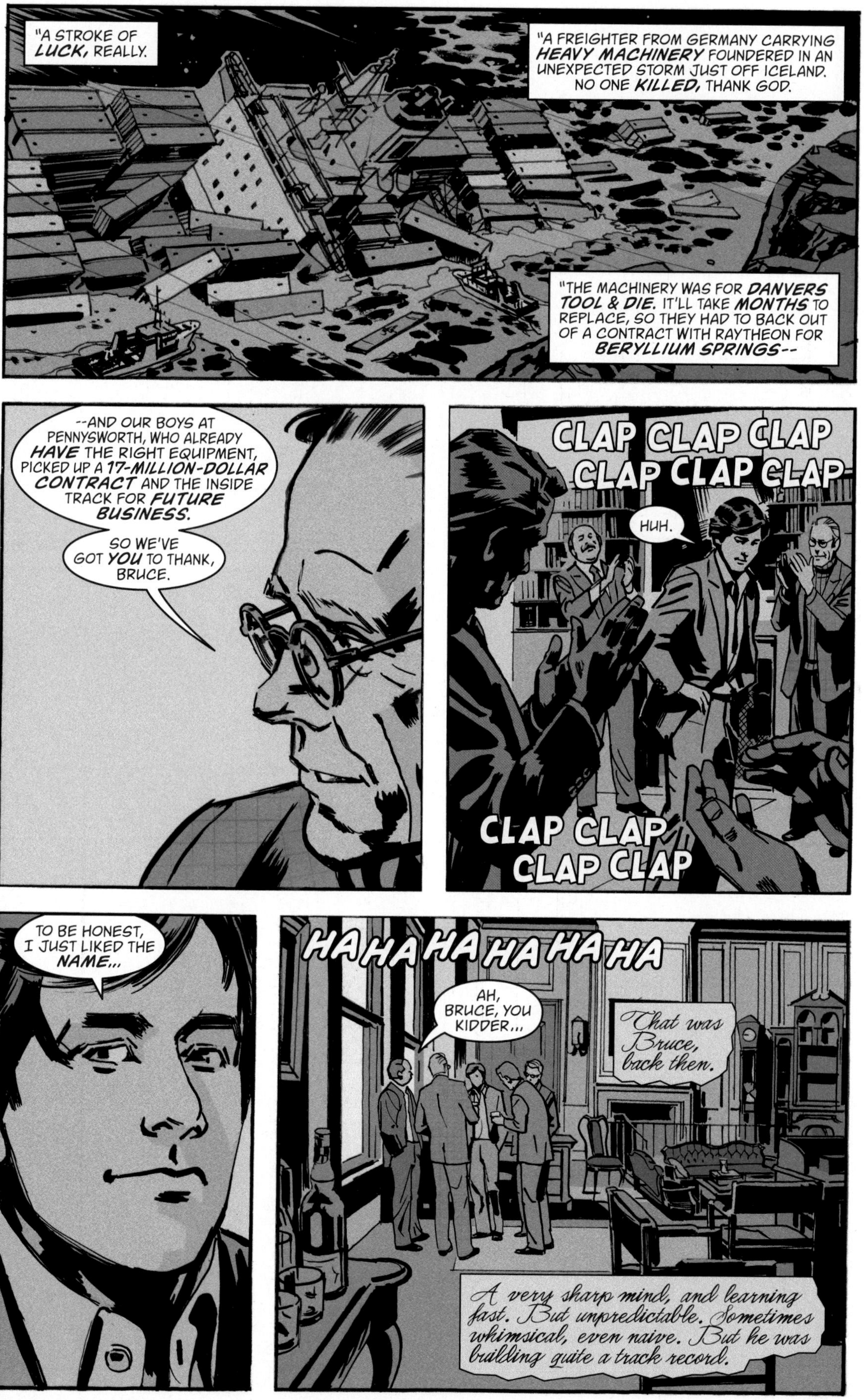
"A STROKE OF LUCK, REALLY.
"A FREIGHTER FROM GERMANY CARRYING HEAVY MACHINERY FOUNDERED IN AN UNEXPECTED STORM JUST OFF ICELAND. NO ONE KILLED, THANK GOD.
"THE MACHINERY WAS FOR DANVERS TOOL & DIE. IT'LL TAKE MONTHS TO REPLACE, SO THEY HAD TO BACK OUT OF A CONTRACT WITH RAYTHEON FOR BERYLLIUM SPRINGS--
--AND OUR BOYS AT PENNYSWORTH, WHO ALREADY HAVE THE RIGHT EQUIPMENT, PICKED UP A 17-MILLION-DOLLAR CONTRACT AND THE INSIDE TRACK FOR FUTURE BUSINESS.
SO WE'VE GOT YOU TO THANK, BRUCE.
CLAP CLAP CLAP CLAP CLAP CLAP
HUH.
CLAP CLAP CLAP CLAP
TO BE HONEST, I JUST LIKED THE NAME...
HA HA HA HA HA HA HA
AH, BRUCE, YOU KIDDER...
That was Bruce, back then.
A very sharp mind, and learning fast. But unpredictable. Sometimes whimsical, even naive. But he was building quite a track record.

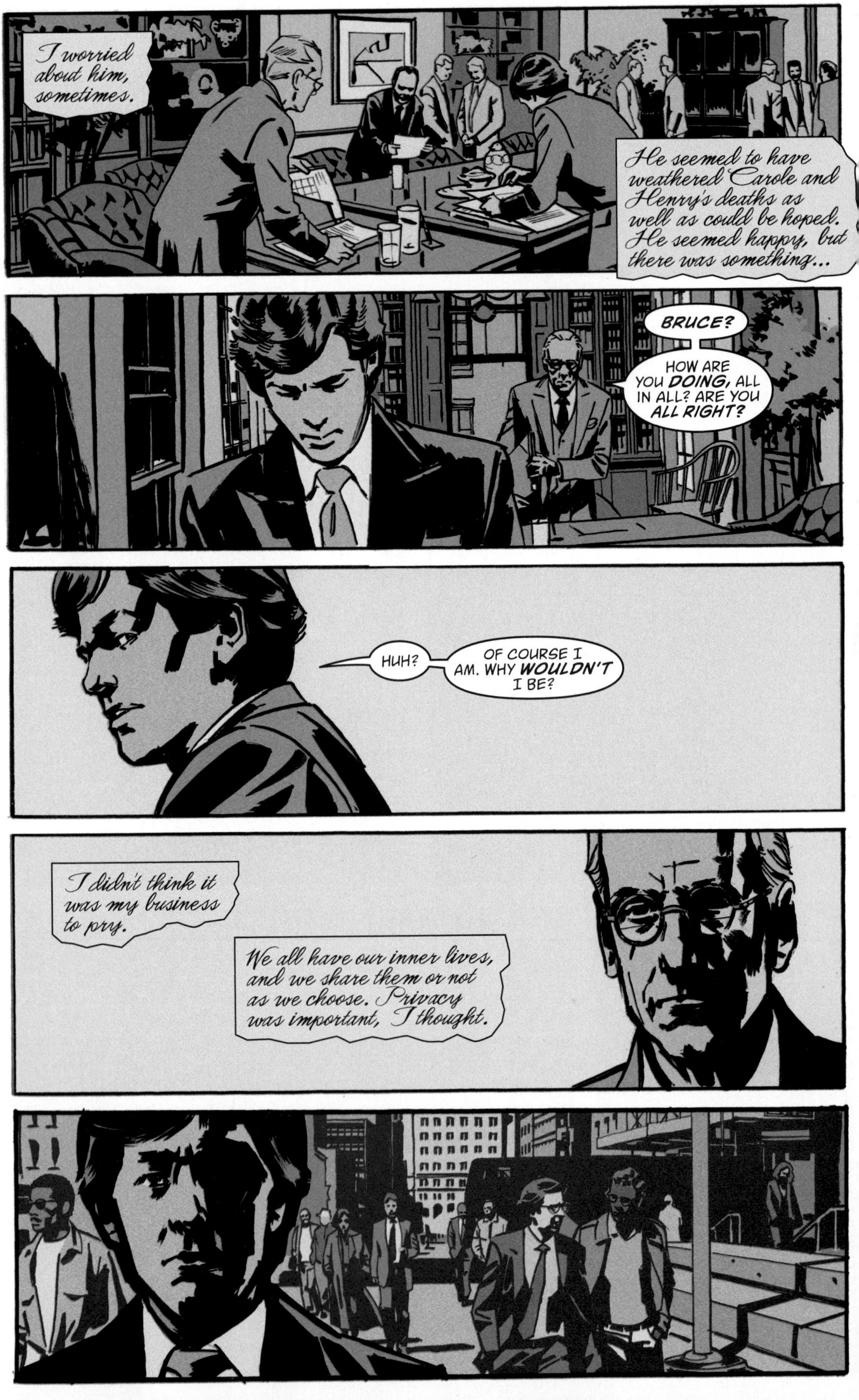
I worried about him, sometimes.
He seemed to have weathered Carole and Henry's deaths as well as could be hoped. He seemed happy, but there was something...
BRUCE?
HOW ARE YOU DOING, ALL IN ALL? ARE YOU ALL RIGHT?
HUH?
OF COURSE I AM. WHY WOULDN'T I BE?
I didn't think it was my business to pry.
We all have our inner lives, and we share them or not as we choose. Privacy was important, I thought.

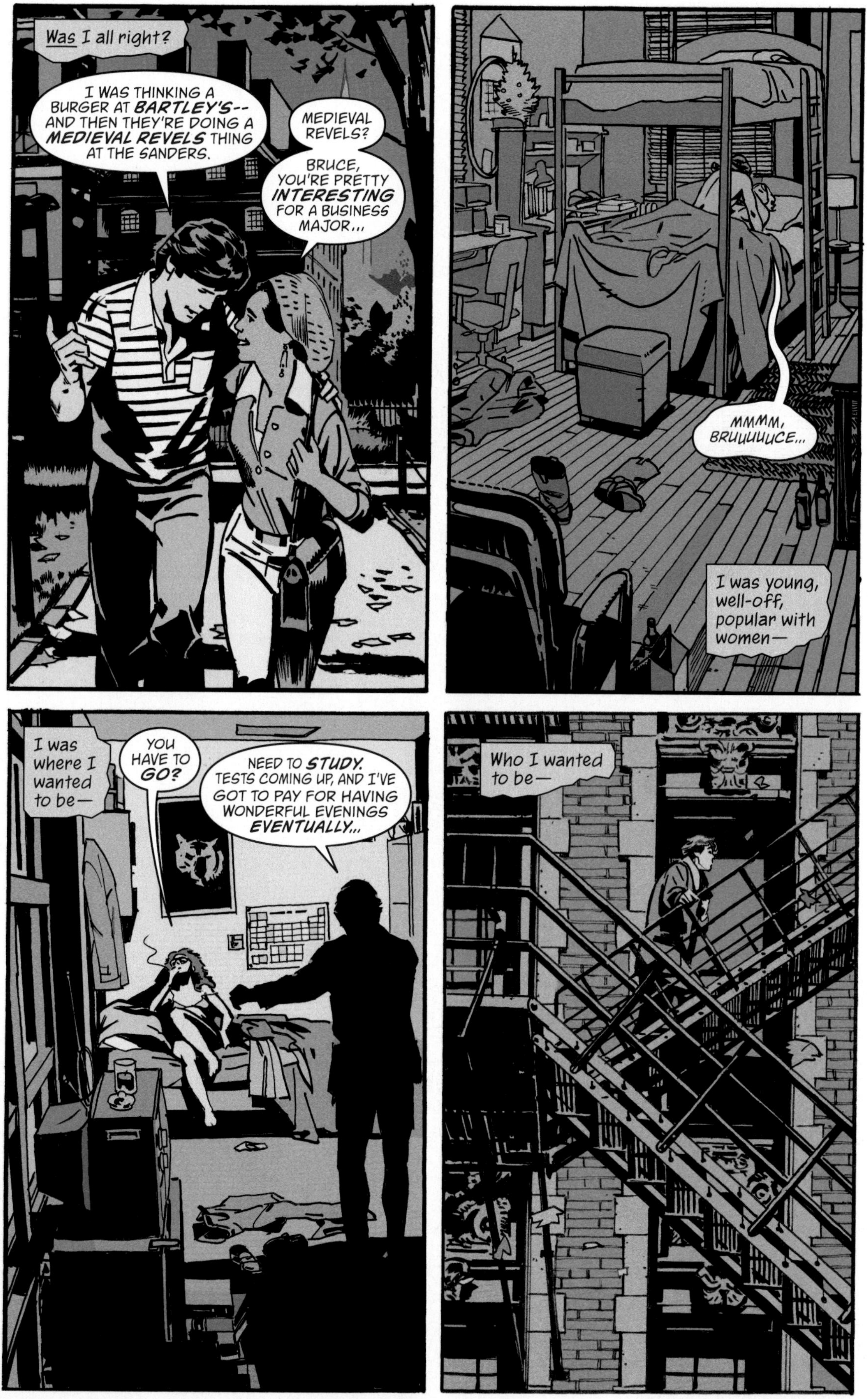
Was I all right?
I WAS THINKING A BURGER AT BARTLEY'S--AND THEN THEY'RE DOING A MEDIEVAL REVELS THING AT THE SANDERS.
MEDIEVAL REVELS?
BRUCE, YOU'RE PRETTY INTERESTING FOR A BUSINESS MAJOR...
MMMM, BRUUUUUCE...
I was young, well-off, popular with women—
I was where I wanted to be—
YOU HAVE TO GO?
NEED TO STUDY. TESTS COMING UP, AND I'VE GOT TO PAY FOR HAVING WONDERFUL EVENINGS EVENTUALLY...
Who I wanted to be—

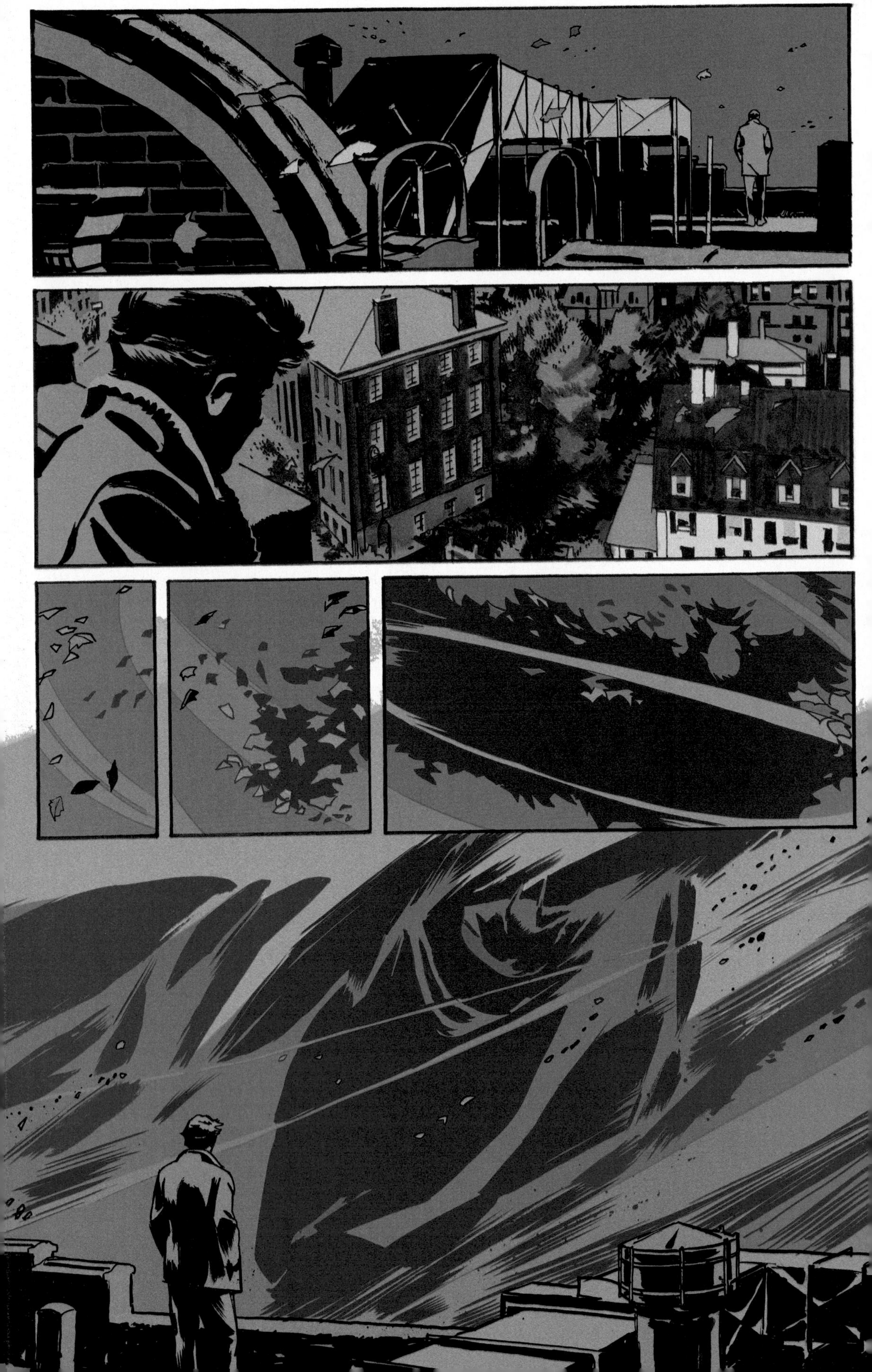

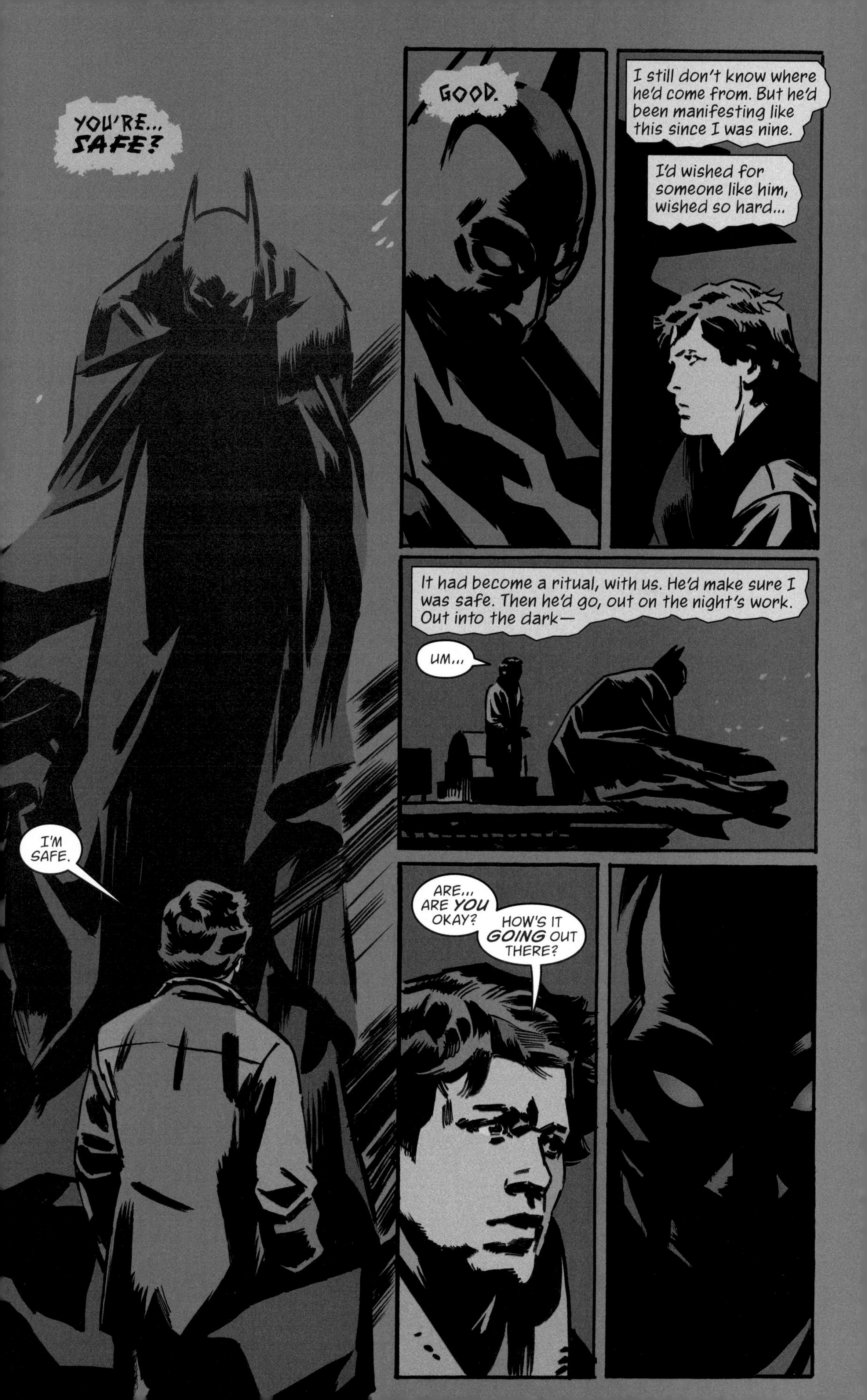
YOU'RE... SAFE?
I'M SAFE.
GOOD.
I still don't know where he'd come from. But he'd been manifesting like this since I was nine.
I'd wished for someone like him, wished so hard...
It had become a ritual, with us. He'd make sure I was safe. Then he'd go, out on the night's work. Out into the dark—
UM...
ARE... ARE YOU OKAY?
HOW'S IT GOING OUT THERE?

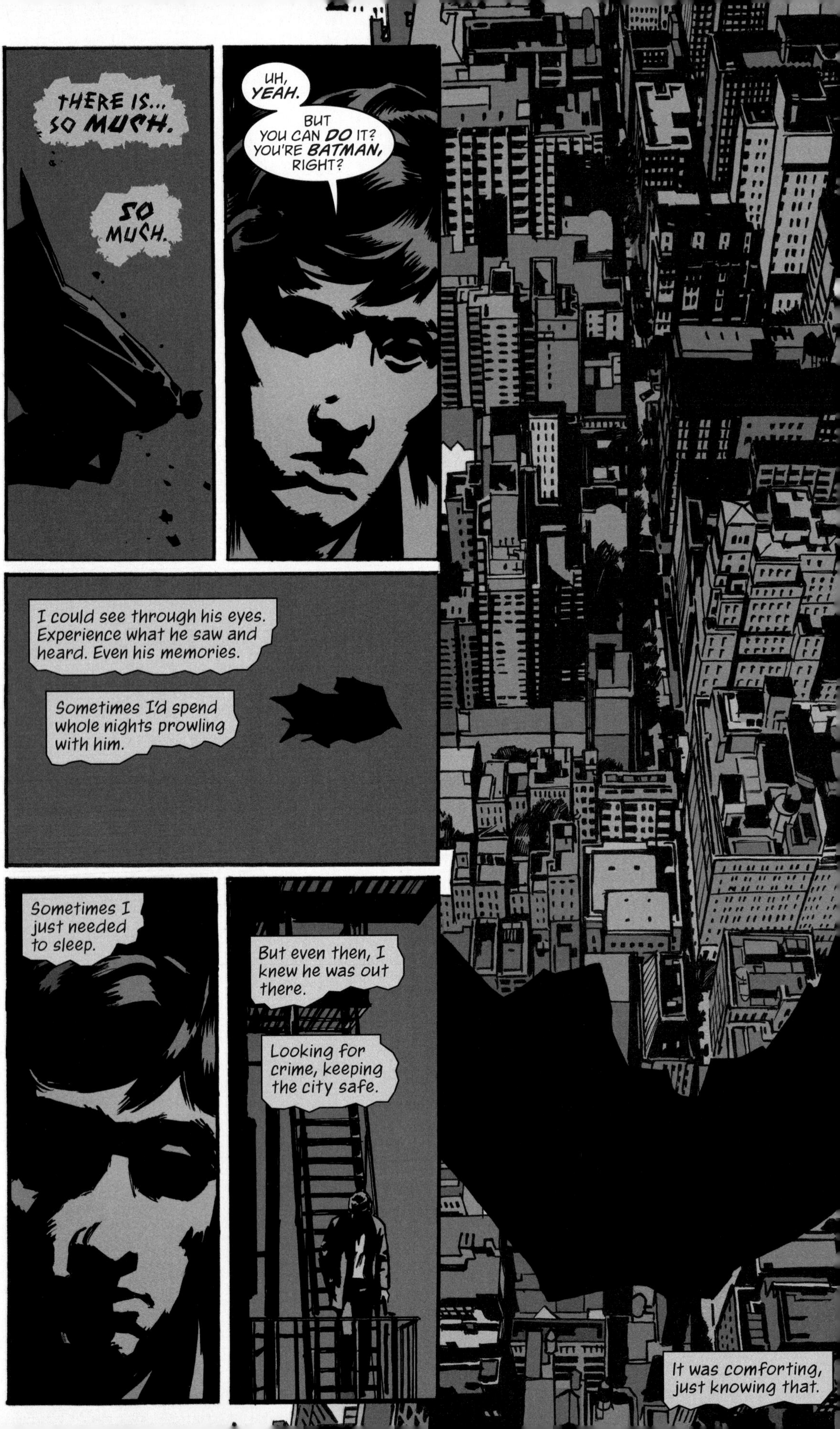
THERE IS... SO MUCH.
SO MUCH.
UH, YEAH.
BUT YOU CAN DO IT? YOU'RE BATMAN, RIGHT?
I could see through his eyes. Experience what he saw and heard. Even his memories.
Sometimes I'd spend whole nights prowling with him.
Sometimes I just needed to sleep.
But even then, I knew he was out there.
Looking for crime, keeping the city safe.
It was comforting, just knowing that.

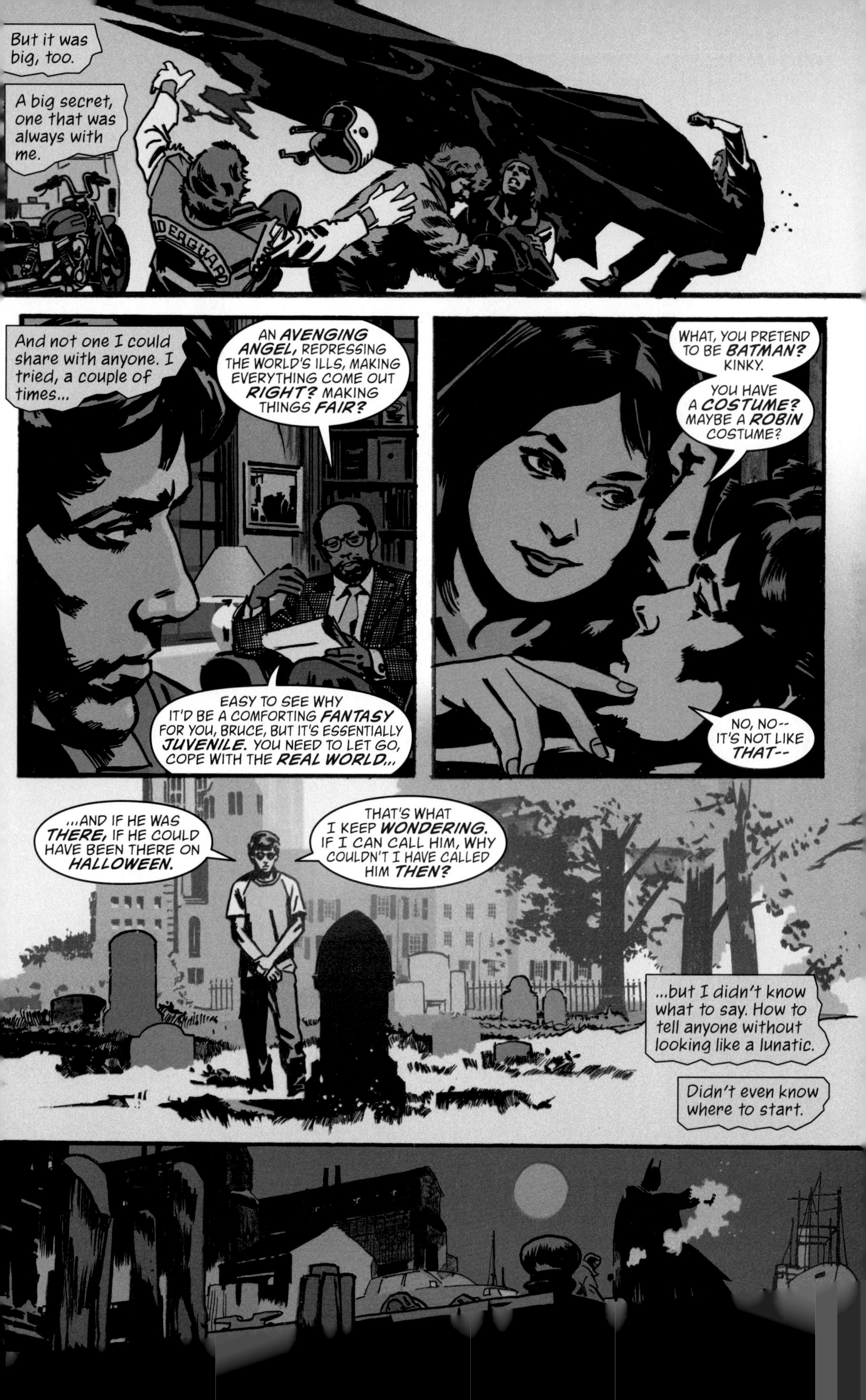

But it was big, too.
A big secret, one that was always with me.
And not one I could share with anyone. I tried, a couple of times...
AN AVENGING ANGEL, REDRESSING THE WORLD'S ILLS, MAKING EVERYTHING COME OUT RIGHT? MAKING THINGS FAIR?
EASY TO SEE WHY IT'D BE A COMFORTING FANTASY FOR YOU, BRUCE, BUT IT'S ESSENTIALLY JUVENILE. YOU NEED TO LET GO, COPE WITH THE REAL WORLD...
WHAT, YOU PRETEND TO BE BATMAN? KINKY.
YOU HAVE A COSTUME? MAYBE A ROBIN COSTUME?
NO, NO-- IT'S NOT LIKE THAT--
...AND IF HE WAS THERE, IF HE COULD HAVE BEEN THERE ON HALLOWEEN.
THAT'S WHAT I KEEP WONDERING. IF I CAN CALL HIM, WHY COULDN'T I HAVE CALLED HIM THEN?
...but I didn't know what to say. How to tell anyone without looking like a lunatic.
Didn't even know where to start.

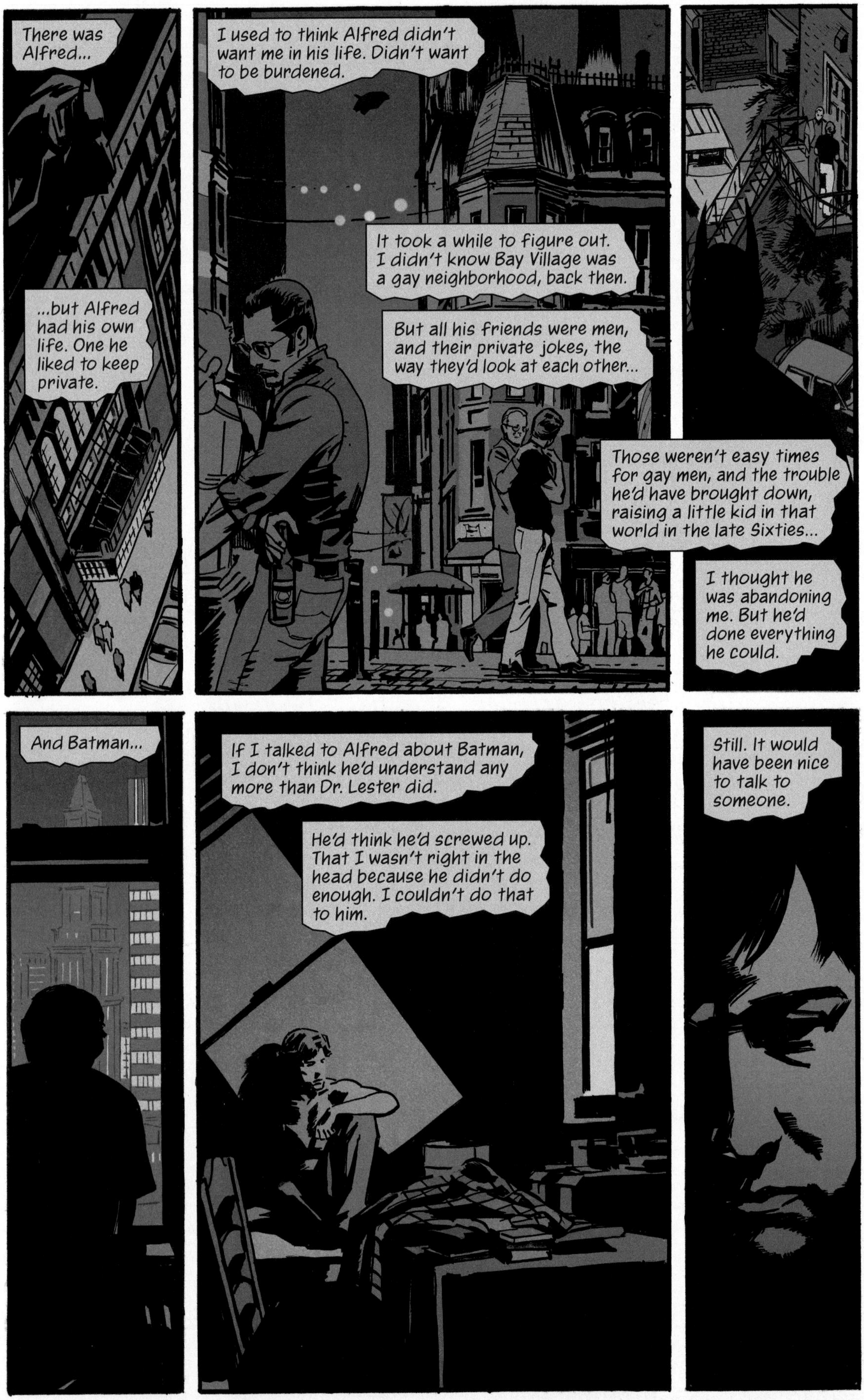
There was Alfred...
...but Alfred had his own life. One he liked to keep private.
I used to think Alfred didn't want me in his life. Didn't want to be burdened.
It took a while to figure out. I didn't know Bay Village was a gay neighborhood, back then.
But all his friends were men, and their private jokes, the way they'd look at each other...
Those weren't easy times for gay men, and the trouble he'd have brought down, raising a little kid in that world in the late Sixties...
I thought he was abandoning me. But he'd done everything he could.
And Batman...
If I talked to Alfred about Batman, I don't think he'd understand any more than Dr. Lester did.
He'd think he'd screwed up. That I wasn't right in the head because he didn't do enough. I couldn't do that to him.
Still. It would have been nice to talk to someone.

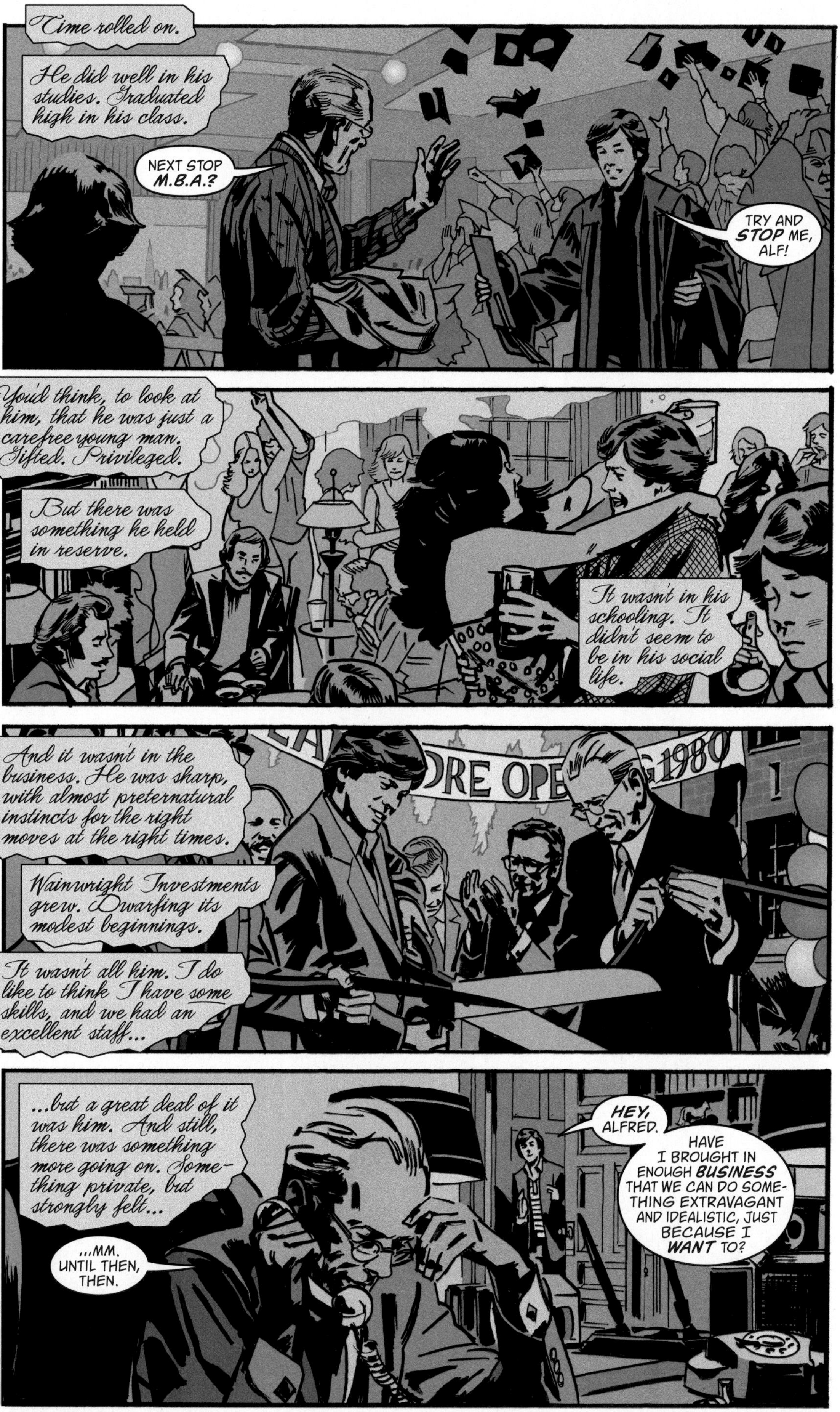
Time rolled on.
He did well in his studies. Graduated high in his class.
NEXT STOP M.B.A.?
TRY AND STOP ME, ALF!
You'd think, to look at him, that he was just a carefree young man. Gifted. Privileged.
But there was something he held in reserve.
It wasn't in his schooling. It didn't seem to be in his social life.
And it wasn't in the business. He was sharp, with almost preternatural instincts for the right moves at the right times.
Wainwright Investments grew. Dwarfing its modest beginnings.
It wasn't all him. I do like to think I have some skills, and we had an excellent staff...
...but a great deal of it was him. And still, there was something more going on. Something private, but strongly felt...
...MM. UNTIL THEN, THEN.
HEY, ALFRED.
HAVE I BROUGHT IN ENOUGH BUSINESS THAT WE CAN DO SOMETHING EXTRAVAGANT AND IDEALISTIC, JUST BECAUSE I WANT TO?

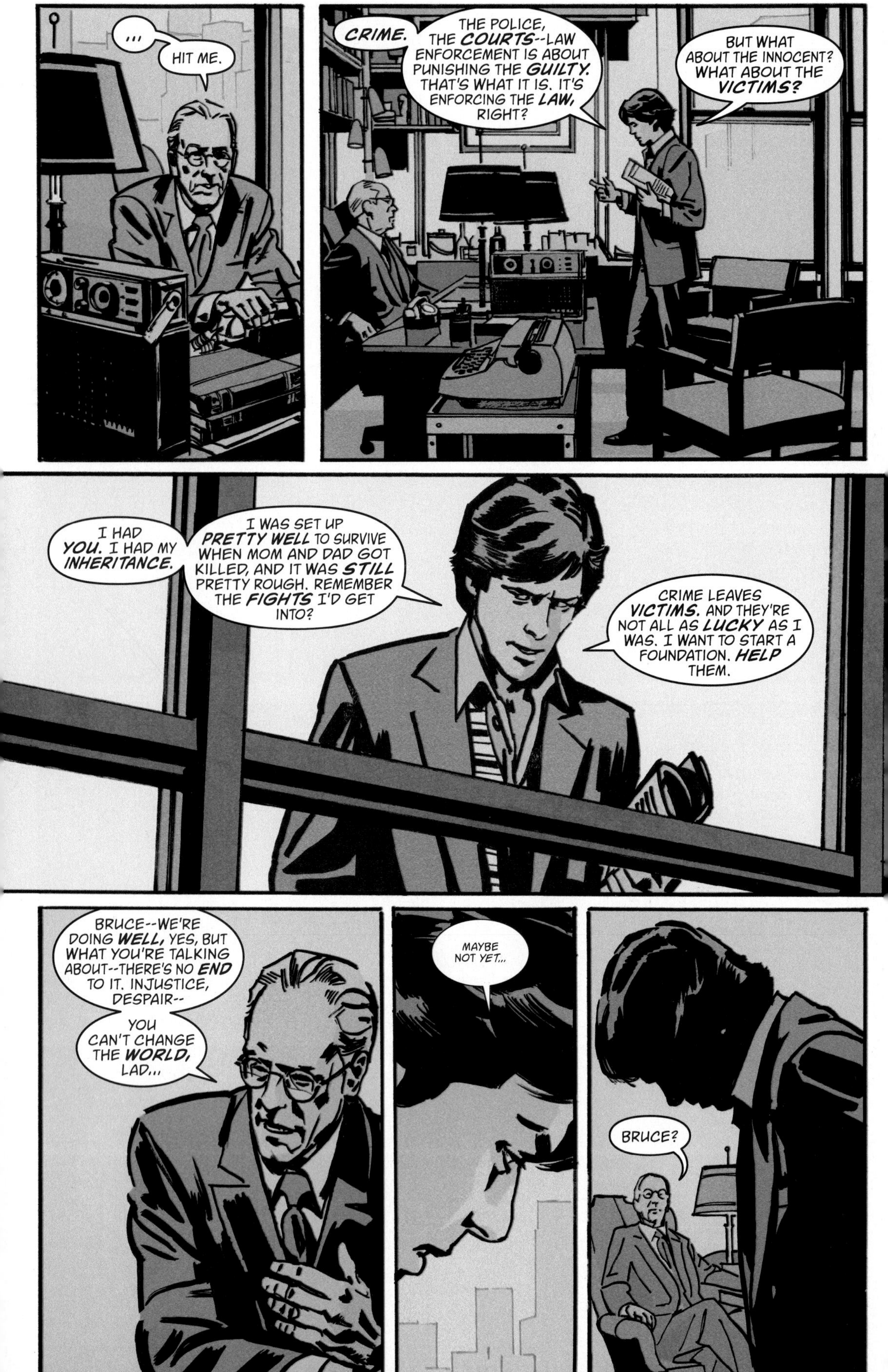
...
HIT ME.
CRIME.
THE POLICE, THE COURTS--LAW ENFORCEMENT IS ABOUT PUNISHING THE GUILTY. THAT'S WHAT IT IS. IT'S ENFORCING THE LAW, RIGHT?
BUT WHAT ABOUT THE INNOCENT? WHAT ABOUT THE VICTIMS?
I HAD YOU. I HAD MY INHERITANCE.
I WAS SET UP PRETTY WELL TO SURVIVE WHEN MOM AND DAD GOT KILLED, AND IT WAS STILL PRETTY ROUGH. REMEMBER THE FIGHTS I'D GET INTO?
CRIME LEAVES VICTIMS. AND THEY'RE NOT ALL AS LUCKY AS I WAS. I WANT TO START A FOUNDATION. HELP THEM.
BRUCE--WE'RE DOING WELL, YES, BUT WHAT YOU'RE TALKING ABOUT--THERE'S NO END TO IT. INJUSTICE, DESPAIR--
YOU CAN'T CHANGE THE WORLD, LAD...
MAYBE NOT YET...
BRUCE?

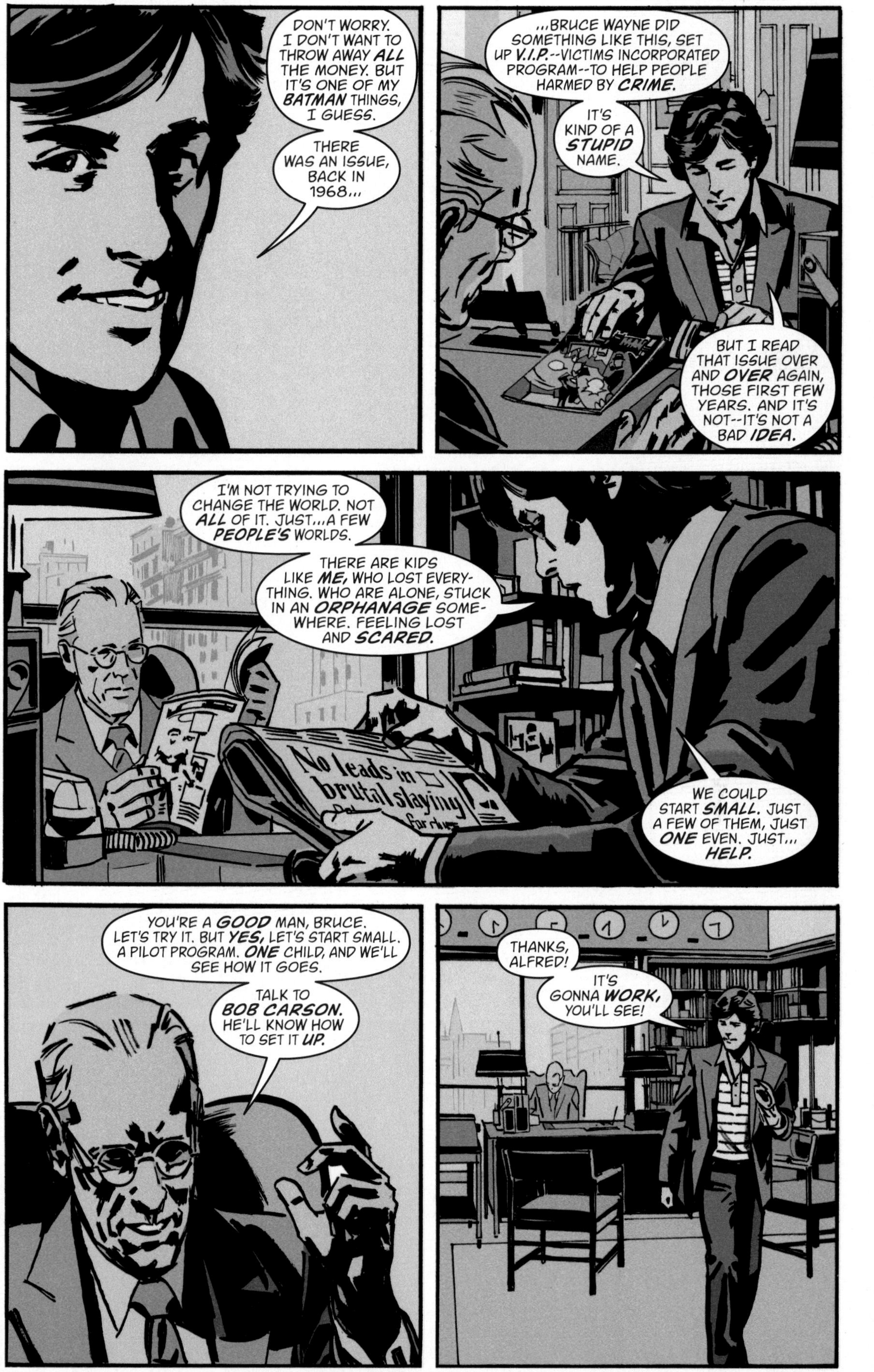
DON'T WORRY. I DON'T WANT TO THROW AWAY ALL THE MONEY. BUT IT'S ONE OF MY BATMAN THINGS, I GUESS.
THERE WAS AN ISSUE, BACK IN 1968...
...BRUCE WAYNE DID SOMETHING LIKE THIS, SET UP V.I.P.--VICTIMS INCORPORATED PROGRAM--TO HELP PEOPLE HARMED BY CRIME.
IT'S KIND OF A STUPID NAME.
BUT I READ THAT ISSUE OVER AND OVER AGAIN, THOSE FIRST FEW YEARS. AND IT'S NOT--IT'S NOT A BAD IDEA.
I'M NOT TRYING TO CHANGE THE WORLD. NOT ALL OF IT. JUST...A FEW PEOPLE'S WORLDS.
THERE ARE KIDS LIKE ME, WHO LOST EVERY-THING. WHO ARE ALONE, STUCK IN AN ORPHANAGE SOME-WHERE. FEELING LOST AND SCARED.
No leads in brutal slaying
WE COULD START SMALL. JUST A FEW OF THEM, JUST ONE EVEN. JUST... HELP.
YOU'RE A GOOD MAN, BRUCE. LET'S TRY IT. BUT YES, LET'S START SMALL. A PILOT PROGRAM. ONE CHILD, AND WE'LL SEE HOW IT GOES.
TALK TO BOB CARSON. HE'LL KNOW HOW TO SET IT UP.
THANKS, ALFRED!
IT'S GONNA WORK, YOU'LL SEE!

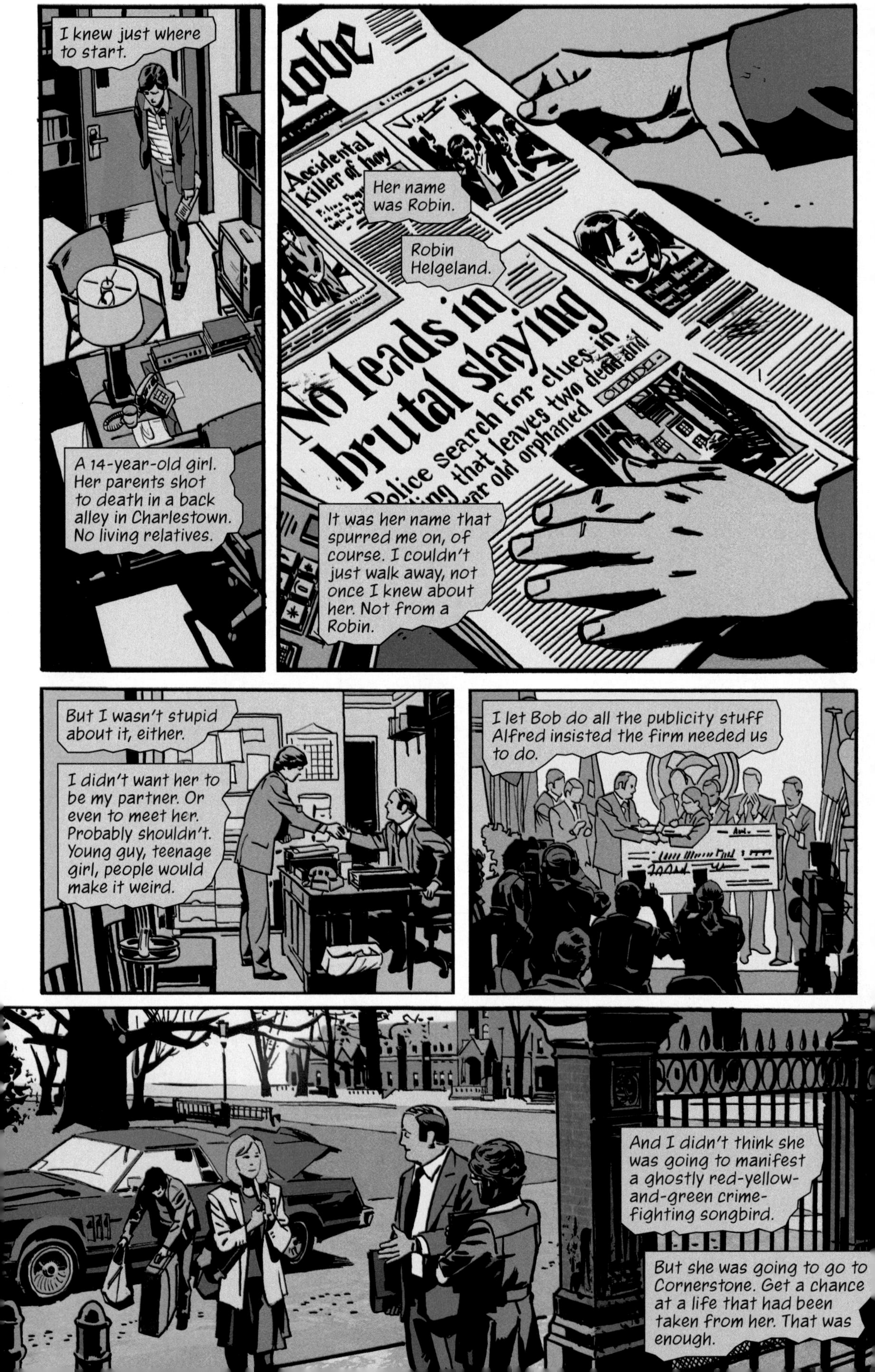

I knew just where to start.
A 14-year-old girl. Her parents shot to death in a back alley in Charlestown. No living relatives.
Her name was Robin.
Robin Helgeland.
No leads in brutal slaying
It was her name that spurred me on, of course. I couldn't just walk away, not once I knew about her. Not from a Robin.
But I wasn't stupid about it, either.
I didn't want her to be my partner. Or even to meet her. Probably shouldn't. Young guy, teenage girl, people would make it weird.
I let Bob do all the publicity stuff Alfred insisted the firm needed us to do.
And I didn't think she was going to manifest a ghostly red-yellow-and-green crime-fighting songbird.
But she was going to go to Cornerstone. Get a chance at a life that had been taken from her. That was enough.

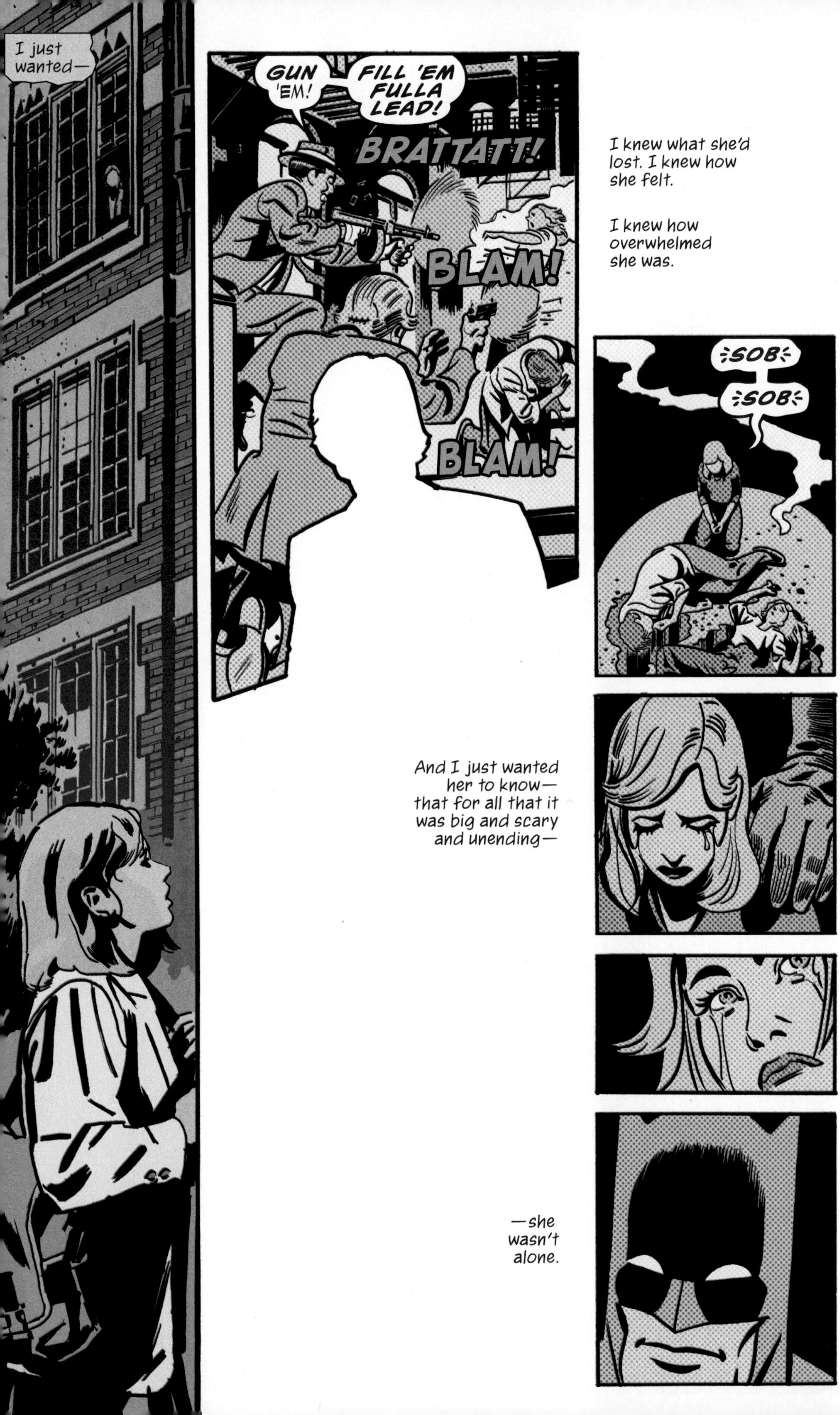
I just wanted—
GUN 'EM!
FILL 'EM FULLA LEAD!
BRATTATT!
BLAM!
BLAM!
I knew what she'd lost. I knew how she felt.
I knew how overwhelmed she was.
SOB
SOB
And I just wanted her to know— that for all that it was big and scary and unending—
—she wasn't alone.

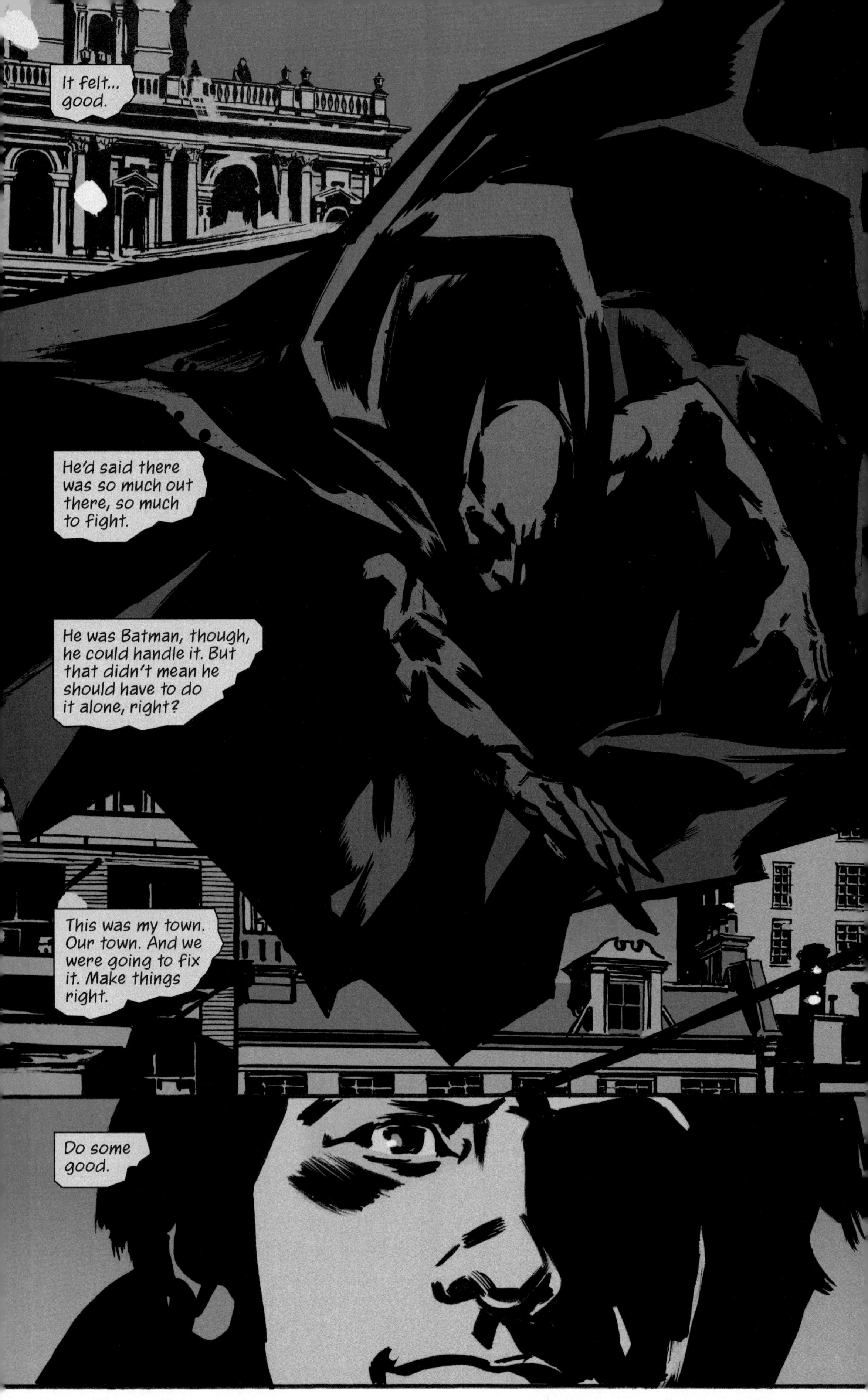
It felt... good.
He'd said there was so much out there, so much to fight.
He was Batman, though, he could handle it. But that didn't mean he should have to do it alone, right?
This was my town. Our town. And we were going to fix it. Make things right.
Do some good.

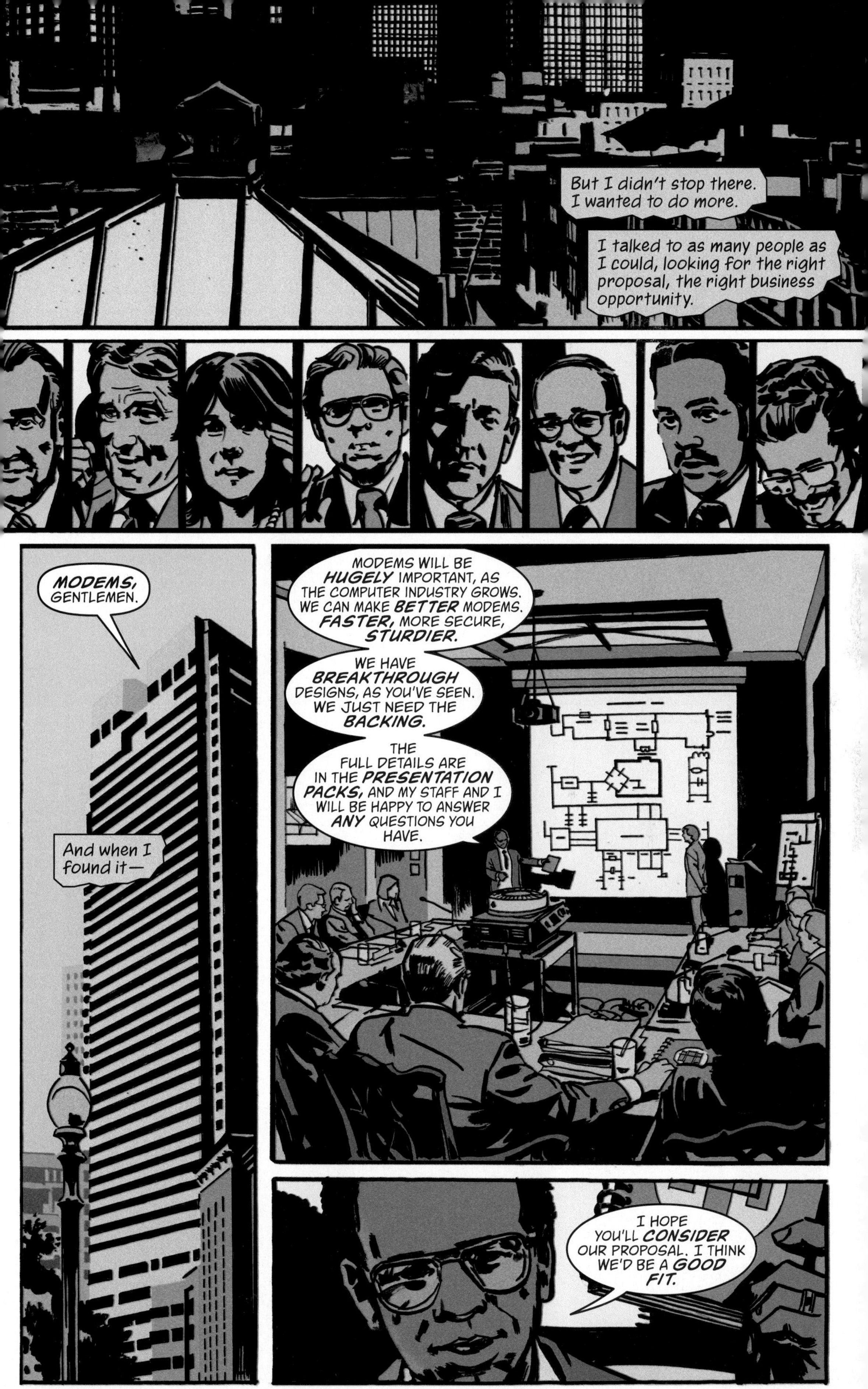
But I didn't stop there. I wanted to do more.
I talked to as many people as I could, looking for the right proposal, the right business opportunity.
MODEMS, GENTLEMEN.
And when I found it—
MODEMS WILL BE HUGELY IMPORTANT, AS THE COMPUTER INDUSTRY GROWS. WE CAN MAKE BETTER MODEMS. FASTER, MORE SECURE, STURDIER.
WE HAVE BREAKTHROUGH DESIGNS, AS YOU'VE SEEN. WE JUST NEED THE BACKING.
THE FULL DETAILS ARE IN THE PRESENTATION PACKS, AND MY STAFF AND I WILL BE HAPPY TO ANSWER ANY QUESTIONS YOU HAVE.
I HOPE YOU'LL CONSIDER OUR PROPOSAL. I THINK WE'D BE A GOOD FIT.

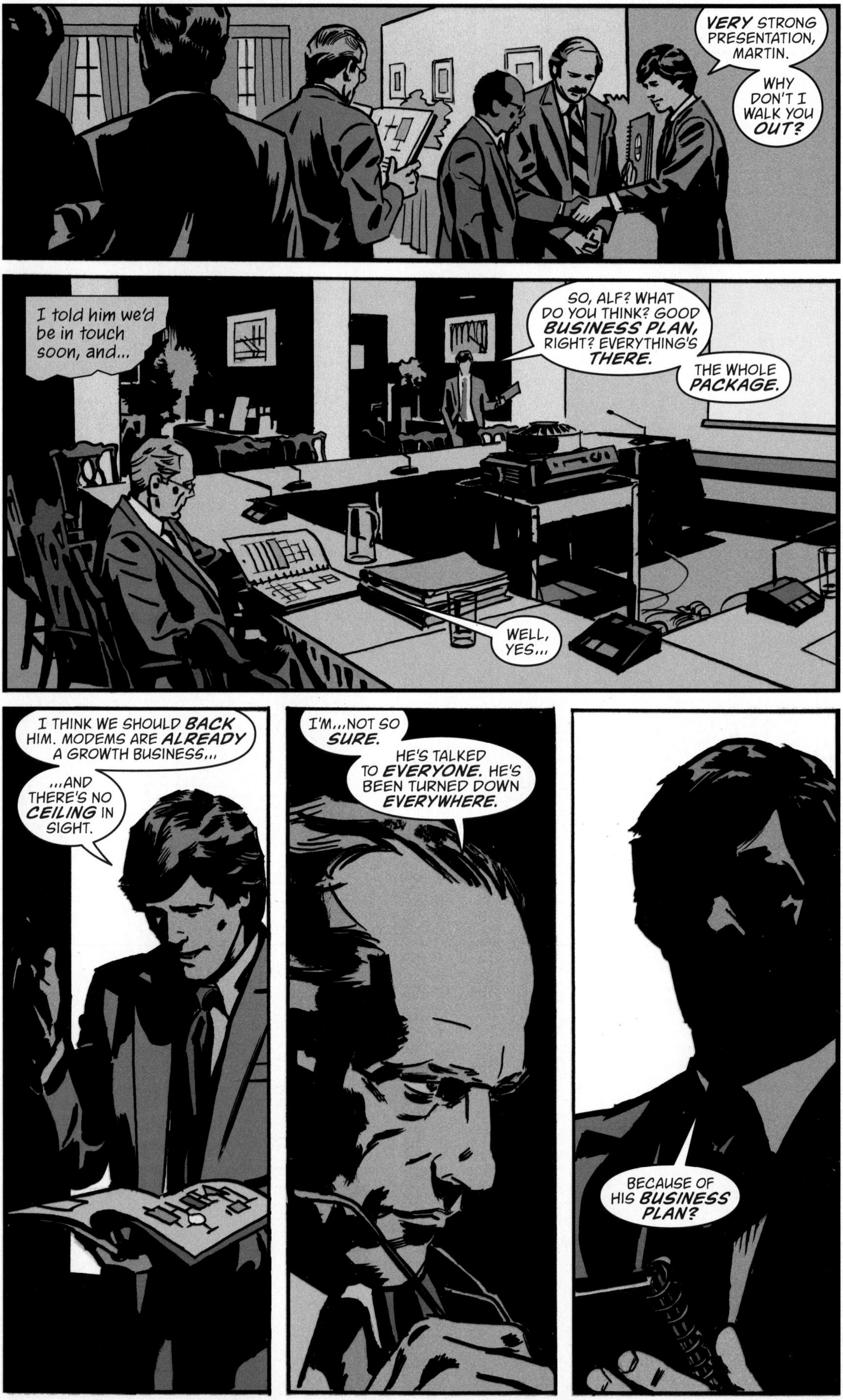

VERY STRONG PRESENTATION, MARTIN.
WHY DON'T I WALK YOU OUT?
I told him we'd be in touch soon, and...
SO, ALF? WHAT DO YOU THINK? GOOD BUSINESS PLAN, RIGHT? EVERYTHING'S THERE.
THE WHOLE PACKAGE.
WELL, YES...
I THINK WE SHOULD BACK HIM. MODEMS ARE ALREADY A GROWTH BUSINESS...
...AND THERE'S NO CEILING IN SIGHT.
I'M...NOT SO SURE.
HE'S TALKED TO EVERYONE. HE'S BEEN TURNED DOWN EVERYWHERE.
BECAUSE OF HIS BUSINESS PLAN?

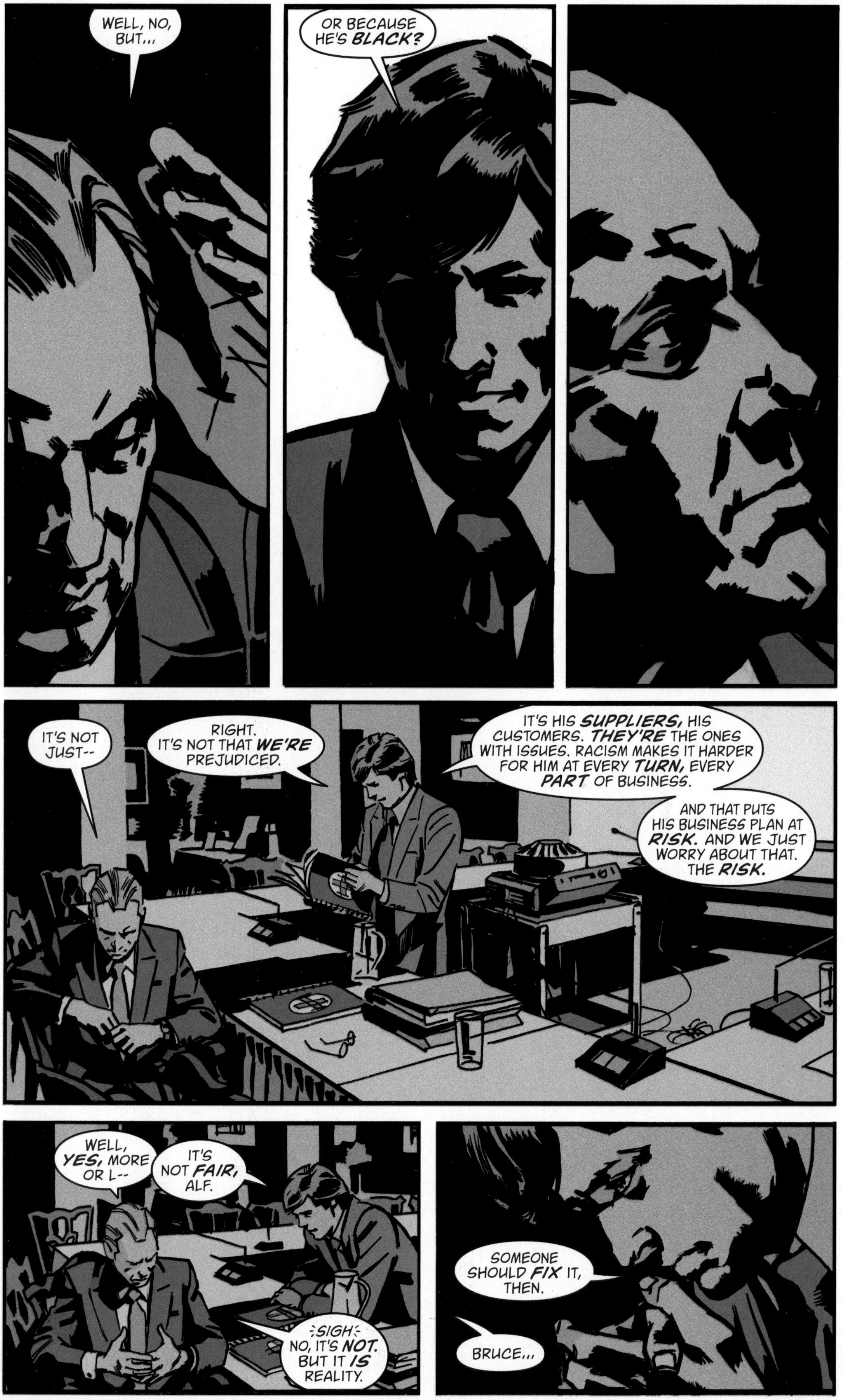
WELL, NO, BUT...
OR BECAUSE HE'S BLACK?
IT'S NOT JUST--
RIGHT. IT'S NOT THAT WE'RE PREJUDICED.
IT'S HIS SUPPLIERS, HIS CUSTOMERS. THEY'RE THE ONES WITH ISSUES. RACISM MAKES IT HARDER FOR HIM AT EVERY TURN, EVERY PART OF BUSINESS.
AND THAT PUTS HIS BUSINESS PLAN AT RISK. AND WE JUST WORRY ABOUT THAT. THE RISK.
WELL, YES, MORE OR L--
IT'S NOT FAIR, ALF.
SIGH
NO, IT'S NOT. BUT IT IS REALITY.
SOMEONE SHOULD FIX IT, THEN.
BRUCE...

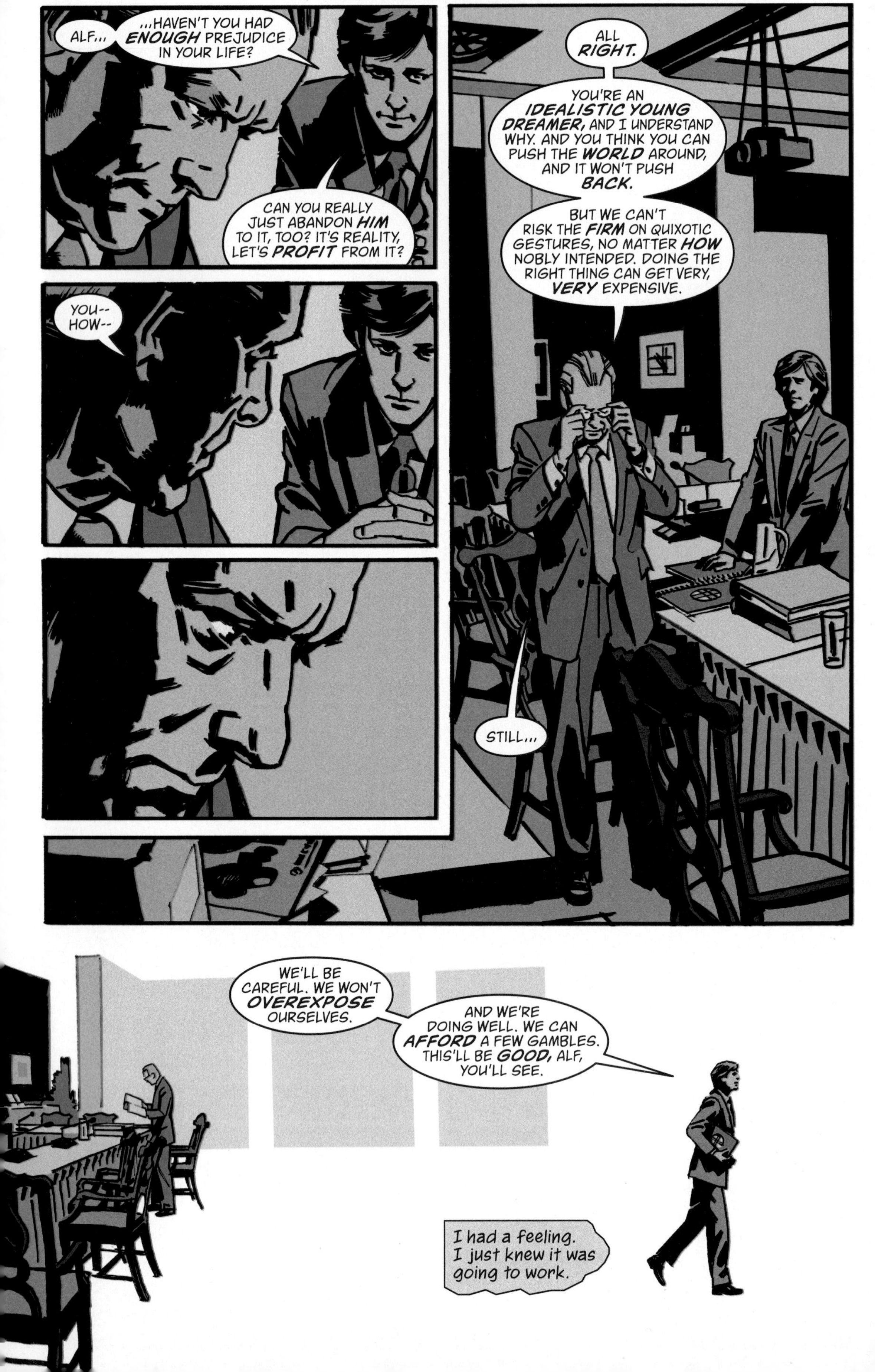
ALF...
...HAVEN'T YOU HAD ENOUGH PREJUDICE IN YOUR LIFE?
CAN YOU REALLY JUST ABANDON HIM TO IT, TOO? IT'S REALITY, LET'S PROFIT FROM IT?
YOU-- HOW--
ALL RIGHT.
YOU'RE AN IDEALISTIC YOUNG DREAMER, AND I UNDERSTAND WHY. AND YOU THINK YOU CAN PUSH THE WORLD AROUND, AND IT WON'T PUSH BACK.
BUT WE CAN'T RISK THE FIRM ON QUIXOTIC GESTURES, NO MATTER HOW NOBLY INTENDED. DOING THE RIGHT THING CAN GET VERY, VERY EXPENSIVE.
STILL...
WE'LL BE CAREFUL. WE WON'T OVEREXPOSE OURSELVES.
AND WE'RE DOING WELL. WE CAN AFFORD A FEW GAMBLES. THIS'LL BE GOOD, ALF, YOU'LL SEE.
I had a feeling. I just knew it was going to work.

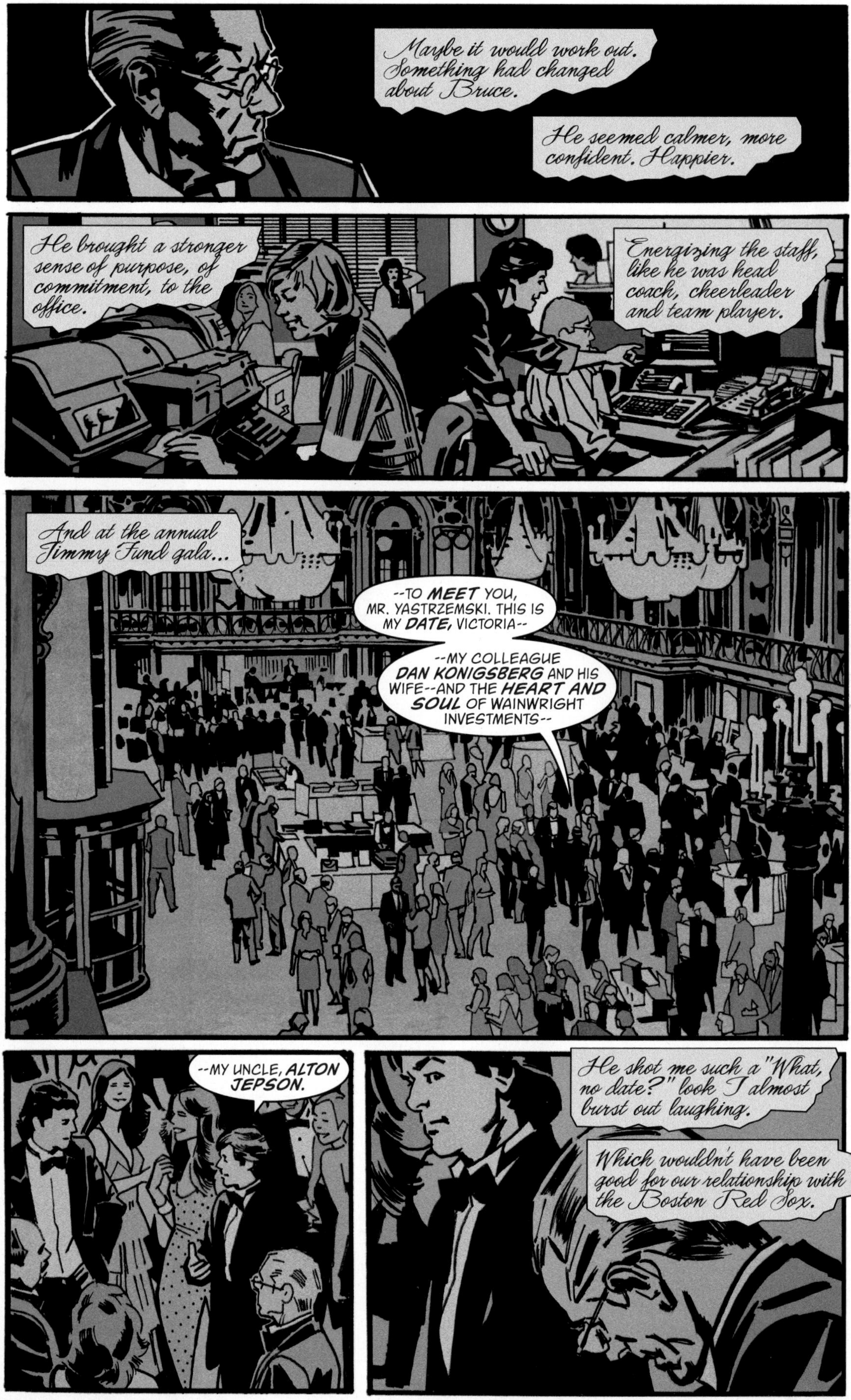

Maybe it would work out. Something had changed about Bruce.
He seemed calmer, more confident. Happier.
He brought a stronger sense of purpose, of commitment, to the office.
Energizing the staff, like he was head coach, cheerleader and team player.
And at the annual Jimmy Fund gala...
--TO MEET YOU, MR. YASTRZEMSKI. THIS IS MY DATE, VICTORIA--
--MY COLLEAGUE DAN KONIGSBERG AND HIS WIFE--AND THE HEART AND SOUL OF WAINWRIGHT INVESTMENTS--
--MY UNCLE, ALTON JEPSON.
He shot me such a "What, no date?" look I almost burst out laughing.
Which wouldn't have been good for our relationship with the Boston Red Sox.

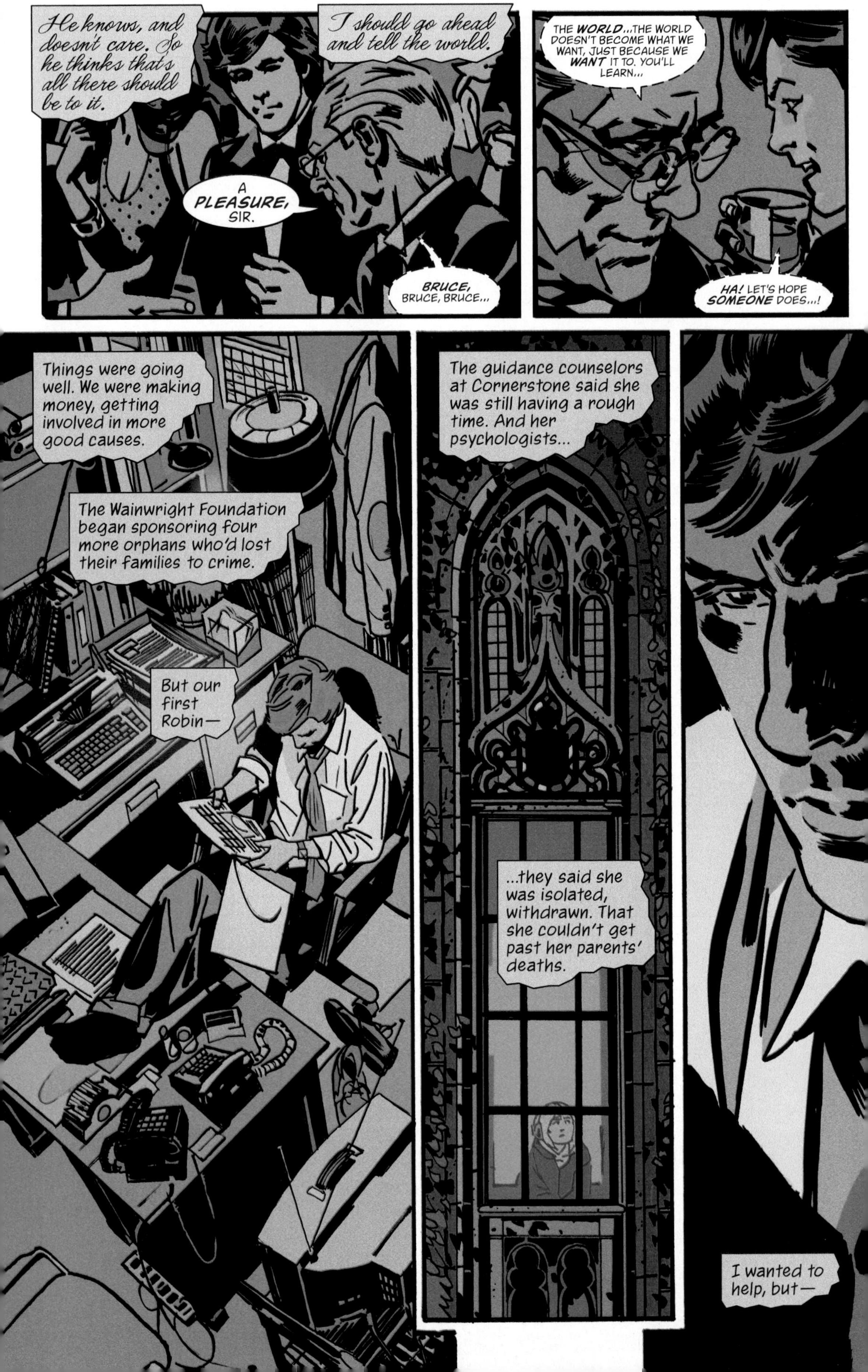

He knows, and doesn't care. So he thinks that's all there should be to it.
I should go ahead and tell the world.
A PLEASURE, SIR.
BRUCE, BRUCE, BRUCE...
THE WORLD...THE WORLD DOESN'T BECOME WHAT WE WANT, JUST BECAUSE WE WANT IT TO. YOU'LL LEARN...
HA! LET'S HOPE SOMEONE DOES...!
Things were going well. We were making money, getting involved in more good causes.
The Wainwright Foundation began sponsoring four more orphans who'd lost their families to crime.
But our first Robin—
The guidance counselors at Cornerstone said she was still having a rough time. And her psychologists...
...they said she was isolated, withdrawn. That she couldn't get past her parents' deaths.
I wanted to help, but—

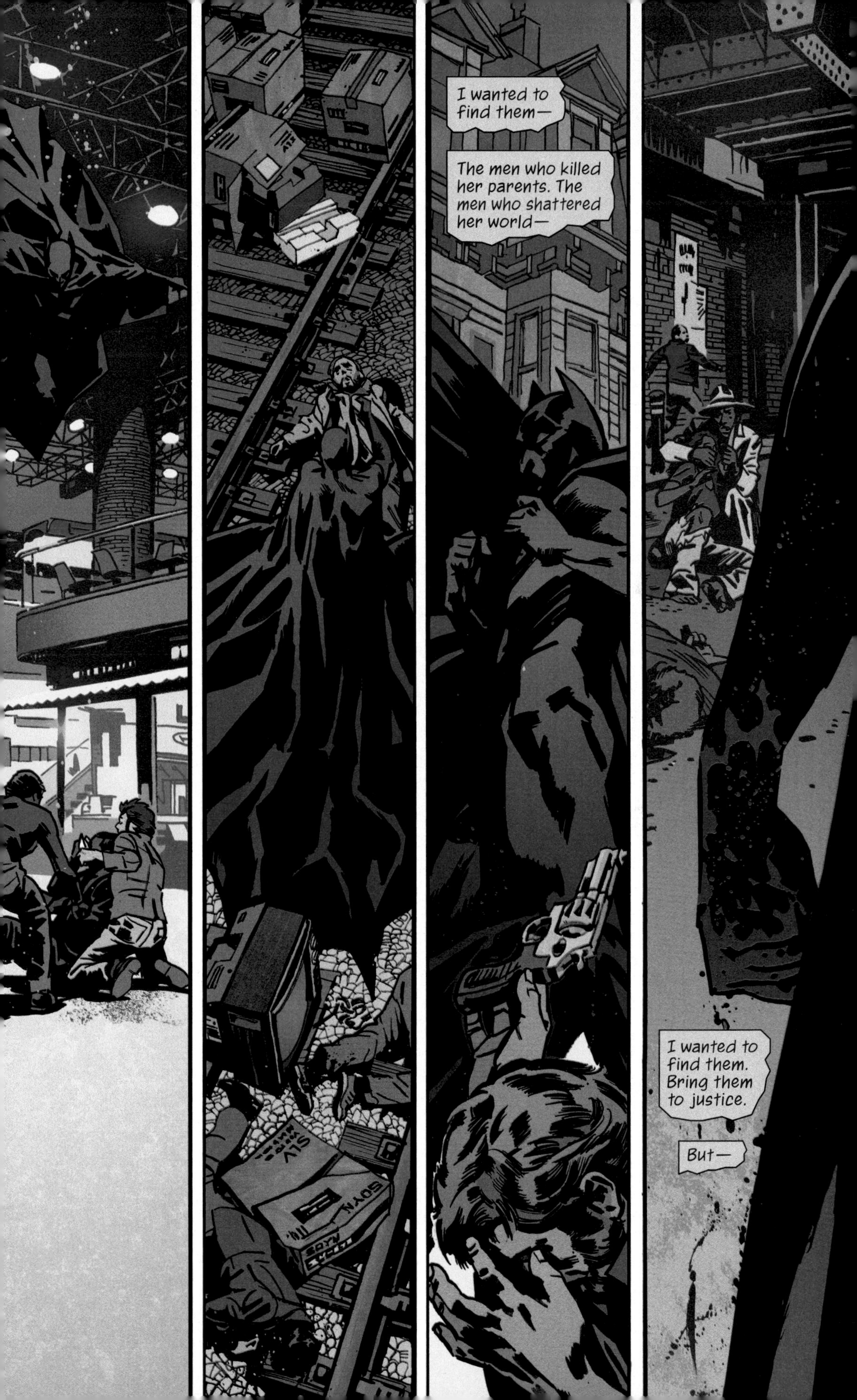
I wanted to find them—
The men who killed her parents. The men who shattered her world—
I wanted to find them. Bring them to justice.
But—

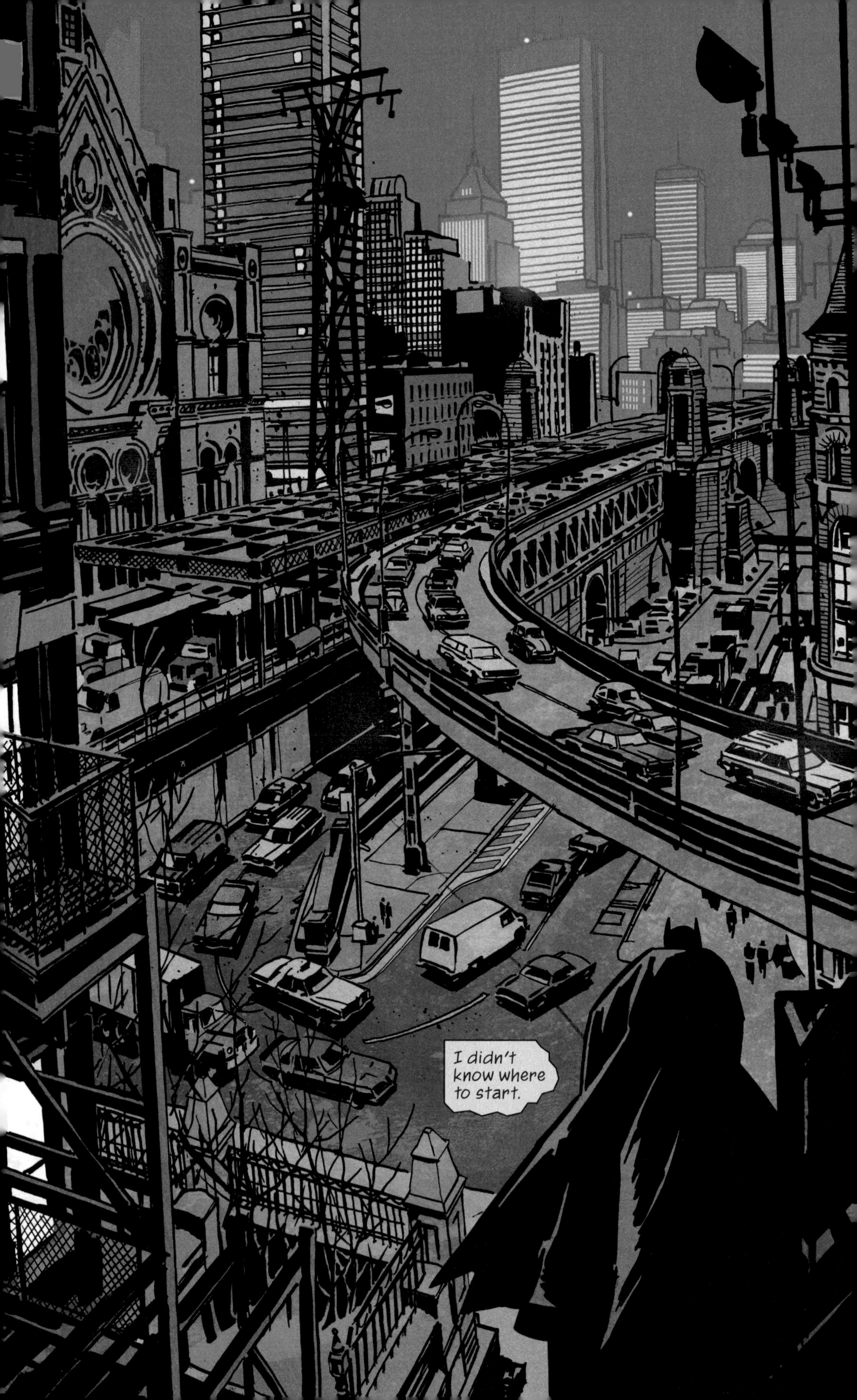
I didn't know where to start.

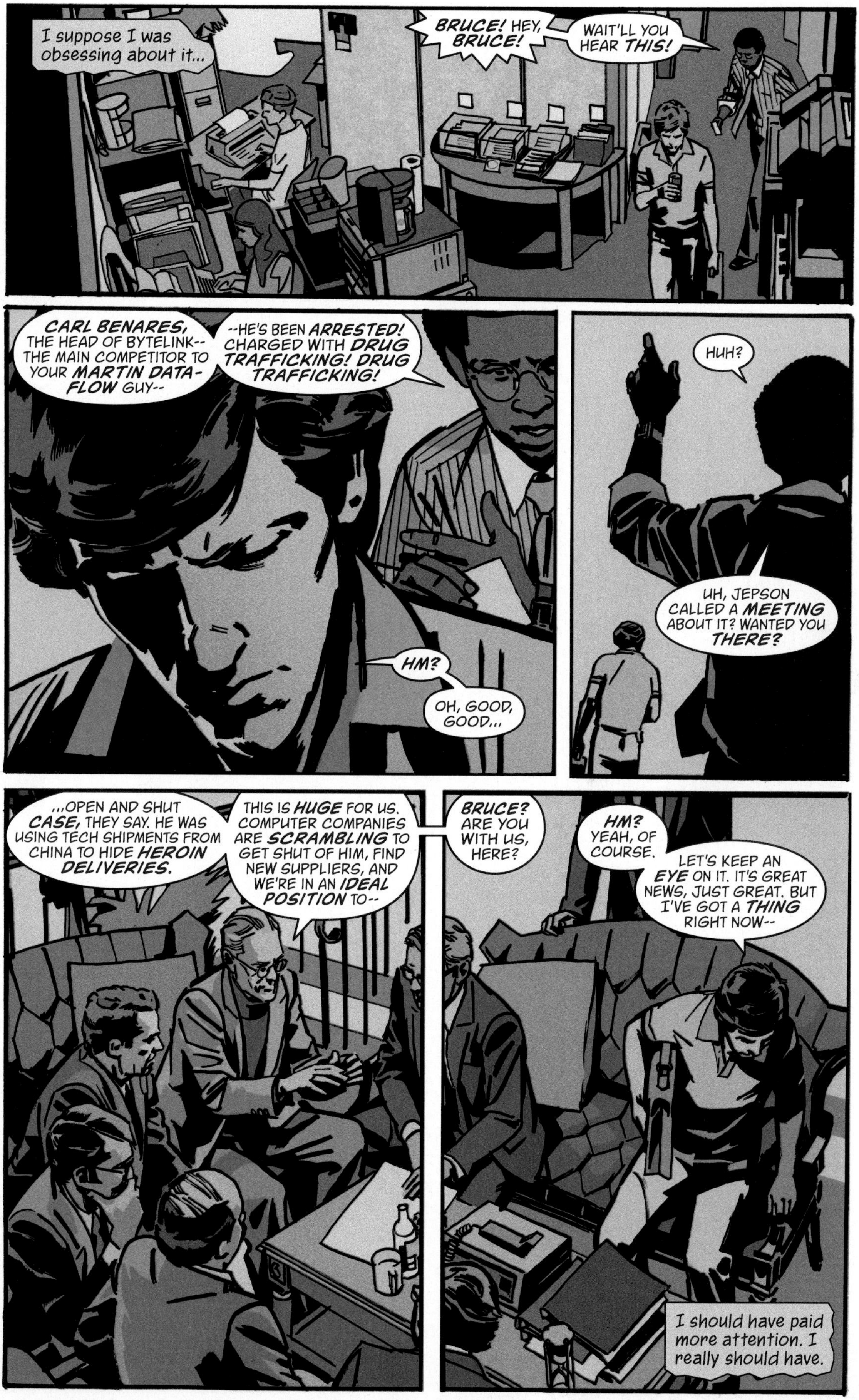
I suppose I was obsessing about it...
BRUCE! HEY, BRUCE!
WAIT'LL YOU HEAR THIS!
CARL BENARES, THE HEAD OF BYTELINK-- THE MAIN COMPETITOR TO YOUR MARTIN DATA-FLOW GUY--
--HE'S BEEN ARRESTED! CHARGED WITH DRUG TRAFFICKING! DRUG TRAFFICKING!
HM?
OH, GOOD, GOOD...
HUH?
UH, JEPSON CALLED A MEETING ABOUT IT? WANTED YOU THERE?
...OPEN AND SHUT CASE, THEY SAY. HE WAS USING TECH SHIPMENTS FROM CHINA TO HIDE HEROIN DELIVERIES.
THIS IS HUGE FOR US. COMPUTER COMPANIES ARE SCRAMBLING TO GET SHUT OF HIM, FIND NEW SUPPLIERS, AND WE'RE IN AN IDEAL POSITION TO--
BRUCE? ARE YOU WITH US, HERE?
HM? YEAH, OF COURSE.
LET'S KEEP AN EYE ON IT. IT'S GREAT NEWS, JUST GREAT. BUT I'VE GOT A THING RIGHT NOW--
I should have paid more attention. I really should have.

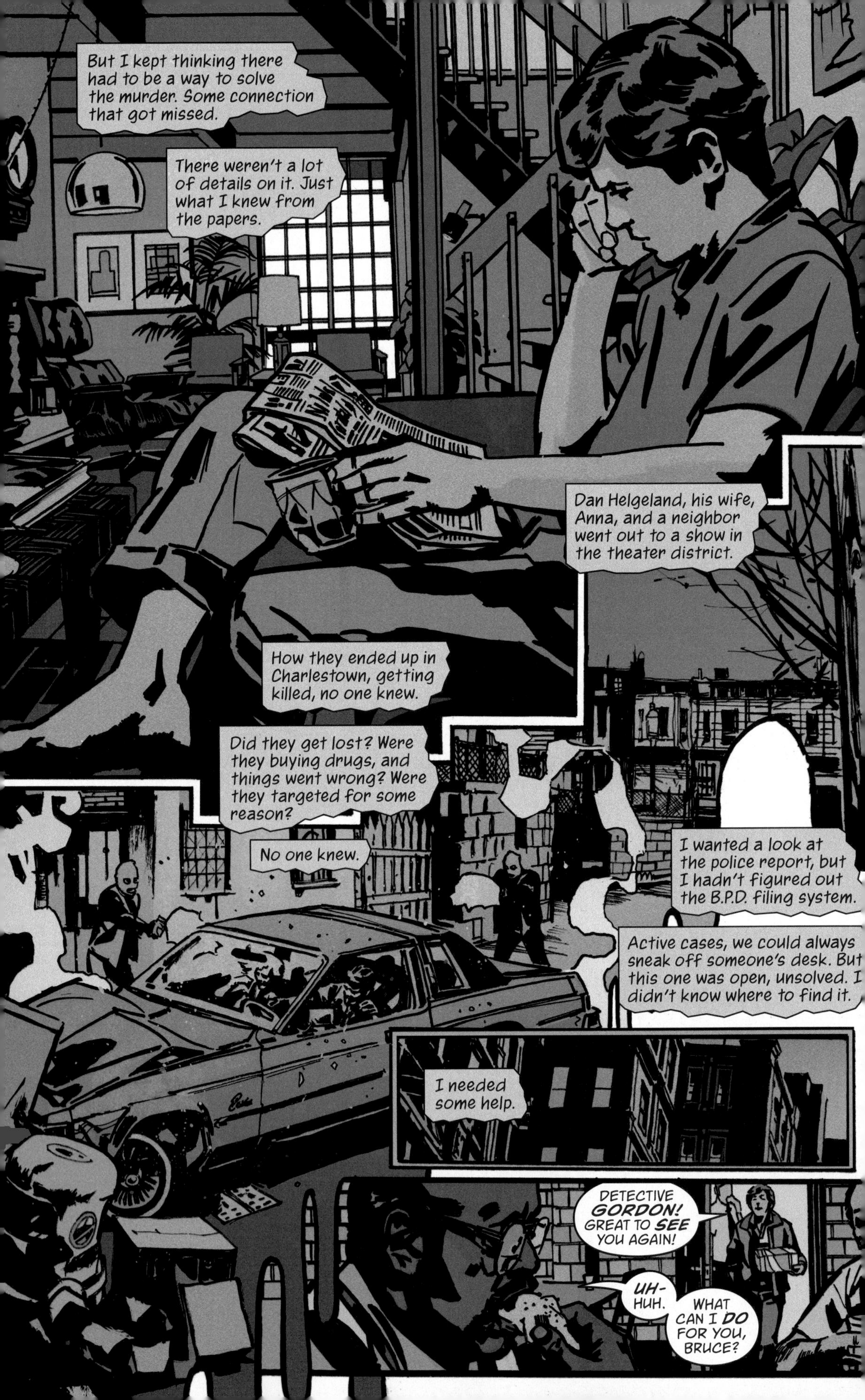
But I kept thinking there had to be a way to solve the murder. Some connection that got missed.
There weren't a lot of details on it. Just what I knew from the papers.
Dan Helgeland, his wife, Anna, and a neighbor went out to a show in the theater district.
How they ended up in Charlestown, getting killed, no one knew.
Did they get lost? Were they buying drugs, and things went wrong? Were they targeted for some reason?
No one knew.
I wanted a look at the police report, but I hadn't figured out the B.P.D. filing system.
Active cases, we could always sneak off someone's desk. But this one was open, unsolved. I didn't know where to find it.
I needed some help.
DETECTIVE GORDON! GREAT TO SEE YOU AGAIN!
UH-HUH.
WHAT CAN I DO FOR YOU, BRUCE?

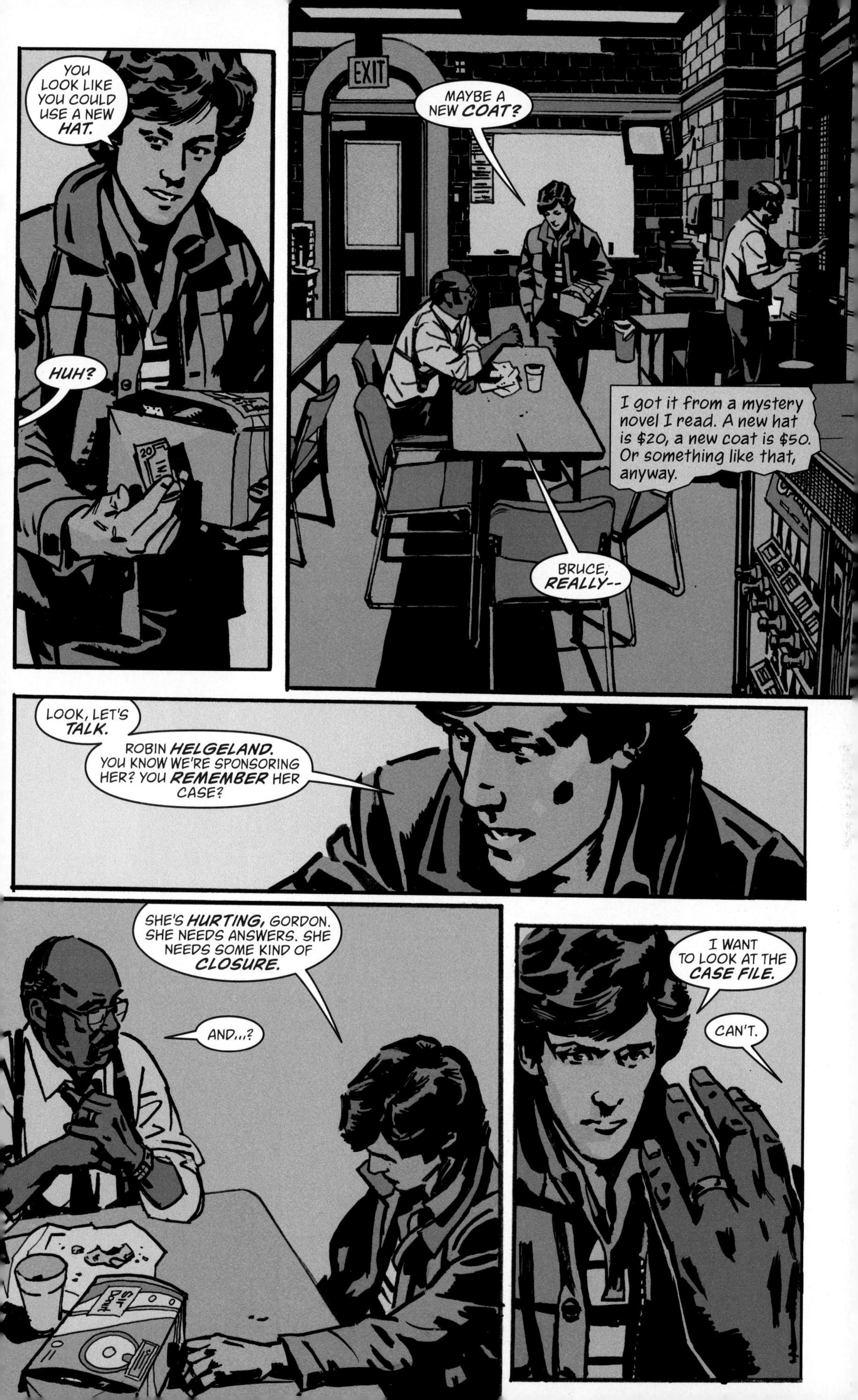
YOU LOOK LIKE YOU COULD USE A NEW *HAT.*
HUH?
MAYBE A NEW *COAT?*
I got it from a mystery novel I read. A new hat is $20, a new coat is $50. Or something like that, anyway.
BRUCE, *REALLY--*
LOOK, LET'S *TALK.*
ROBIN *HELGELAND.* YOU KNOW WE'RE SPONSORING HER? YOU *REMEMBER* HER CASE?
SHE'S *HURTING,* GORDON. SHE NEEDS ANSWERS. SHE NEEDS SOME KIND OF *CLOSURE.*
AND...?
I WANT TO LOOK AT THE *CASE FILE.*
CAN'T.

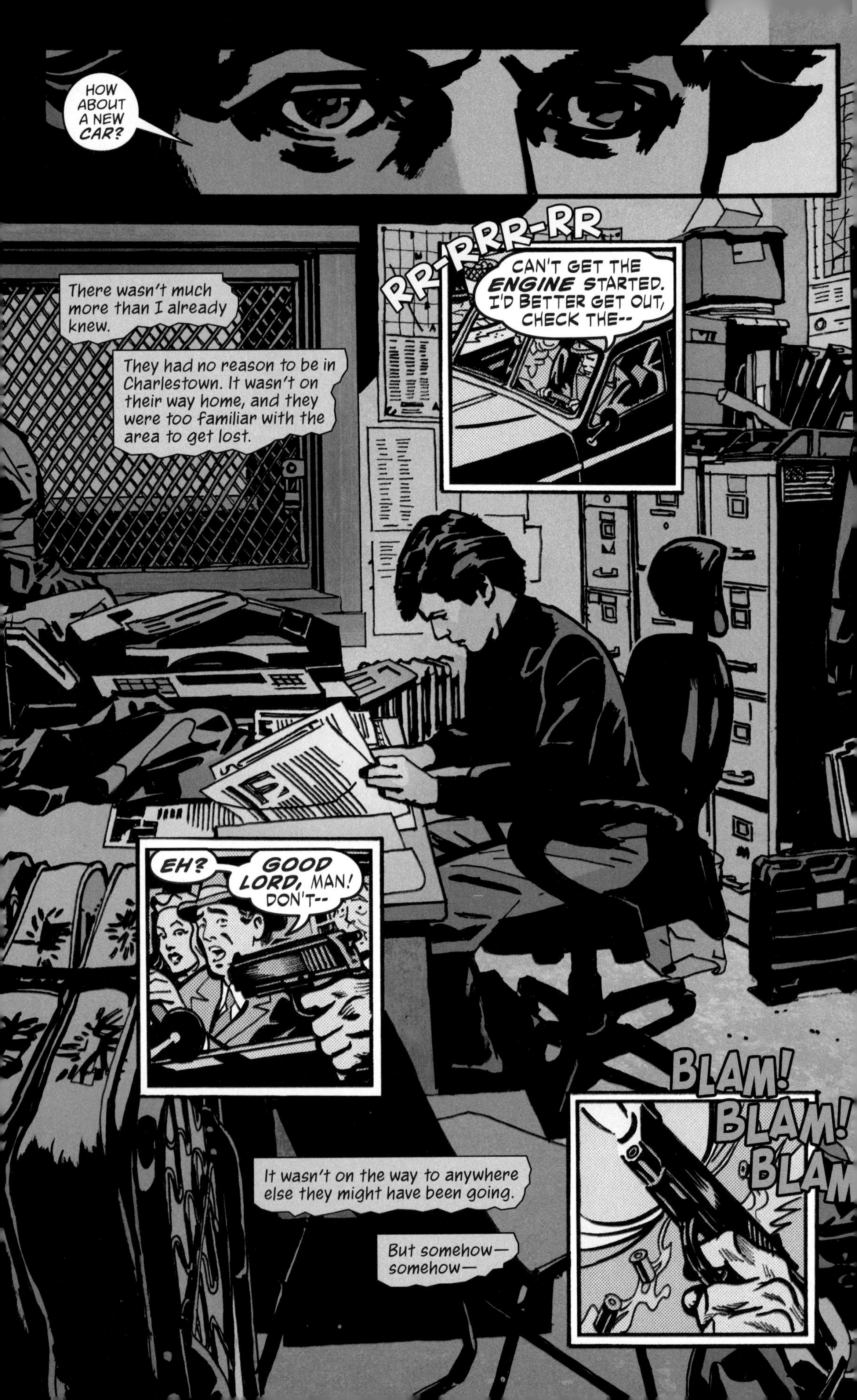

HOW ABOUT A NEW CAR?
There wasn't much more than I already knew.
They had no reason to be in Charlestown. It wasn't on their way home, and they were too familiar with the area to get lost.
RR-RRR-RR
CAN'T GET THE ENGINE STARTED. I'D BETTER GET OUT, CHECK THE--
EH?
GOOD LORD, MAN! DON'T--
BLAM! BLAM! BLAM
It wasn't on the way to anywhere else they might have been going.
But somehow—somehow—

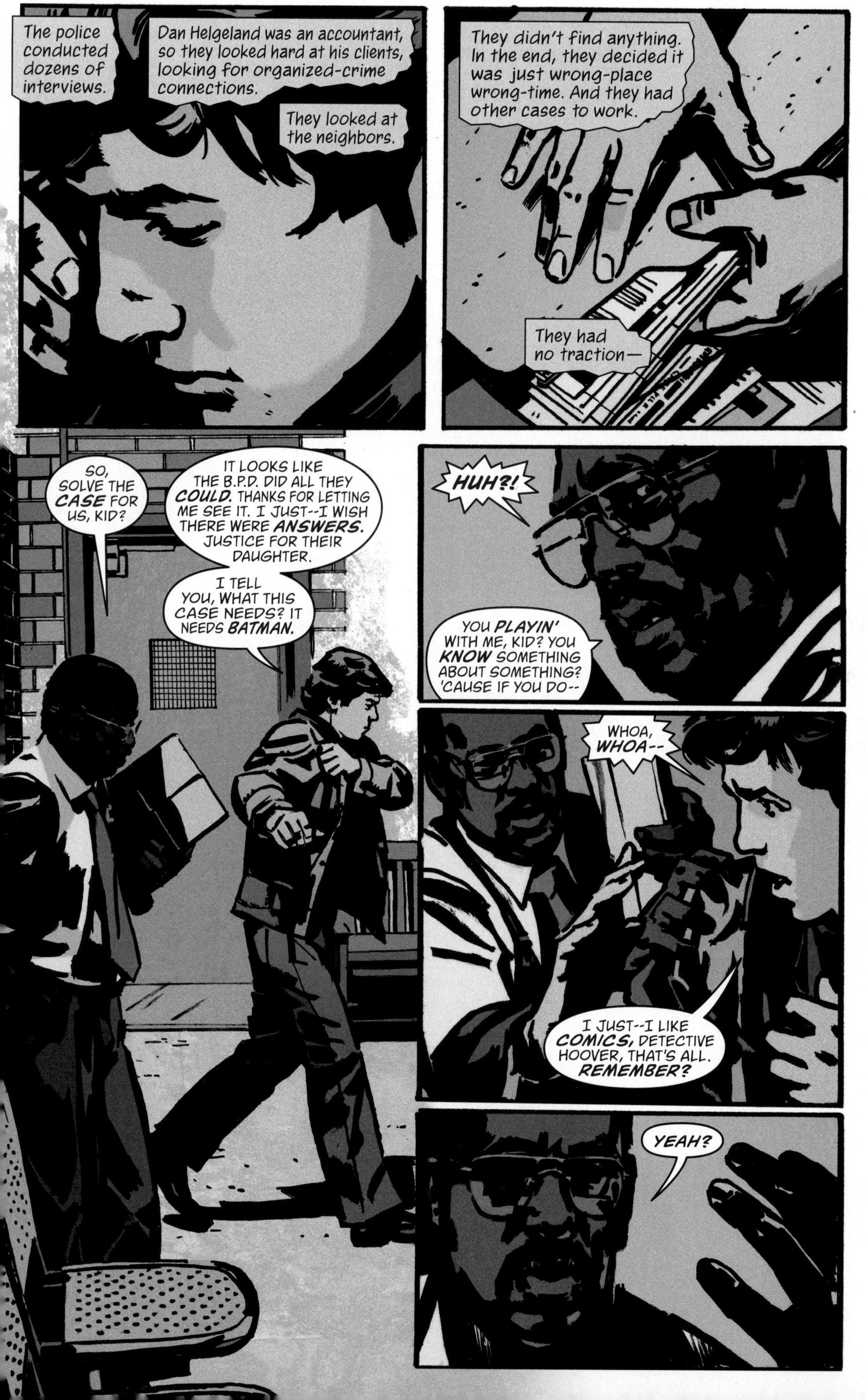

The police conducted dozens of interviews.
Dan Helgeland was an accountant, so they looked hard at his clients, looking for organized-crime connections.
They looked at the neighbors.
They didn't find anything. In the end, they decided it was just wrong-place wrong-time. And they had other cases to work.
They had no traction—
SO, SOLVE THE CASE FOR US, KID?
IT LOOKS LIKE THE B.P.D. DID ALL THEY COULD. THANKS FOR LETTING ME SEE IT. I JUST--I WISH THERE WERE ANSWERS. JUSTICE FOR THEIR DAUGHTER.
I TELL YOU, WHAT THIS CASE NEEDS? IT NEEDS BATMAN.
HUH?!
YOU PLAYIN' WITH ME, KID? YOU KNOW SOMETHING ABOUT SOMETHING? 'CAUSE IF YOU DO--
WHOA, WHOA--
I JUST--I LIKE COMICS, DETECTIVE HOOVER, THAT'S ALL. REMEMBER?
YEAH?

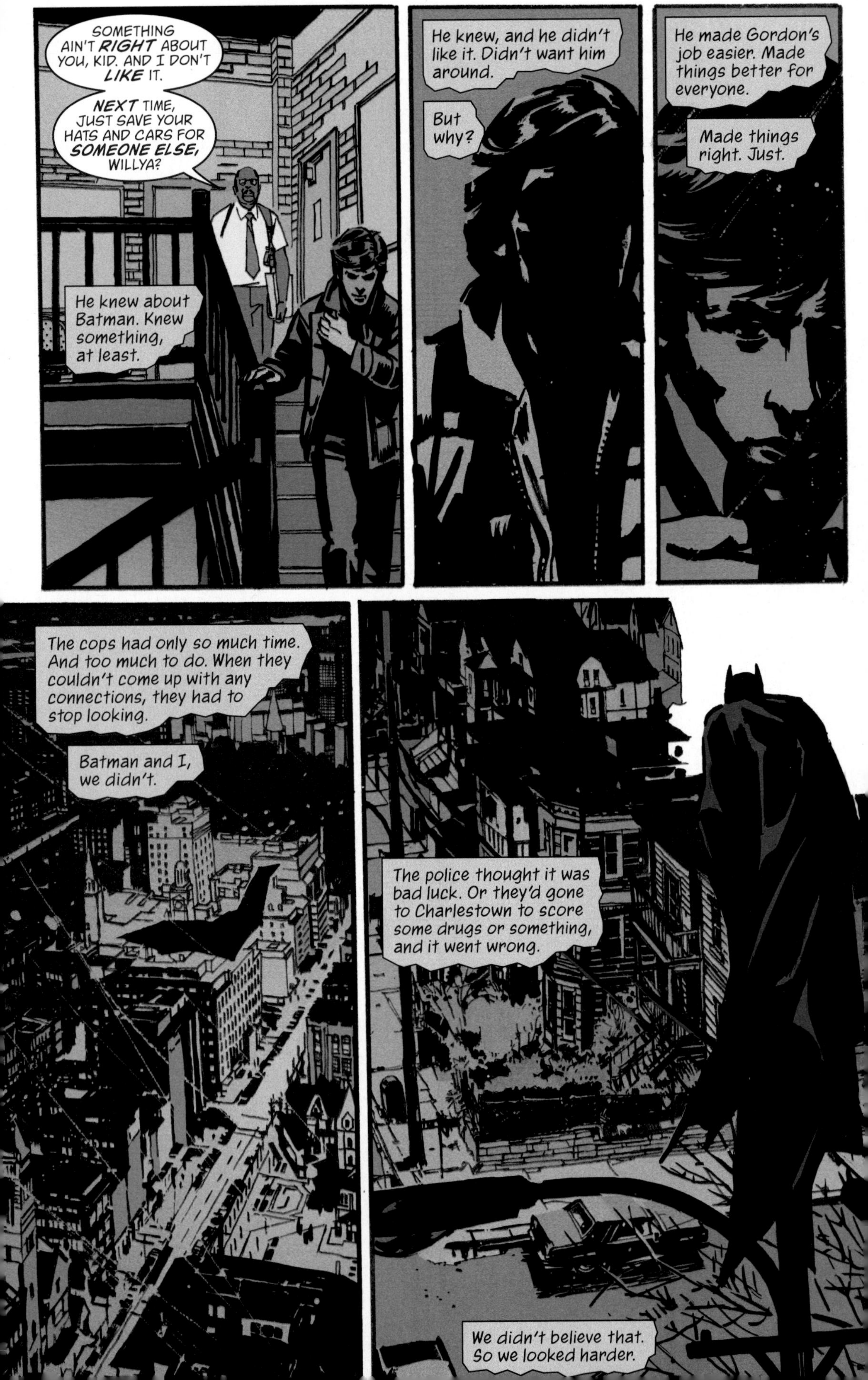

SOMETHING AIN'T RIGHT ABOUT YOU, KID. AND I DON'T LIKE IT.
NEXT TIME, JUST SAVE YOUR HATS AND CARS FOR SOMEONE ELSE, WILLYA?
He knew about Batman. Knew something, at least.
He knew, and he didn't like it. Didn't want him around.
But why?
He made Gordon's job easier. Made things better for everyone.
Made things right. Just.
The cops had only so much time. And too much to do. When they couldn't come up with any connections, they had to stop looking.
Batman and I, we didn't.
The police thought it was bad luck. Or they'd gone to Charlestown to score some drugs or something, and it went wrong.
We didn't believe that. So we looked harder.

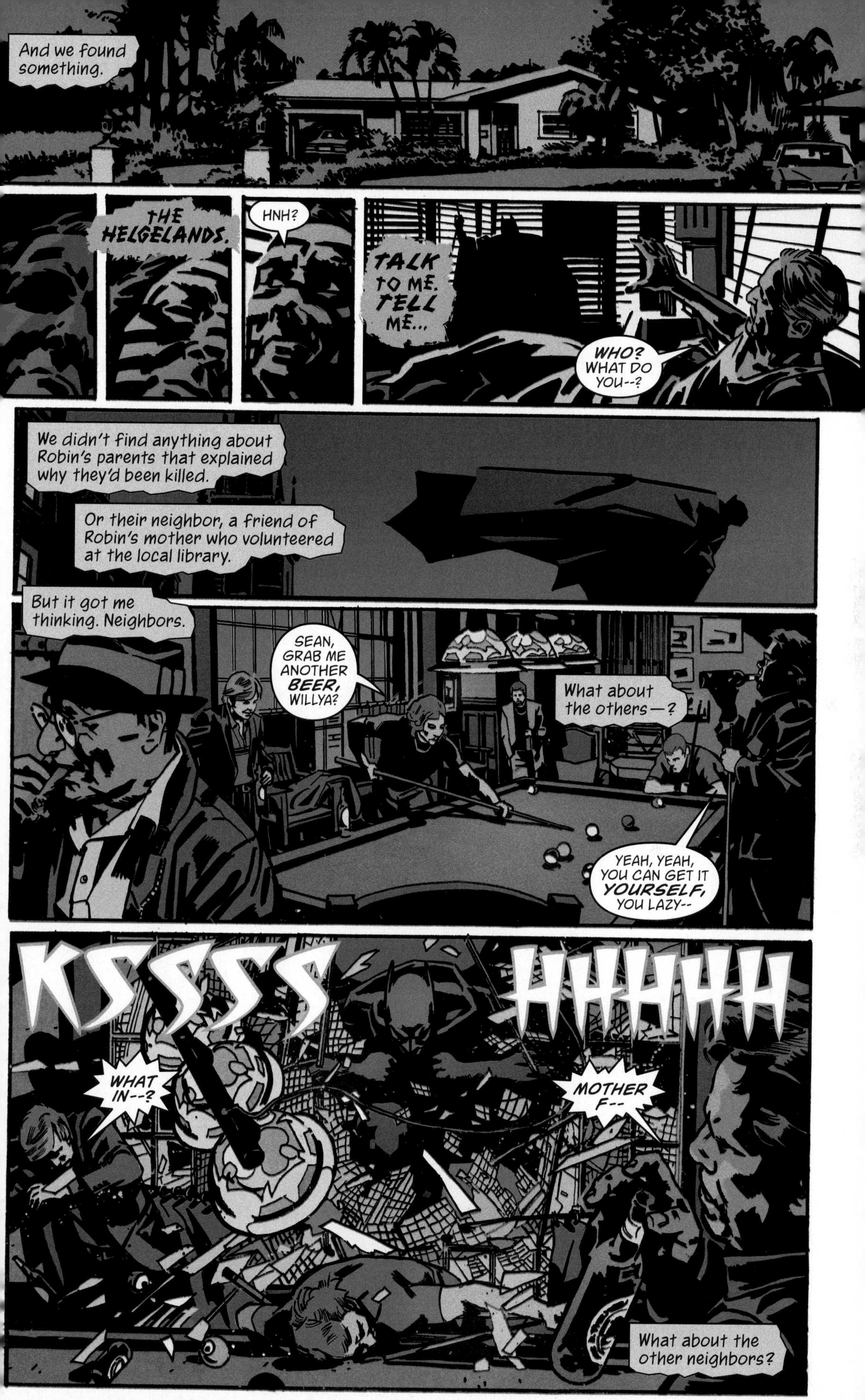

And we found something.
THE HELGELANDS.
HNH?
TALK TO ME. TELL ME...
WHO? WHAT DO YOU--?
We didn't find anything about Robin's parents that explained why they'd been killed.
Or their neighbor, a friend of Robin's mother who volunteered at the local library.
But it got me thinking. Neighbors.
SEAN, GRAB ME ANOTHER BEER, WILLYA?
What about the others—?
YEAH, YEAH, YOU CAN GET IT YOURSELF, YOU LAZY--
KSSSS
HHHHH
WHAT IN--?
MOTHER F--
What about the other neighbors?

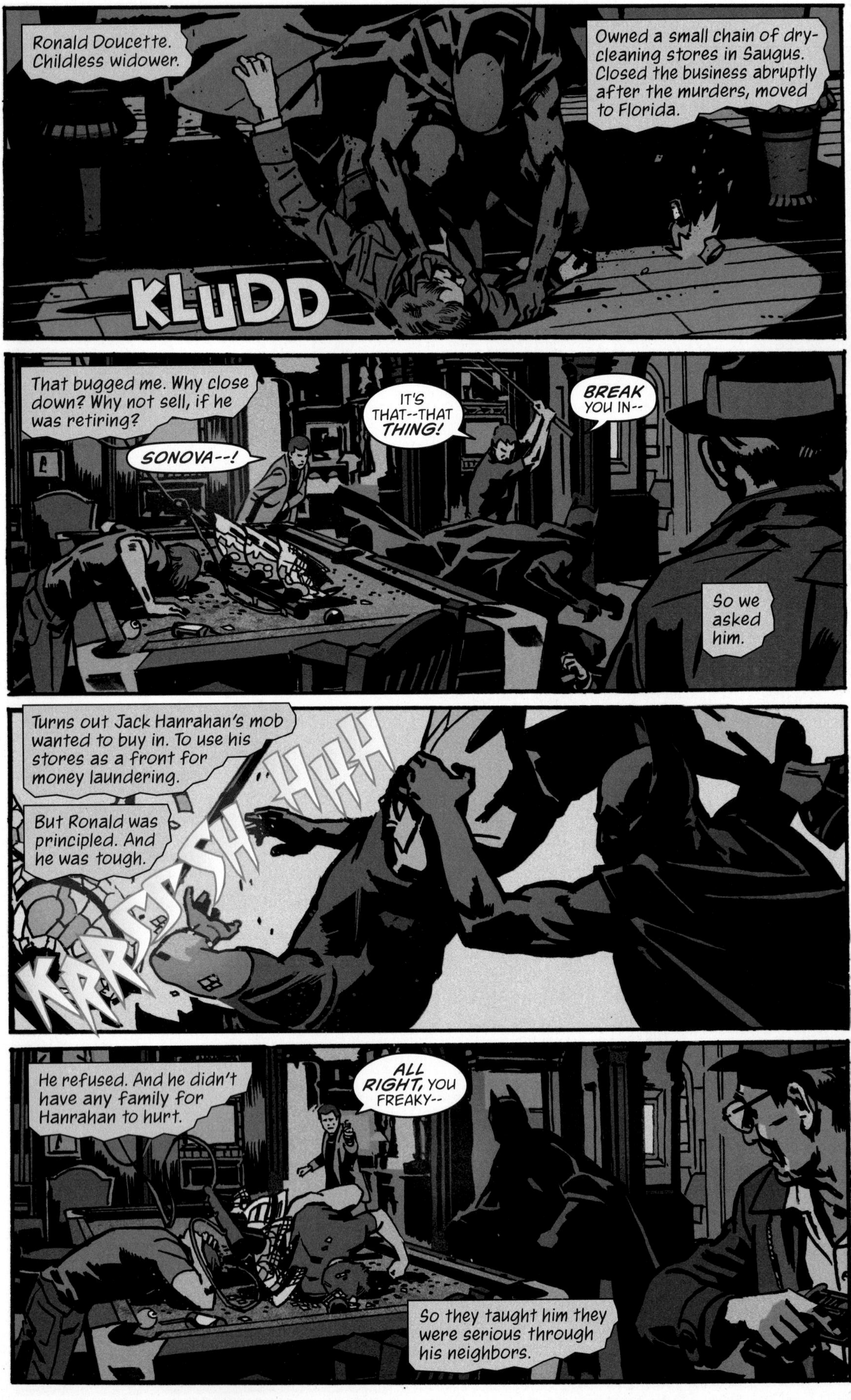
Ronald Doucette. Childless widower.
Owned a small chain of dry-cleaning stores in Saugus. Closed the business abruptly after the murders, moved to Florida.
KLUDD
That bugged me. Why close down? Why not sell, if he was retiring?
SONOVA--!
IT'S THAT--THAT THING!
BREAK YOU IN--
So we asked him.
Turns out Jack Hanrahan's mob wanted to buy in. To use his stores as a front for money laundering.
But Ronald was principled. And he was tough.
KRRSSSH
He refused. And he didn't have any family for Hanrahan to hurt.
ALL RIGHT, YOU FREAKY--
So they taught him they were serious through his neighbors.

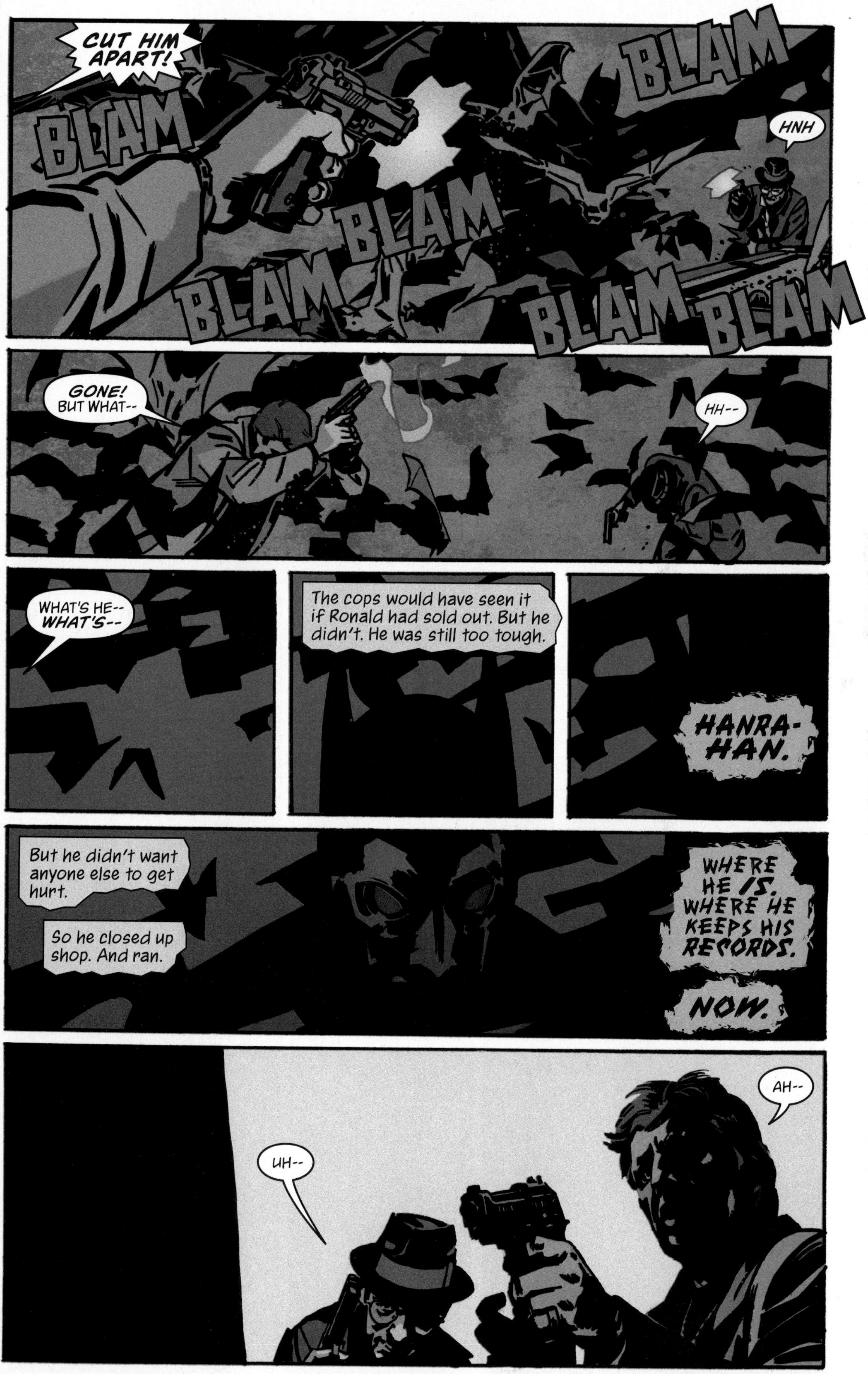
CUT HIM APART!
BLAM
BLAM
HNH
BLAM
BLAM
BLAM
BLAM
GONE! BUT WHAT--
HH--
WHAT'S HE-- WHAT'S--
The cops would have seen it if Ronald had sold out. But he didn't. He was still too tough.
HANRA-HAN.
But he didn't want anyone else to get hurt.
So he closed up shop. And ran.
WHERE HE IS. WHERE HE KEEPS HIS RECORDS.
NOW.
AH--
UH--

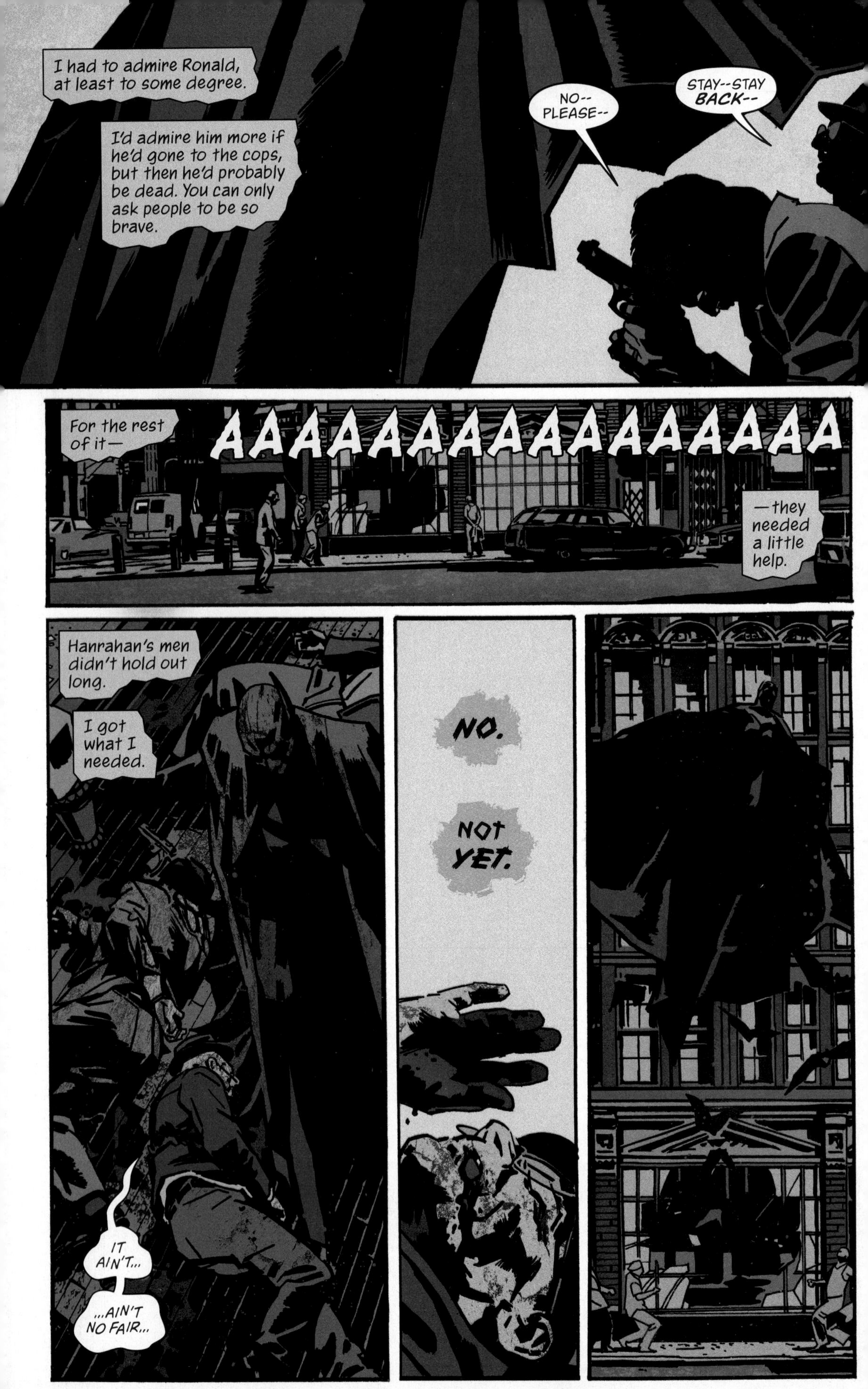
I had to admire Ronald, at least to some degree.
I'd admire him more if he'd gone to the cops, but then he'd probably be dead. You can only ask people to be so brave.
NO-- PLEASE--
STAY--STAY BACK--
For the rest of it—
AAAAAAAAAAAAAAA
—they needed a little help.
Hanrahan's men didn't hold out long.
I got what I needed.
IT AIN'T...
...AIN'T NO FAIR...
NO.
NOT YET.

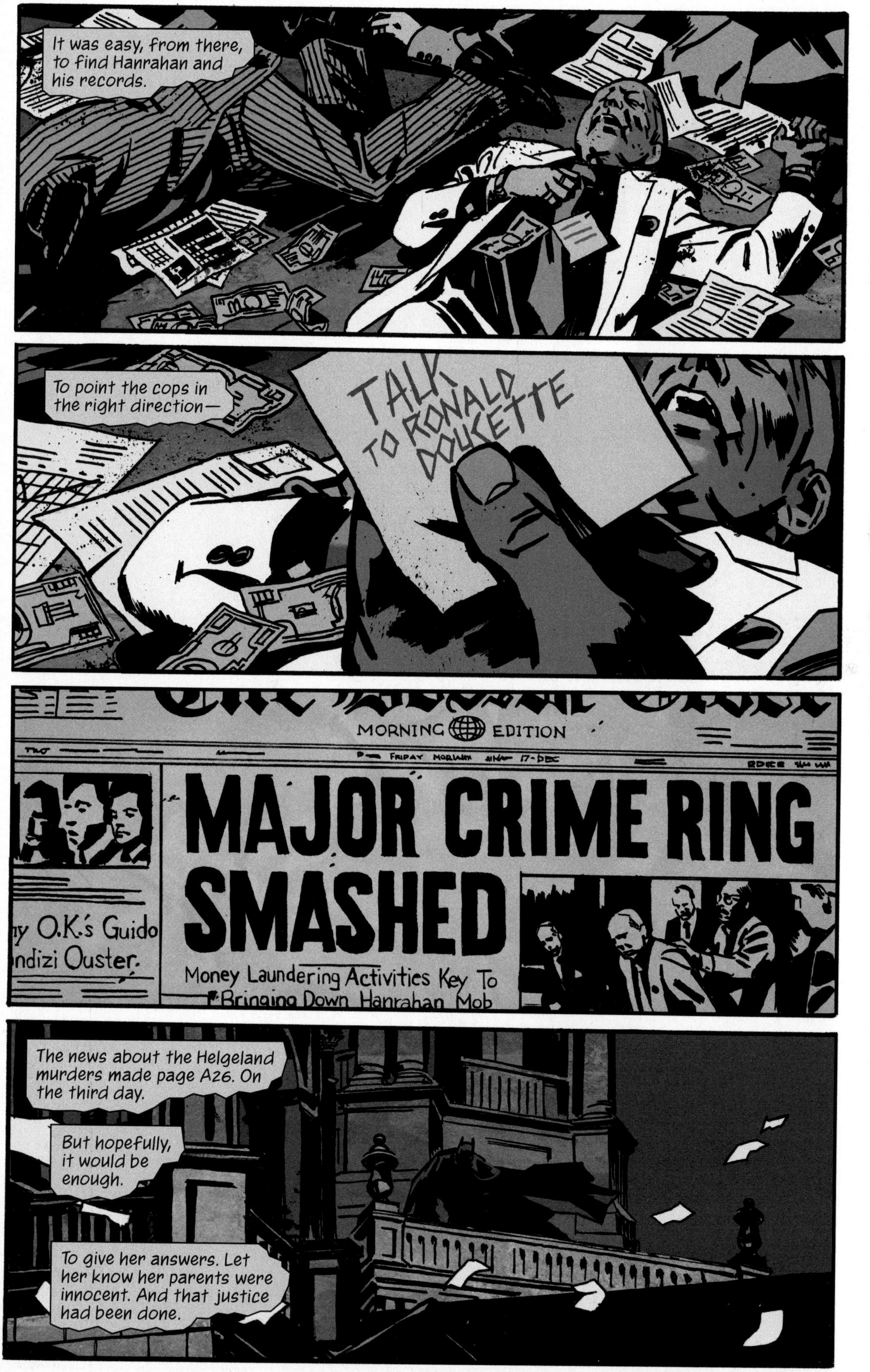

It was easy, from there, to find Hanrahan and his records.
To point the cops in the right direction—
TALK TO RONALD DOUCETTE
MORNING EDITION
MAJOR CRIME RING SMASHED
ny O.K.'s Guido
ndizi Ouster.
Money Laundering Activities Key To Bringing Down Hanrahan Mob
The news about the Helgeland murders made page A26. On the third day.
But hopefully, it would be enough.
To give her answers. Let her know her parents were innocent. And that justice had been done.

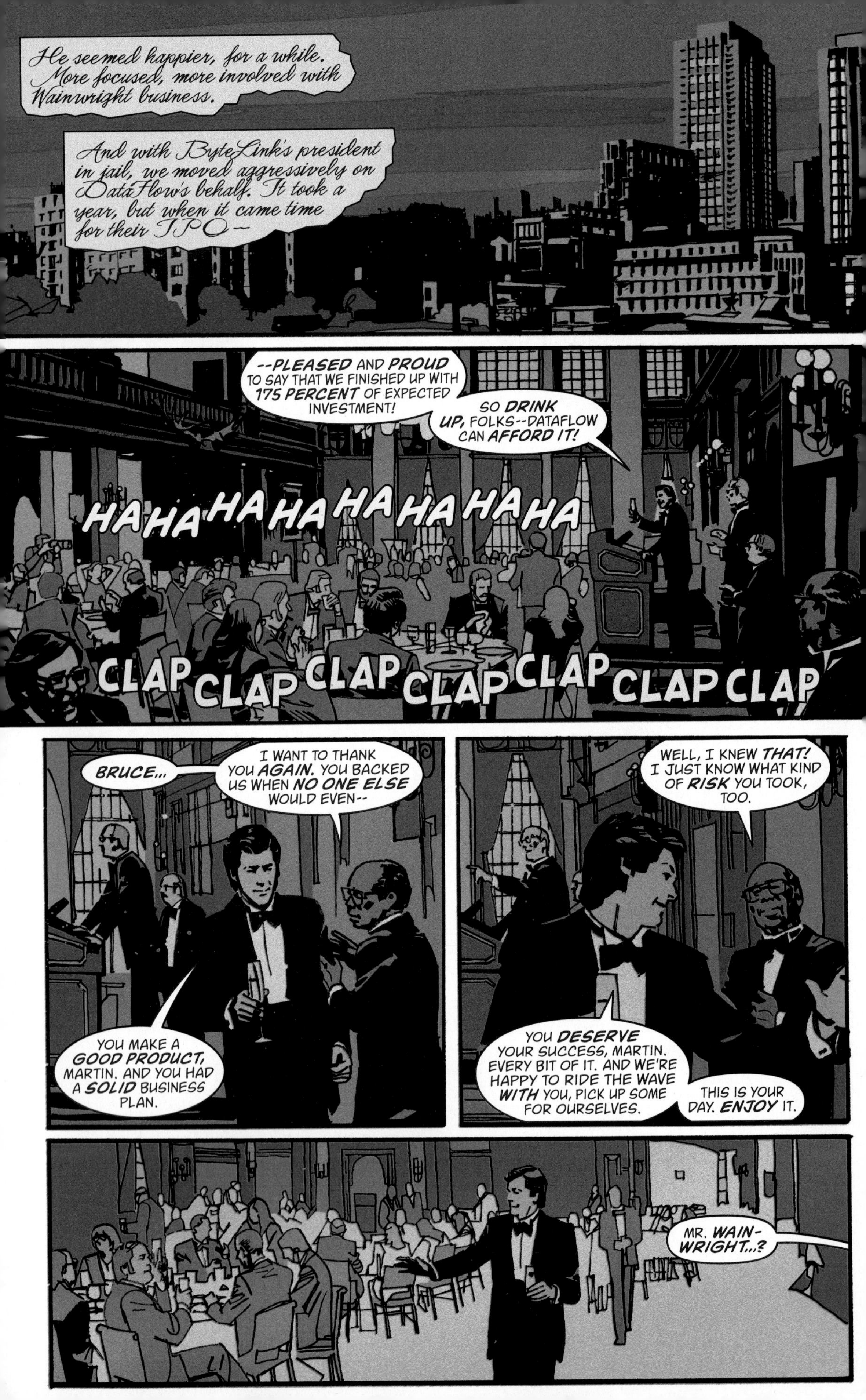
He seemed happier, for a while. More focused, more involved with Wainwright business.
And with ByteLink's president in jail, we moved aggressively on DataFlow's behalf. It took a year, but when it came time for their IPO--
--PLEASED AND PROUD TO SAY THAT WE FINISHED UP WITH 175 PERCENT OF EXPECTED INVESTMENT!
SO DRINK UP, FOLKS--DATAFLOW CAN AFFORD IT!
HAHAHAHAHAHAHAHAHAHAHA
CLAP CLAP CLAP CLAP CLAP CLAP CLAP
BRUCE...
I WANT TO THANK YOU AGAIN. YOU BACKED US WHEN NO ONE ELSE WOULD EVEN--
YOU MAKE A GOOD PRODUCT, MARTIN. AND YOU HAD A SOLID BUSINESS PLAN.
WELL, I KNEW THAT! I JUST KNOW WHAT KIND OF RISK YOU TOOK, TOO.
YOU DESERVE YOUR SUCCESS, MARTIN. EVERY BIT OF IT. AND WE'RE HAPPY TO RIDE THE WAVE WITH YOU, PICK UP SOME FOR OURSELVES.
THIS IS YOUR DAY. ENJOY IT.
MR. WAIN-WRIGHT...?

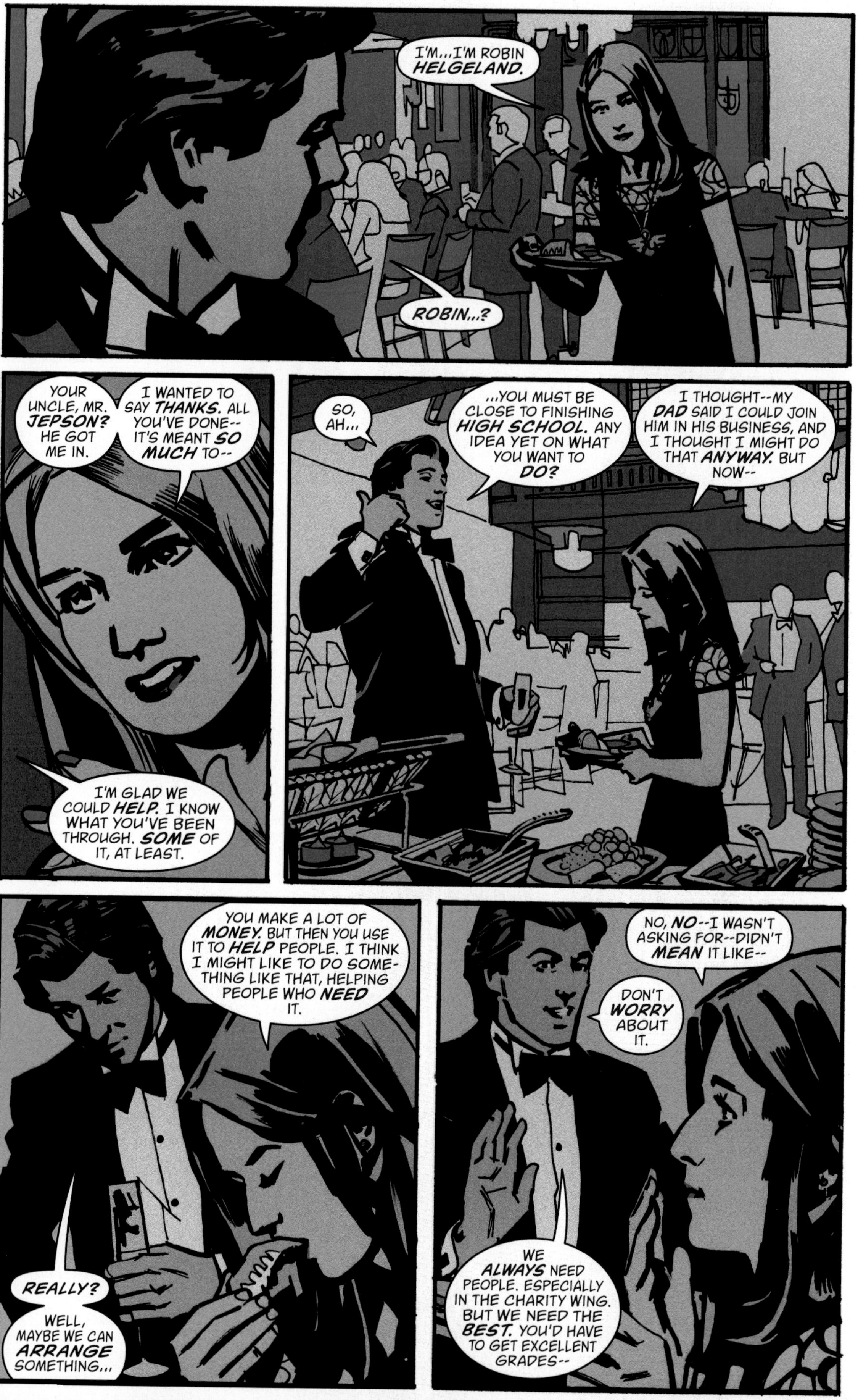
I'M...I'M ROBIN HELGELAND.
ROBIN...?
YOUR UNCLE, MR. JEPSON? HE GOT ME IN.
I WANTED TO SAY THANKS. ALL YOU'VE DONE-- IT'S MEANT SO MUCH TO--
I'M GLAD WE COULD HELP. I KNOW WHAT YOU'VE BEEN THROUGH. SOME OF IT, AT LEAST.
SO, AH...
...YOU MUST BE CLOSE TO FINISHING HIGH SCHOOL. ANY IDEA YET ON WHAT YOU WANT TO DO?
I THOUGHT--MY DAD SAID I COULD JOIN HIM IN HIS BUSINESS, AND I THOUGHT I MIGHT DO THAT ANYWAY. BUT NOW--
YOU MAKE A LOT OF MONEY. BUT THEN YOU USE IT TO HELP PEOPLE. I THINK I MIGHT LIKE TO DO SOMETHING LIKE THAT, HELPING PEOPLE WHO NEED IT.
REALLY?
WELL, MAYBE WE CAN ARRANGE SOMETHING...
NO, NO--I WASN'T ASKING FOR--DIDN'T MEAN IT LIKE--
DON'T WORRY ABOUT IT.
WE ALWAYS NEED PEOPLE. ESPECIALLY IN THE CHARITY WING. BUT WE NEED THE BEST. YOU'D HAVE TO GET EXCELLENT GRADES--

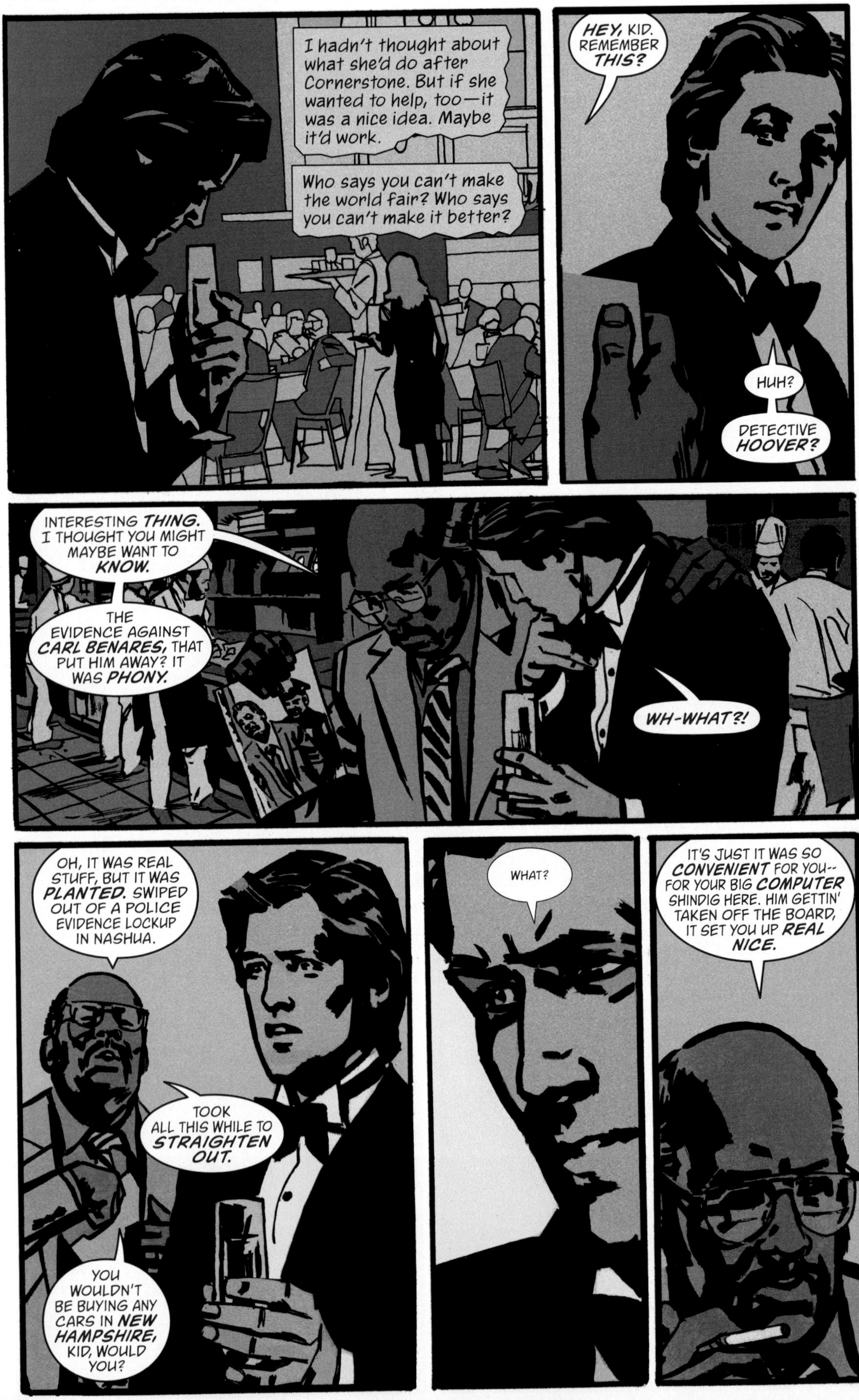
I hadn't thought about what she'd do after Cornerstone. But if she wanted to help, too—it was a nice idea. Maybe it'd work.
Who says you can't make the world fair? Who says you can't make it better?
HEY, KID. REMEMBER THIS?
HUH?
DETECTIVE HOOVER?
INTERESTING THING. I THOUGHT YOU MIGHT MAYBE WANT TO KNOW.
THE EVIDENCE AGAINST CARL BENARES, THAT PUT HIM AWAY? IT WAS PHONY.
WH-WHAT?!
OH, IT WAS REAL STUFF, BUT IT WAS PLANTED. SWIPED OUT OF A POLICE EVIDENCE LOCKUP IN NASHUA.
TOOK ALL THIS WHILE TO STRAIGHTEN OUT.
YOU WOULDN'T BE BUYING ANY CARS IN NEW HAMPSHIRE, KID, WOULD YOU?
WHAT?
IT'S JUST IT WAS SO CONVENIENT FOR YOU-- FOR YOUR BIG COMPUTER SHINDIG HERE. HIM GETTIN' TAKEN OFF THE BOARD, IT SET YOU UP REAL NICE.

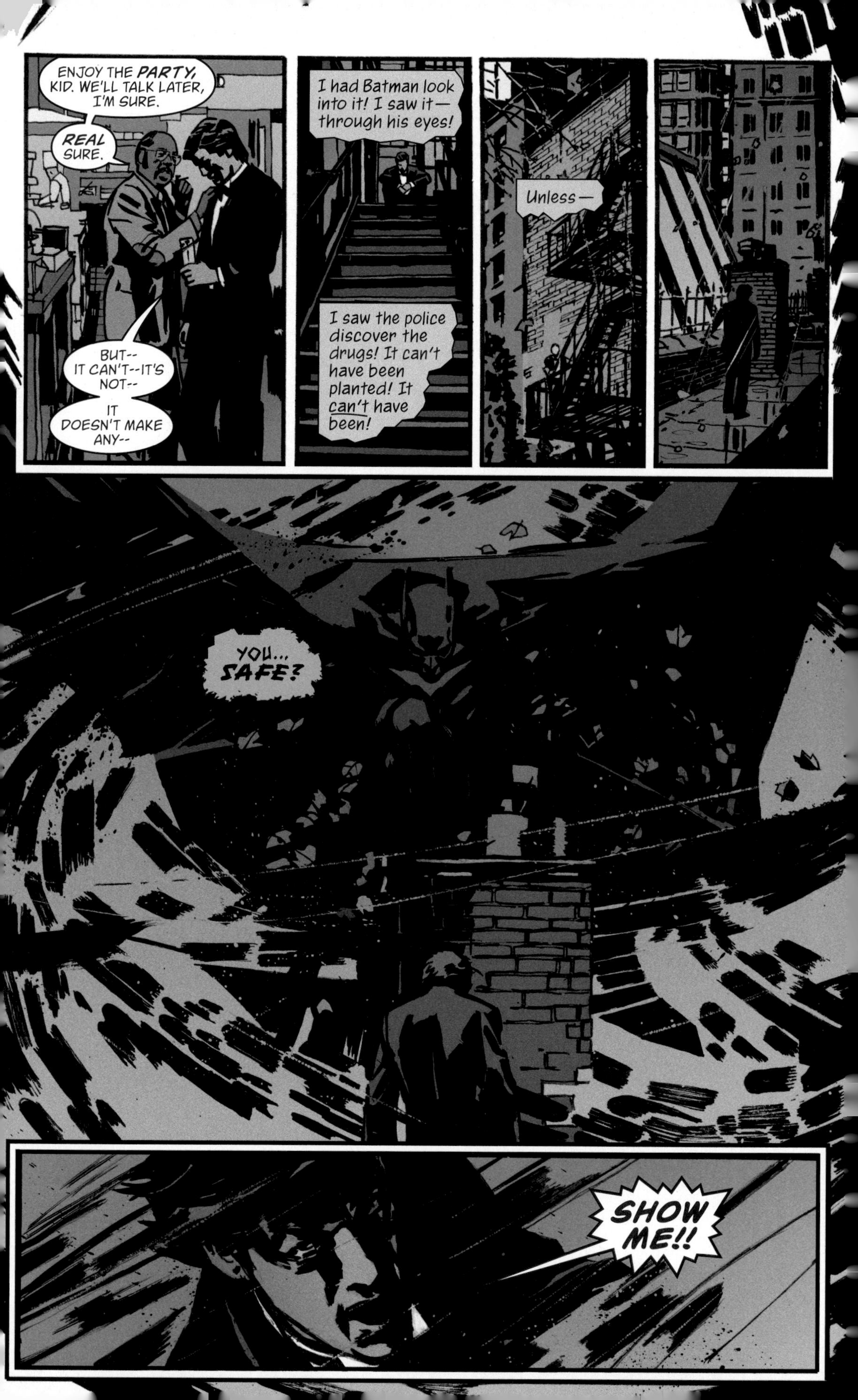

ENJOY THE PARTY, KID. WE'LL TALK LATER, I'M SURE.
REAL SURE.
BUT-- IT CAN'T--IT'S NOT--
IT DOESN'T MAKE ANY--
I had Batman look into it! I saw it— through his eyes!
I saw the police discover the drugs! It can't have been planted! It can't have been!
Unless—
YOU... SAFE?
SHOW ME!!

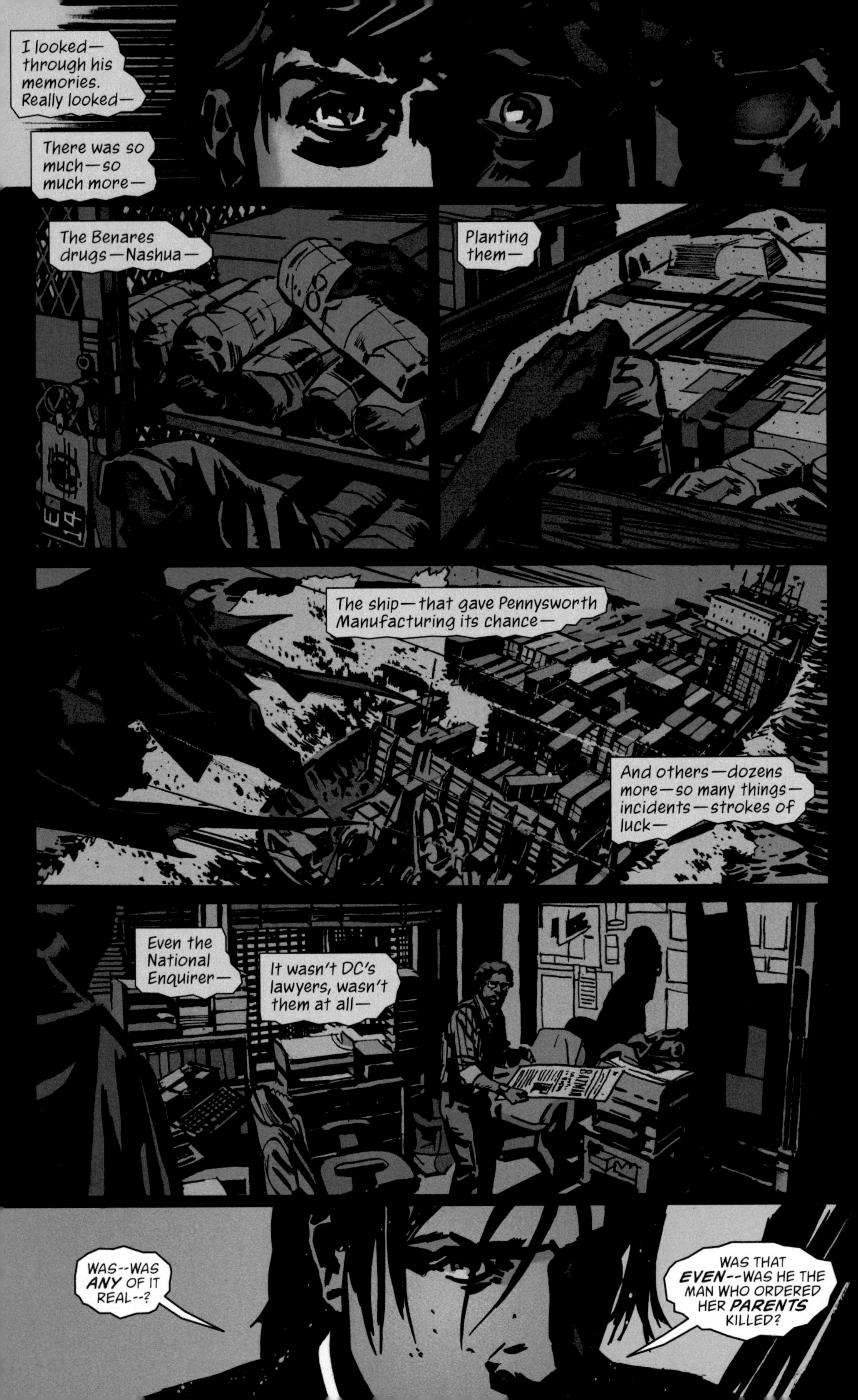
I looked—through his memories. Really looked—
There was so much—so much more—
The Benares drugs—Nashua—
Planting them—
The ship—that gave Pennysworth Manufacturing its chance—
And others—dozens more—so many things—incidents—strokes of luck—
Even the National Enquirer—
It wasn't DC's lawyers, wasn't them at all—
WAS--WAS ANY OF IT REAL--?
WAS THAT EVEN--WAS HE THE MAN WHO ORDERED HER PARENTS KILLED?

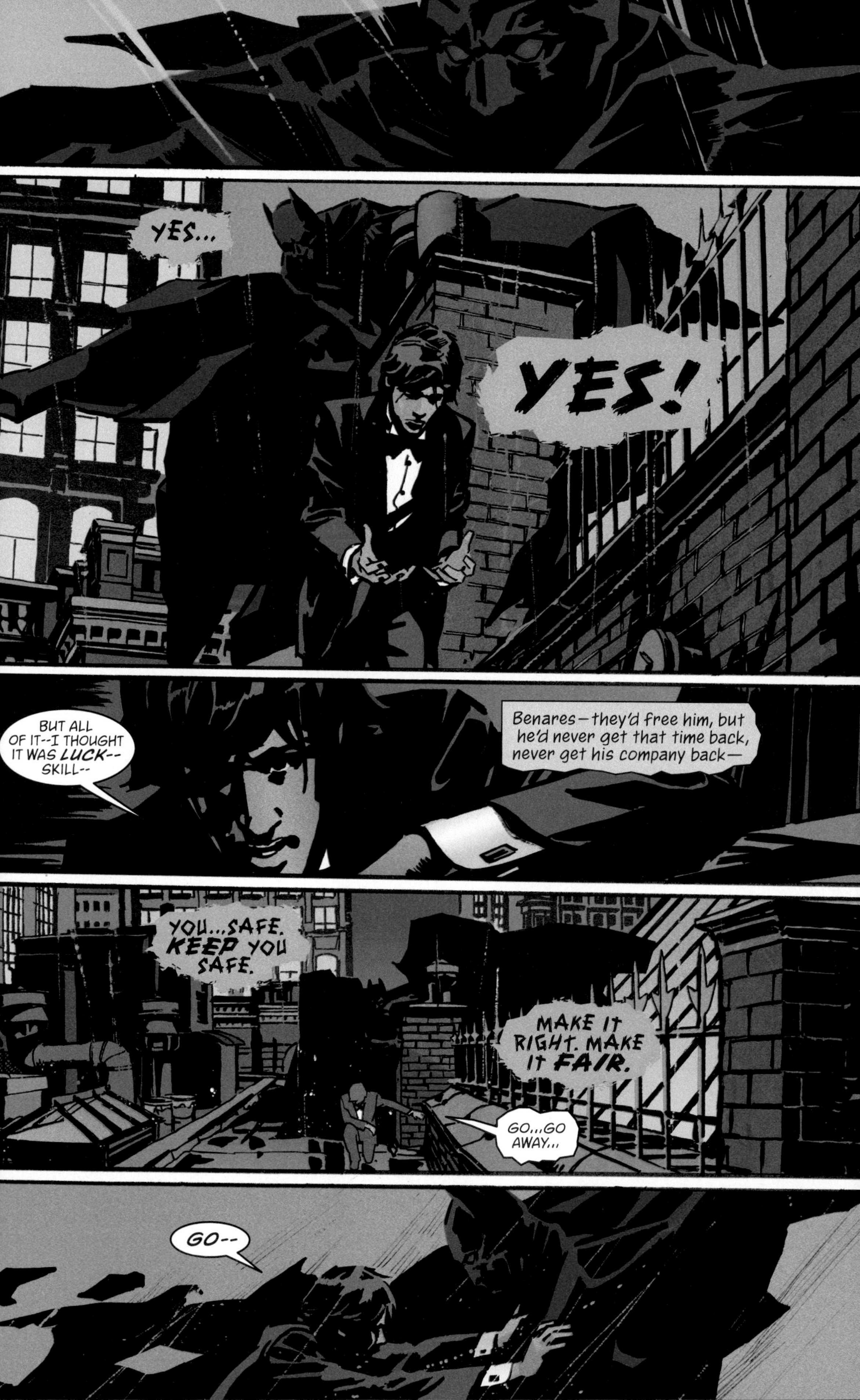

YES...
YES!
BUT ALL OF IT--I THOUGHT IT WAS LUCK-- SKILL--
Benares—they'd free him, but he'd never get that time back, never get his company back—
YOU...SAFE. KEEP YOU SAFE.
MAKE IT RIGHT. MAKE IT FAIR.
GO...GO AWAY...
GO--

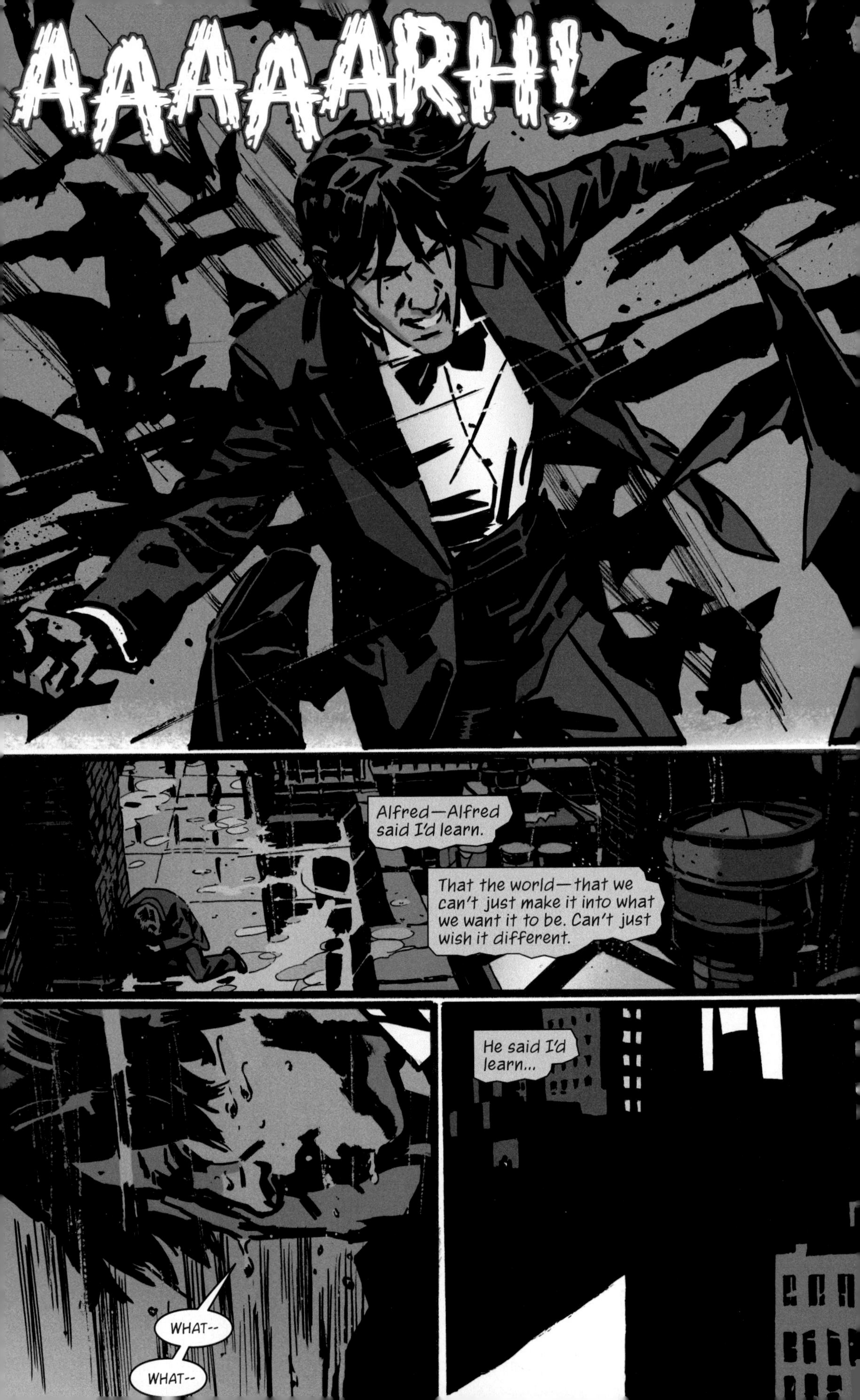
AAAAARH!
Alfred—Alfred said I'd learn.
That the world—that we can't just make it into what we want it to be. Can't just wish it different.
He said I'd learn...
WHAT--
WHAT--

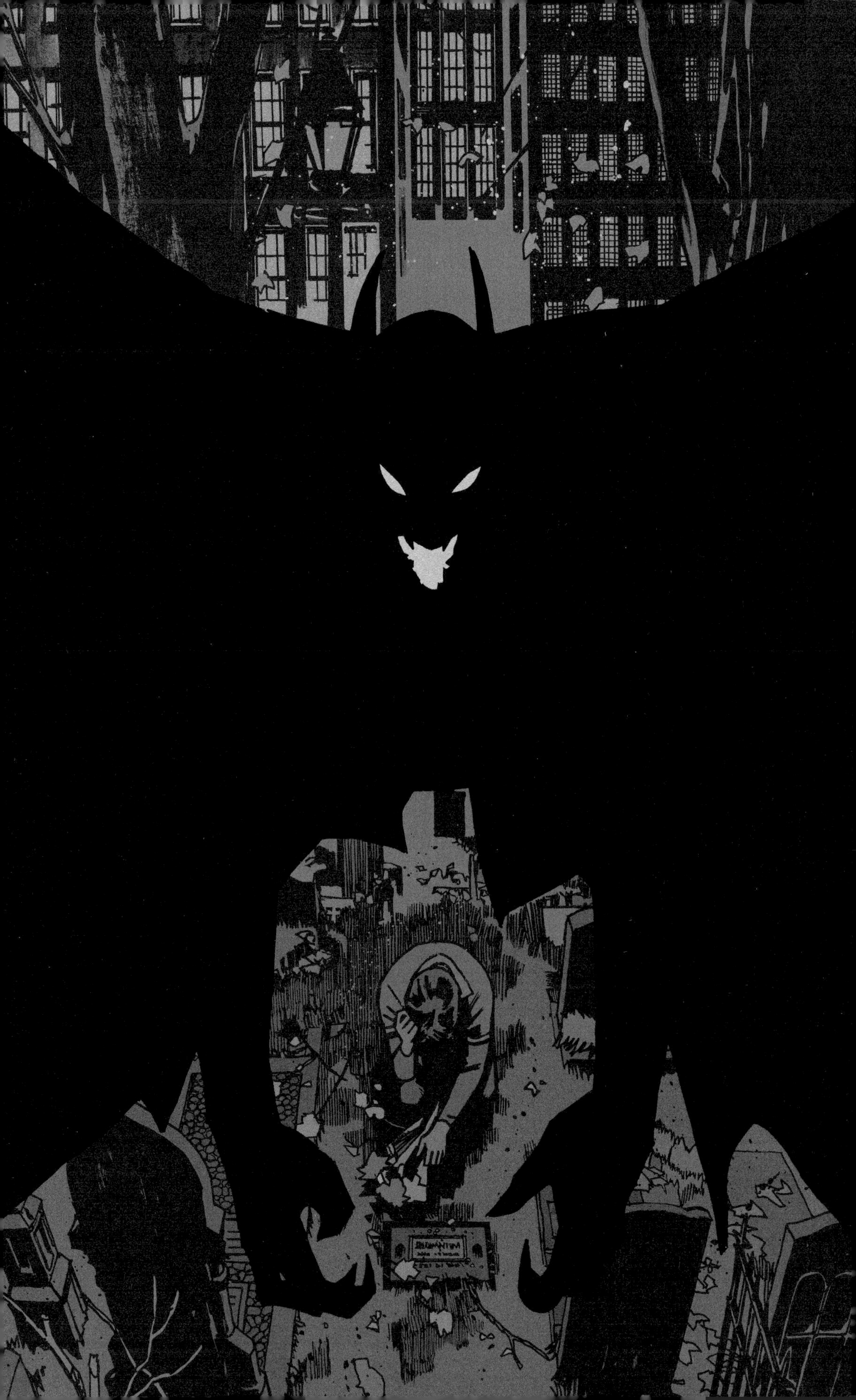

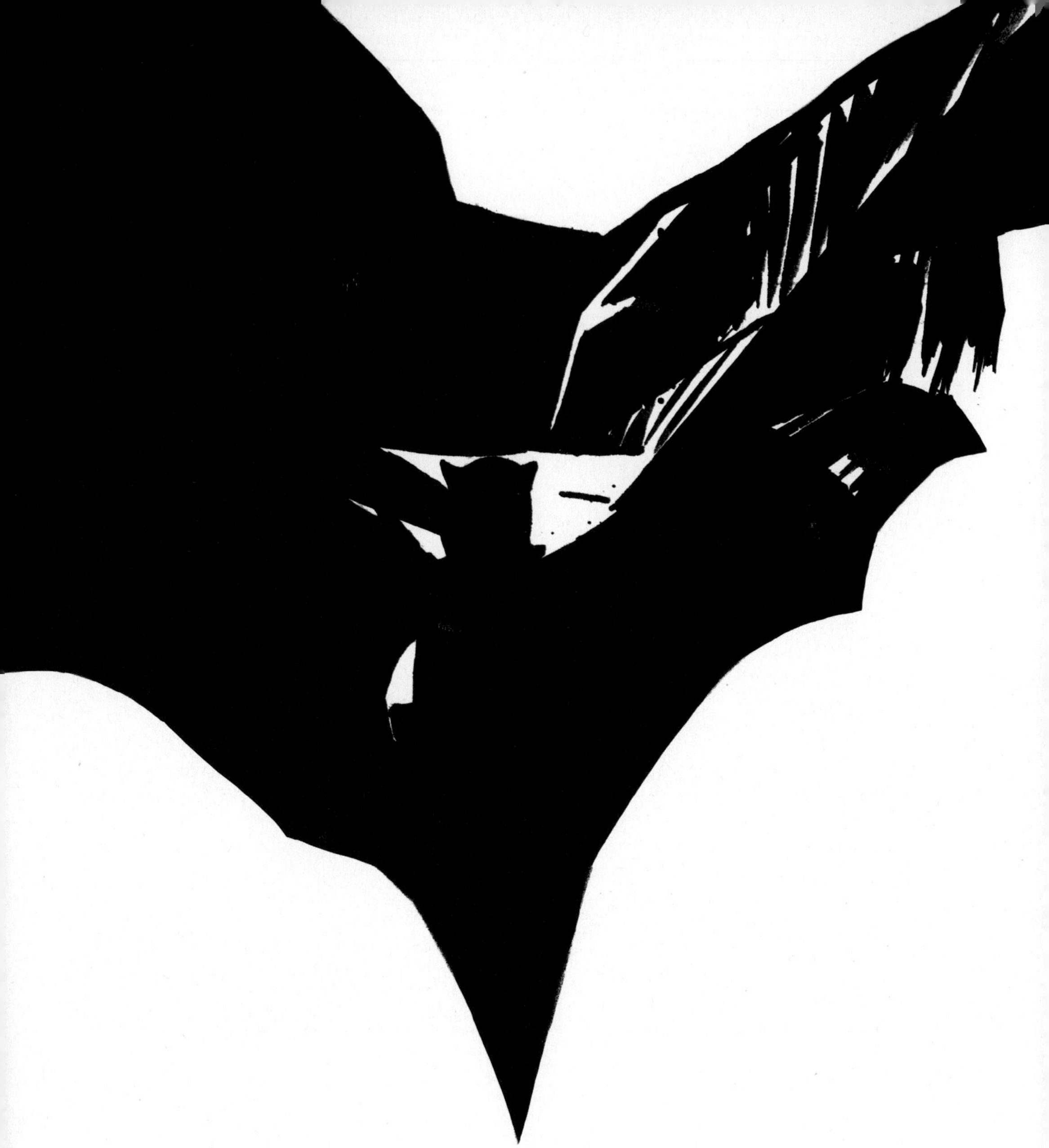

BOOK THREE: **CRUSADER**

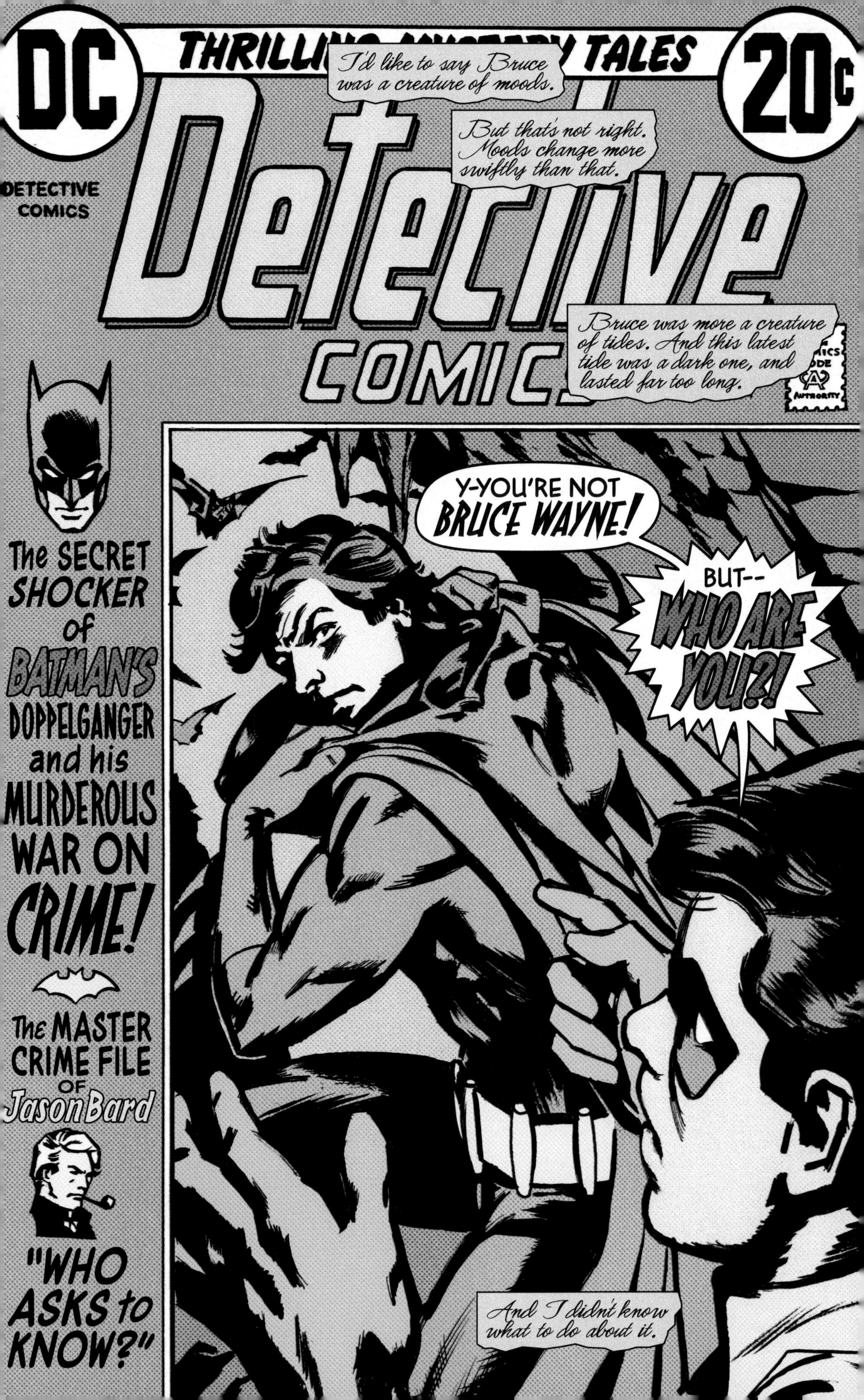

DC
TALES
20c
I'd like to say Bruce was a creature of moods.
But that's not right. Moods change more swiftly than that.
DETECTIVE COMICS
Detective Comics
Bruce was more a creature of tides. And this latest tide was a dark one, and lasted far too long.
The SECRET SHOCKER of BATMAN'S DOPPELGANGER and his MURDEROUS WAR ON CRIME!
Y-YOU'RE NOT BRUCE WAYNE!
BUT-- WHO ARE YOU?!
The MASTER CRIME FILE OF Jason Bard
"WHO ASKS to KNOW?"
And I didn't know what to do about it.

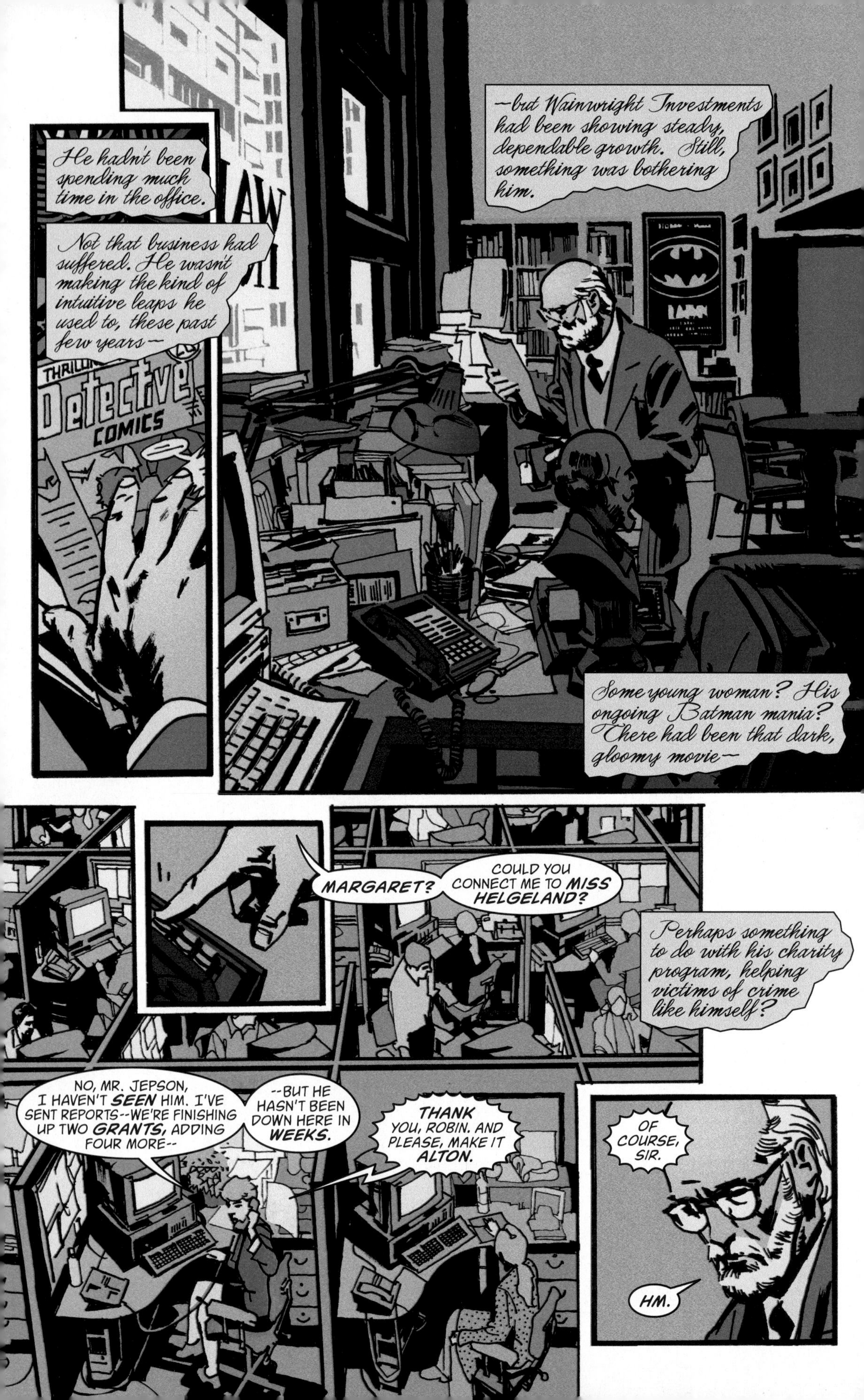
He hadn't been spending much time in the office.
Not that business had suffered. He wasn't making the kind of intuitive leaps he used to, these past few years—
—but Wainwright Investments had been showing steady, dependable growth. Still, something was bothering him.
Some young woman? His ongoing Batman mania? There had been that dark, gloomy movie—
MARGARET?
COULD YOU CONNECT ME TO MISS HELGELAND?
Perhaps something to do with his charity program, helping victims of crime like himself?
NO, MR. JEPSON, I HAVEN'T SEEN HIM. I'VE SENT REPORTS--WE'RE FINISHING UP TWO GRANTS, ADDING FOUR MORE--
--BUT HE HASN'T BEEN DOWN HERE IN WEEKS.
THANK YOU, ROBIN. AND PLEASE, MAKE IT ALTON.
OF COURSE, SIR.
HM.

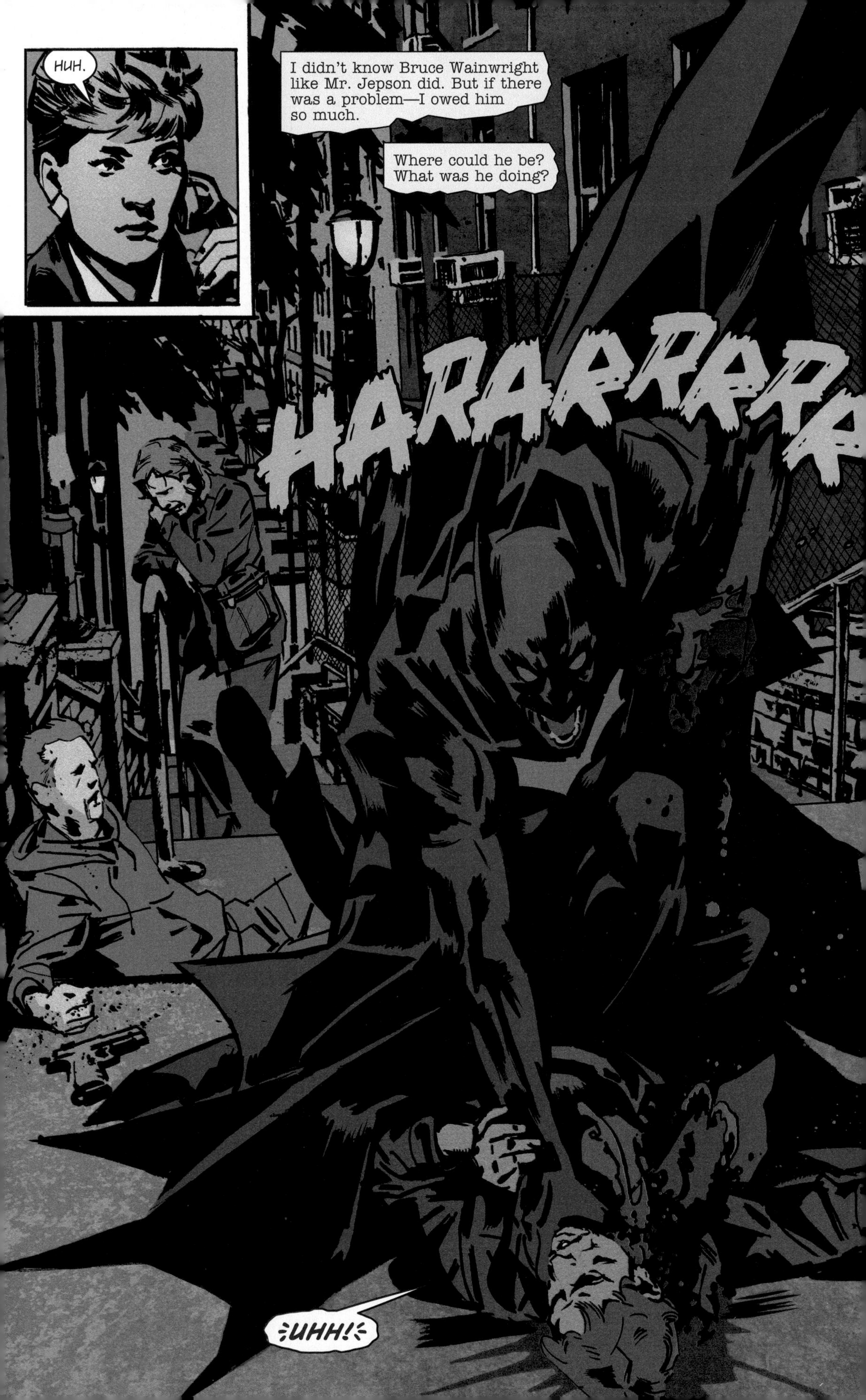
HUH.
I didn't know Bruce Wainwright like Mr. Jepson did. But if there was a problem—I owed him so much.
Where could he be? What was he doing?
HARARRRRR
UHH!

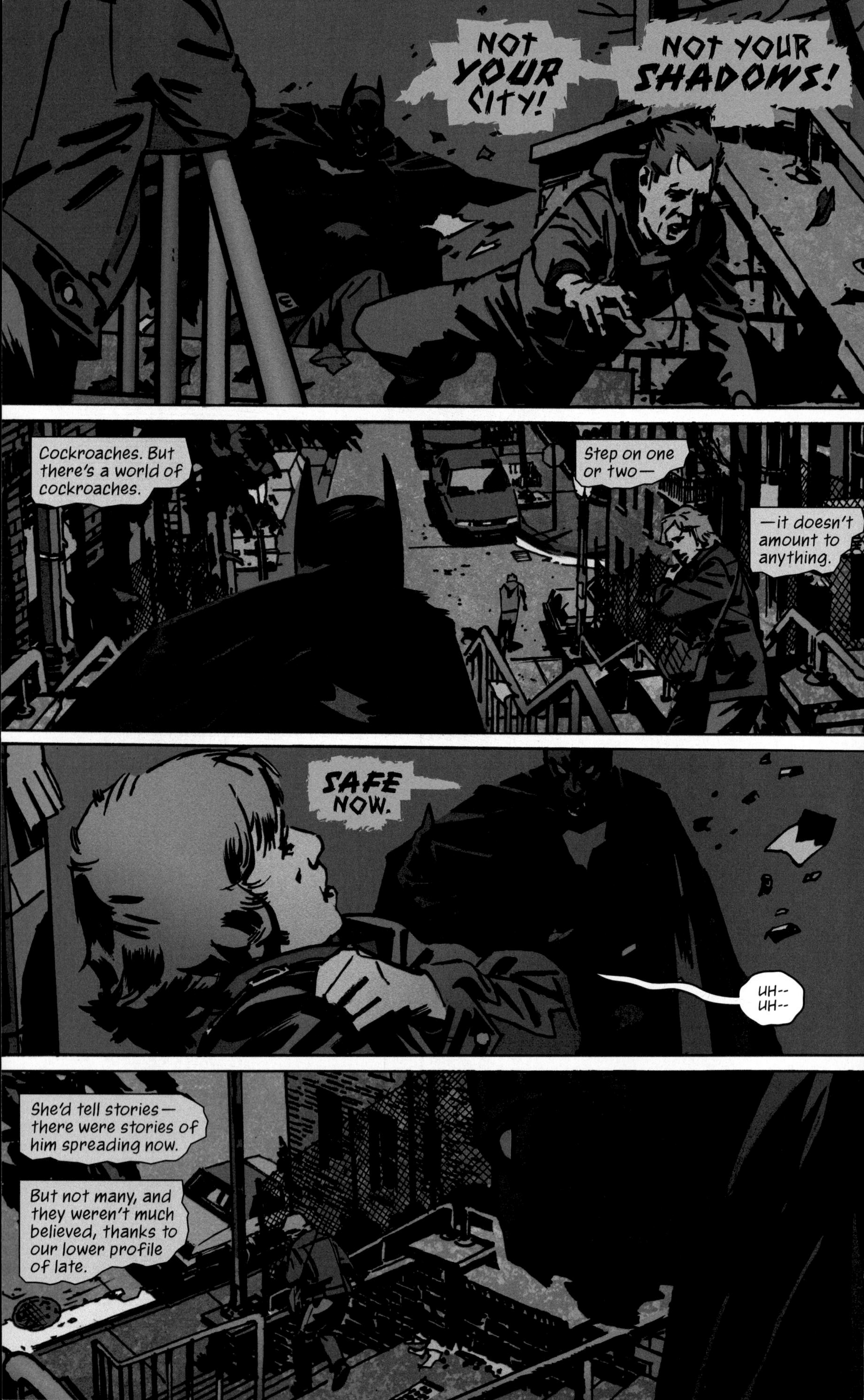
NOT YOUR CITY!
NOT YOUR SHADOWS!
Cockroaches. But there's a world of cockroaches.
Step on one or two—
—it doesn't amount to anything.
SAFE NOW.
UH-- UH--
She'd tell stories—there were stories of him spreading now.
But not many, and they weren't much believed, thanks to our lower profile of late.

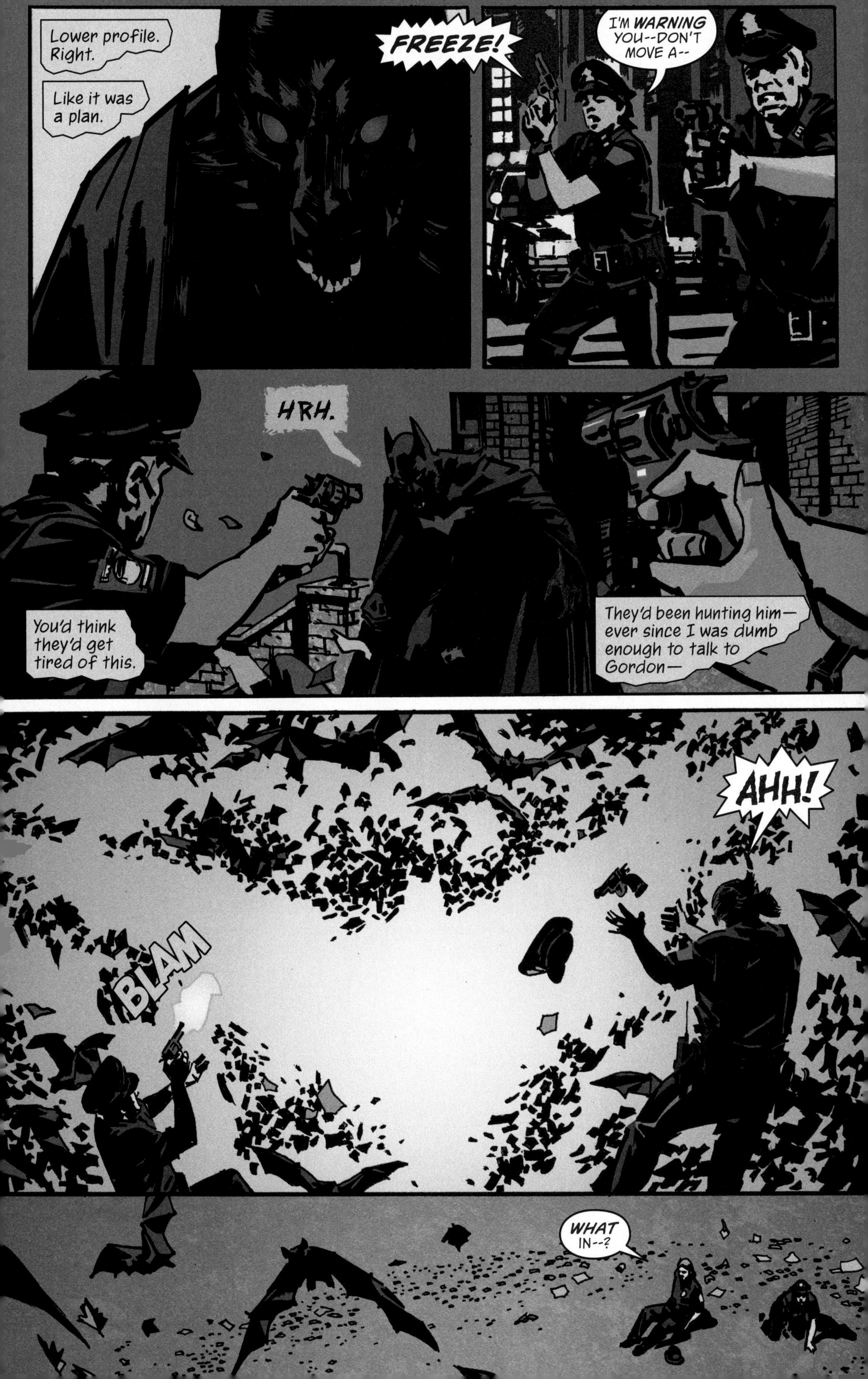
Lower profile. Right.
Like it was a plan.
FREEZE!
I'M WARNING YOU--DON'T MOVE A--
HRH.
You'd think they'd get tired of this.
They'd been hunting him— ever since I was dumb enough to talk to Gordon—
AHH!
BLAM
WHAT IN--?

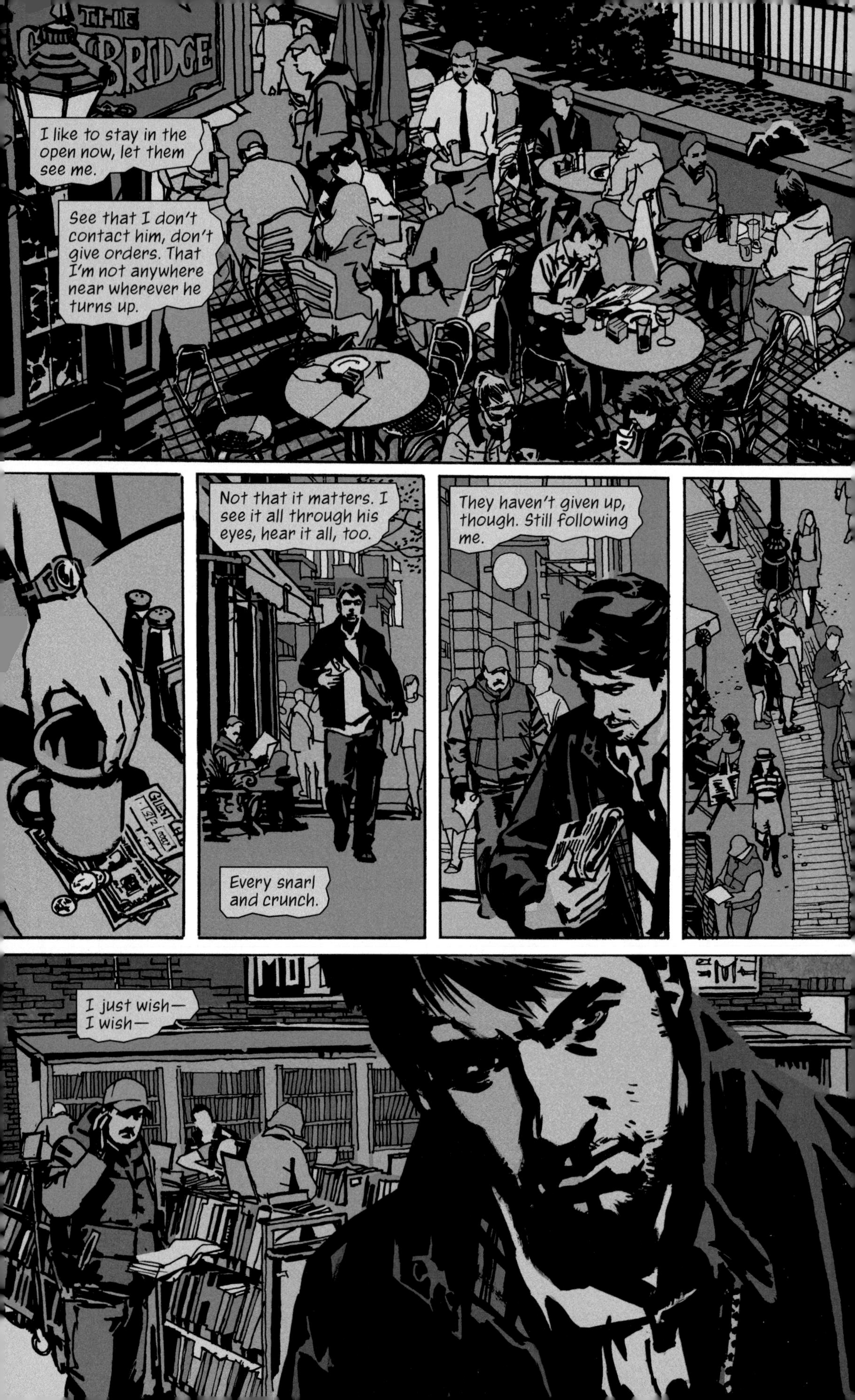
THE
BRIDGE
I like to stay in the open now, let them see me.
See that I don't contact him, don't give orders. That I'm not anywhere near wherever he turns up.
Not that it matters. I see it all through his eyes, hear it all, too.
Every snarl and crunch.
They haven't given up, though. Still following me.
I just wish—
I wish—

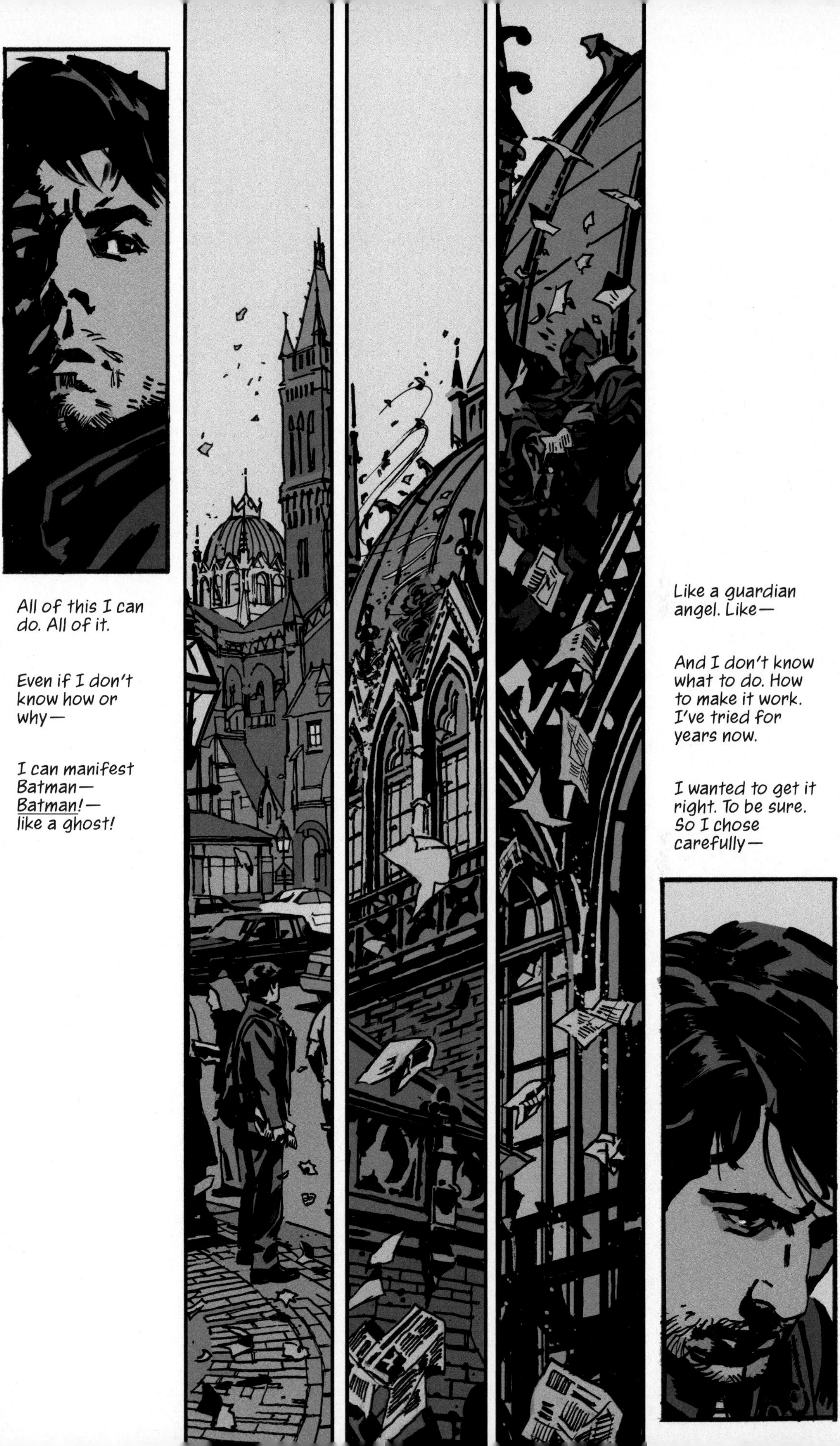
All of this I can do. All of it.
Even if I don't know how or why—
I can manifest Batman— Batman!— like a ghost!
Like a guardian angel. Like—
And I don't know what to do. How to make it work. I've tried for years now.
I wanted to get it right. To be sure. So I chose carefully—

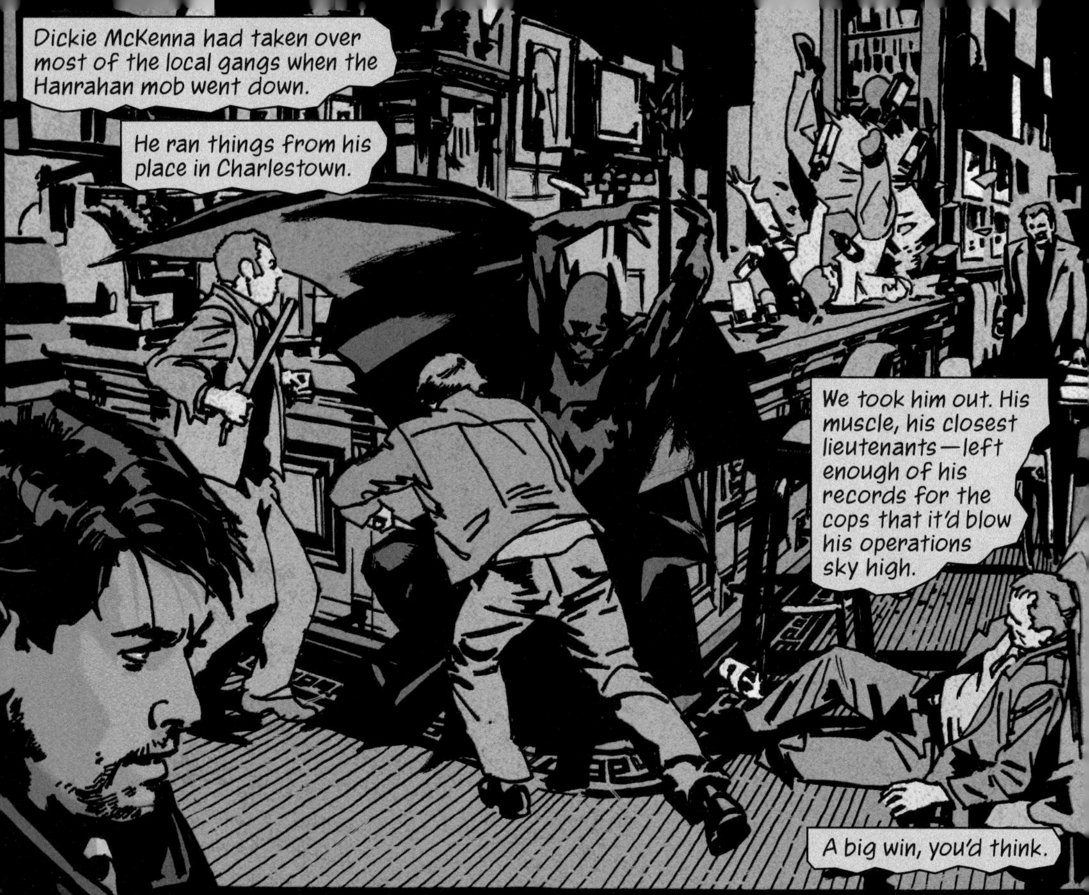
Dickie McKenna had taken over most of the local gangs when the Hanrahan mob went down.
He ran things from his place in Charlestown.
We took him out. His muscle, his closest lieutenants—left enough of his records for the cops that it'd blow his operations sky high.
A big win, you'd think.

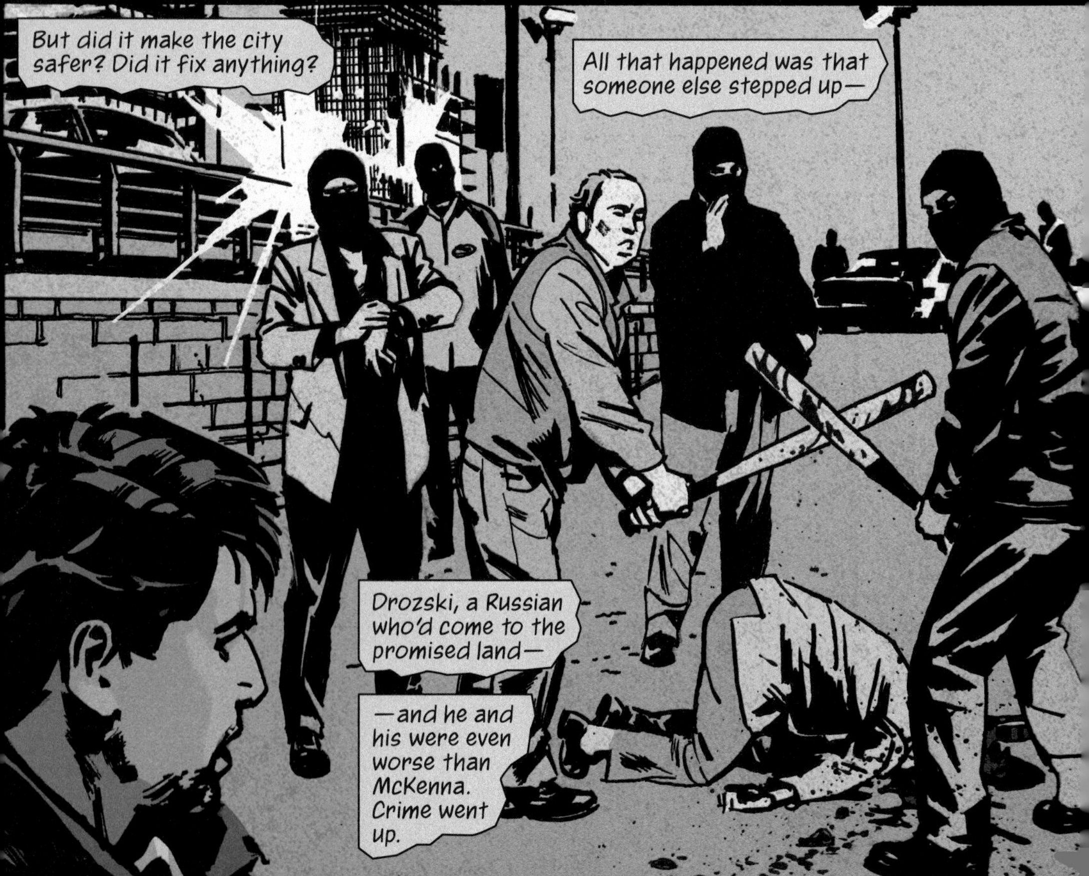
But did it make the city safer? Did it fix anything?
All that happened was that someone else stepped up—
Drozski, a Russian who'd come to the promised land—
—and he and his were even worse than McKenna. Crime went up.

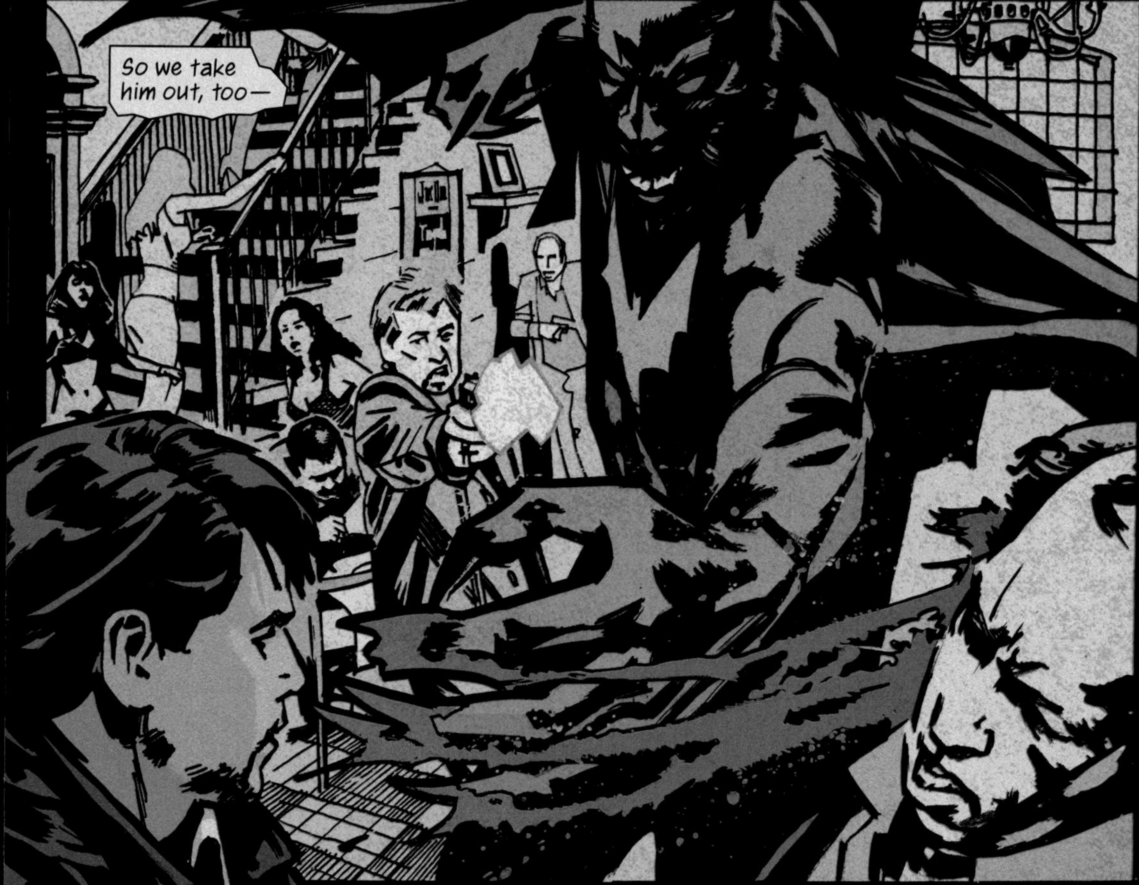
So we take him out, too—

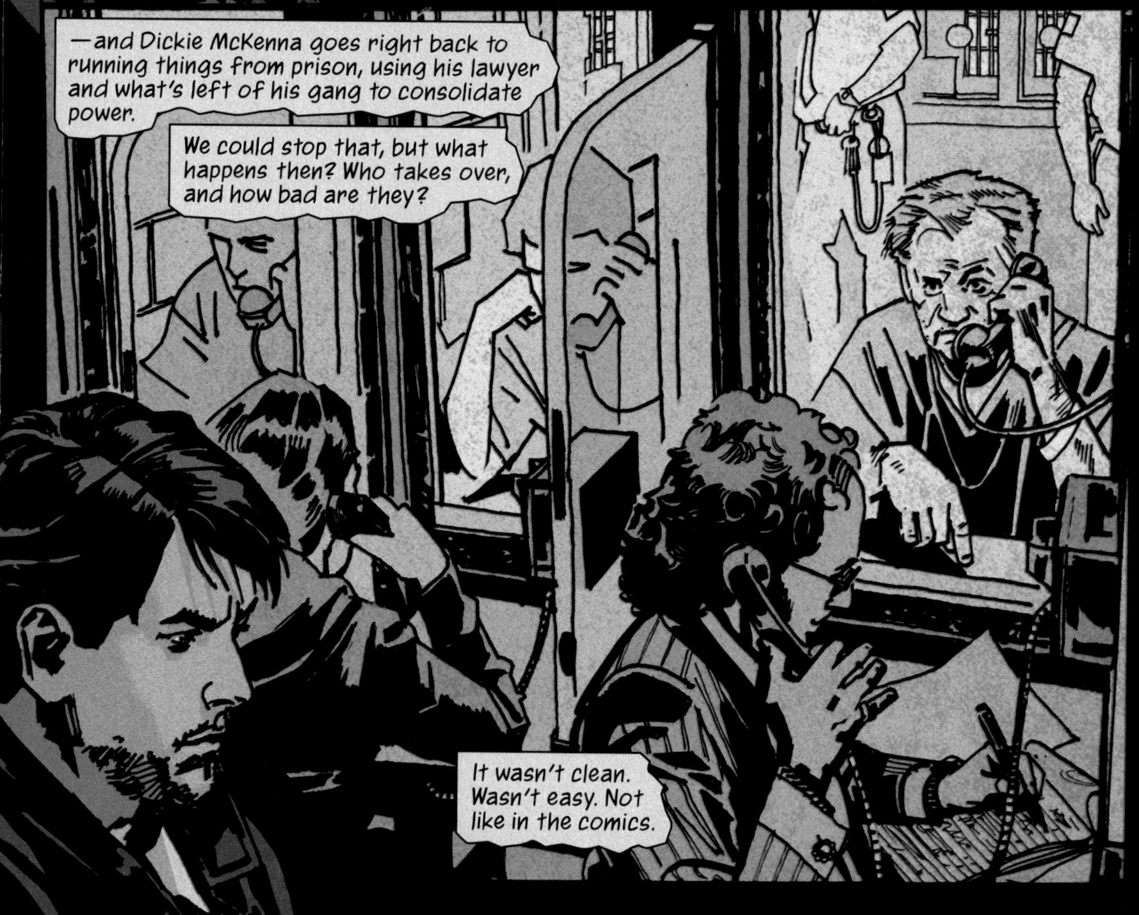
—and Dickie McKenna goes right back to running things from prison, using his lawyer and what's left of his gang to consolidate power.
We could stop that, but what happens then? Who takes over, and how bad are they?
It wasn't clean. Wasn't easy. Not like in the comics.

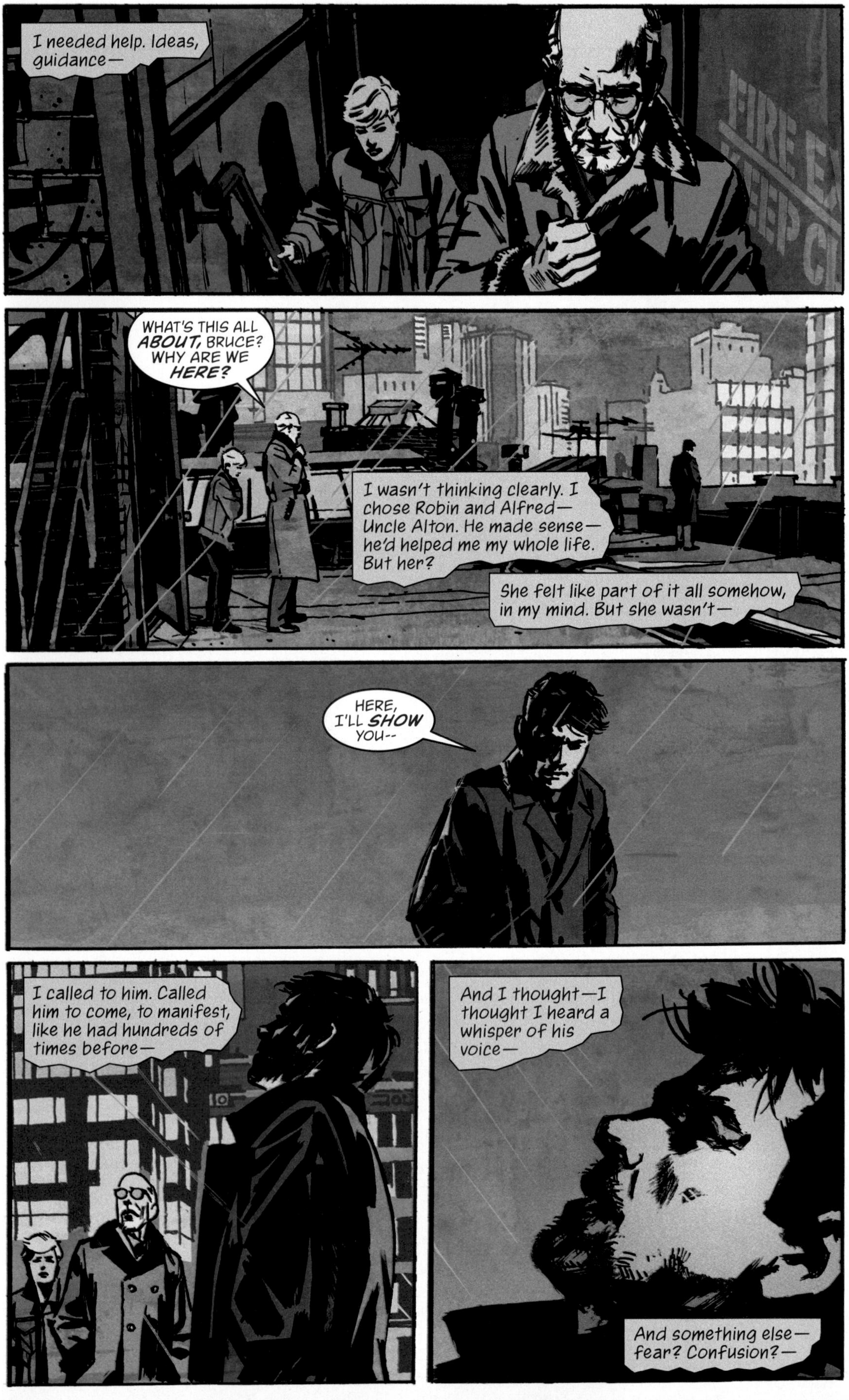
I needed help. Ideas, guidance—
WHAT'S THIS ALL ABOUT, BRUCE? WHY ARE WE HERE?
I wasn't thinking clearly. I chose Robin and Alfred—Uncle Alton. He made sense—he'd helped me my whole life. But her?
She felt like part of it all somehow, in my mind. But she wasn't—
HERE, I'LL SHOW YOU--
I called to him. Called him to come, to manifest, like he had hundreds of times before—
And I thought—I thought I heard a whisper of his voice—
And something else—fear? Confusion?—

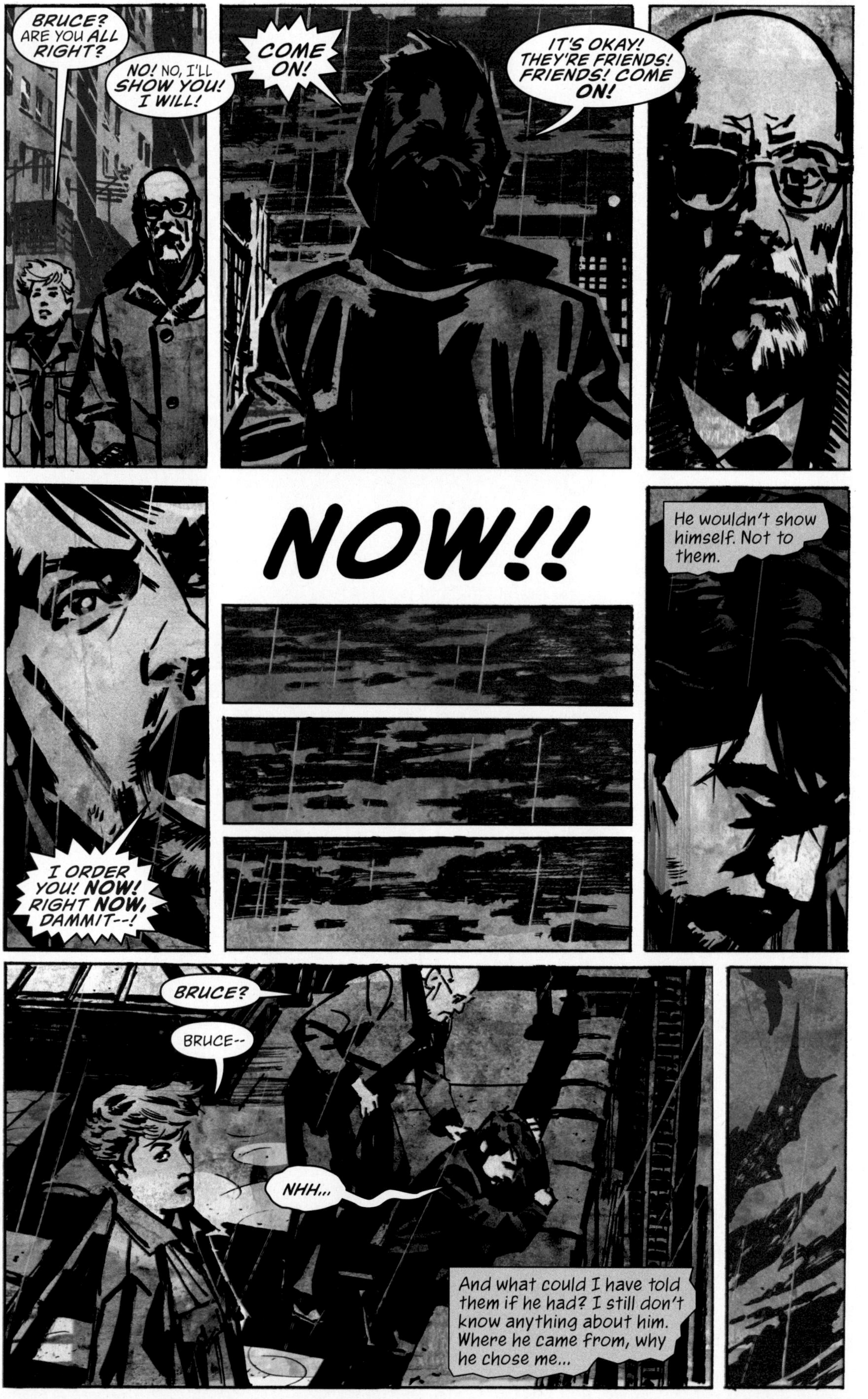
BRUCE? ARE YOU ALL RIGHT?
NO! NO, I'LL SHOW YOU! I WILL!
COME ON!
IT'S OKAY! THEY'RE FRIENDS! FRIENDS! COME ON!
NOW!!
He wouldn't show himself. Not to them.
I ORDER YOU! NOW! RIGHT NOW, DAMMIT--!
BRUCE?
BRUCE--
NHH...
And what could I have told them if he had? I still don't know anything about him. Where he came from, why he chose me...

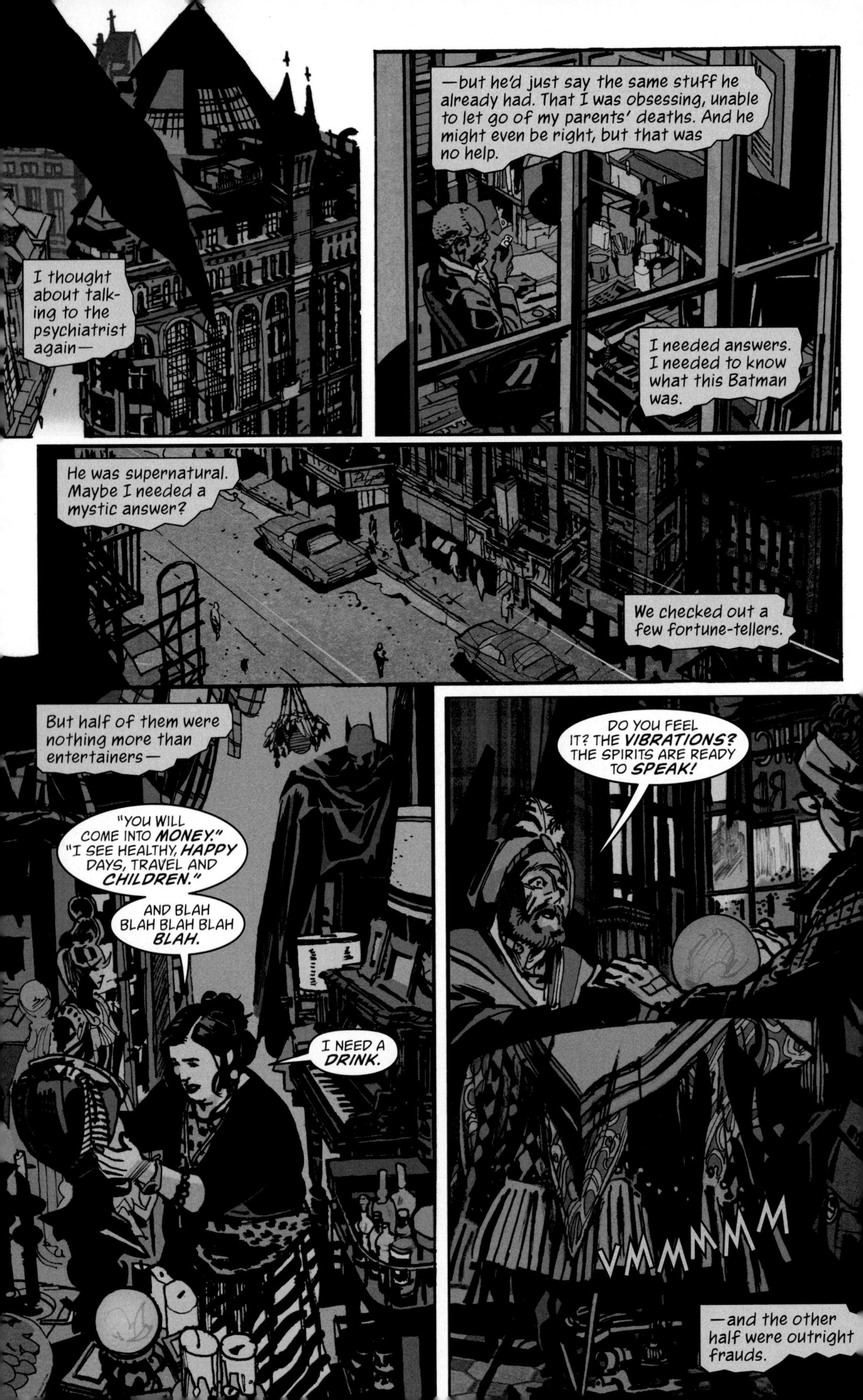
I thought about talk-ing to the psychiatrist again—
—but he'd just say the same stuff he already had. That I was obsessing, unable to let go of my parents' deaths. And he might even be right, but that was no help.
I needed answers. I needed to know what this Batman was.
He was supernatural. Maybe I needed a mystic answer?
We checked out a few fortune-tellers.
But half of them were nothing more than entertainers—
"YOU WILL COME INTO MONEY." "I SEE HEALTHY, HAPPY DAYS, TRAVEL AND CHILDREN."
AND BLAH BLAH BLAH BLAH BLAH.
I NEED A DRINK.
DO YOU FEEL IT? THE VIBRATIONS? THE SPIRITS ARE READY TO SPEAK!
VMMMMMM
—and the other half were outright frauds.

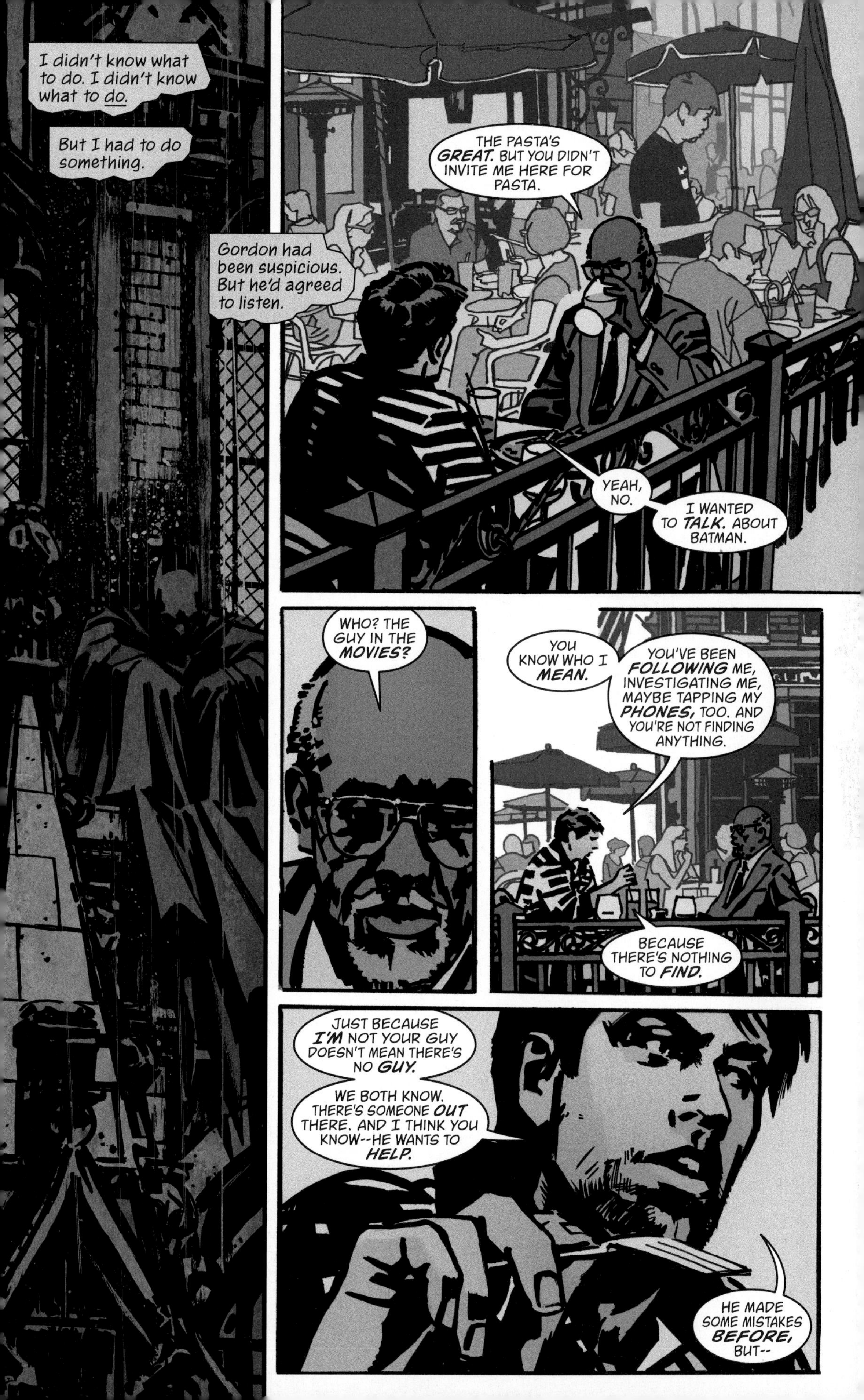
I didn't know what to do. I didn't know what to do.
But I had to do something.
THE PASTA'S GREAT. BUT YOU DIDN'T INVITE ME HERE FOR PASTA.
Gordon had been suspicious. But he'd agreed to listen.
YEAH, NO.
I WANTED TO TALK. ABOUT BATMAN.
WHO? THE GUY IN THE MOVIES?
YOU KNOW WHO I MEAN.
YOU'VE BEEN FOLLOWING ME, INVESTIGATING ME, MAYBE TAPPING MY PHONES, TOO. AND YOU'RE NOT FINDING ANYTHING.
BECAUSE THERE'S NOTHING TO FIND.
JUST BECAUSE I'M NOT YOUR GUY DOESN'T MEAN THERE'S NO GUY.
WE BOTH KNOW. THERE'S SOMEONE OUT THERE. AND I THINK YOU KNOW--HE WANTS TO HELP.
HE MADE SOME MISTAKES BEFORE, BUT--

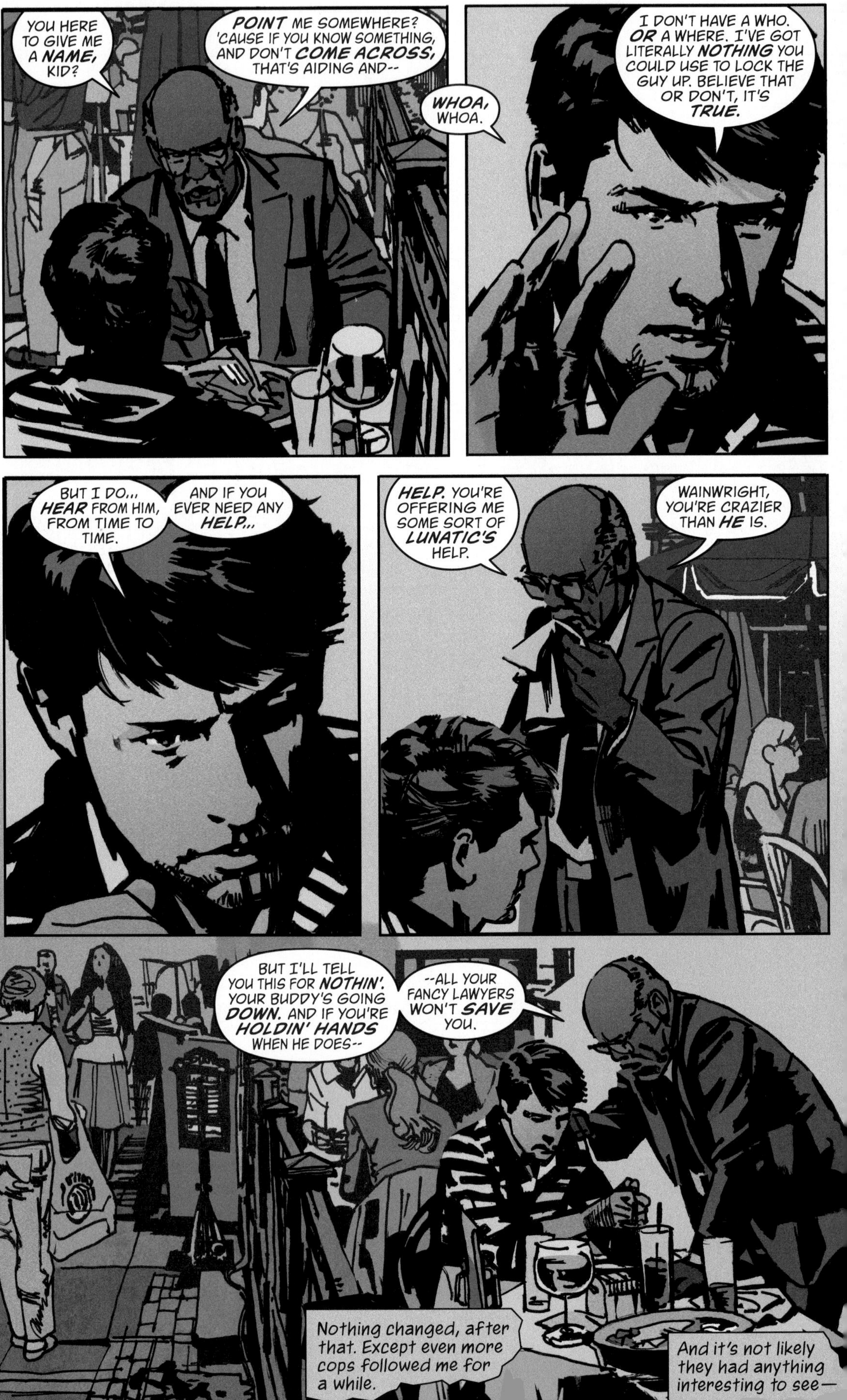
YOU HERE TO GIVE ME A NAME, KID?
POINT ME SOMEWHERE? 'CAUSE IF YOU KNOW SOMETHING, AND DON'T COME ACROSS, THAT'S AIDING AND--
WHOA, WHOA.
I DON'T HAVE A WHO. OR A WHERE. I'VE GOT LITERALLY NOTHING YOU COULD USE TO LOCK THE GUY UP. BELIEVE THAT OR DON'T, IT'S TRUE.
BUT I DO... HEAR FROM HIM, FROM TIME TO TIME.
AND IF YOU EVER NEED ANY HELP...
HELP. YOU'RE OFFERING ME SOME SORT OF LUNATIC'S HELP.
WAINWRIGHT, YOU'RE CRAZIER THAN HE IS.
BUT I'LL TELL YOU THIS FOR NOTHIN'. YOUR BUDDY'S GOING DOWN. AND IF YOU'RE HOLDIN' HANDS WHEN HE DOES--
--ALL YOUR FANCY LAWYERS WON'T SAVE YOU.
Nothing changed, after that. Except even more cops followed me for a while.
And it's not likely they had anything interesting to see—

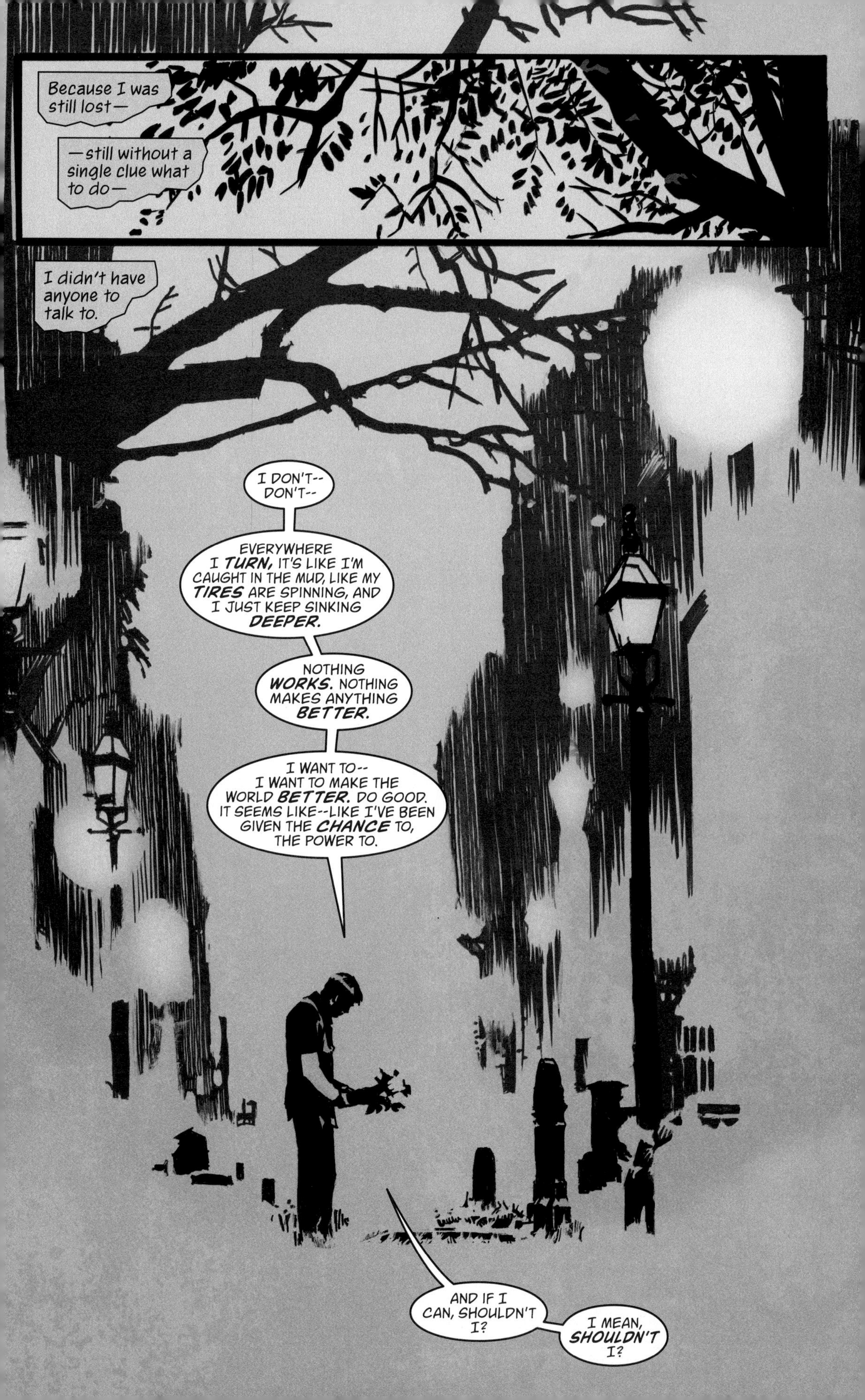
Because I was still lost—
—still without a single clue what to do—
I didn't have anyone to talk to.
I DON'T-- DON'T--
EVERYWHERE I TURN, IT'S LIKE I'M CAUGHT IN THE MUD, LIKE MY TIRES ARE SPINNING, AND I JUST KEEP SINKING DEEPER.
NOTHING WORKS. NOTHING MAKES ANYTHING BETTER.
I WANT TO-- I WANT TO MAKE THE WORLD BETTER. DO GOOD. IT SEEMS LIKE--LIKE I'VE BEEN GIVEN THE CHANCE TO, THE POWER TO.
AND IF I CAN, SHOULDN'T I?
I MEAN, SHOULDN'T I?

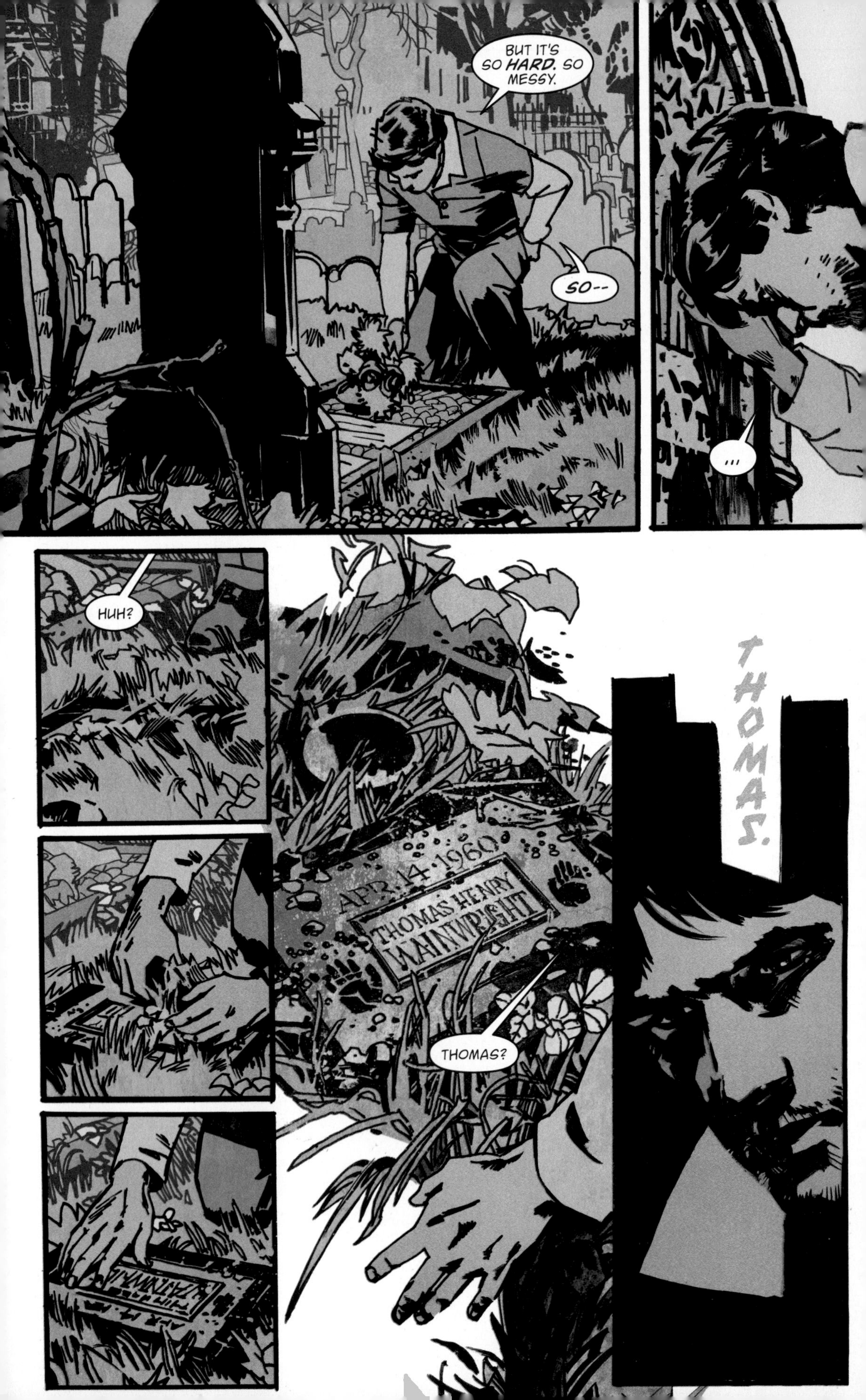
BUT IT'S SO HARD. SO MESSY.
SO--
...
HUH?
APR. 14 · 1960
THOMAS HENRY WAINWRIGHT
THOMAS?
THOMAS.

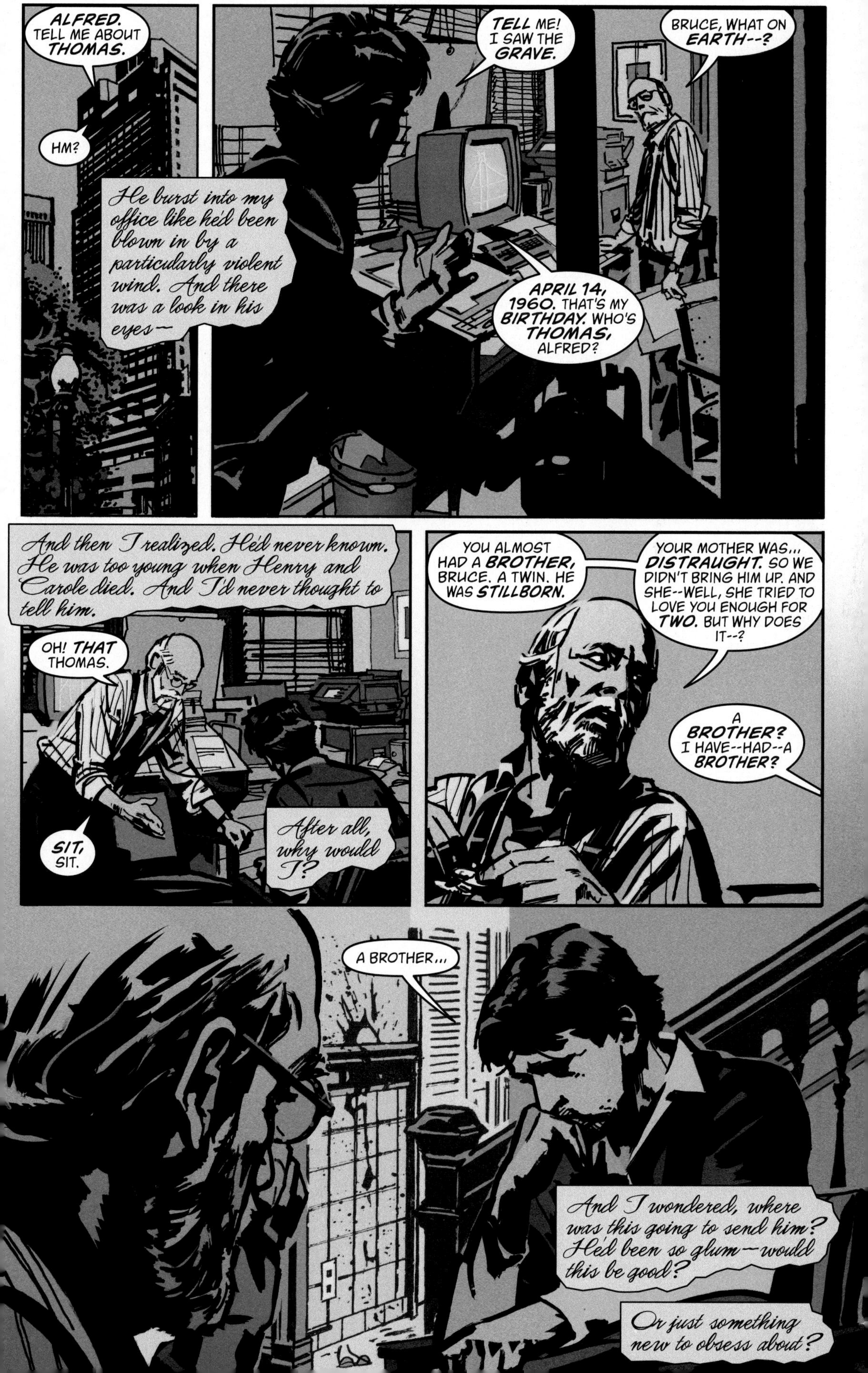
ALFRED. TELL ME ABOUT THOMAS.
HM?
He burst into my office like he'd been blown in by a particularly violent wind. And there was a look in his eyes—
TELL ME! I SAW THE GRAVE.
APRIL 14, 1960. THAT'S MY BIRTHDAY. WHO'S THOMAS, ALFRED?
BRUCE, WHAT ON EARTH--?
And then I realized. He'd never known. He was too young when Henry and Carole died. And I'd never thought to tell him.
OH! THAT THOMAS.
SIT, SIT.
After all, why would I?
YOU ALMOST HAD A BROTHER, BRUCE. A TWIN. HE WAS STILLBORN.
YOUR MOTHER WAS... DISTRAUGHT. SO WE DIDN'T BRING HIM UP. AND SHE--WELL, SHE TRIED TO LOVE YOU ENOUGH FOR TWO. BUT WHY DOES IT--?
A BROTHER? I HAVE--HAD--A BROTHER?
A BROTHER...
And I wondered, where was this going to send him? He'd been so glum—would this be good?
Or just something new to obsess about?

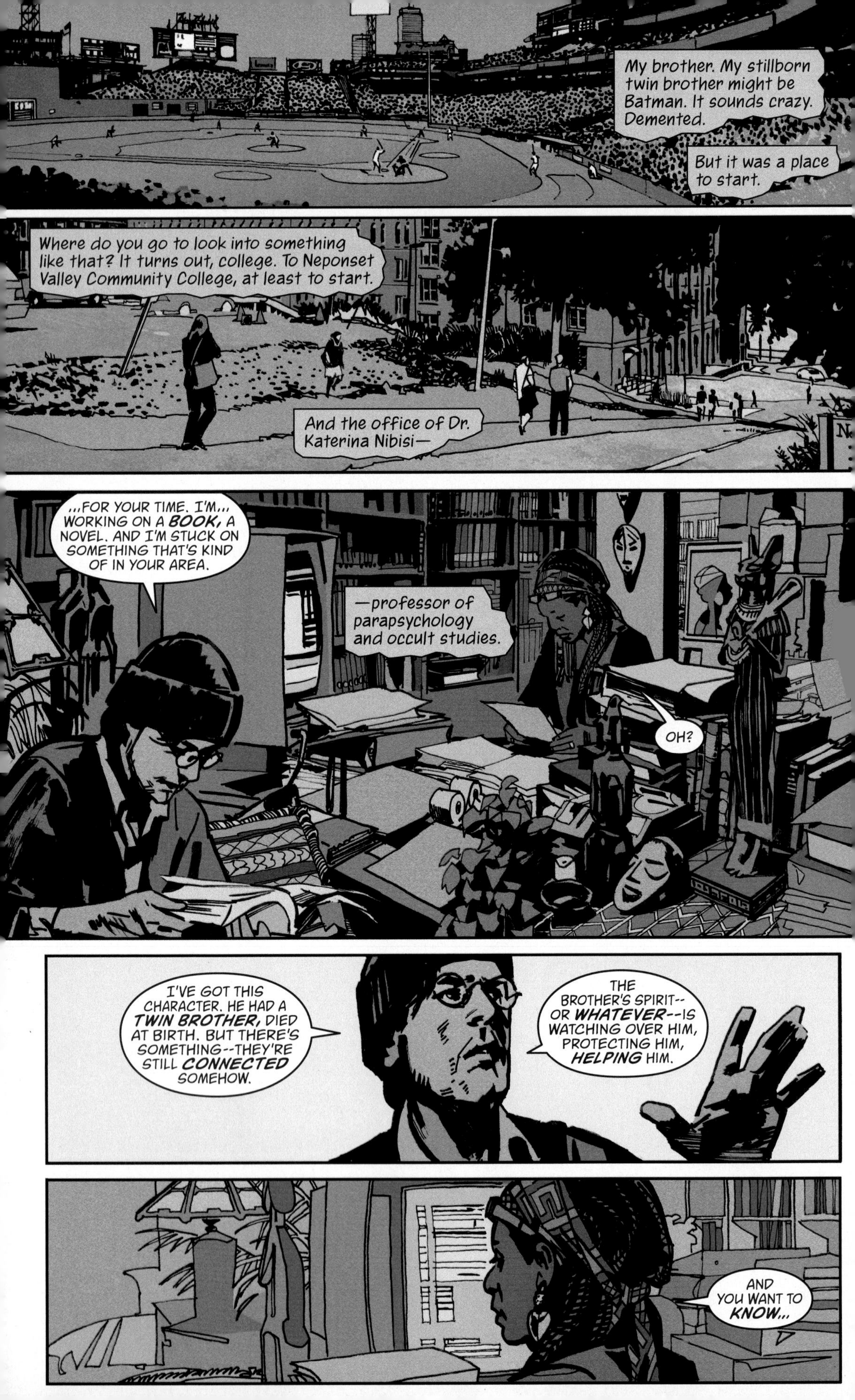

My brother. My stillborn twin brother might be Batman. It sounds crazy. Demented.
But it was a place to start.
Where do you go to look into something like that? It turns out, college. To Neponset Valley Community College, at least to start.
And the office of Dr. Katerina Nibisi—
...FOR YOUR TIME. I'M... WORKING ON A BOOK, A NOVEL. AND I'M STUCK ON SOMETHING THAT'S KIND OF IN YOUR AREA.
—professor of parapsychology and occult studies.
OH?
I'VE GOT THIS CHARACTER. HE HAD A TWIN BROTHER, DIED AT BIRTH. BUT THERE'S SOMETHING--THEY'RE STILL CONNECTED SOMEHOW.
THE BROTHER'S SPIRIT--OR WHATEVER--IS WATCHING OVER HIM, PROTECTING HIM, HELPING HIM.
AND YOU WANT TO KNOW...

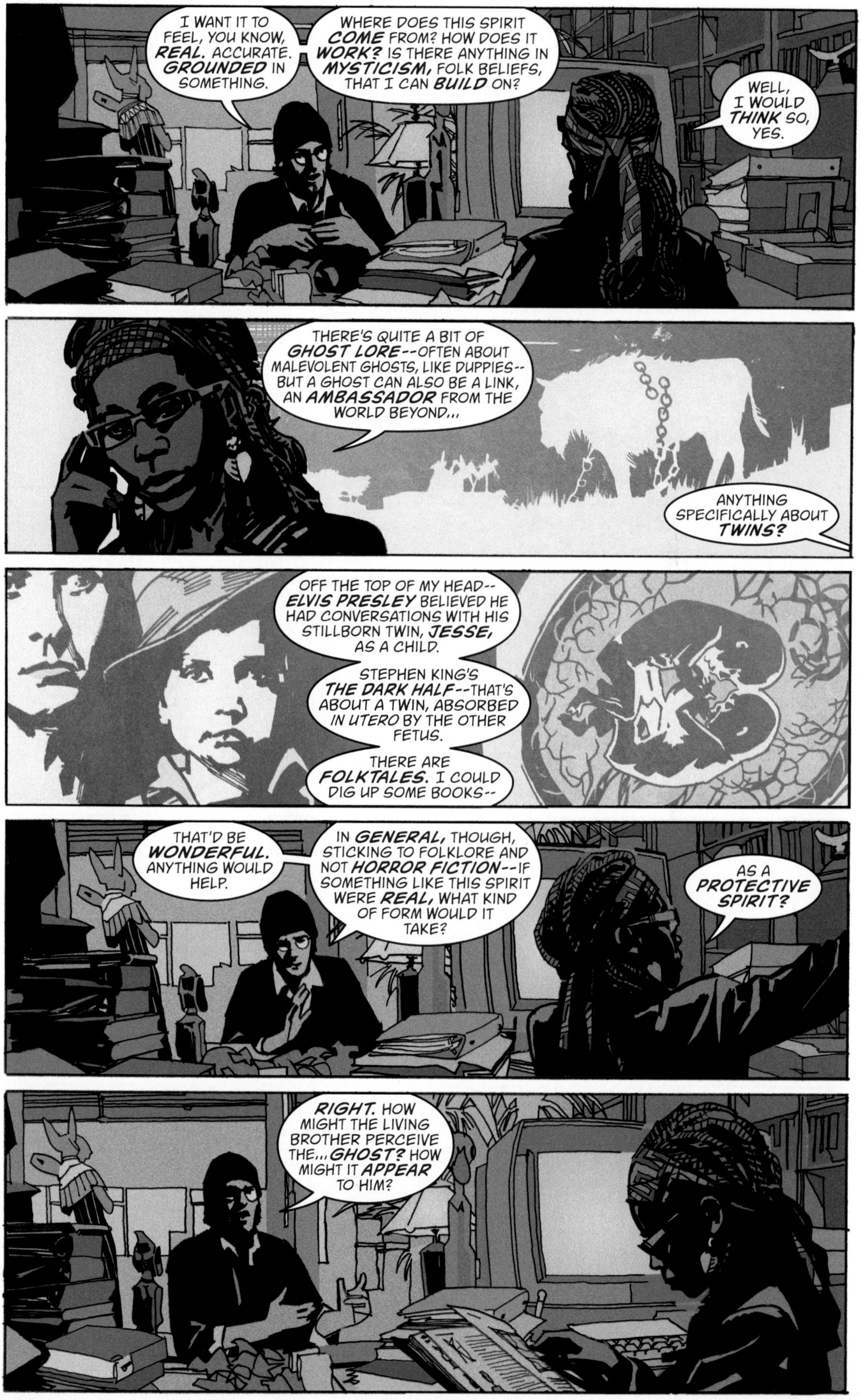
I WANT IT TO FEEL, YOU KNOW, REAL. ACCURATE. GROUNDED IN SOMETHING.
WHERE DOES THIS SPIRIT COME FROM? HOW DOES IT WORK? IS THERE ANYTHING IN MYSTICISM, FOLK BELIEFS, THAT I CAN BUILD ON?
WELL, I WOULD THINK SO, YES.
THERE'S QUITE A BIT OF GHOST LORE--OFTEN ABOUT MALEVOLENT GHOSTS, LIKE DUPPIES--BUT A GHOST CAN ALSO BE A LINK, AN AMBASSADOR FROM THE WORLD BEYOND...
ANYTHING SPECIFICALLY ABOUT TWINS?
OFF THE TOP OF MY HEAD--ELVIS PRESLEY BELIEVED HE HAD CONVERSATIONS WITH HIS STILLBORN TWIN, JESSE, AS A CHILD.
STEPHEN KING'S THE DARK HALF--THAT'S ABOUT A TWIN, ABSORBED IN UTERO BY THE OTHER FETUS.
THERE ARE FOLKTALES. I COULD DIG UP SOME BOOKS--
THAT'D BE WONDERFUL. ANYTHING WOULD HELP.
IN GENERAL, THOUGH, STICKING TO FOLKLORE AND NOT HORROR FICTION--IF SOMETHING LIKE THIS SPIRIT WERE REAL, WHAT KIND OF FORM WOULD IT TAKE?
AS A PROTECTIVE SPIRIT?
RIGHT. HOW MIGHT THE LIVING BROTHER PERCEIVE THE...GHOST? HOW MIGHT IT APPEAR TO HIM?

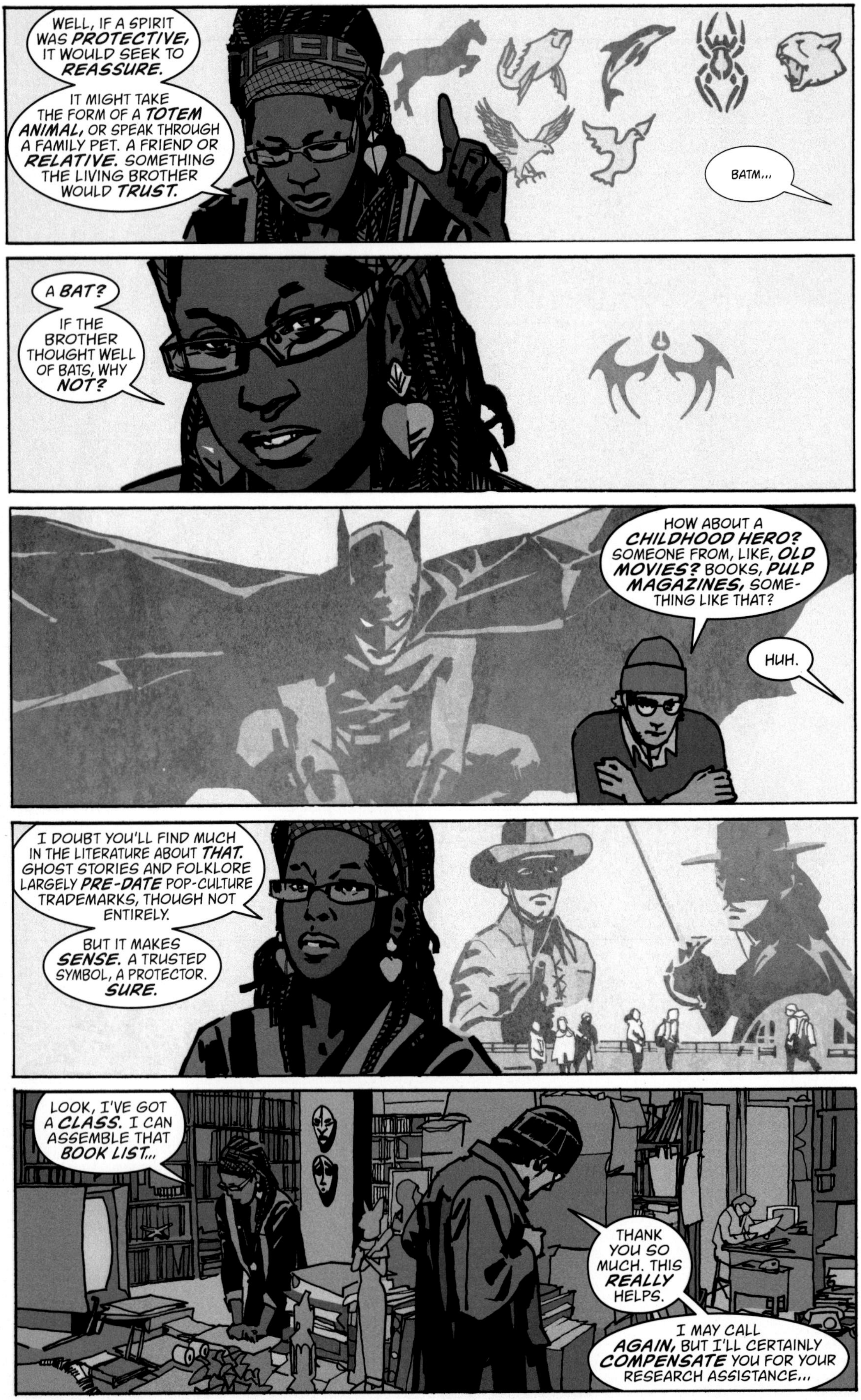
WELL, IF A SPIRIT WAS PROTECTIVE, IT WOULD SEEK TO REASSURE.
IT MIGHT TAKE THE FORM OF A TOTEM ANIMAL, OR SPEAK THROUGH A FAMILY PET. A FRIEND OR RELATIVE. SOMETHING THE LIVING BROTHER WOULD TRUST.
BATM...
A BAT?
IF THE BROTHER THOUGHT WELL OF BATS, WHY NOT?
HOW ABOUT A CHILDHOOD HERO? SOMEONE FROM, LIKE, OLD MOVIES? BOOKS, PULP MAGAZINES, SOME-THING LIKE THAT?
HUH.
I DOUBT YOU'LL FIND MUCH IN THE LITERATURE ABOUT THAT. GHOST STORIES AND FOLKLORE LARGELY PRE-DATE POP-CULTURE TRADEMARKS, THOUGH NOT ENTIRELY.
BUT IT MAKES SENSE. A TRUSTED SYMBOL, A PROTECTOR. SURE.
LOOK, I'VE GOT A CLASS. I CAN ASSEMBLE THAT BOOK LIST...
THANK YOU SO MUCH. THIS REALLY HELPS.
I MAY CALL AGAIN, BUT I'LL CERTAINLY COMPENSATE YOU FOR YOUR RESEARCH ASSISTANCE...

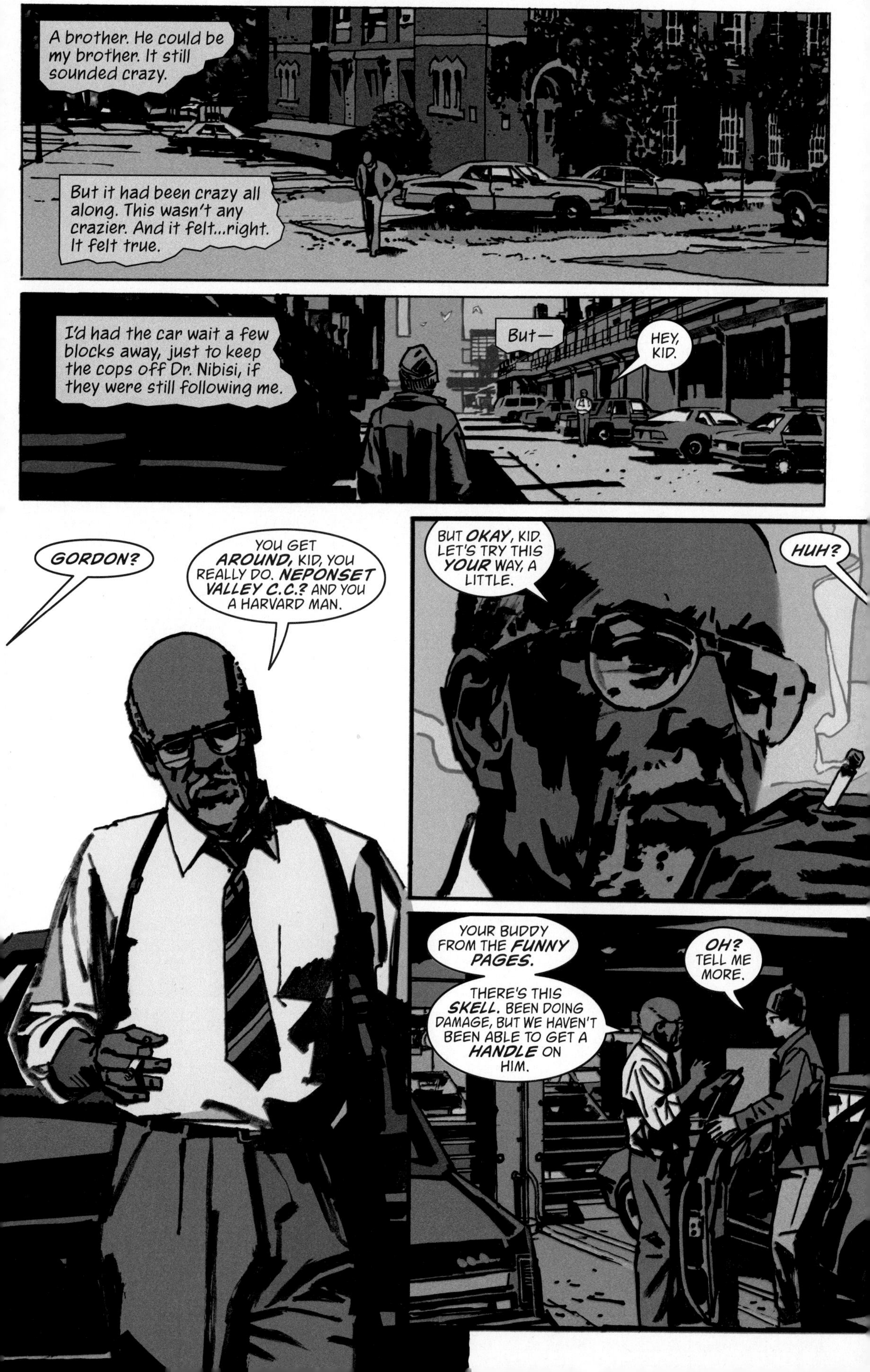
A brother. He could be my brother. It still sounded crazy.
But it had been crazy all along. This wasn't any crazier. And it felt...right. It felt true.
I'd had the car wait a few blocks away, just to keep the cops off Dr. Nibisi, if they were still following me.
But—
HEY, KID.
GORDON?
YOU GET AROUND, KID, YOU REALLY DO. NEPONSET VALLEY C.C.? AND YOU A HARVARD MAN.
BUT OKAY, KID. LET'S TRY THIS YOUR WAY, A LITTLE.
HUH?
YOUR BUDDY FROM THE FUNNY PAGES.
THERE'S THIS SKELL. BEEN DOING DAMAGE, BUT WE HAVEN'T BEEN ABLE TO GET A HANDLE ON HIM.
OH? TELL ME MORE.

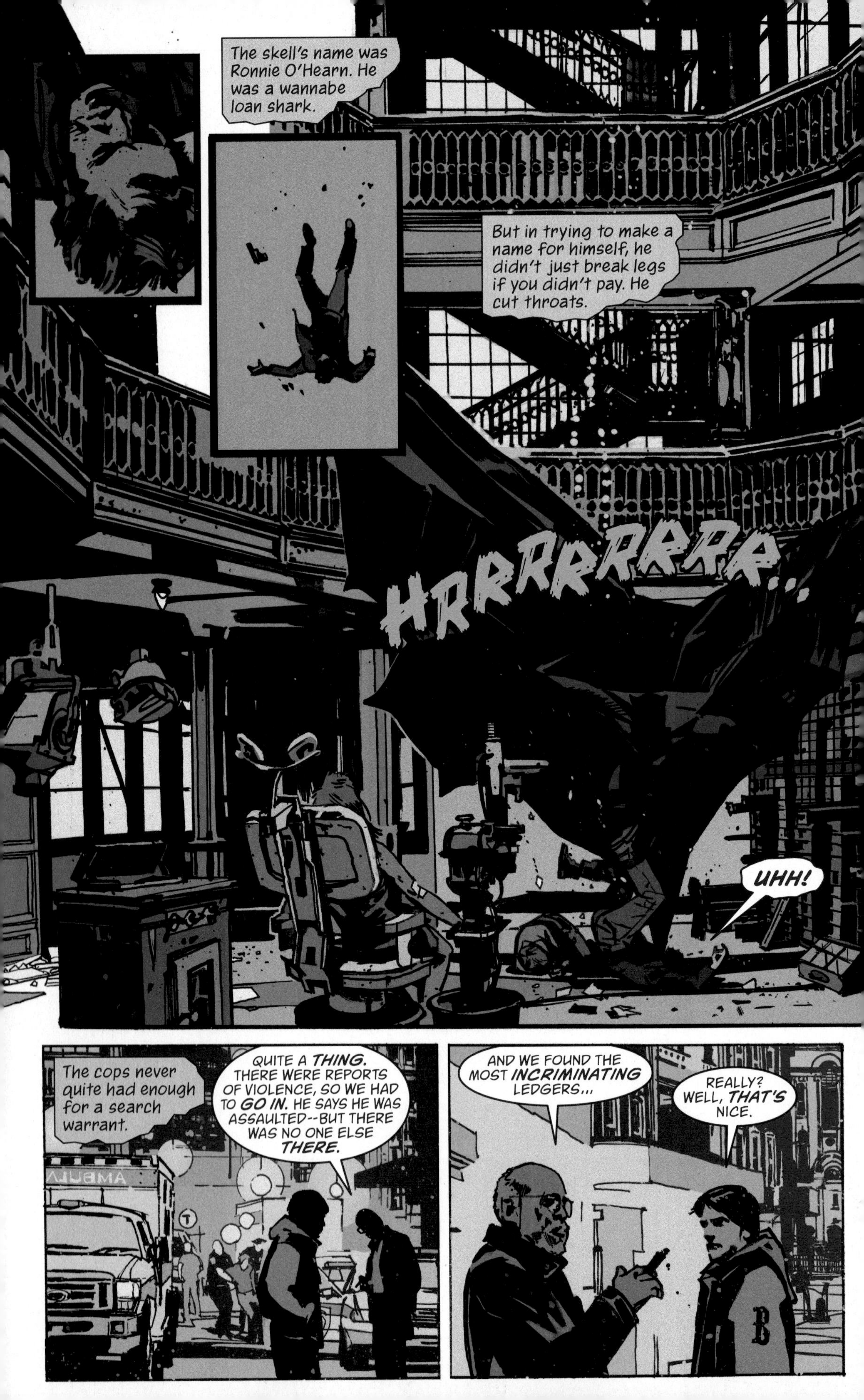
The skell's name was Ronnie O'Hearn. He was a wannabe loan shark.
But in trying to make a name for himself, he didn't just break legs if you didn't pay. He cut throats.
HRRRRRRRR...
UHH!
The cops never quite had enough for a search warrant.
QUITE A THING. THERE WERE REPORTS OF VIOLENCE, SO WE HAD TO GO IN. HE SAYS HE WAS ASSAULTED--BUT THERE WAS NO ONE ELSE THERE.
AMBULA
AND WE FOUND THE MOST INCRIMINATING LEDGERS...
REALLY? WELL, THAT'S NICE.

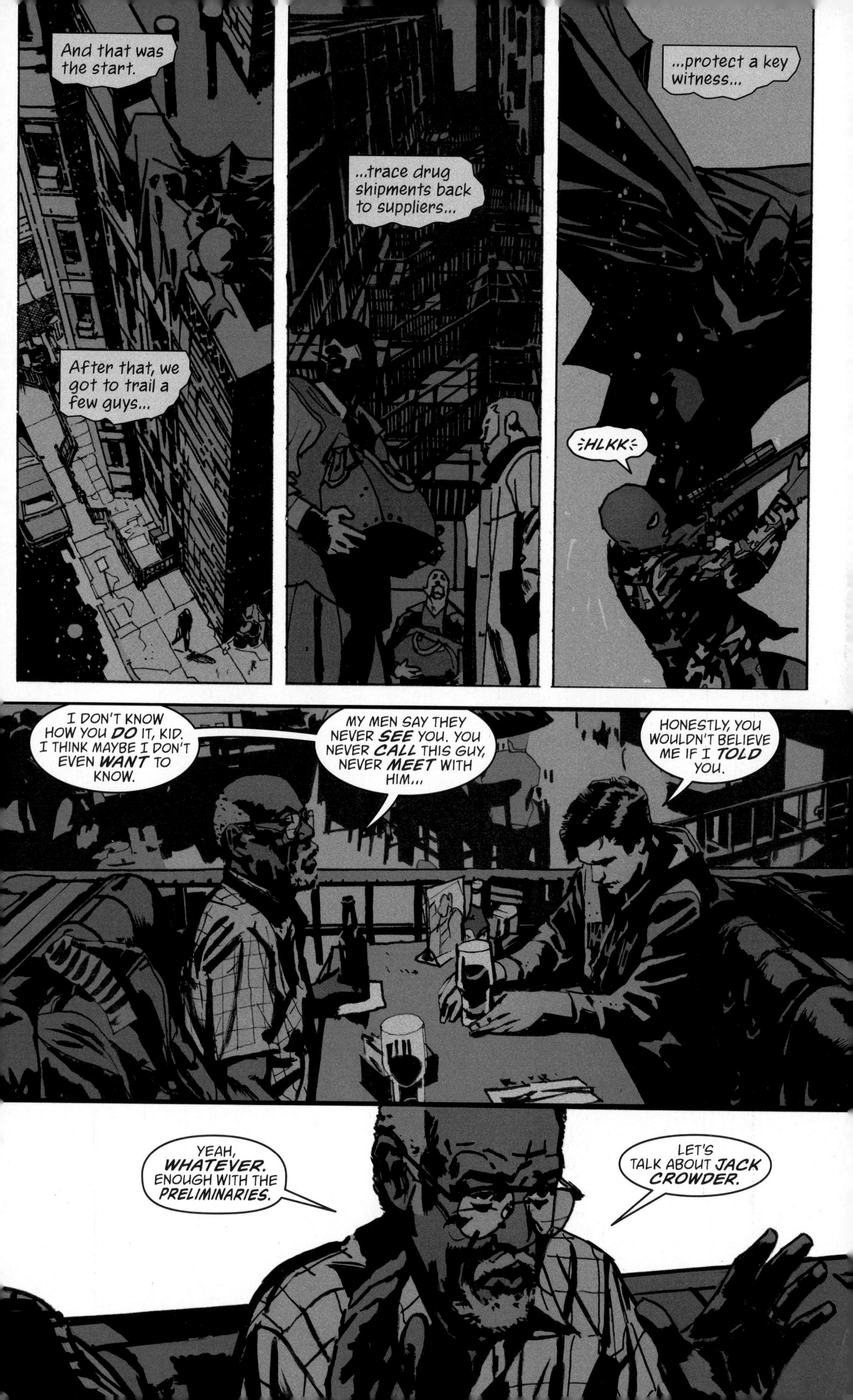
And that was the start.
After that, we got to trail a few guys...
...trace drug shipments back to suppliers...
...protect a key witness...
HLKK
I DON'T KNOW HOW YOU DO IT, KID. I THINK MAYBE I DON'T EVEN WANT TO KNOW.
MY MEN SAY THEY NEVER SEE YOU. YOU NEVER CALL THIS GUY, NEVER MEET WITH HIM...
HONESTLY, YOU WOULDN'T BELIEVE ME IF I TOLD YOU.
YEAH, WHATEVER. ENOUGH WITH THE PRELIMINARIES.
LET'S TALK ABOUT JACK CROWDER.

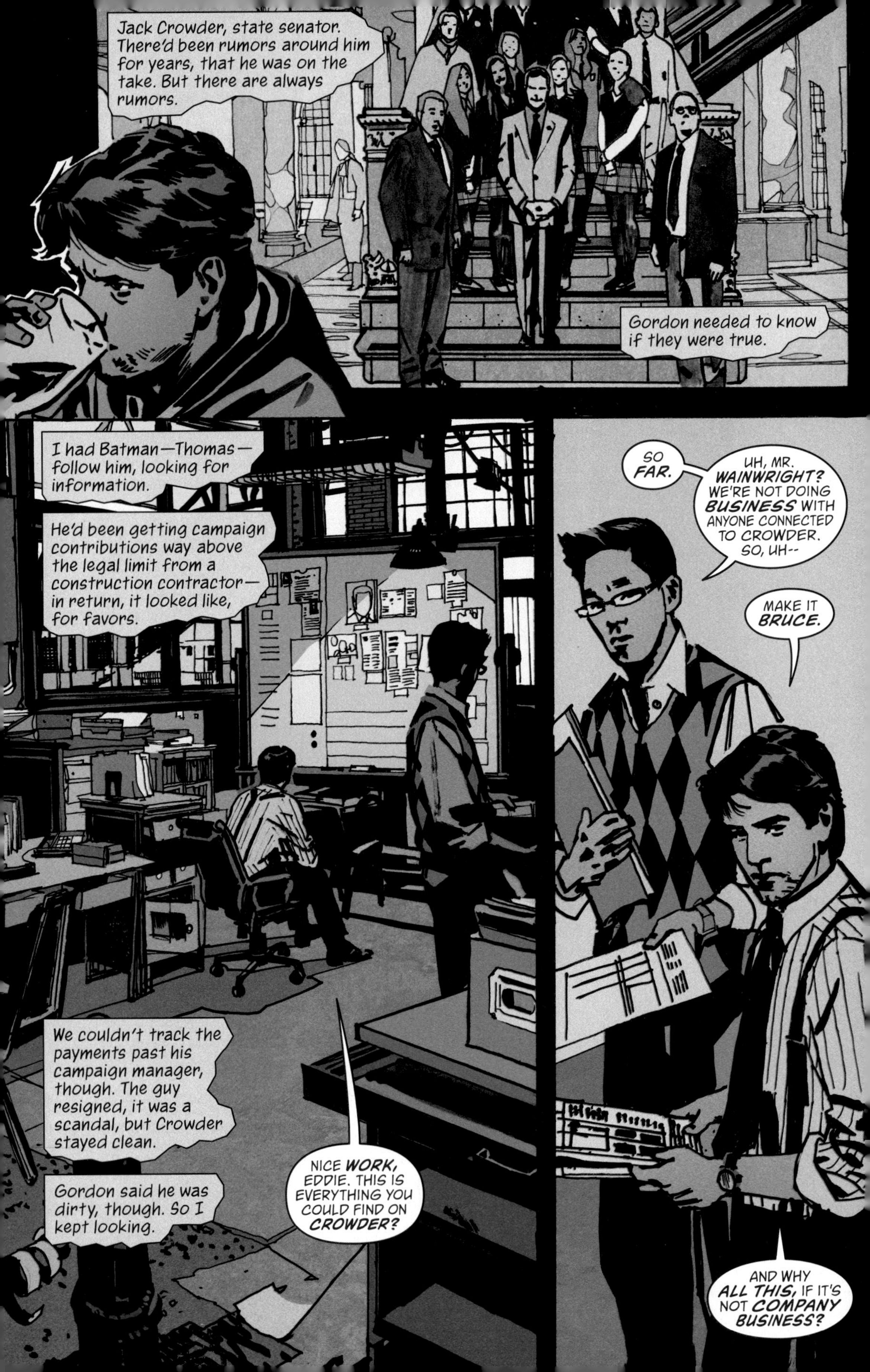

Jack Crowder, state senator. There'd been rumors around him for years, that he was on the take. But there are always rumors.
Gordon needed to know if they were true.
I had Batman—Thomas—follow him, looking for information.
He'd been getting campaign contributions way above the legal limit from a construction contractor—in return, it looked like, for favors.
We couldn't track the payments past his campaign manager, though. The guy resigned, it was a scandal, but Crowder stayed clean.
Gordon said he was dirty, though. So I kept looking.
NICE WORK, EDDIE. THIS IS EVERYTHING YOU COULD FIND ON CROWDER?
SO FAR.
UH, MR. WAINWRIGHT? WE'RE NOT DOING BUSINESS WITH ANYONE CONNECTED TO CROWDER. SO, UH--
MAKE IT BRUCE.
AND WHY ALL THIS, IF IT'S NOT COMPANY BUSINESS?

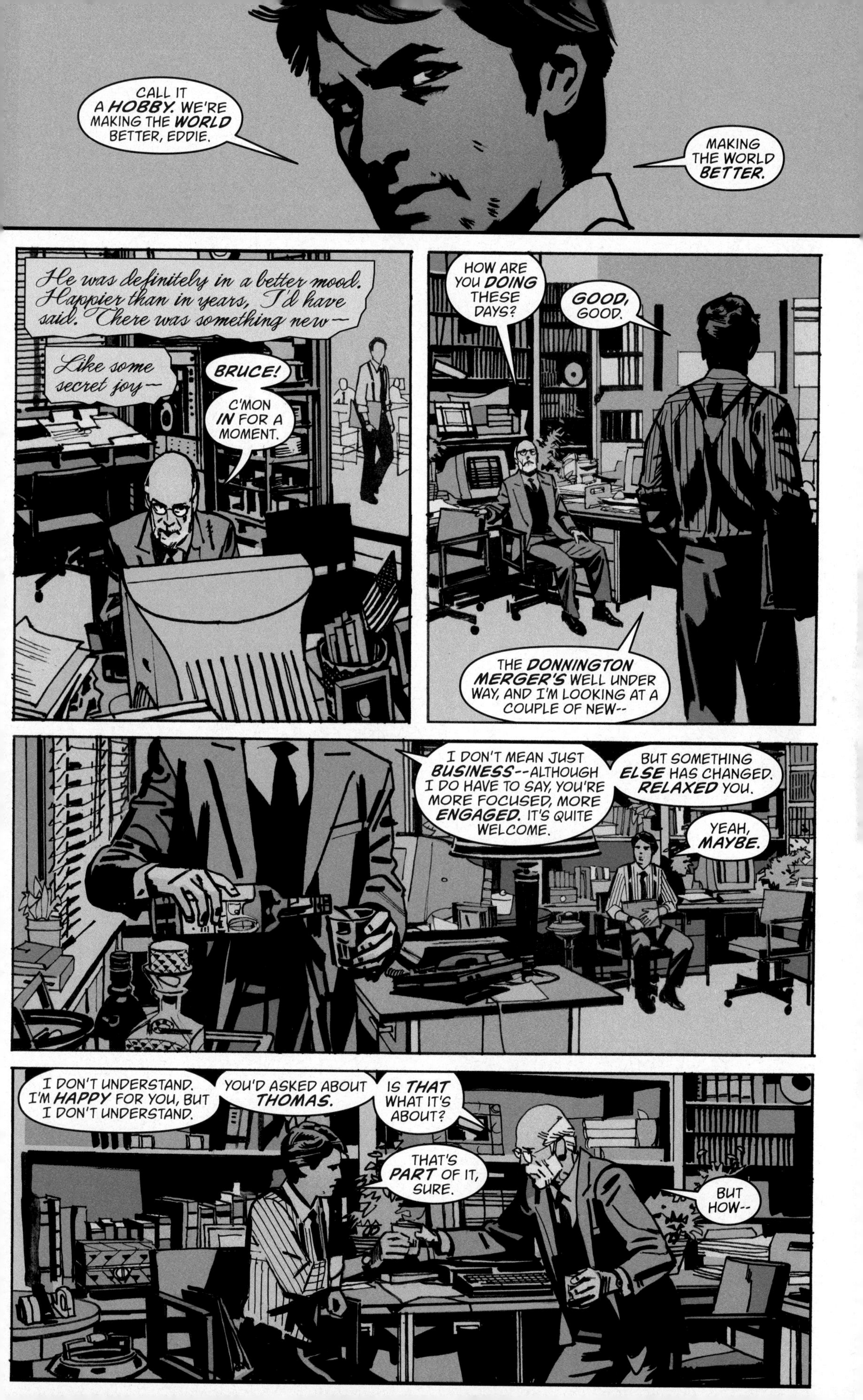
CALL IT A HOBBY. WE'RE MAKING THE WORLD BETTER, EDDIE.
MAKING THE WORLD BETTER.
He was definitely in a better mood. Happier than in years, I'd have said. There was something new~
Like some secret joy~
BRUCE!
C'MON IN FOR A MOMENT.
HOW ARE YOU DOING THESE DAYS?
GOOD, GOOD.
THE DONNINGTON MERGER'S WELL UNDER WAY, AND I'M LOOKING AT A COUPLE OF NEW--
I DON'T MEAN JUST BUSINESS--ALTHOUGH I DO HAVE TO SAY, YOU'RE MORE FOCUSED, MORE ENGAGED. IT'S QUITE WELCOME.
BUT SOMETHING ELSE HAS CHANGED. RELAXED YOU.
YEAH, MAYBE.
I DON'T UNDERSTAND. I'M HAPPY FOR YOU, BUT I DON'T UNDERSTAND.
YOU'D ASKED ABOUT THOMAS.
IS THAT WHAT IT'S ABOUT?
THAT'S PART OF IT, SURE.
BUT HOW--

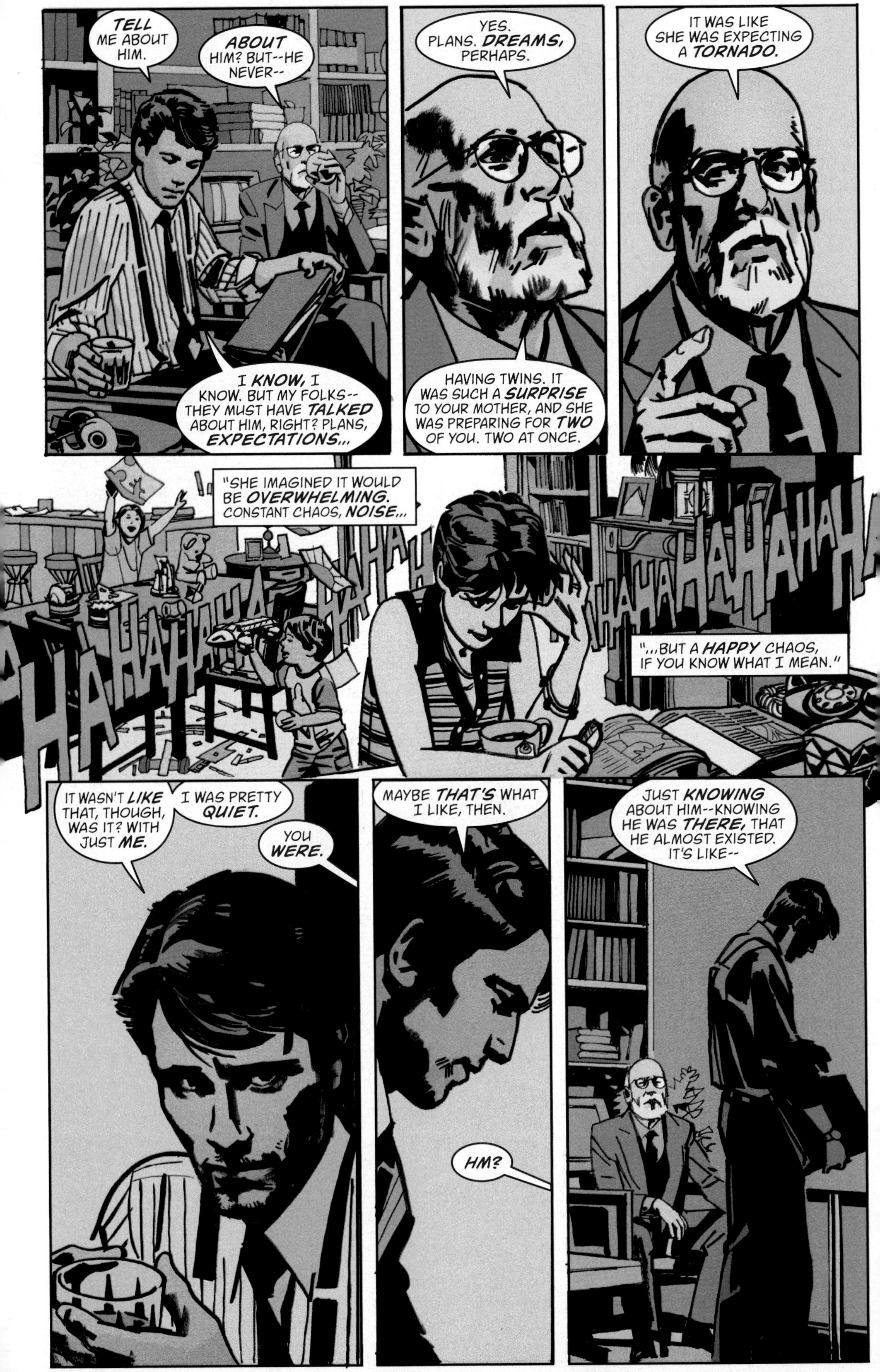
TELL ME ABOUT HIM.
ABOUT HIM? BUT--HE NEVER--
I KNOW, I KNOW. BUT MY FOLKS--THEY MUST HAVE TALKED ABOUT HIM, RIGHT? PLANS, EXPECTATIONS...
YES. PLANS. DREAMS, PERHAPS.
HAVING TWINS. IT WAS SUCH A SURPRISE TO YOUR MOTHER, AND SHE WAS PREPARING FOR TWO OF YOU. TWO AT ONCE.
IT WAS LIKE SHE WAS EXPECTING A TORNADO.
"SHE IMAGINED IT WOULD BE OVERWHELMING. CONSTANT CHAOS, NOISE...
HAHAHAHAHAHAHAHAHAHAHAHAHAHAHAHAHAHAHAHA
"...BUT A HAPPY CHAOS, IF YOU KNOW WHAT I MEAN."
IT WASN'T LIKE THAT, THOUGH, WAS IT? WITH JUST ME.
I WAS PRETTY QUIET.
YOU WERE.
MAYBE THAT'S WHAT I LIKE, THEN.
HM?
JUST KNOWING ABOUT HIM--KNOWING HE WAS THERE, THAT HE ALMOST EXISTED. IT'S LIKE--

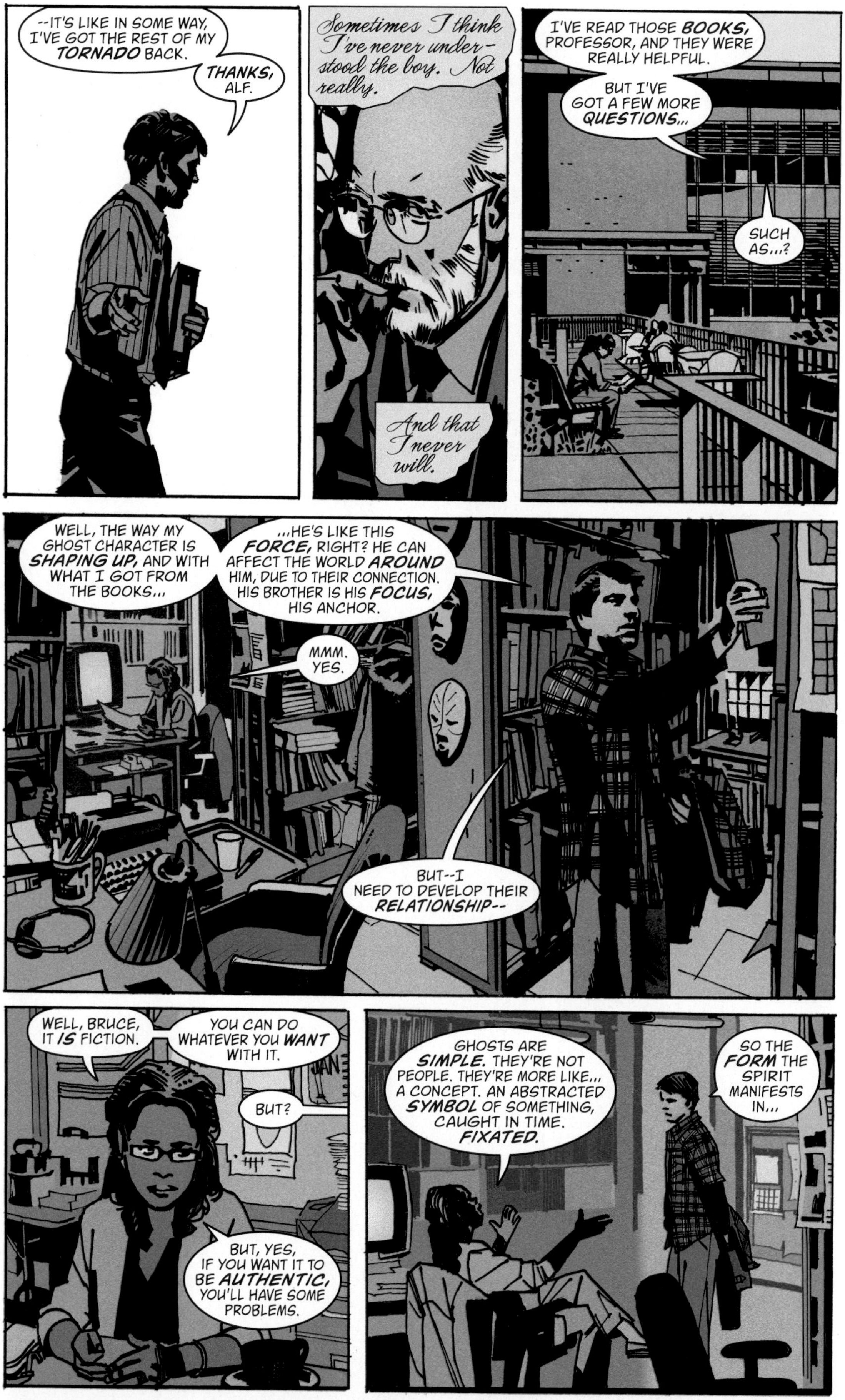
--IT'S LIKE IN SOME WAY, I'VE GOT THE REST OF MY TORNADO BACK.
THANKS, ALF.
Sometimes I think I've never under-stood the boy. Not really.
And that I never will.
I'VE READ THOSE BOOKS, PROFESSOR, AND THEY WERE REALLY HELPFUL.
BUT I'VE GOT A FEW MORE QUESTIONS...
SUCH AS...?
WELL, THE WAY MY GHOST CHARACTER IS SHAPING UP, AND WITH WHAT I GOT FROM THE BOOKS...
...HE'S LIKE THIS FORCE, RIGHT? HE CAN AFFECT THE WORLD AROUND HIM, DUE TO THEIR CONNECTION. HIS BROTHER IS HIS FOCUS, HIS ANCHOR.
MMM. YES.
BUT--I NEED TO DEVELOP THEIR RELATIONSHIP--
WELL, BRUCE, IT IS FICTION.
YOU CAN DO WHATEVER YOU WANT WITH IT.
BUT?
BUT, YES, IF YOU WANT IT TO BE AUTHENTIC, YOU'LL HAVE SOME PROBLEMS.
GHOSTS ARE SIMPLE. THEY'RE NOT PEOPLE. THEY'RE MORE LIKE... A CONCEPT. AN ABSTRACTED SYMBOL OF SOMETHING, CAUGHT IN TIME. FIXATED.
SO THE FORM THE SPIRIT MANIFESTS IN...

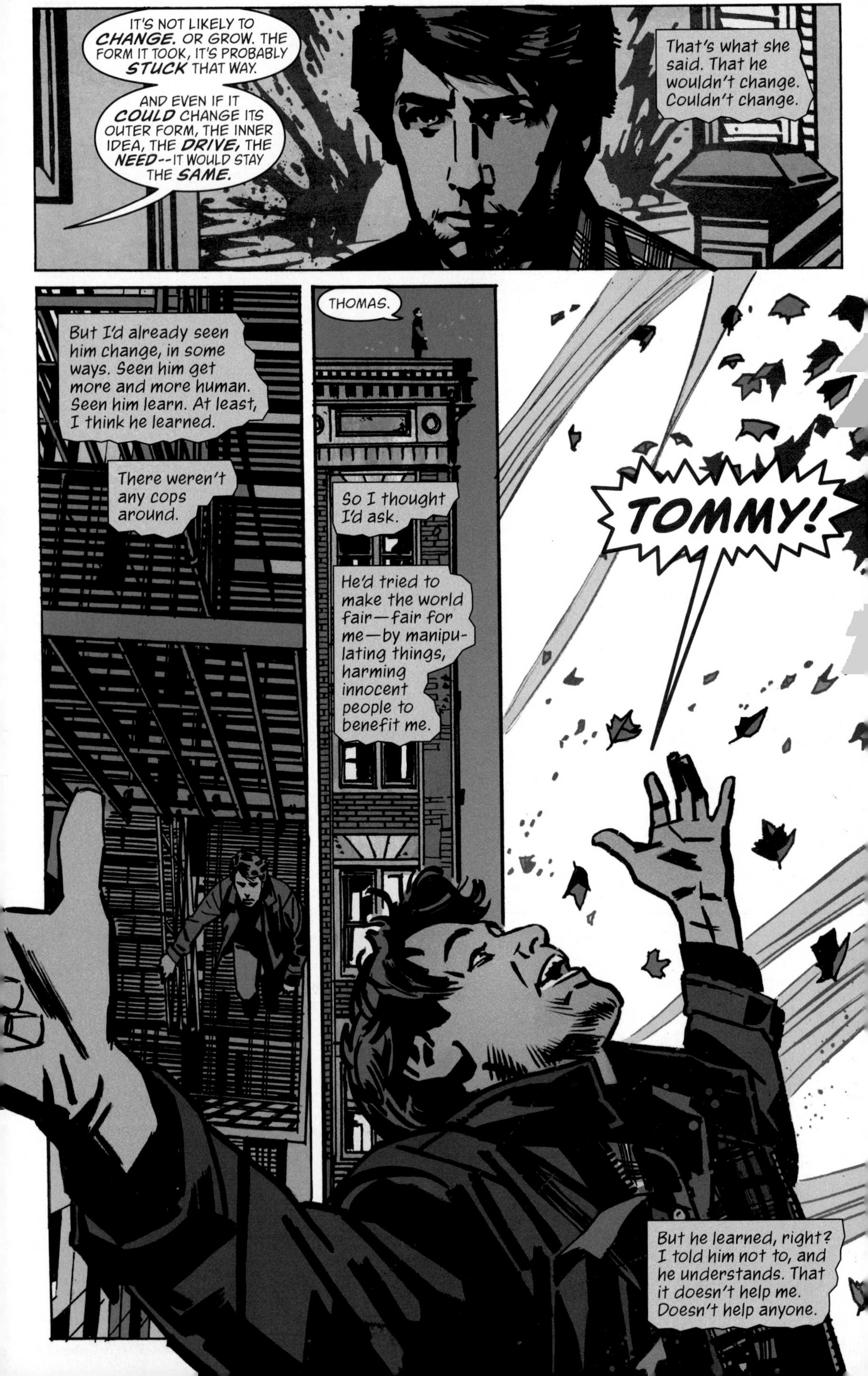

IT'S NOT LIKELY TO CHANGE. OR GROW. THE FORM IT TOOK, IT'S PROBABLY STUCK THAT WAY.
AND EVEN IF IT COULD CHANGE ITS OUTER FORM, THE INNER IDEA, THE DRIVE, THE NEED--IT WOULD STAY THE SAME.
That's what she said. That he wouldn't change. Couldn't change.
But I'd already seen him change, in some ways. Seen him get more and more human. Seen him learn. At least, I think he learned.
There weren't any cops around.
THOMAS.
So I thought I'd ask.
He'd tried to make the world fair—fair for me—by manipulating things, harming innocent people to benefit me.
TOMMY!
But he learned, right? I told him not to, and he understands. That it doesn't help me. Doesn't help anyone.

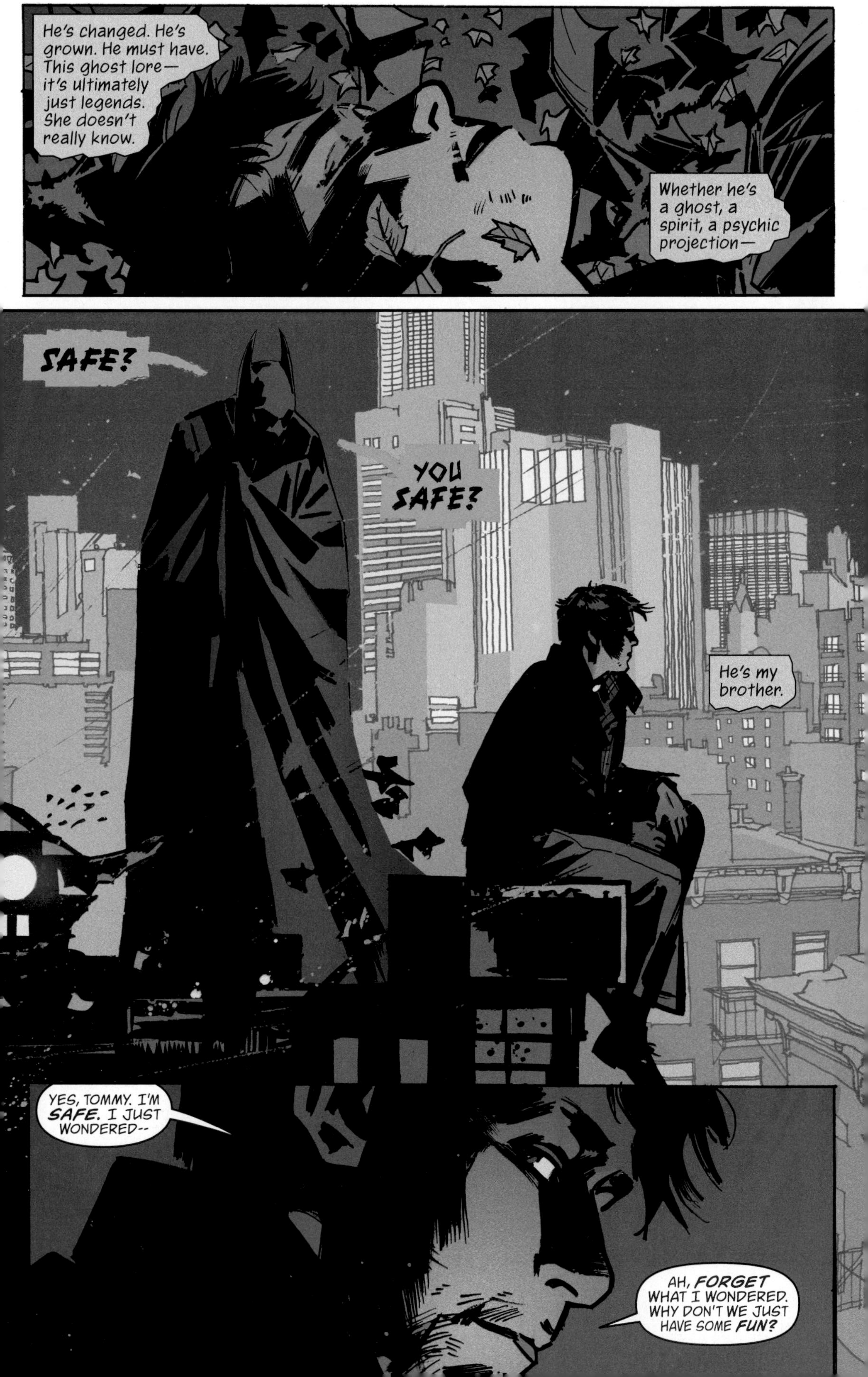
He's changed. He's grown. He must have. This ghost lore— it's ultimately just legends. She doesn't really know.
Whether he's a ghost, a spirit, a psychic projection—
SAFE?
YOU SAFE?
He's my brother.
YES, TOMMY. I'M SAFE. I JUST WONDERED--
AH, FORGET WHAT I WONDERED. WHY DON'T WE JUST HAVE SOME FUN?

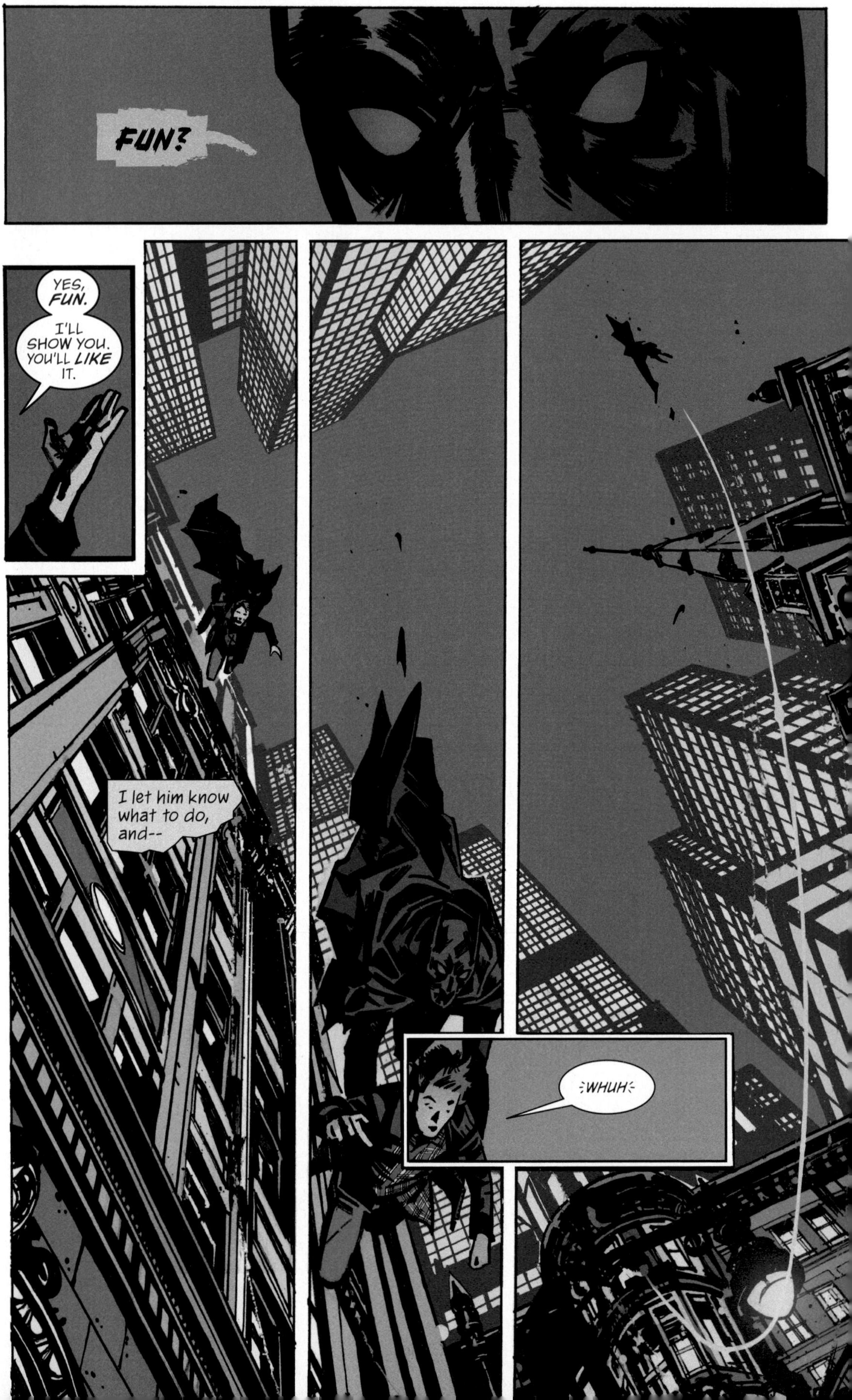
FUN?
YES, FUN.
I'LL SHOW YOU. YOU'LL LIKE IT.
I let him know what to do, and--
WHUH

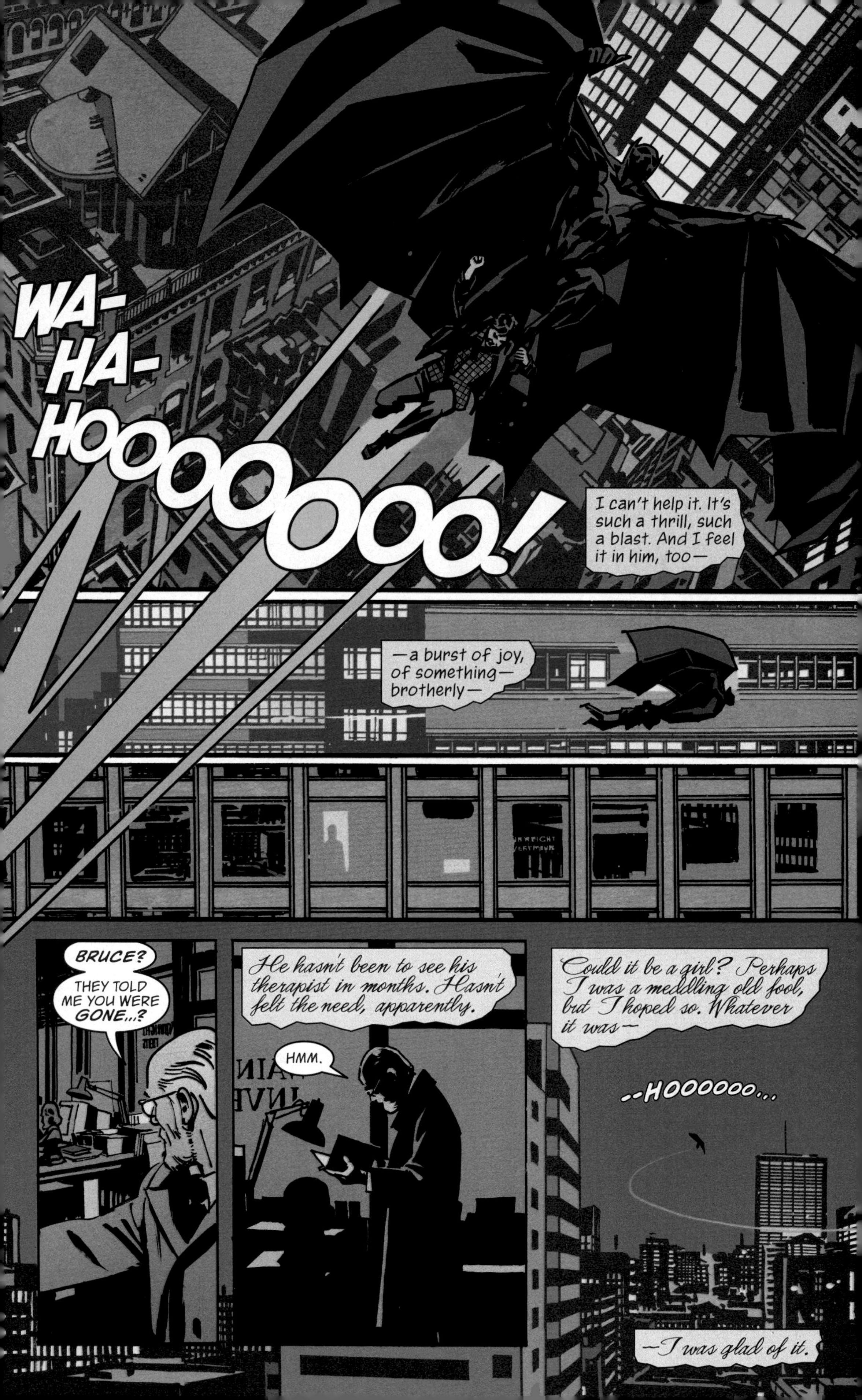

WA-
HA-
HOOOOOOOO!
I can't help it. It's such a thrill, such a blast. And I feel it in him, too—
—a burst of joy, of something—brotherly—
BRUCE?
THEY TOLD ME YOU WERE GONE...?
He hasn't been to see his therapist in months. Hasn't felt the need, apparently.
HMM.
Could it be a girl? Perhaps I was a meddling old fool, but I hoped so. Whatever it was—
--HOOOOOO...
—I was glad of it.

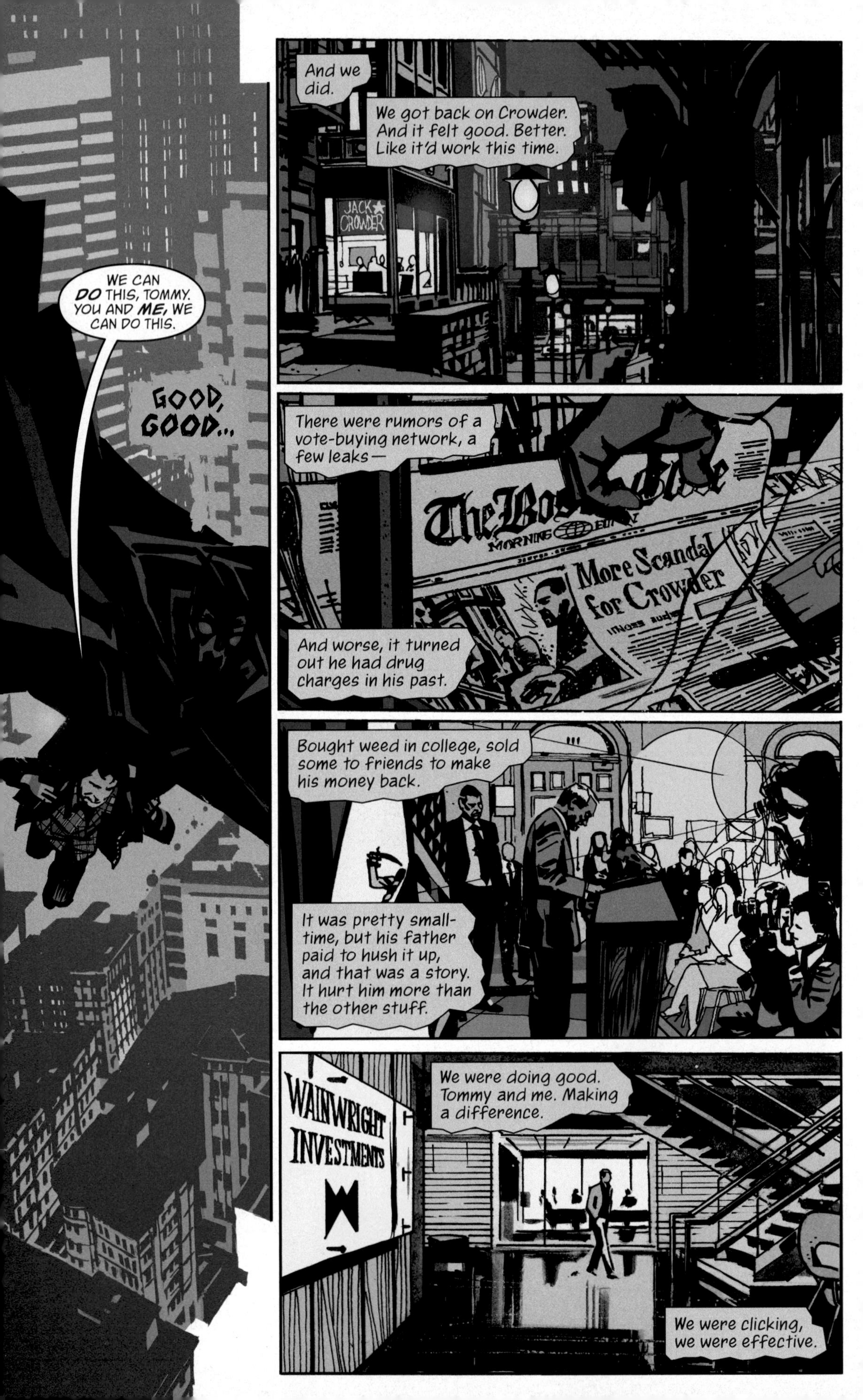
WE CAN DO THIS, TOMMY. YOU AND ME, WE CAN DO THIS.
GOOD, GOOD...
And we did.
We got back on Crowder. And it felt good. Better. Like it'd work this time.
JACK CROWDER
There were rumors of a vote-buying network, a few leaks—
More Scandal for Crowder
And worse, it turned out he had drug charges in his past.
Bought weed in college, sold some to friends to make his money back.
It was pretty small-time, but his father paid to hush it up, and that was a story. It hurt him more than the other stuff.
WAINWRIGHT INVESTMENTS
We were doing good. Tommy and me. Making a difference.
We were clicking, we were effective.

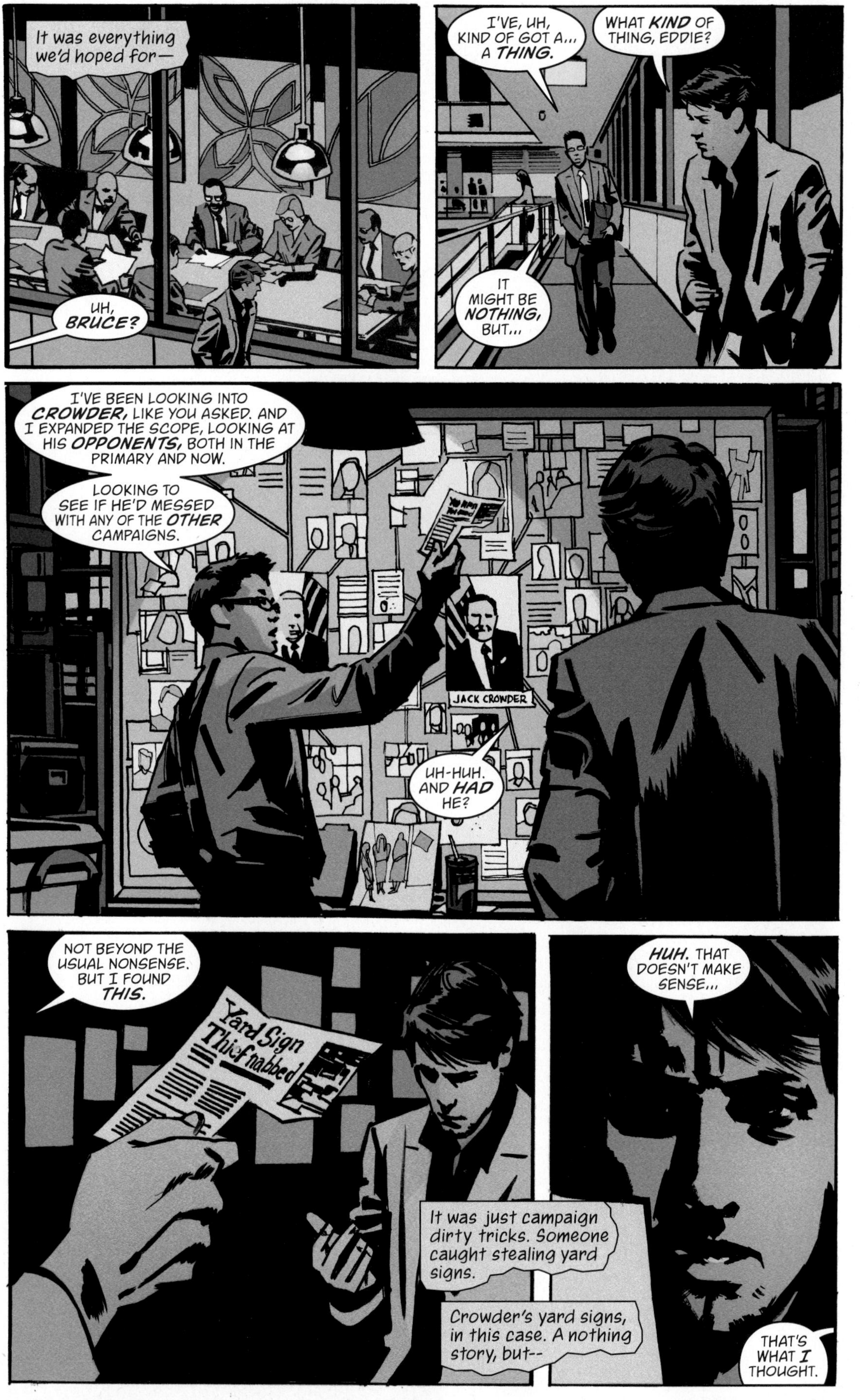
It was everything we'd hoped for—
UH, BRUCE?
I'VE, UH, KIND OF GOT A... A THING.
WHAT KIND OF THING, EDDIE?
IT MIGHT BE NOTHING, BUT...
I'VE BEEN LOOKING INTO CROWDER, LIKE YOU ASKED. AND I EXPANDED THE SCOPE, LOOKING AT HIS OPPONENTS, BOTH IN THE PRIMARY AND NOW.
LOOKING TO SEE IF HE'D MESSED WITH ANY OF THE OTHER CAMPAIGNS.
JACK CROWDER
UH-HUH. AND HAD HE?
NOT BEYOND THE USUAL NONSENSE. BUT I FOUND THIS.
Yard Sign Thief nabbed
It was just campaign dirty tricks. Someone caught stealing yard signs.
Crowder's yard signs, in this case. A nothing story, but--
HUH. THAT DOESN'T MAKE SENSE...
THAT'S WHAT I THOUGHT.

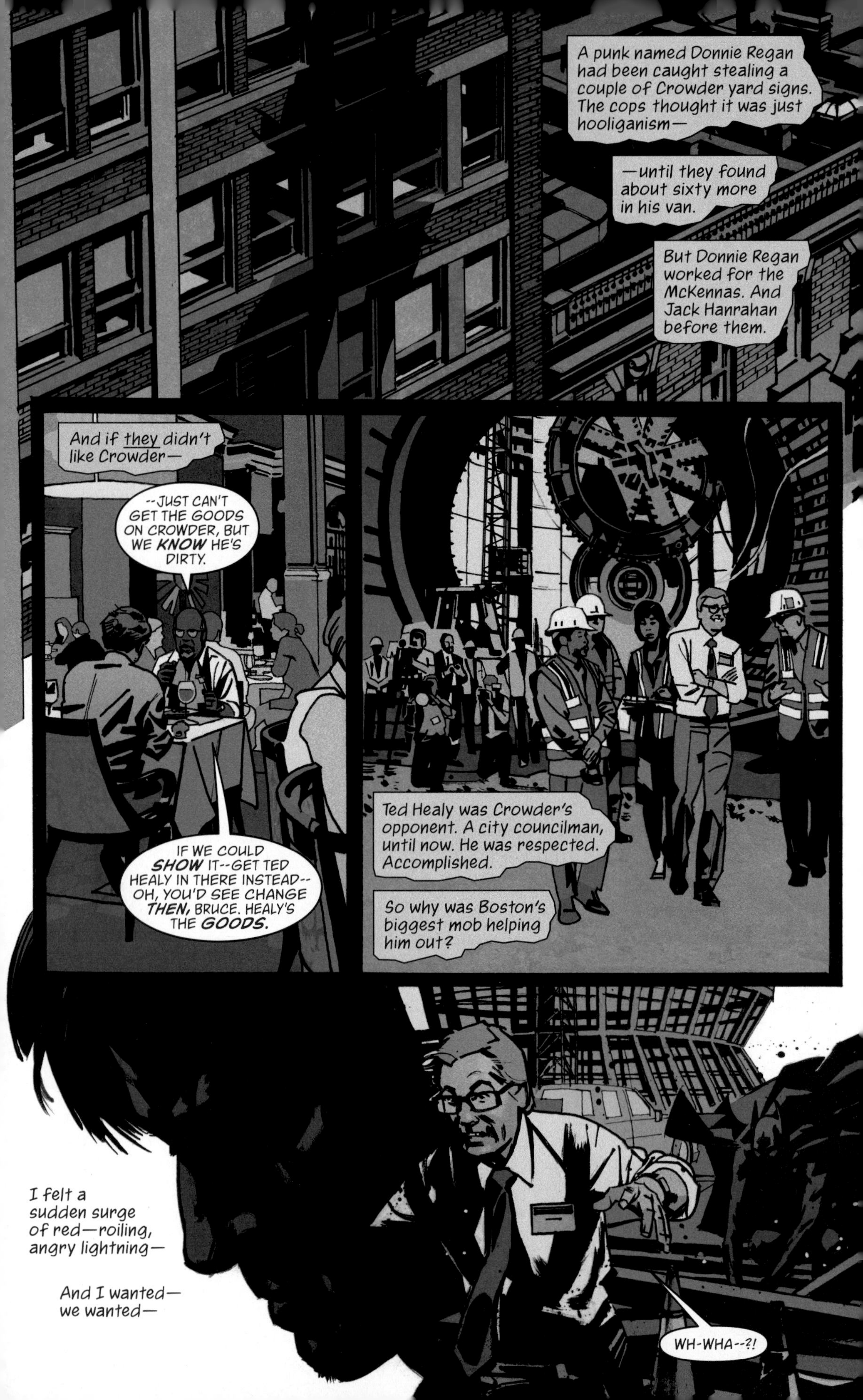

A punk named Donnie Regan had been caught stealing a couple of Crowder yard signs. The cops thought it was just hooliganism—
—until they found about sixty more in his van.
But Donnie Regan worked for the McKennas. And Jack Hanrahan before them.
And if they didn't like Crowder—
--JUST CAN'T GET THE GOODS ON CROWDER, BUT WE KNOW HE'S DIRTY.
IF WE COULD SHOW IT--GET TED HEALY IN THERE INSTEAD--OH, YOU'D SEE CHANGE THEN, BRUCE. HEALY'S THE GOODS.
Ted Healy was Crowder's opponent. A city councilman, until now. He was respected. Accomplished.
So why was Boston's biggest mob helping him out?
I felt a sudden surge of red—roiling, angry lightning—
And I wanted—we wanted—
WH-WHA--?!

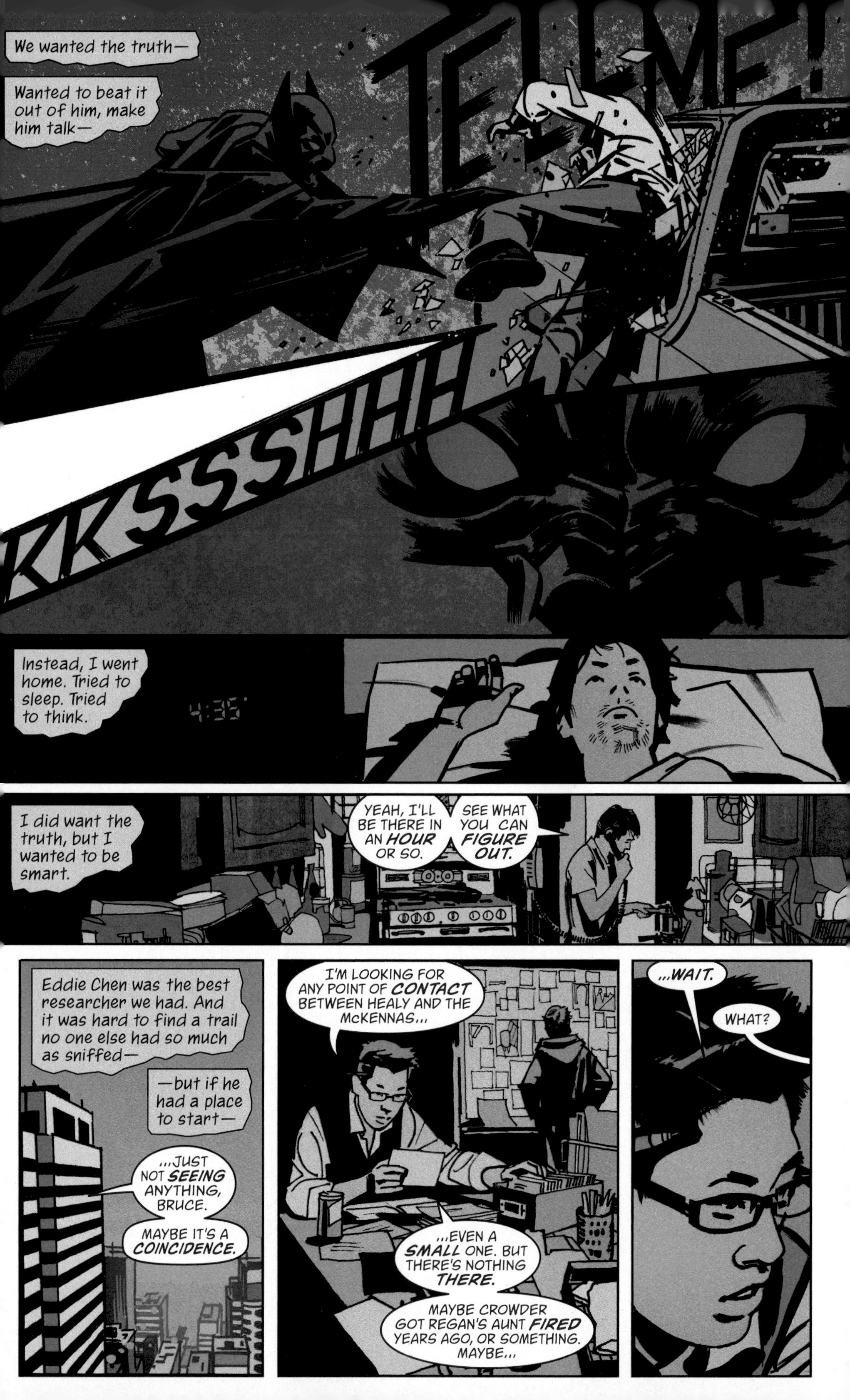

We wanted the truth—
Wanted to beat it out of him, make him talk—
TELL ME!
KKSSSHHH
Instead, I went home. Tried to sleep. Tried to think.
I did want the truth, but I wanted to be smart.
YEAH, I'LL BE THERE IN AN *HOUR* OR SO.
SEE WHAT YOU CAN *FIGURE OUT.*
Eddie Chen was the best researcher we had. And it was hard to find a trail no one else had so much as sniffed—
—but if he had a place to start—
...JUST NOT *SEEING* ANYTHING, BRUCE.
MAYBE IT'S A *COINCIDENCE.*
I'M LOOKING FOR ANY POINT OF *CONTACT* BETWEEN HEALY AND THE McKENNAS...
...EVEN A *SMALL* ONE. BUT THERE'S NOTHING *THERE.*
MAYBE CROWDER GOT REGAN'S AUNT *FIRED* YEARS AGO, OR SOMETHING. MAYBE...
...*WAIT.*
WHAT?

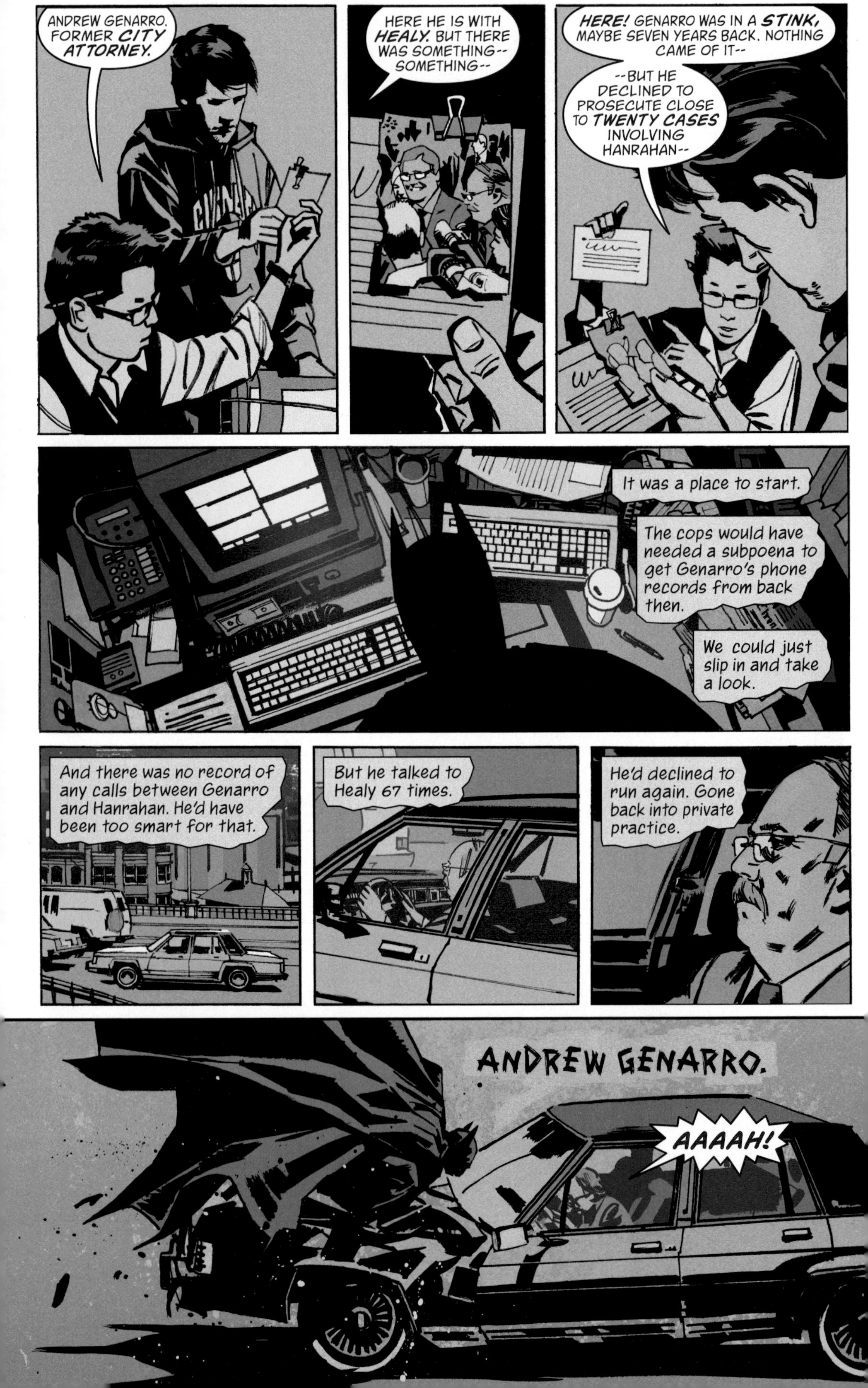
ANDREW GENARRO. FORMER CITY ATTORNEY.
HERE HE IS WITH HEALY. BUT THERE WAS SOMETHING-- SOMETHING--
HERE! GENARRO WAS IN A STINK, MAYBE SEVEN YEARS BACK. NOTHING CAME OF IT--
--BUT HE DECLINED TO PROSECUTE CLOSE TO TWENTY CASES INVOLVING HANRAHAN--
It was a place to start.
The cops would have needed a subpoena to get Genarro's phone records from back then.
We could just slip in and take a look.
And there was no record of any calls between Genarro and Hanrahan. He'd have been too smart for that.
But he talked to Healy 67 times.
He'd declined to run again. Gone back into private practice.
ANDREW GENARRO.
AAAAH!

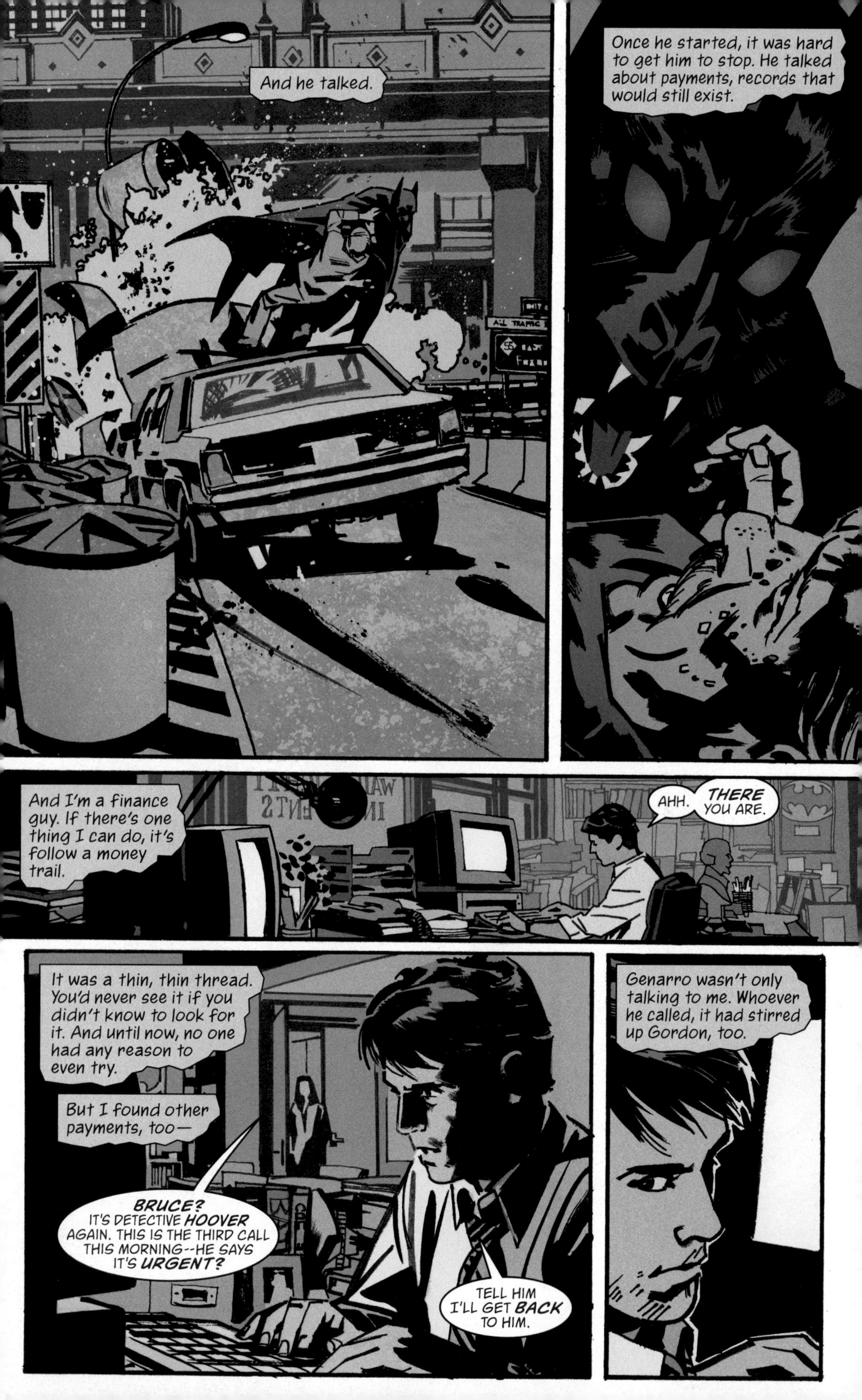
And he talked.
Once he started, it was hard to get him to stop. He talked about payments, records that would still exist.
And I'm a finance guy. If there's one thing I can do, it's follow a money trail.
AHH. THERE YOU ARE.
It was a thin, thin thread. You'd never see it if you didn't know to look for it. And until now, no one had any reason to even try.
But I found other payments, too—
BRUCE? IT'S DETECTIVE HOOVER AGAIN. THIS IS THE THIRD CALL THIS MORNING--HE SAYS IT'S URGENT?
TELL HIM I'LL GET BACK TO HIM.
Genarro wasn't only talking to me. Whoever he called, it had stirred up Gordon, too.

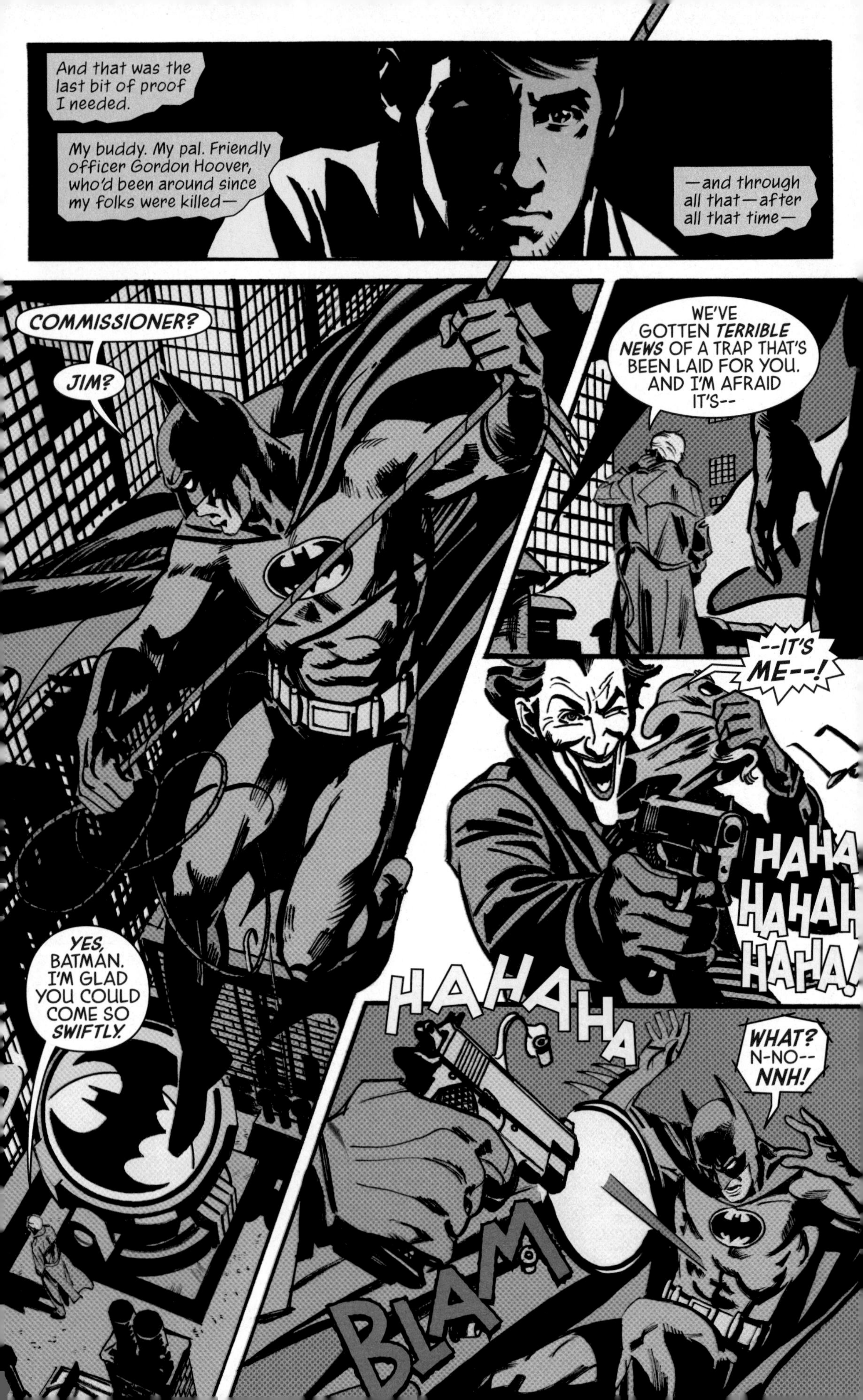

And that was the last bit of proof I needed.
My buddy. My pal. Friendly officer Gordon Hoover, who'd been around since my folks were killed—
—and through all that—after all that time—
COMMISSIONER?
JIM?
WE'VE GOTTEN TERRIBLE NEWS OF A TRAP THAT'S BEEN LAID FOR YOU. AND I'M AFRAID IT'S--
--IT'S ME--!
HAHA HAHAH HAHA!
YES, BATMAN. I'M GLAD YOU COULD COME SO SWIFTLY.
HAHAHA
WHAT? N-NO-- NNH!
BLAM

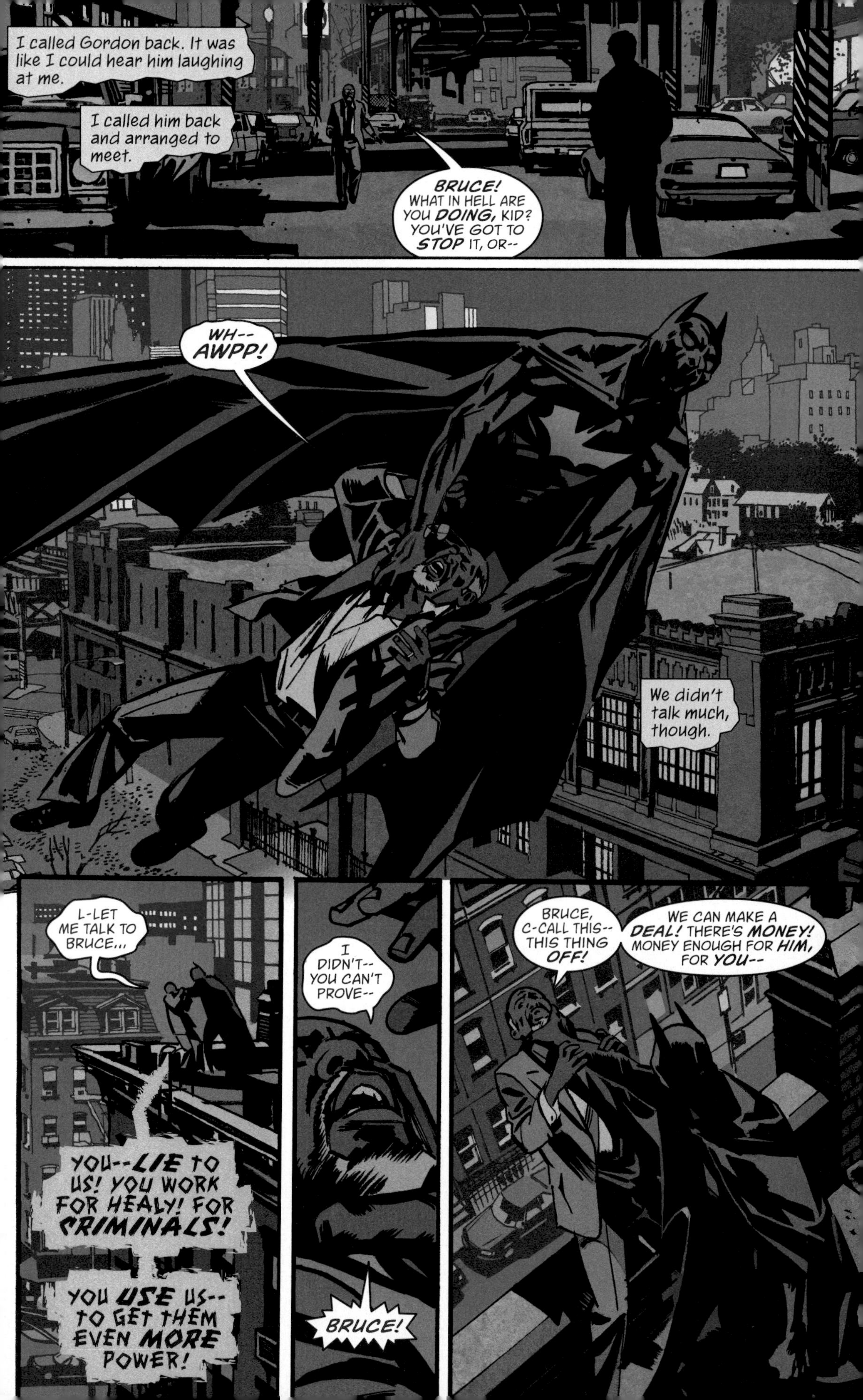
I called Gordon back. It was like I could hear him laughing at me.
I called him back and arranged to meet.
BRUCE! WHAT IN HELL ARE YOU DOING, KID? YOU'VE GOT TO STOP IT, OR--
WH-- AWPP!
We didn't talk much, though.
L-LET ME TALK TO BRUCE...
YOU--LIE TO US! YOU WORK FOR HEALY! FOR CRIMINALS!
YOU USE US-- TO GET THEM EVEN MORE POWER!
I DIDN'T-- YOU CAN'T PROVE--
BRUCE!
BRUCE, C-CALL THIS-- THIS THING OFF!
WE CAN MAKE A DEAL! THERE'S MONEY! MONEY ENOUGH FOR HIM, FOR YOU--

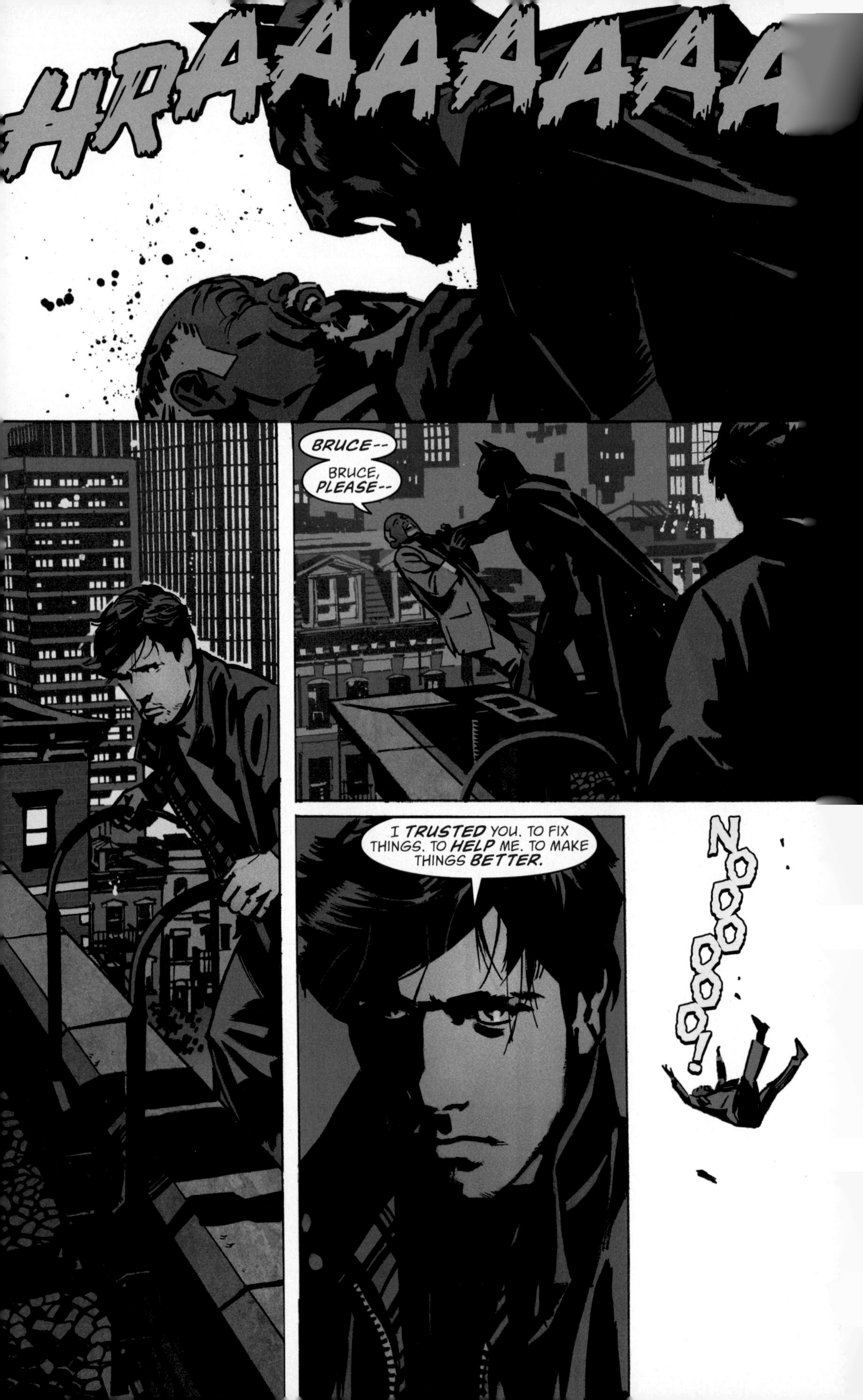
HRAAAAAAA
BRUCE--
BRUCE, PLEASE--
I TRUSTED YOU. TO FIX THINGS. TO HELP ME. TO MAKE THINGS BETTER.
NOOOOO!

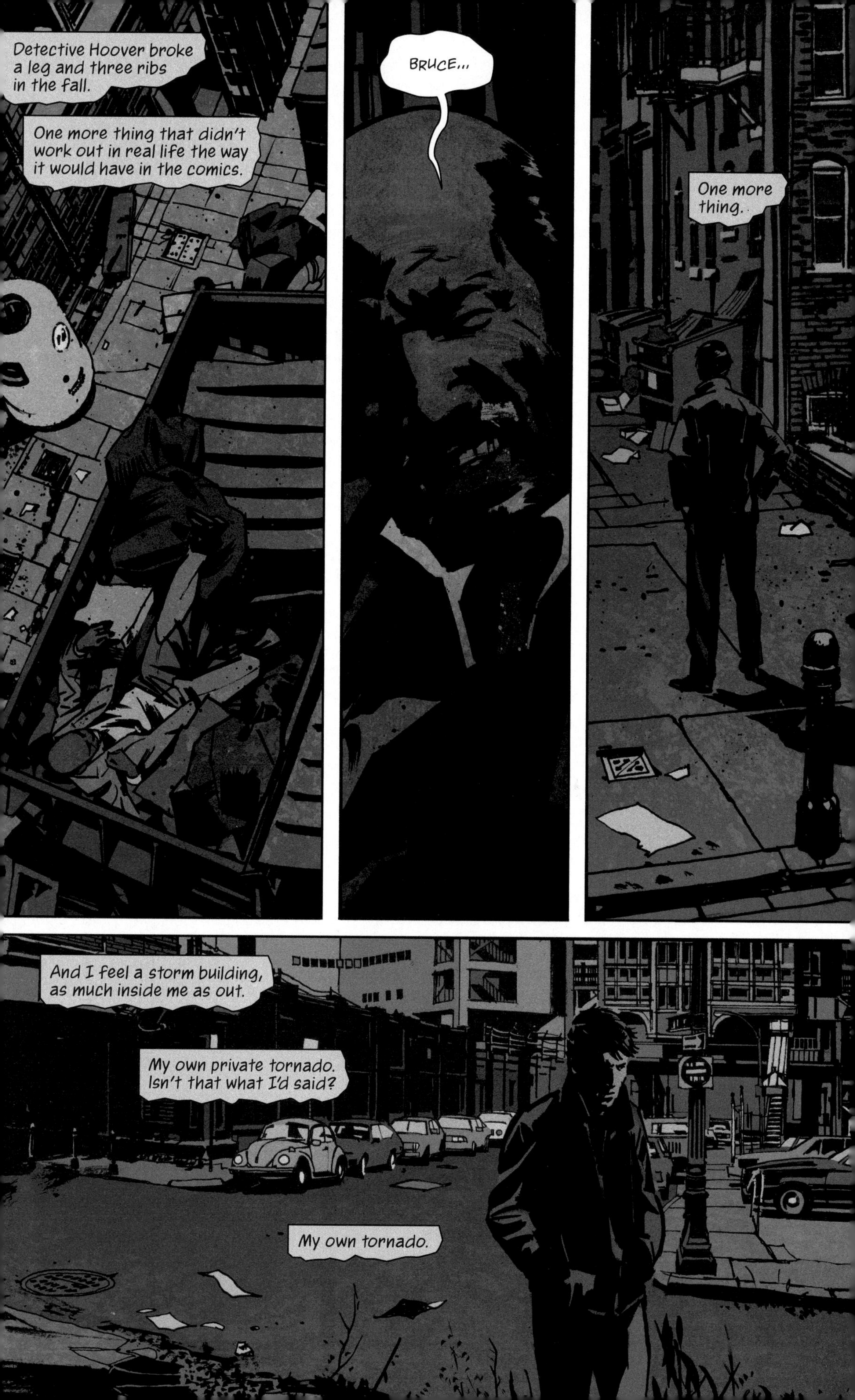
Detective Hoover broke a leg and three ribs in the fall.
One more thing that didn't work out in real life the way it would have in the comics.
BRUCE...
One more thing.
And I feel a storm building, as much inside me as out.
My own private tornado. Isn't that what I'd said?
My own tornado.

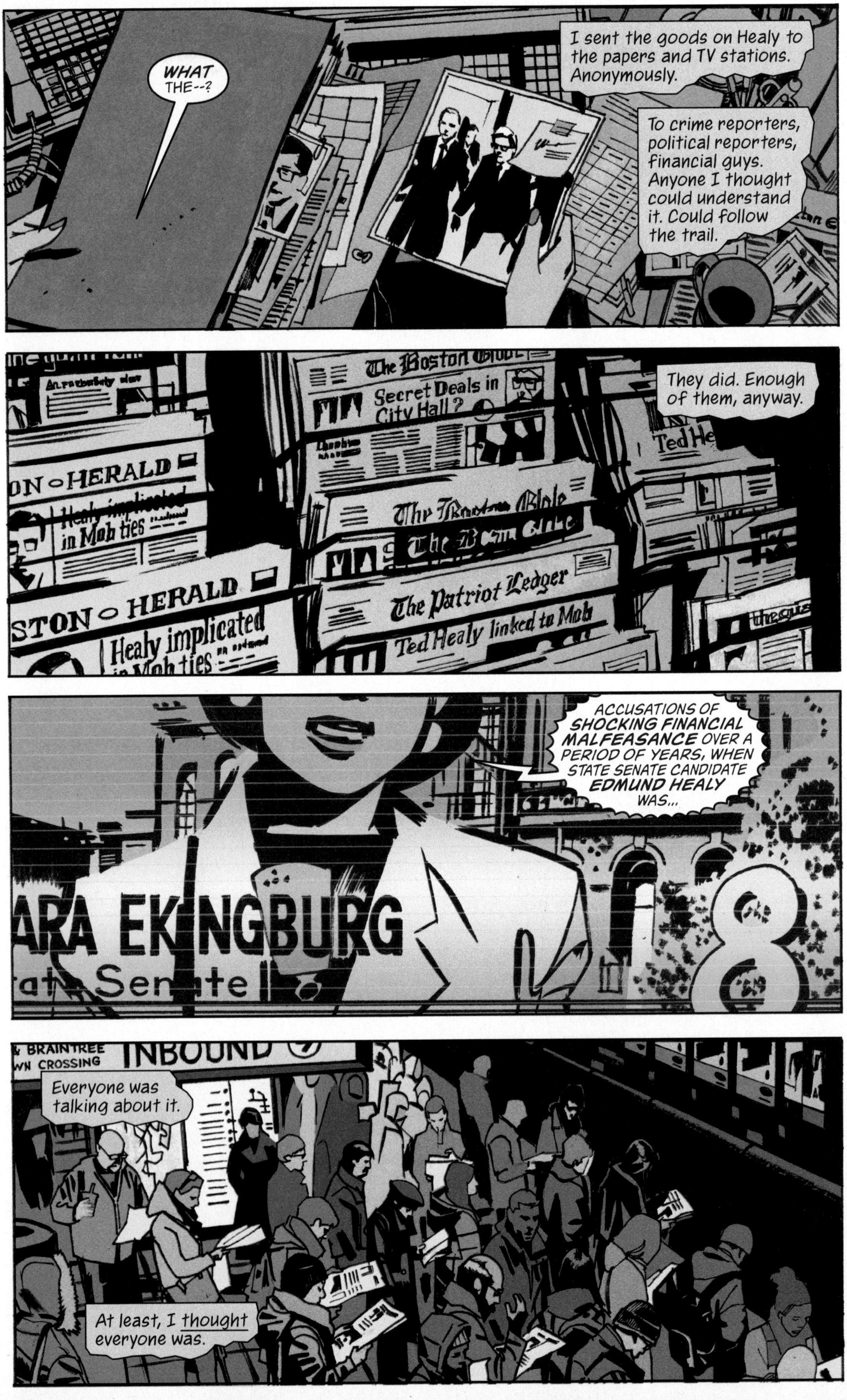

WHAT THE--?
I sent the goods on Healy to the papers and TV stations. Anonymously.
To crime reporters, political reporters, financial guys. Anyone I thought could understand it. Could follow the trail.
They did. Enough of them, anyway.
The Boston Globe
Secret Deals in City Hall?
HERALD
Healy implicated in Mob ties
The Patriot Ledger
Ted Healy linked to Mob
ACCUSATIONS OF SHOCKING FINANCIAL MALFEASANCE OVER A PERIOD OF YEARS, WHEN STATE SENATE CANDIDATE EDMUND HEALY WAS...
ARA EKINGBURG
State Senate
8
& BRAINTREE
WN CROSSING
INBOUND
Everyone was talking about it.
At least, I thought everyone was.

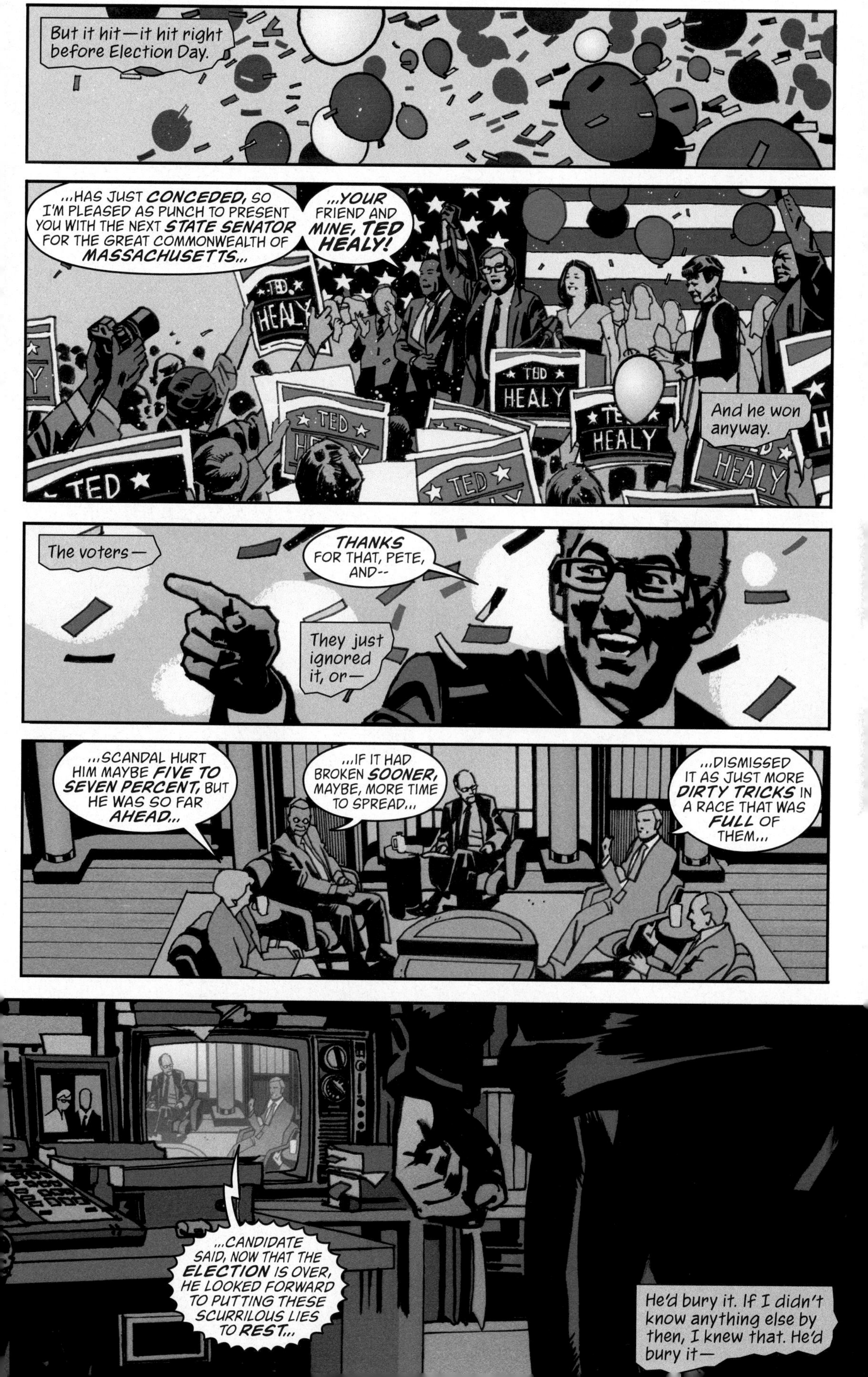

But it hit—it hit right before Election Day.
...HAS JUST CONCEDED, SO I'M PLEASED AS PUNCH TO PRESENT YOU WITH THE NEXT STATE SENATOR FOR THE GREAT COMMONWEALTH OF MASSACHUSETTS...
...YOUR FRIEND AND MINE, TED HEALY!
TED HEALY
And he won anyway.
The voters—
THANKS FOR THAT, PETE, AND--
They just ignored it, or—
...SCANDAL HURT HIM MAYBE FIVE TO SEVEN PERCENT, BUT HE WAS SO FAR AHEAD...
...IF IT HAD BROKEN SOONER, MAYBE, MORE TIME TO SPREAD...
...DISMISSED IT AS JUST MORE DIRTY TRICKS IN A RACE THAT WAS FULL OF THEM...
...CANDIDATE SAID, NOW THAT THE ELECTION IS OVER, HE LOOKED FORWARD TO PUTTING THESE SCURRILOUS LIES TO REST...
He'd bury it. If I didn't know anything else by then, I knew that. He'd bury it—

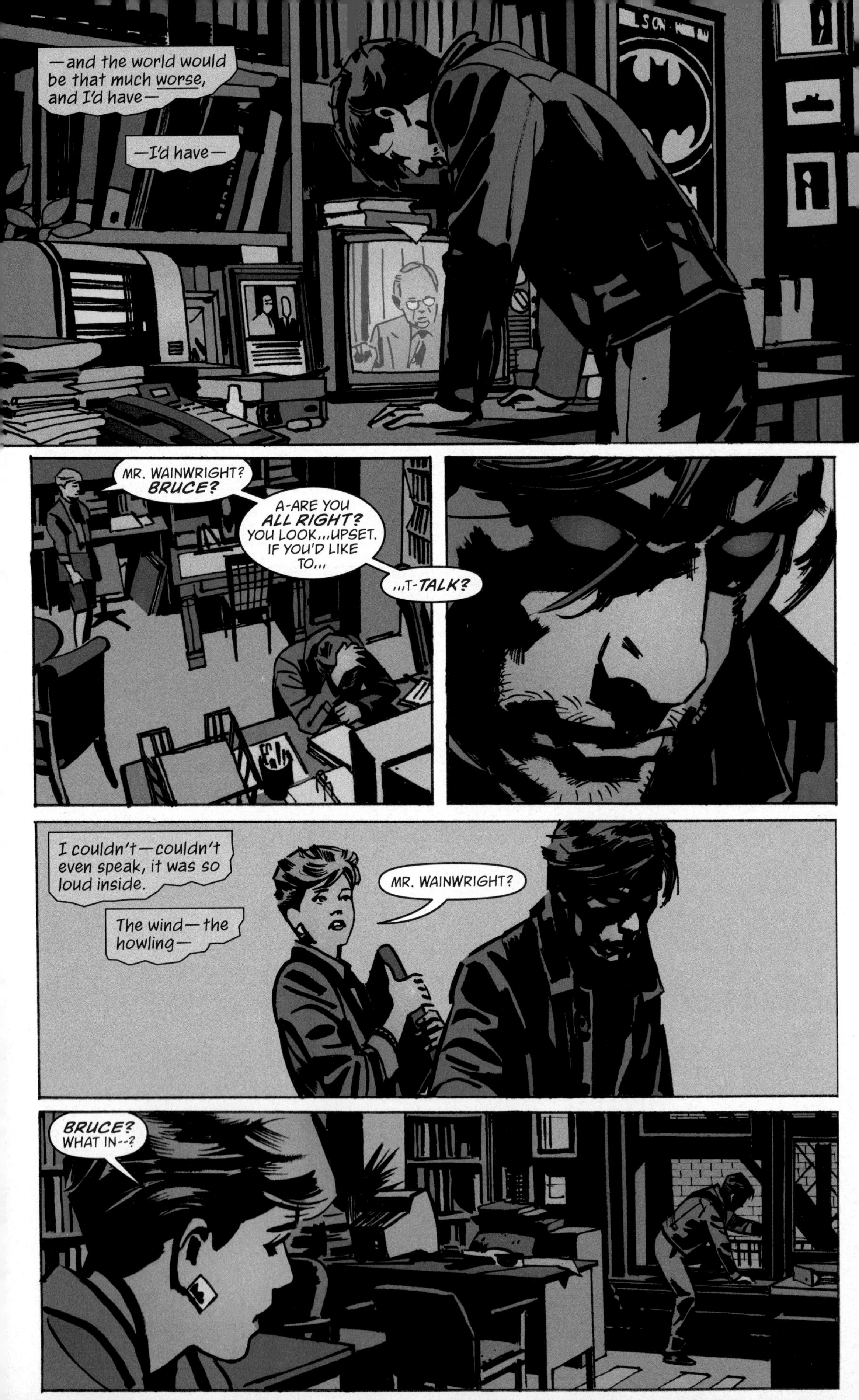
—and the world would be that much worse, and I'd have—
—I'd have—
MR. WAINWRIGHT? BRUCE?
A-ARE YOU ALL RIGHT? YOU LOOK...UPSET. IF YOU'D LIKE TO...
...T-TALK?
I couldn't—couldn't even speak, it was so loud inside.
The wind—the howling—
MR. WAINWRIGHT?
BRUCE? WHAT IN--?

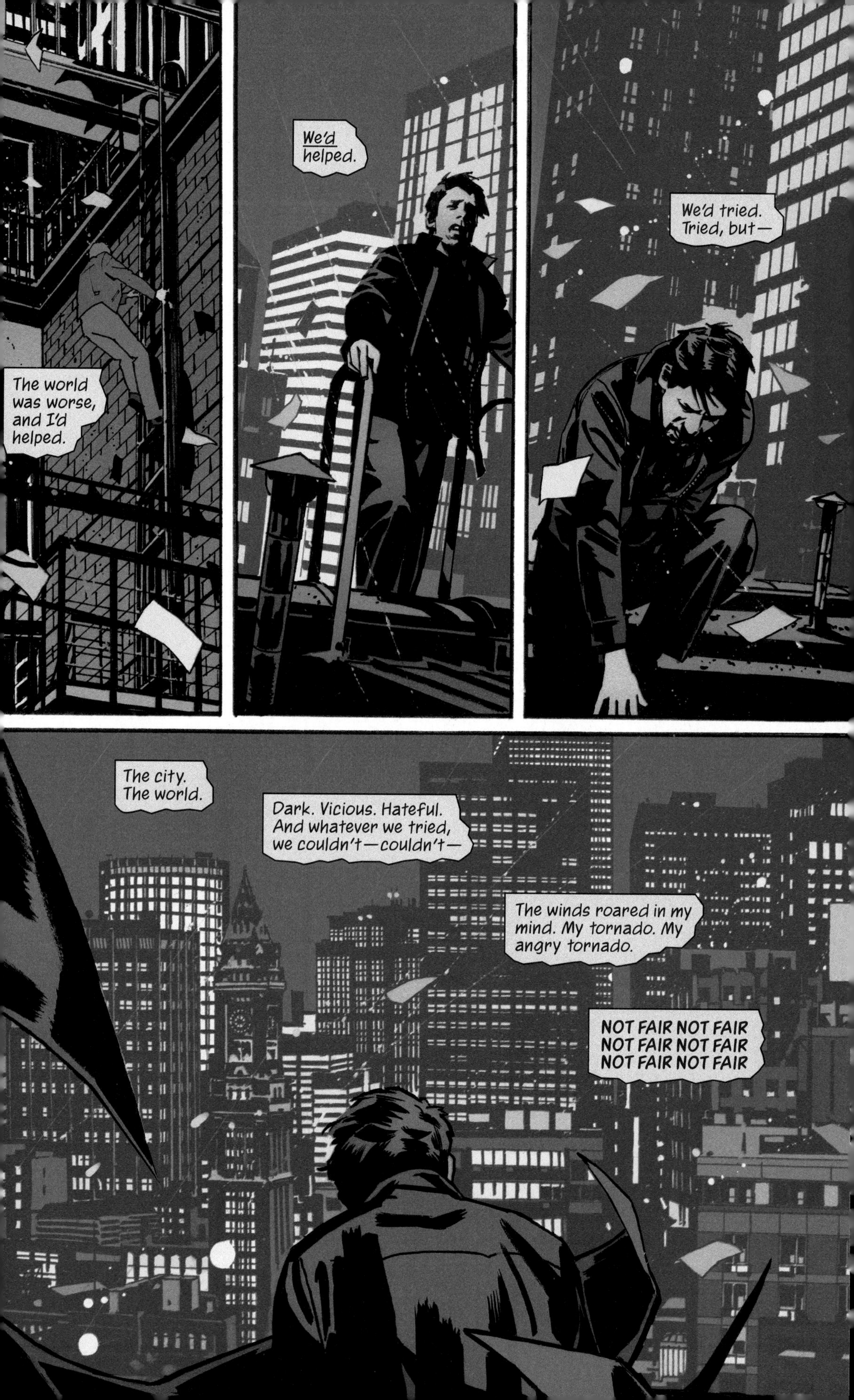
The world was worse, and I'd helped.
We'd helped.
We'd tried. Tried, but—
The city. The world.
Dark. Vicious. Hateful. And whatever we tried, we couldn't—couldn't—
The winds roared in my mind. My tornado. My angry tornado.
NOT FAIR NOT FAIR NOT FAIR NOT FAIR NOT FAIR NOT FAIR

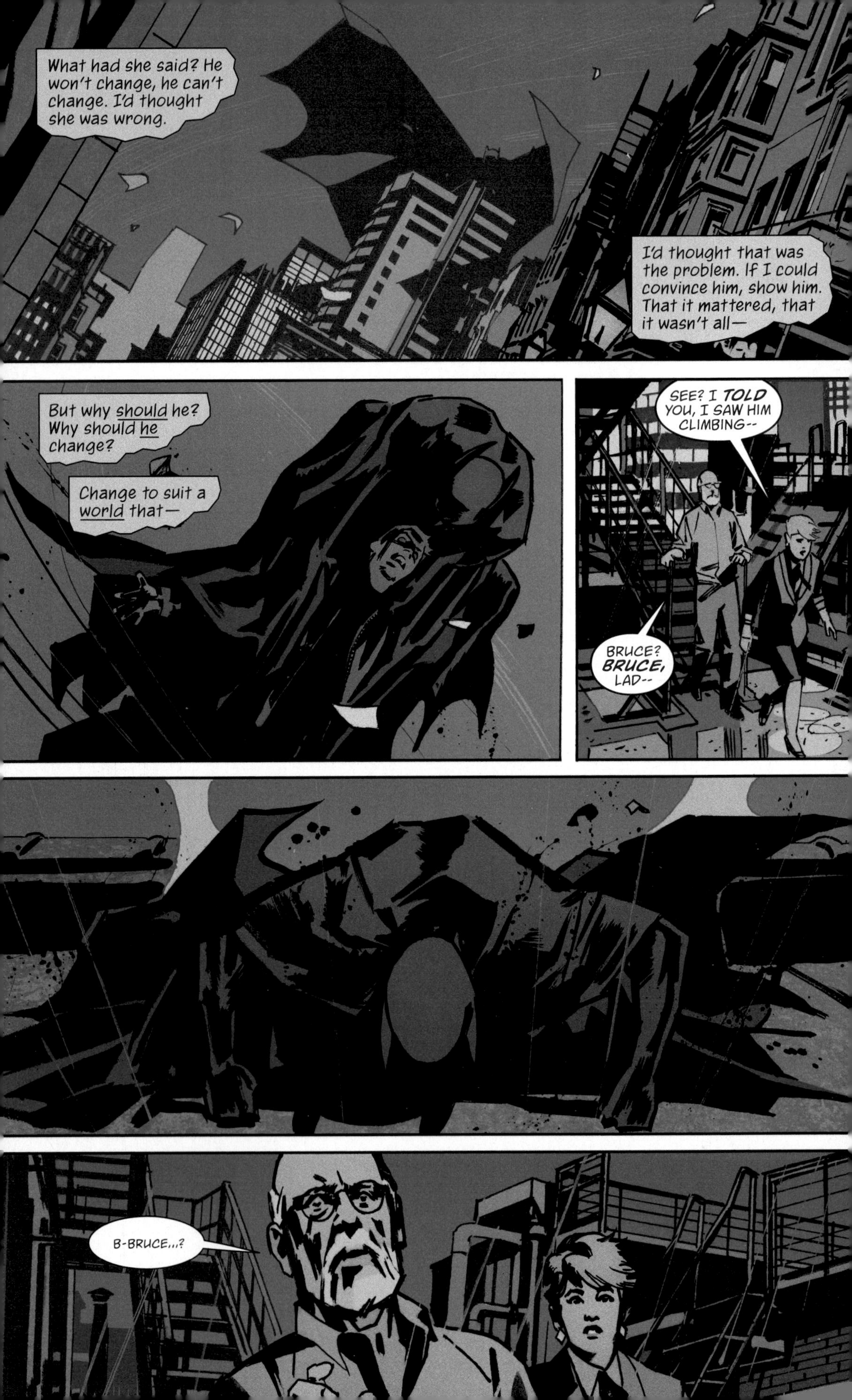
What had she said? He won't change, he can't change. I'd thought she was wrong.
I'd thought that was the problem. If I could convince him, show him. That it mattered, that it wasn't all—
But why should he? Why should he change?
Change to suit a world that—
SEE? I TOLD YOU, I SAW HIM CLIMBING--
BRUCE? BRUCE, LAD--
B-BRUCE...?

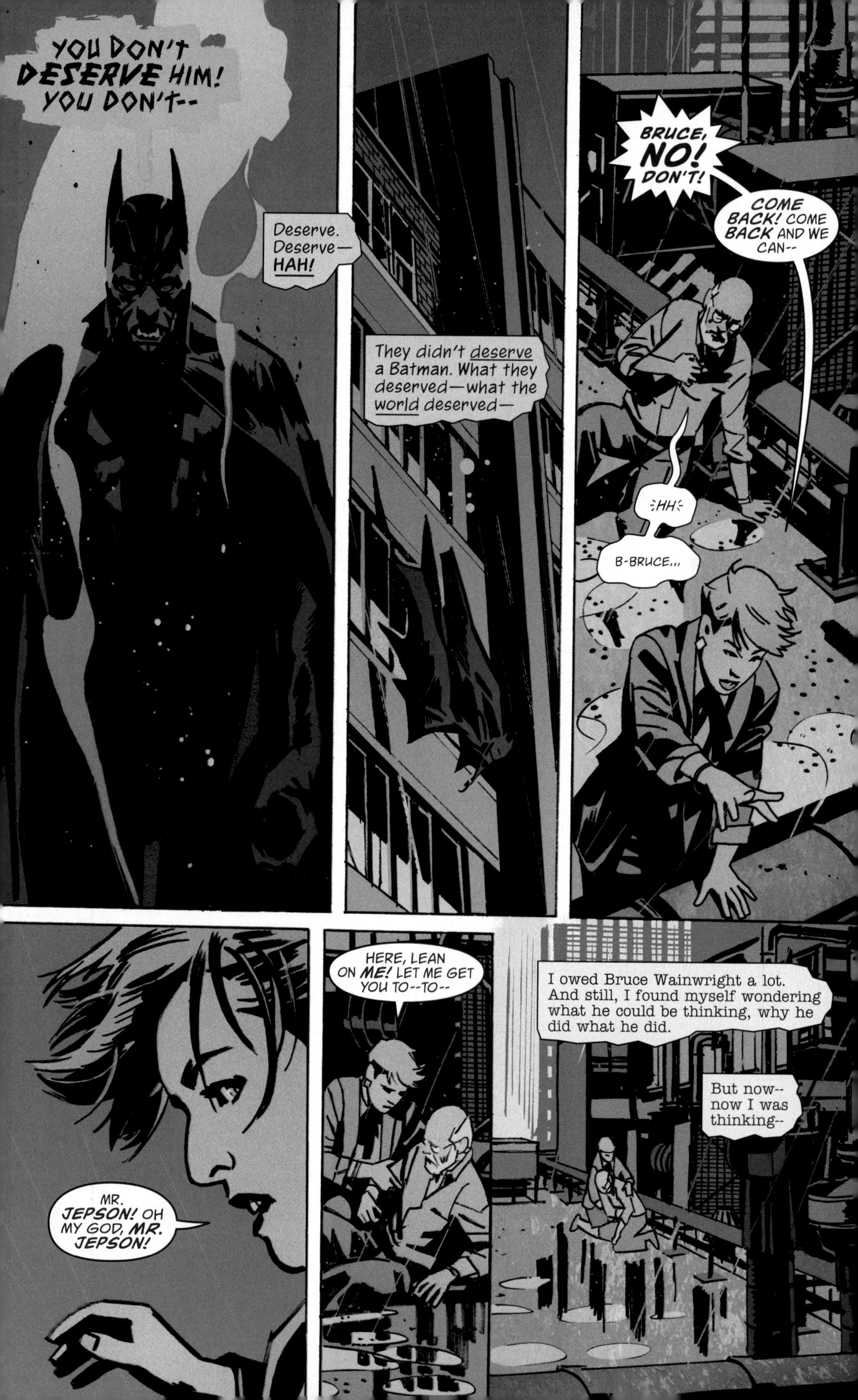

YOU DON'T DESERVE HIM! YOU DON'T--
Deserve. Deserve— HAH!
They didn't deserve a Batman. What they deserved—what the world deserved—
BRUCE, NO! DON'T!
COME BACK! COME BACK AND WE CAN--
HH
B-BRUCE...
MR. JEPSON! OH MY GOD, MR. JEPSON!
HERE, LEAN ON ME! LET ME GET YOU TO--TO--
I owed Bruce Wainwright a lot. And still, I found myself wondering what he could be thinking, why he did what he did.
But now-- now I was thinking--

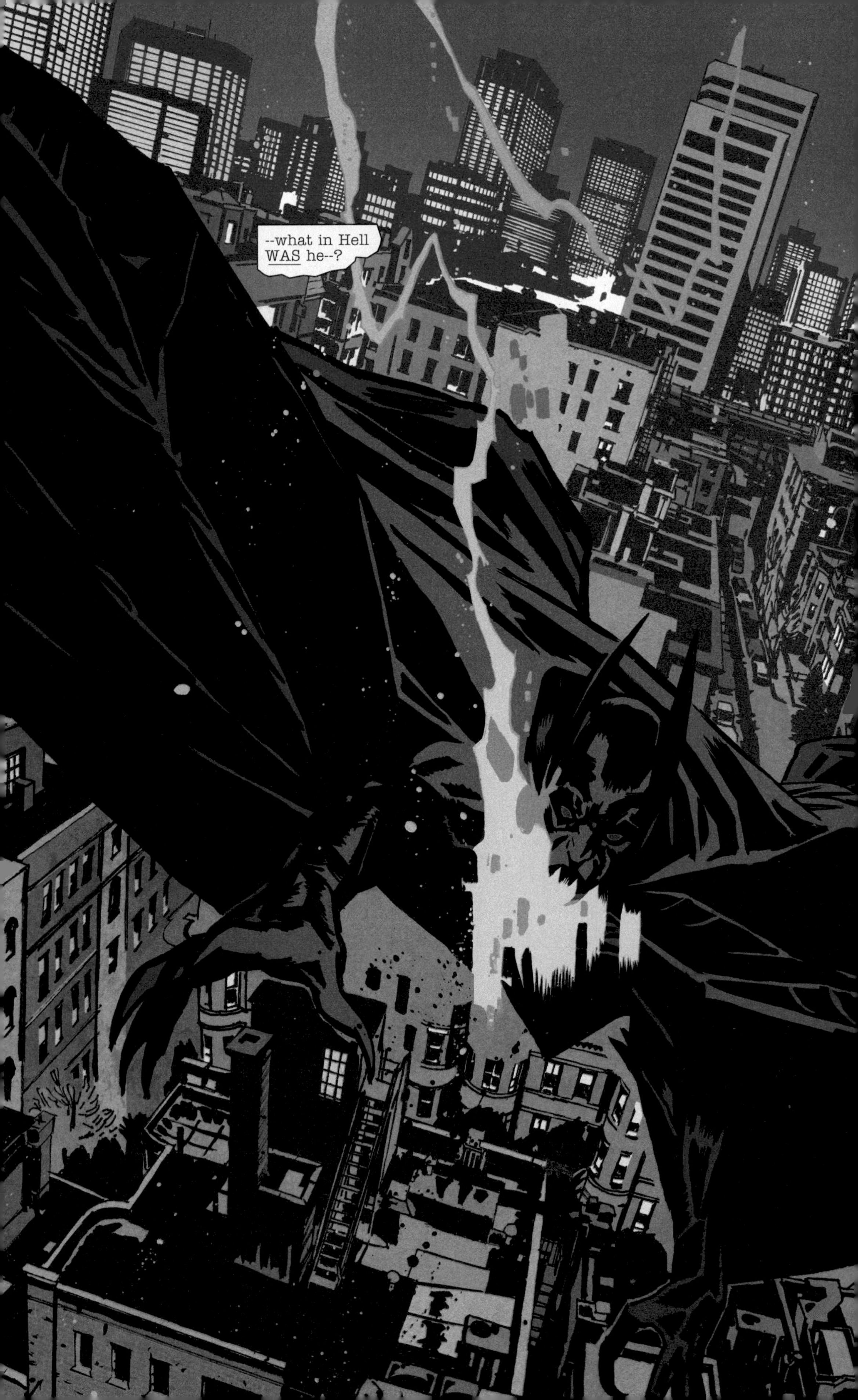
--what in Hell WAS he--?

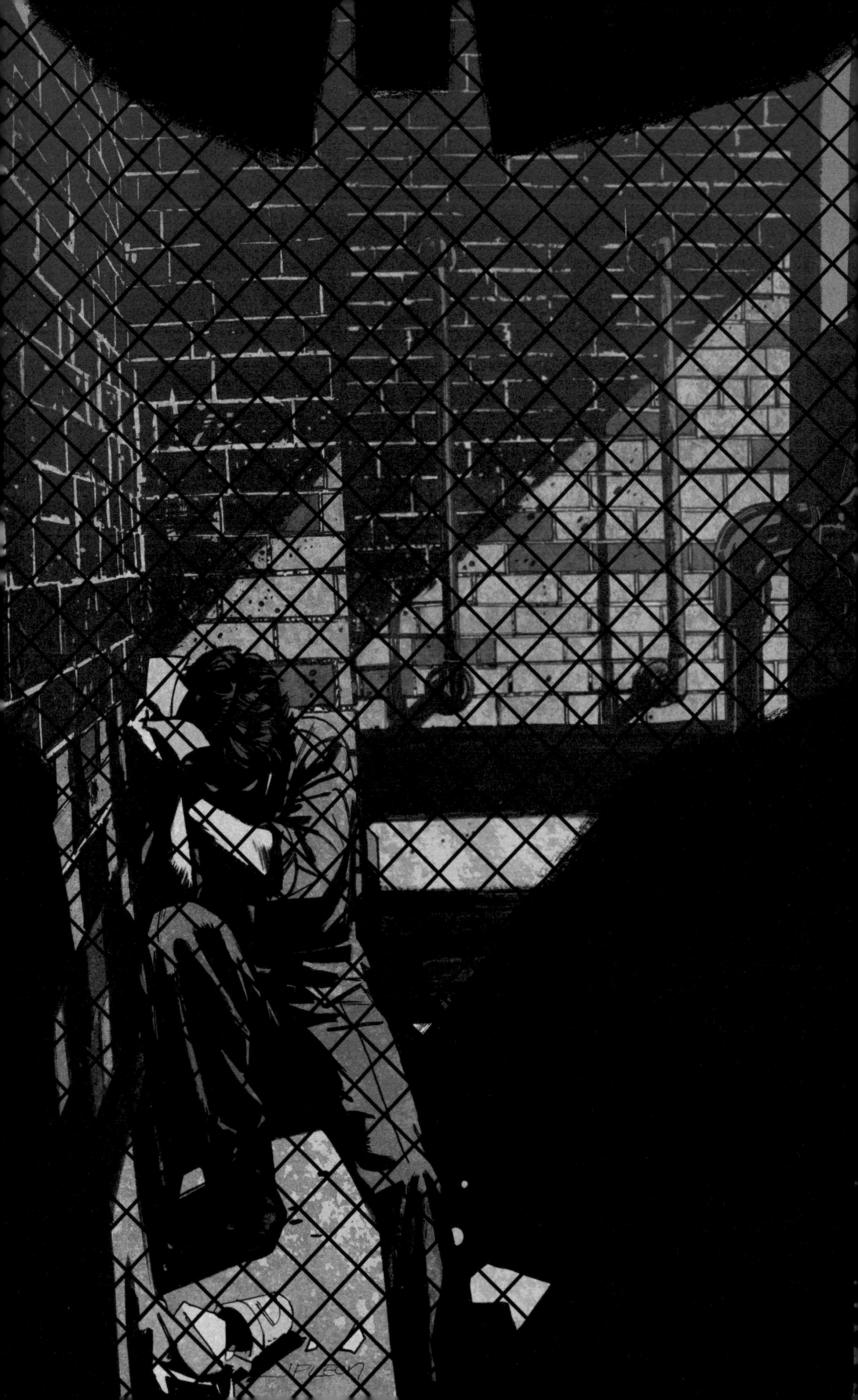

BOOK FOUR: **DARK KNIGHT**

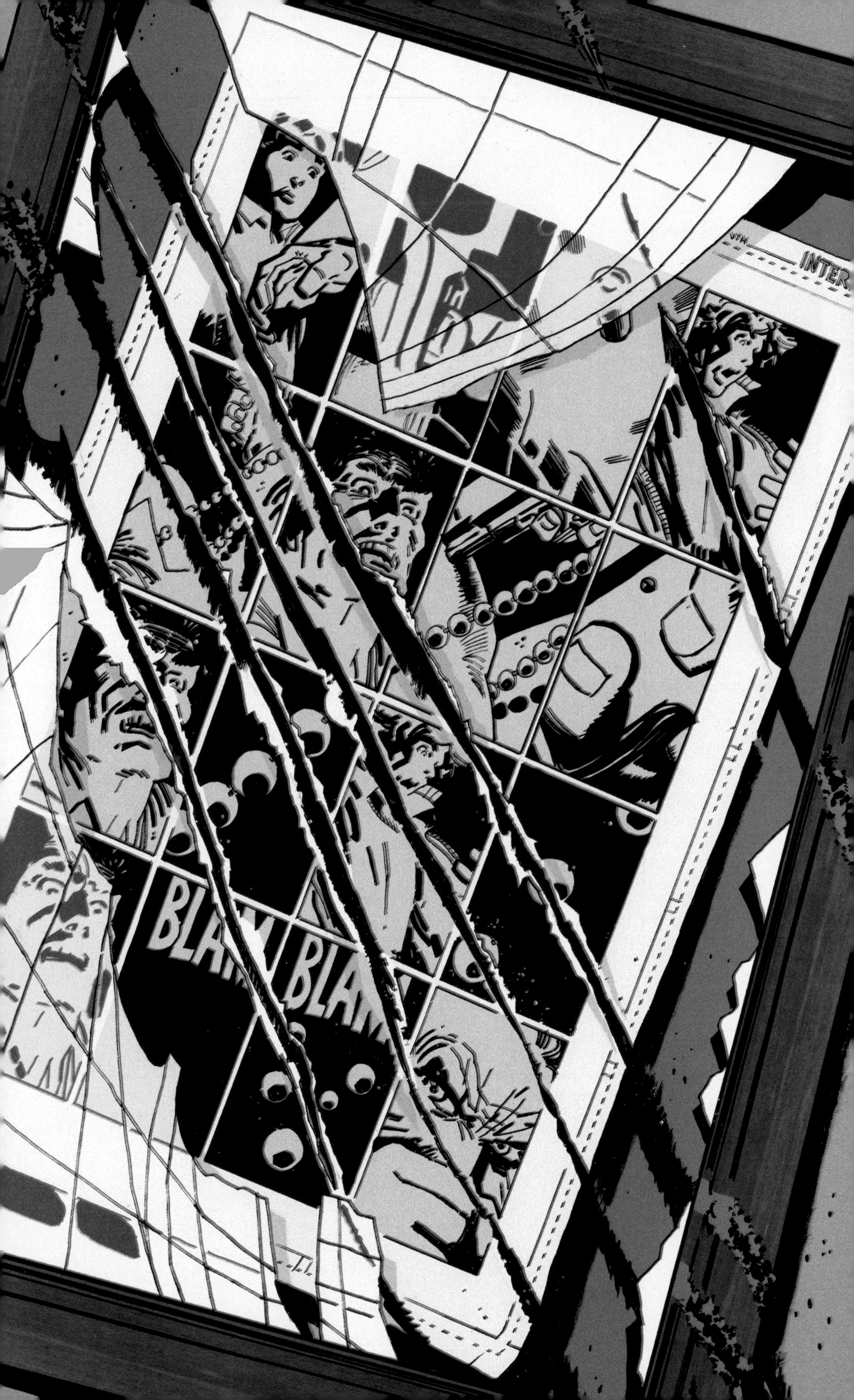
INTER

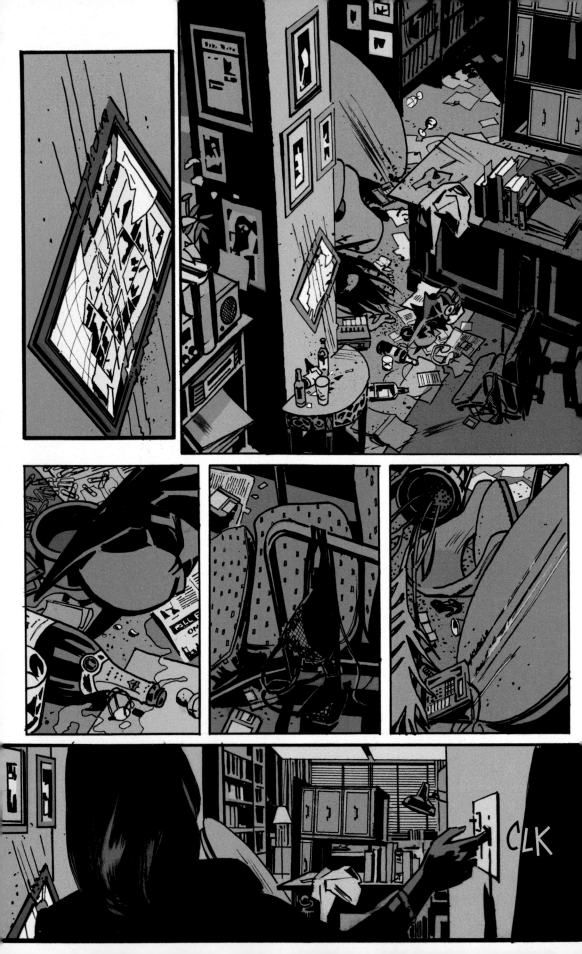

CLK

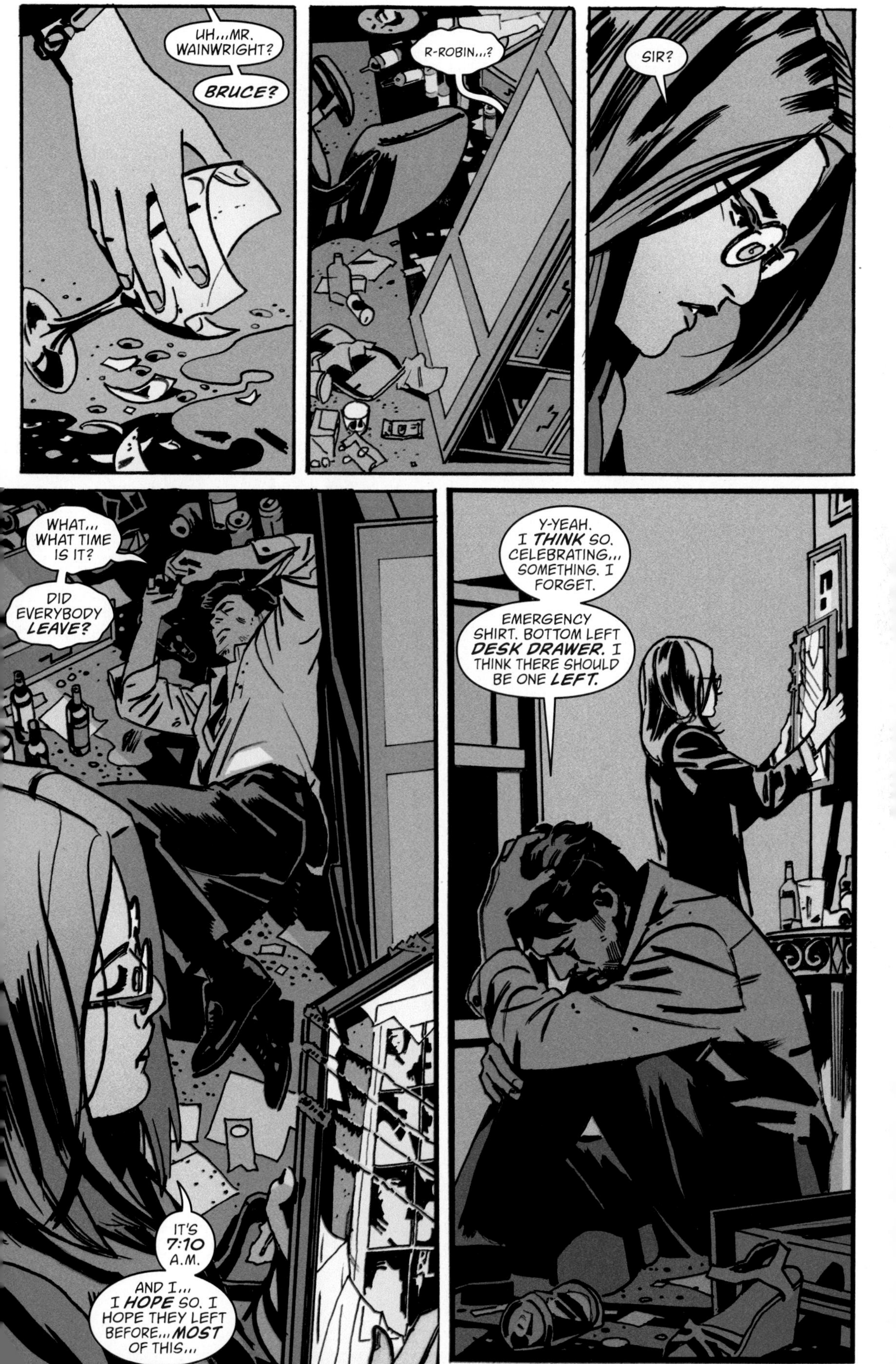
UH...MR. WAINWRIGHT?
BRUCE?
R-ROBIN...?
SIR?
WHAT... WHAT TIME IS IT?
DID EVERYBODY LEAVE?
IT'S 7:10 A.M.
AND I... I HOPE SO. I HOPE THEY LEFT BEFORE... MOST OF THIS...
Y-YEAH. I THINK SO. CELEBRATING... SOMETHING. I FORGET.
EMERGENCY SHIRT. BOTTOM LEFT DESK DRAWER. I THINK THERE SHOULD BE ONE LEFT.

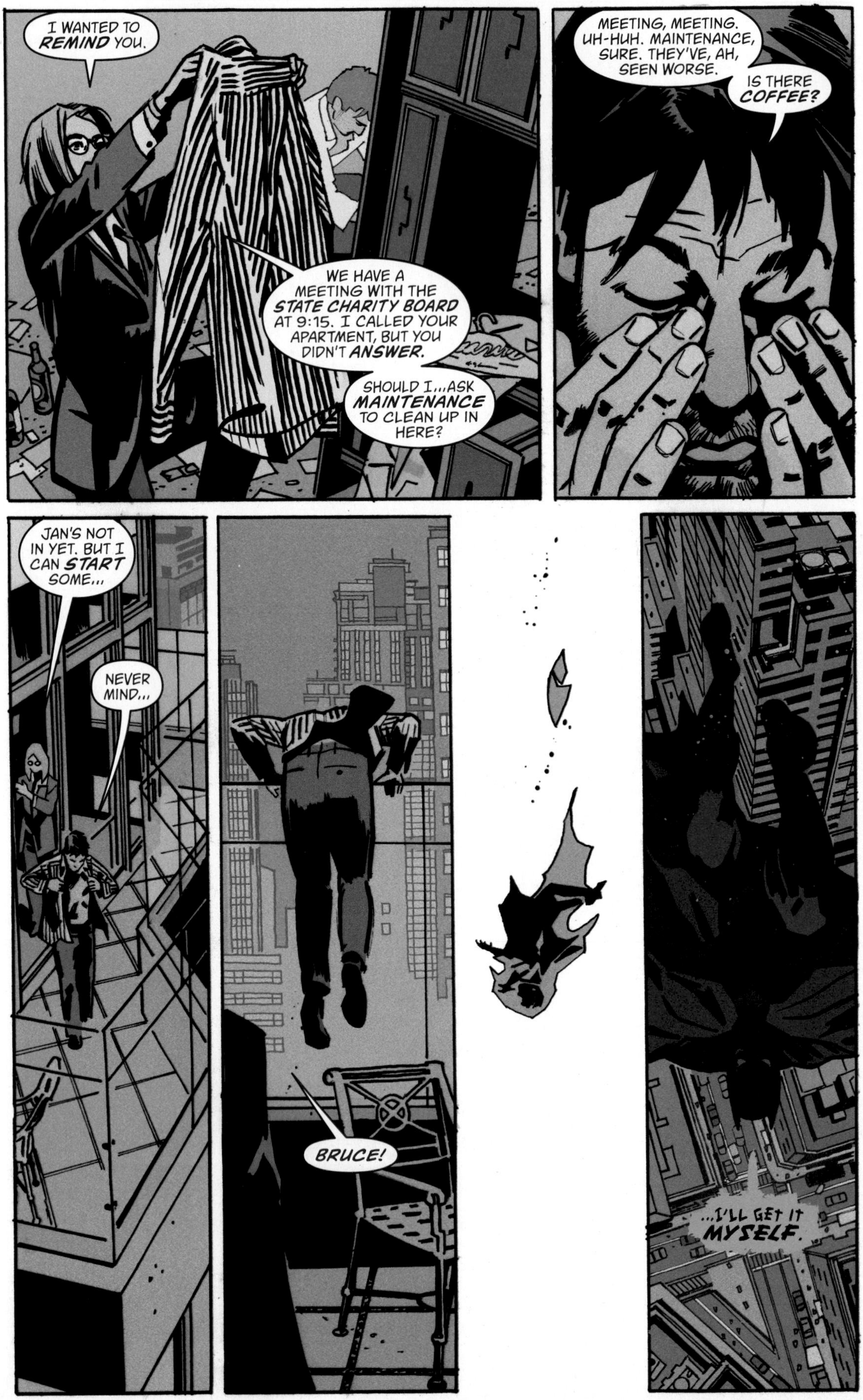

I WANTED TO REMIND YOU.
WE HAVE A MEETING WITH THE STATE CHARITY BOARD AT 9:15. I CALLED YOUR APARTMENT, BUT YOU DIDN'T ANSWER.
SHOULD I...ASK MAINTENANCE TO CLEAN UP IN HERE?
MEETING, MEETING. UH-HUH. MAINTENANCE, SURE. THEY'VE, AH, SEEN WORSE.
IS THERE COFFEE?
JAN'S NOT IN YET. BUT I CAN START SOME...
NEVER MIND...
BRUCE!
...I'LL GET IT MYSELF.

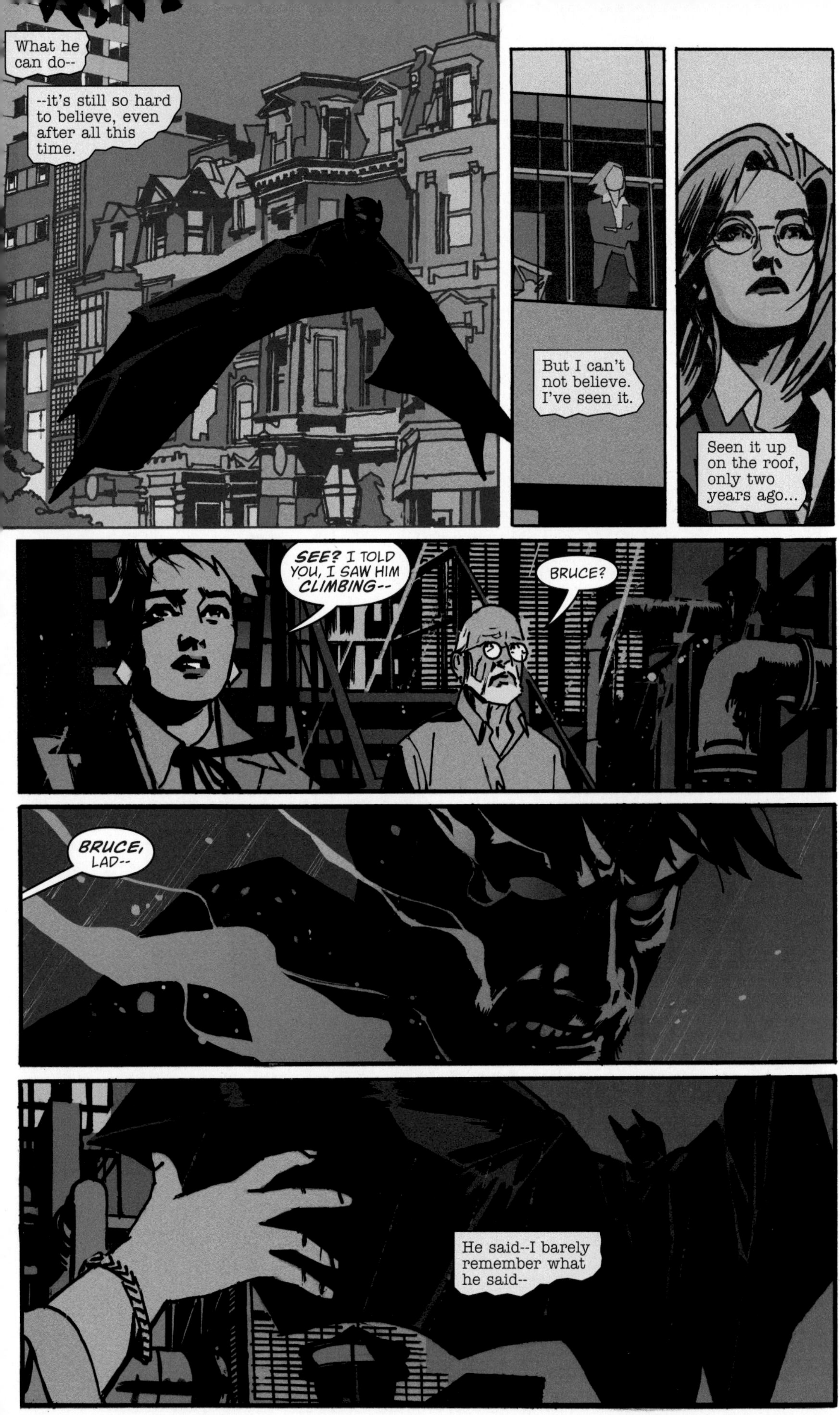
What he can do--
--it's still so hard to believe, even after all this time.
But I can't not believe. I've seen it.
Seen it up on the roof, only two years ago...
SEE? I TOLD YOU, I SAW HIM CLIMBING--
BRUCE?
BRUCE, LAD--
He said--I barely remember what he said--

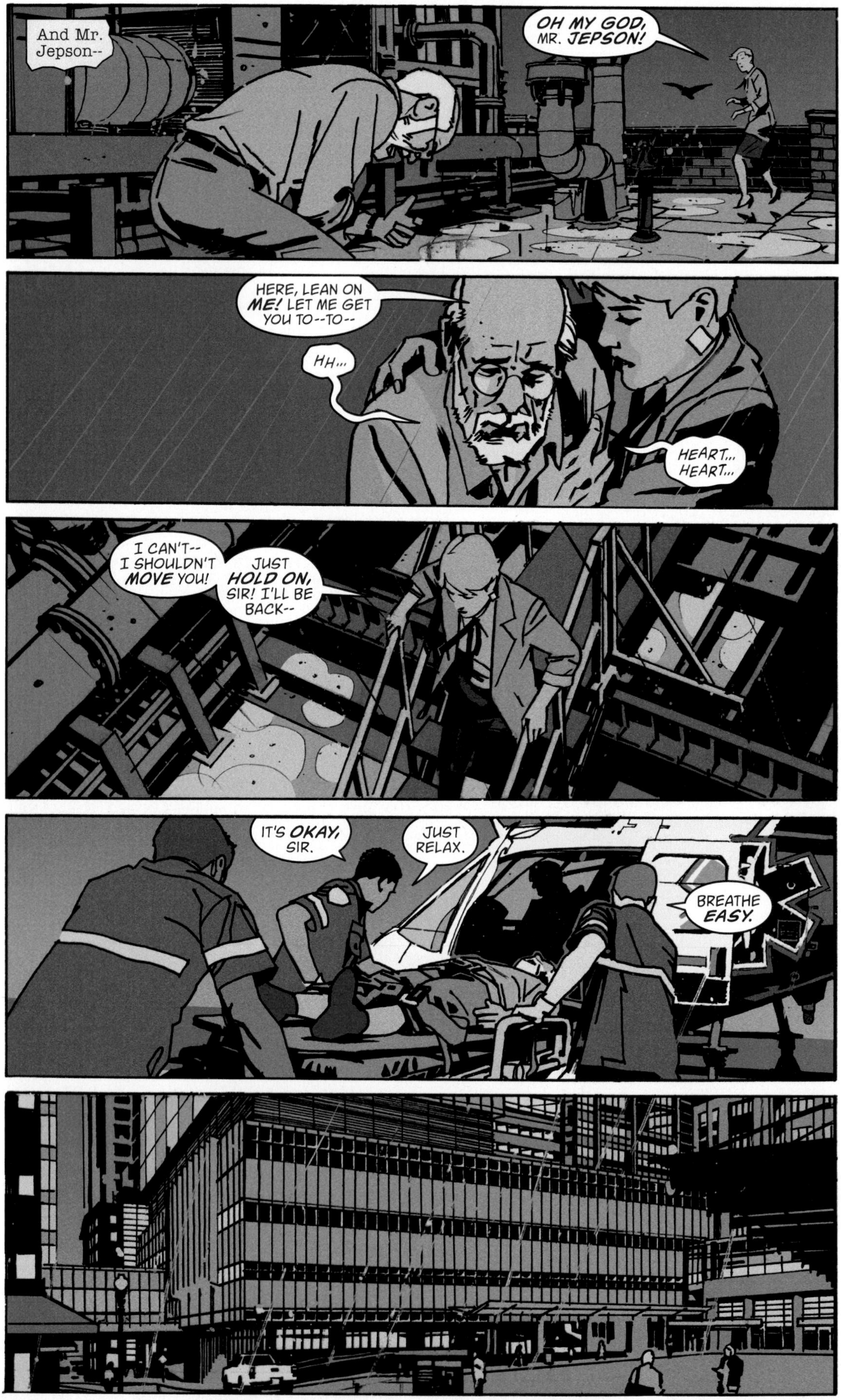
And Mr. Jepson--
OH MY GOD, MR. JEPSON!
HERE, LEAN ON ME! LET ME GET YOU TO--TO--
HH...
HEART... HEART...
I CAN'T-- I SHOULDN'T MOVE YOU!
JUST HOLD ON, SIR! I'LL BE BACK--
IT'S OKAY, SIR.
JUST RELAX.
BREATHE EASY.

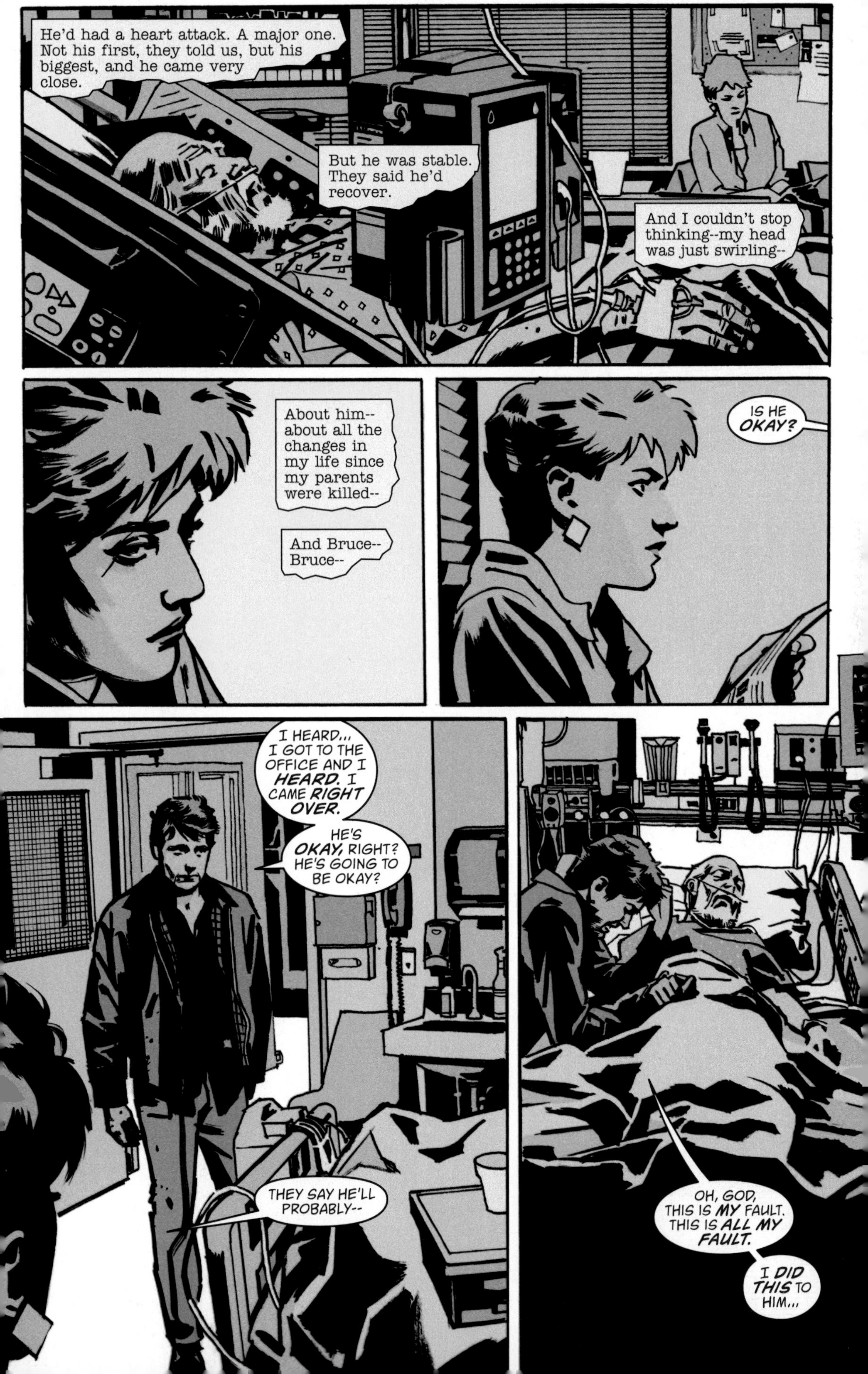
He'd had a heart attack. A major one. Not his first, they told us, but his biggest, and he came very close.
But he was stable. They said he'd recover.
And I couldn't stop thinking--my head was just swirling--
About him--about all the changes in my life since my parents were killed--
And Bruce--Bruce--
IS HE OKAY?
I HEARD... I GOT TO THE OFFICE AND I HEARD. I CAME RIGHT OVER.
HE'S OKAY, RIGHT? HE'S GOING TO BE OKAY?
THEY SAY HE'LL PROBABLY--
OH, GOD, THIS IS MY FAULT. THIS IS ALL MY FAULT.
I DID THIS TO HIM...

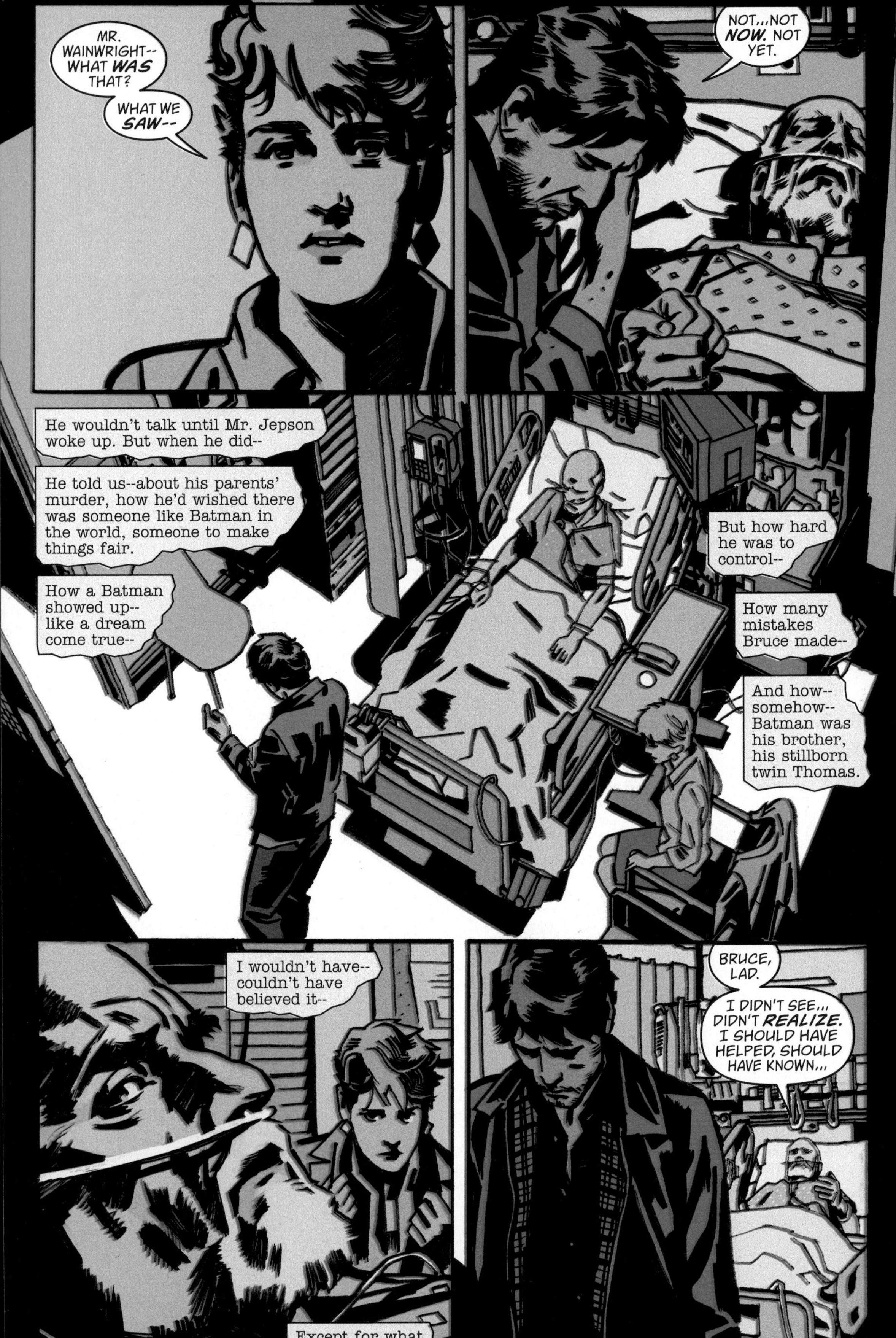
MR. WAINWRIGHT--WHAT WAS THAT?
WHAT WE SAW--
NOT...NOT NOW. NOT YET.
He wouldn't talk until Mr. Jepson woke up. But when he did--
He told us--about his parents' murder, how he'd wished there was someone like Batman in the world, someone to make things fair.
How a Batman showed up--like a dream come true--
But how hard he was to control--
How many mistakes Bruce made--
And how--somehow--Batman was his brother, his stillborn twin Thomas.
I wouldn't have--couldn't have believed it--
Except for what we'd seen--
BRUCE, LAD.
I DIDN'T SEE... DIDN'T REALIZE. I SHOULD HAVE HELPED, SHOULD HAVE KNOWN...

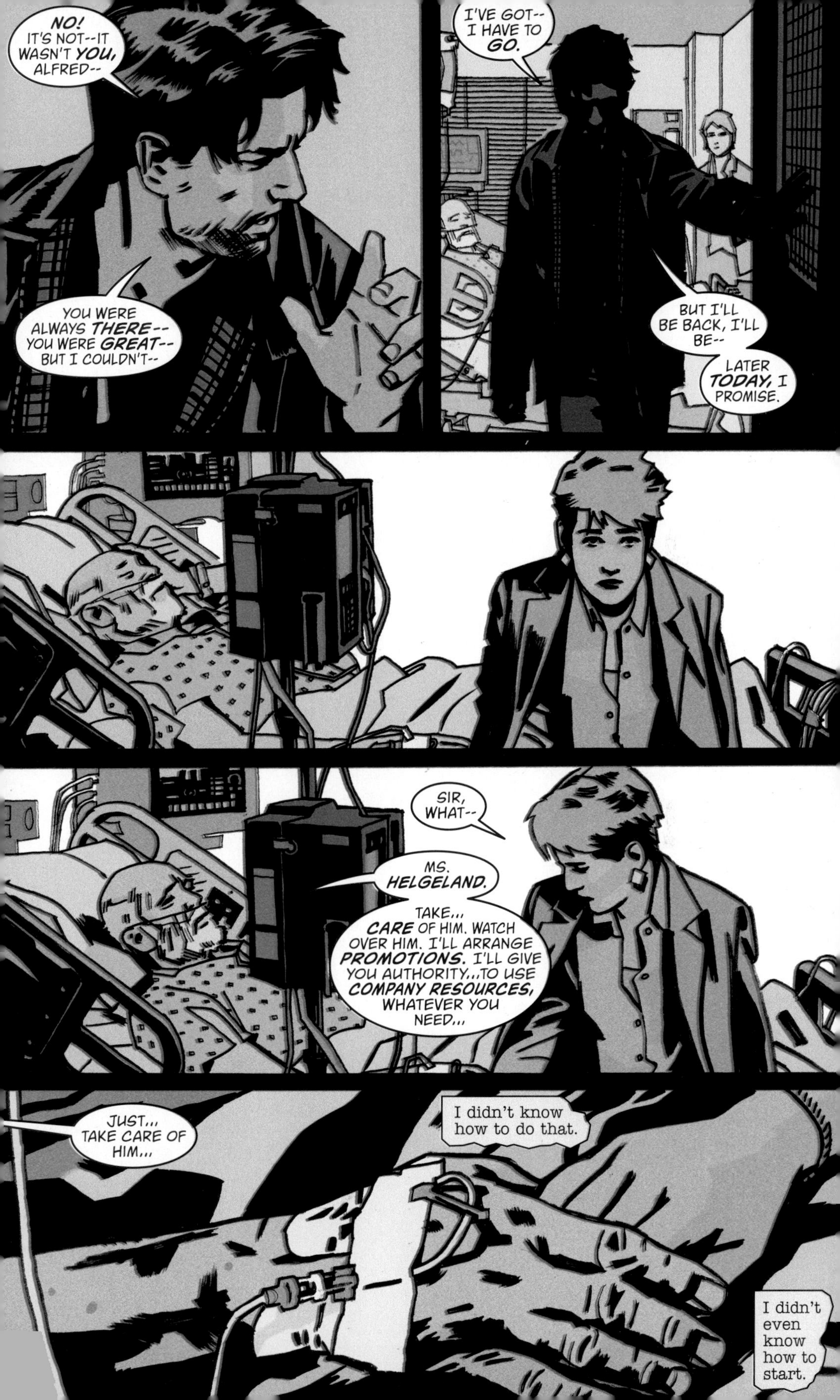
NO! IT'S NOT--IT WASN'T YOU, ALFRED--
YOU WERE ALWAYS THERE--YOU WERE GREAT--BUT I COULDN'T--
I'VE GOT--I HAVE TO GO.
BUT I'LL BE BACK, I'LL BE--
LATER TODAY, I PROMISE.
SIR, WHAT--
MS. HELGELAND.
TAKE... CARE OF HIM. WATCH OVER HIM. I'LL ARRANGE PROMOTIONS. I'LL GIVE YOU AUTHORITY...TO USE COMPANY RESOURCES, WHATEVER YOU NEED...
JUST... TAKE CARE OF HIM...
I didn't know how to do that.
I didn't even know how to start.

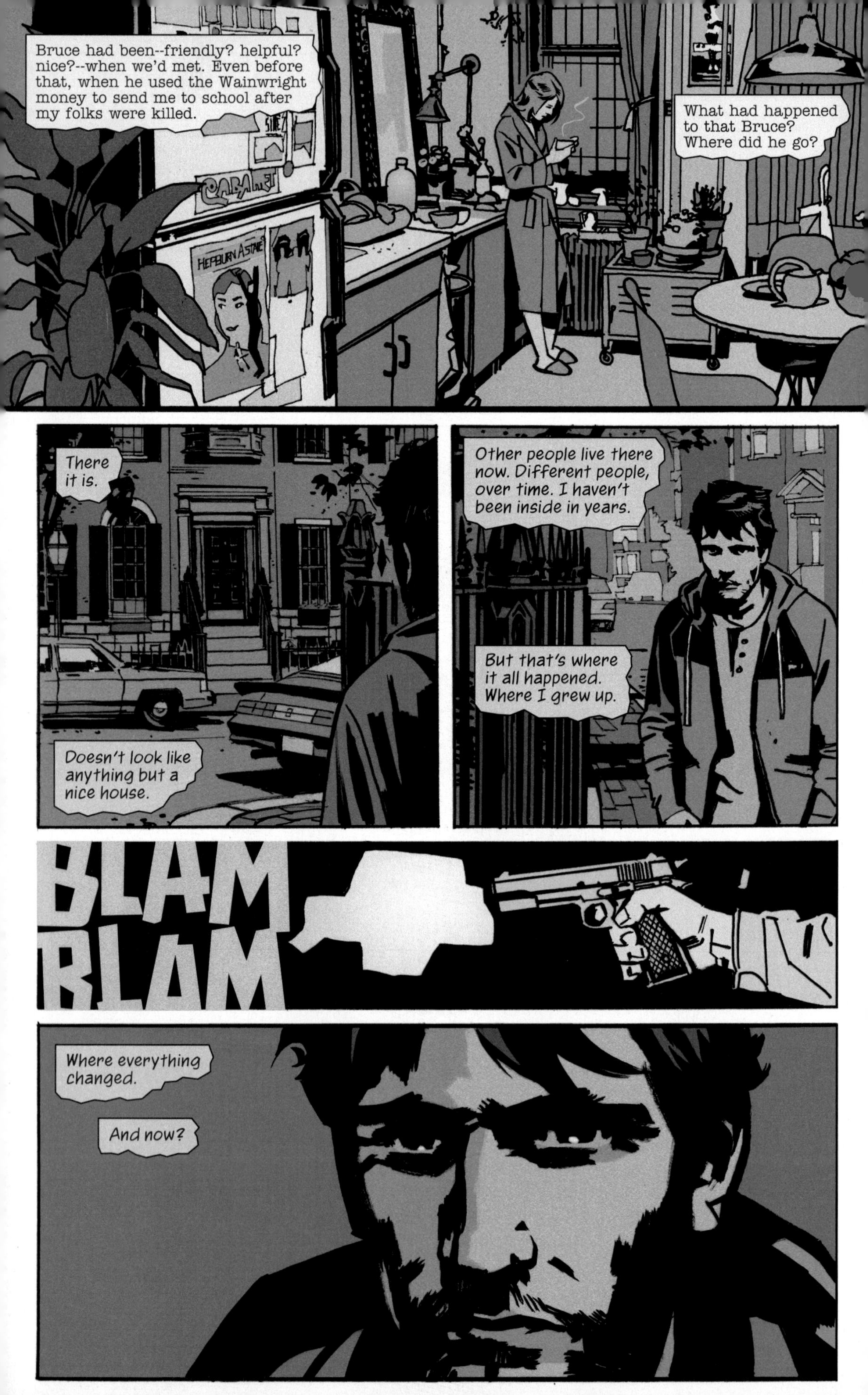

Bruce had been--friendly? helpful? nice?--when we'd met. Even before that, when he used the Wainwright money to send me to school after my folks were killed.
What had happened to that Bruce? Where did he go?
HEPBURN ASTAIRE
There it is.
Doesn't look like anything but a nice house.
Other people live there now. Different people, over time. I haven't been inside in years.
But that's where it all happened. Where I grew up.
BLAM
BLAM
Where everything changed.
And now?

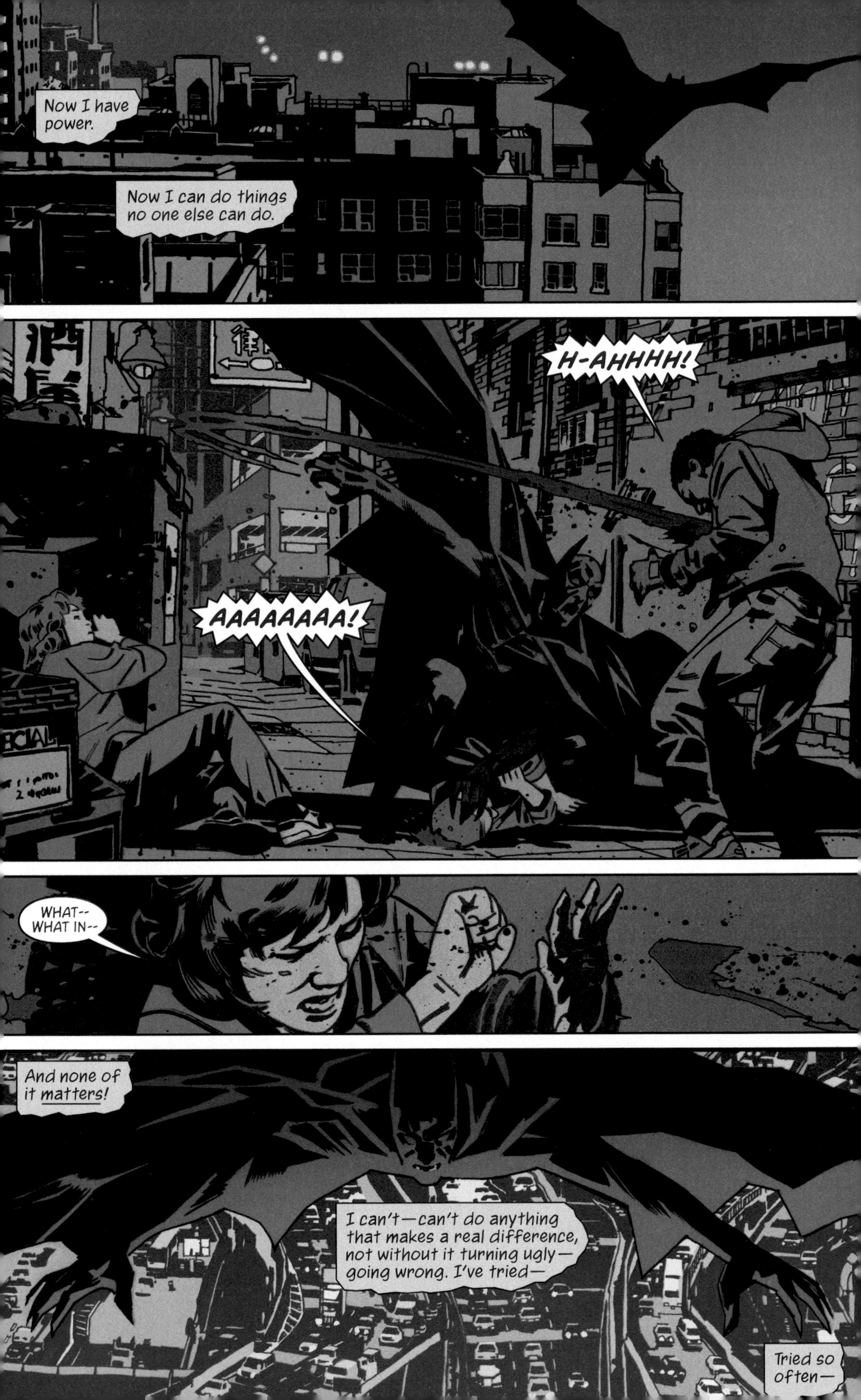

Now I have power.
Now I can do things no one else can do.
H-AHHHH!
AAAAAAAA!
WHAT--
WHAT IN--
And none of it matters!
I can't—can't do anything that makes a real difference, not without it turning ugly—going wrong. I've tried—
Tried so often—

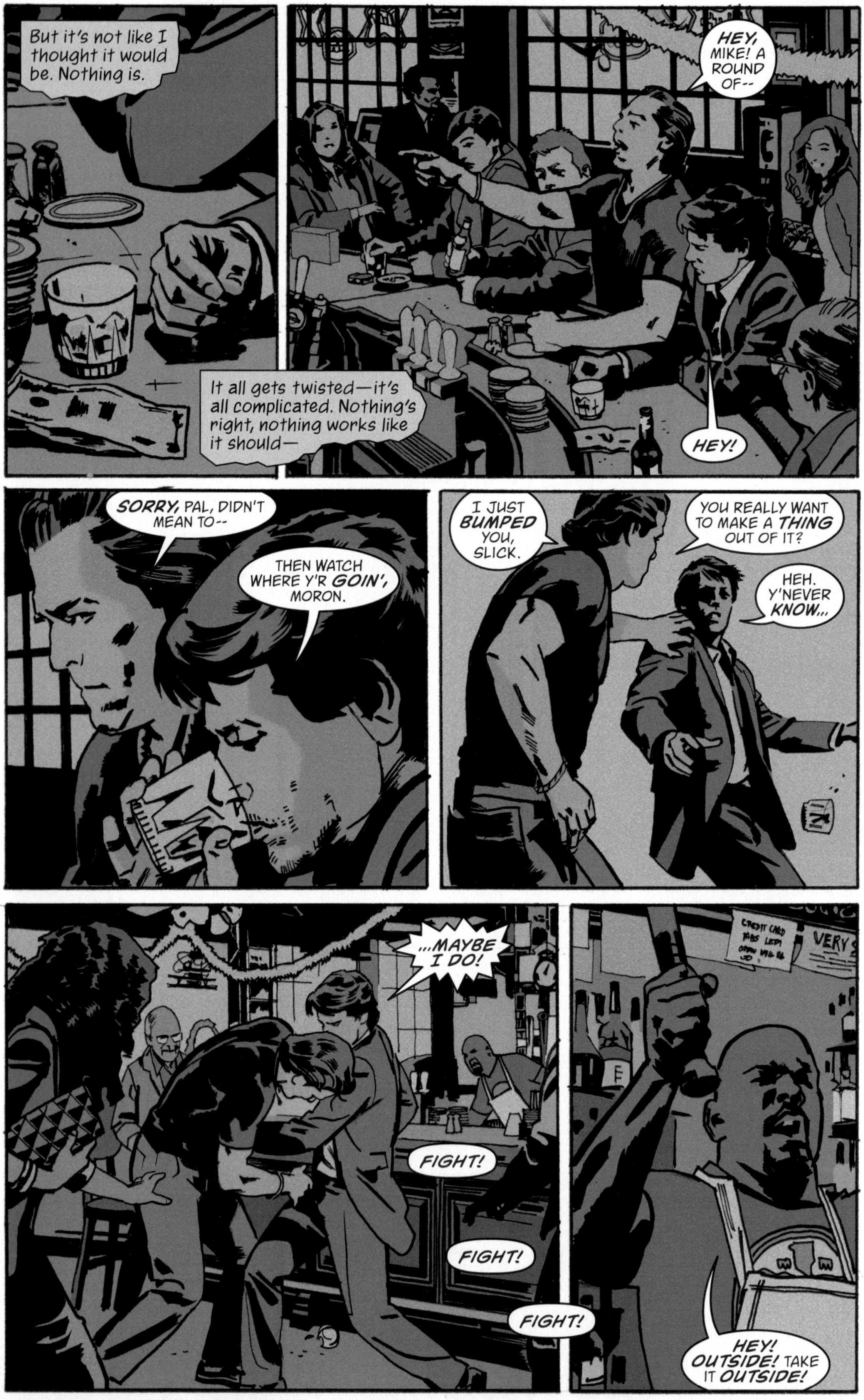
But it's not like I thought it would be. Nothing is.
HEY, MIKE! A ROUND OF--
It all gets twisted—it's all complicated. Nothing's right, nothing works like it should—
HEY!
SORRY, PAL, DIDN'T MEAN TO--
THEN WATCH WHERE Y'R GOIN', MORON.
I JUST BUMPED YOU, SLICK.
YOU REALLY WANT TO MAKE A THING OUT OF IT?
HEH. Y'NEVER KNOW...
...MAYBE I DO!
FIGHT!
FIGHT!
FIGHT!
CREDIT CARD
VERY
HEY! OUTSIDE! TAKE IT OUTSIDE!

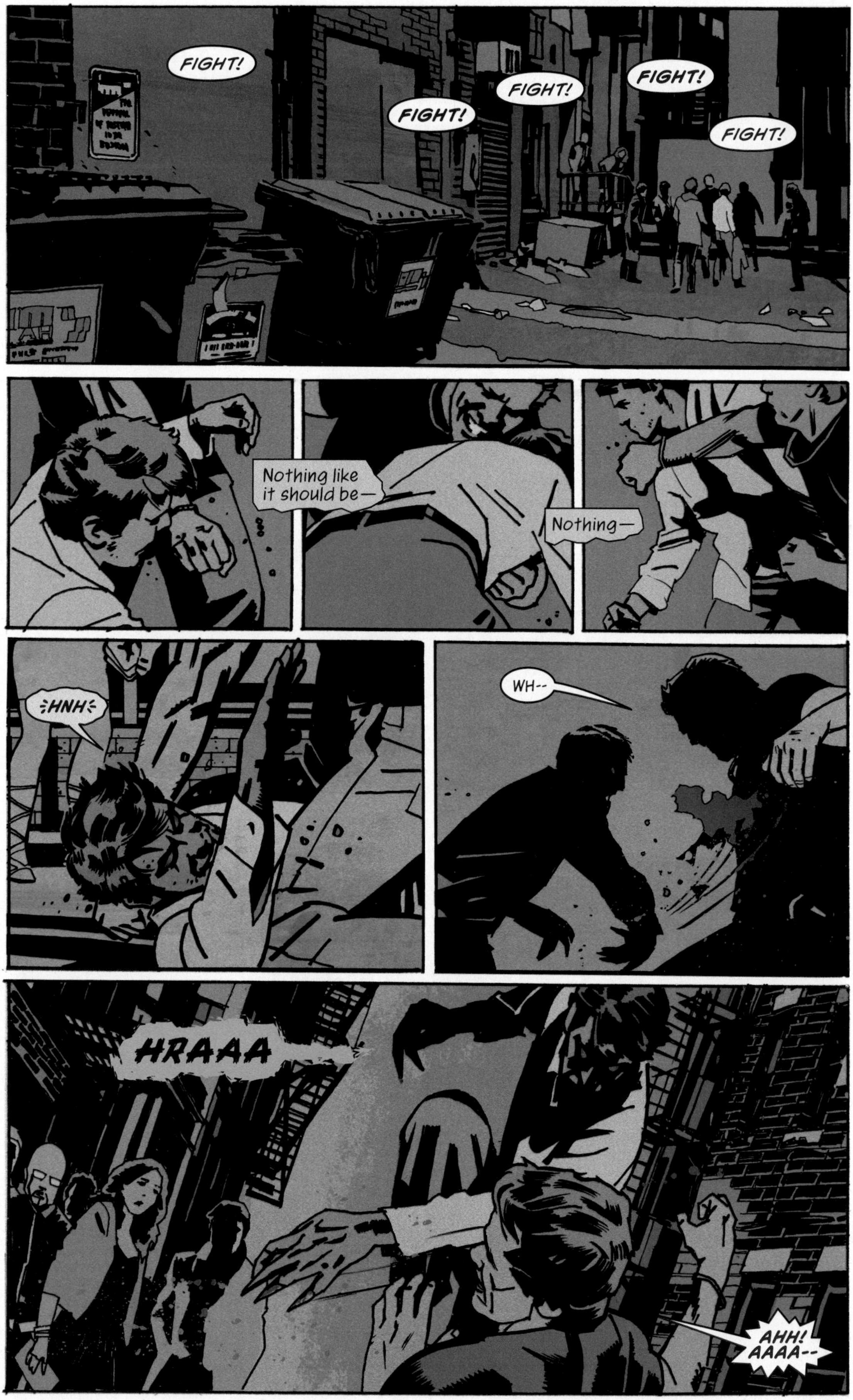
FIGHT!
FIGHT!
FIGHT!
FIGHT!
FIGHT!
Nothing like it should be—
Nothing—
HNH
WH--
HRAAA
AHH! AAAA--

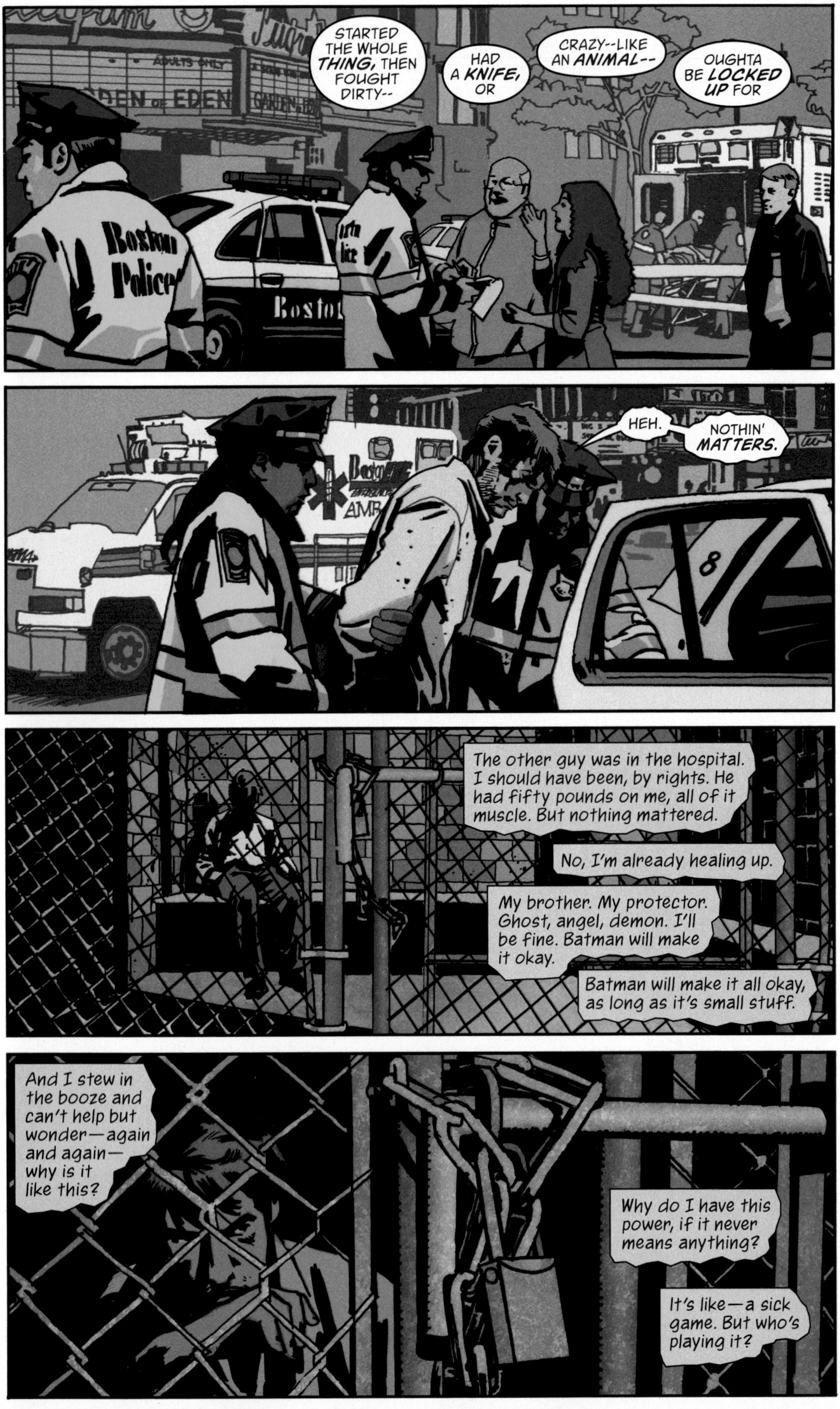
STARTED THE WHOLE THING, THEN FOUGHT DIRTY--
HAD A KNIFE, OR
CRAZY--LIKE AN ANIMAL--
OUGHTA BE LOCKED UP FOR
ADULTS ONLY
Boston Police
HEH.
NOTHIN' MATTERS.
The other guy was in the hospital. I should have been, by rights. He had fifty pounds on me, all of it muscle. But nothing mattered.
No, I'm already healing up.
My brother. My protector. Ghost, angel, demon. I'll be fine. Batman will make it okay.
Batman will make it all okay, as long as it's small stuff.
And I stew in the booze and can't help but wonder—again and again—why is it like this?
Why do I have this power, if it never means anything?
It's like—a sick game. But who's playing it?

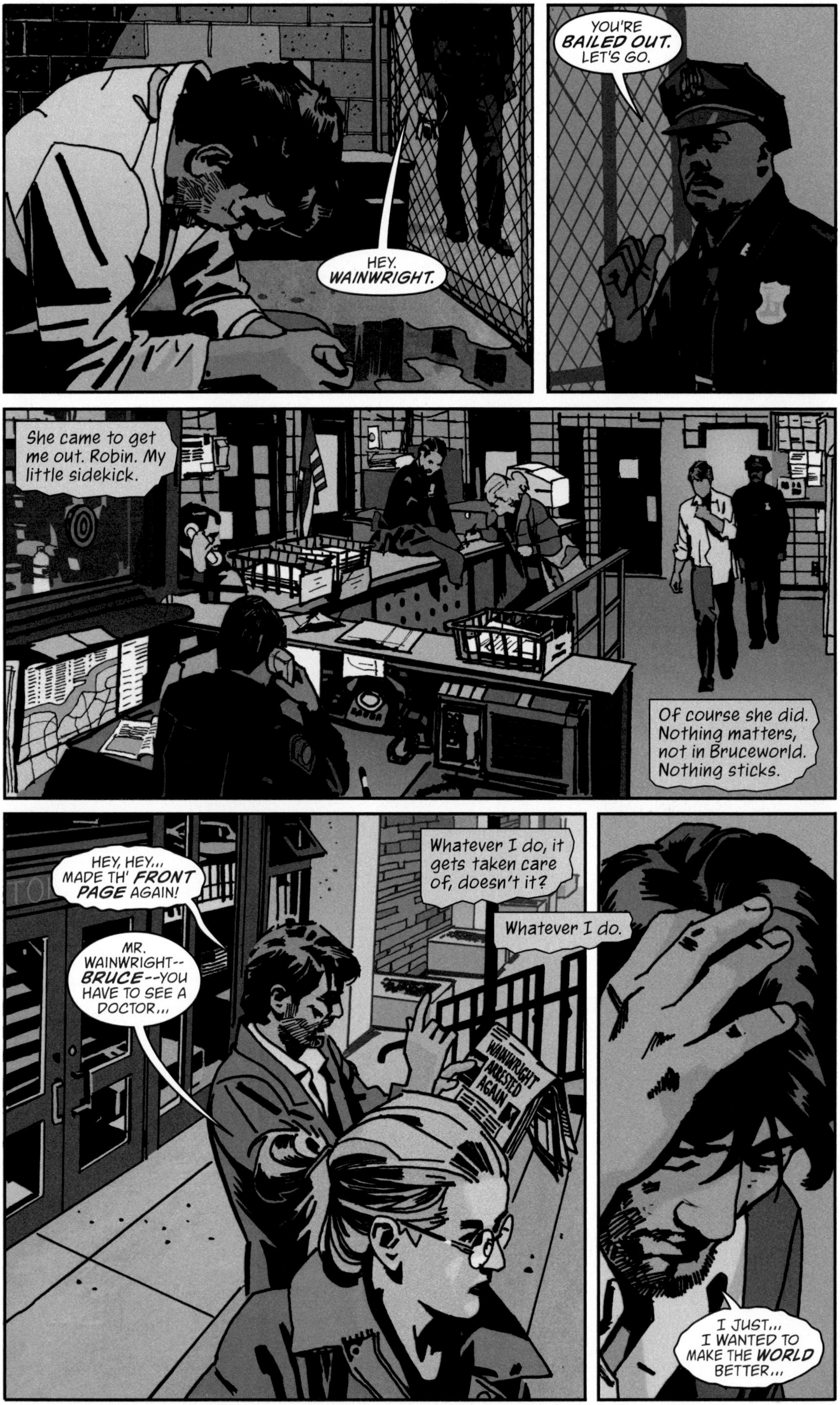
HEY. WAINWRIGHT.
YOU'RE BAILED OUT. LET'S GO.
She came to get me out. Robin. My little sidekick.
Of course she did. Nothing matters, not in Bruceworld. Nothing sticks.
HEY, HEY... MADE TH' FRONT PAGE AGAIN!
MR. WAINWRIGHT--BRUCE--YOU HAVE TO SEE A DOCTOR...
Whatever I do, it gets taken care of, doesn't it?
Whatever I do.
WAINWRIGHT ARRESTED AGAIN
I JUST... I WANTED TO MAKE THE WORLD BETTER...

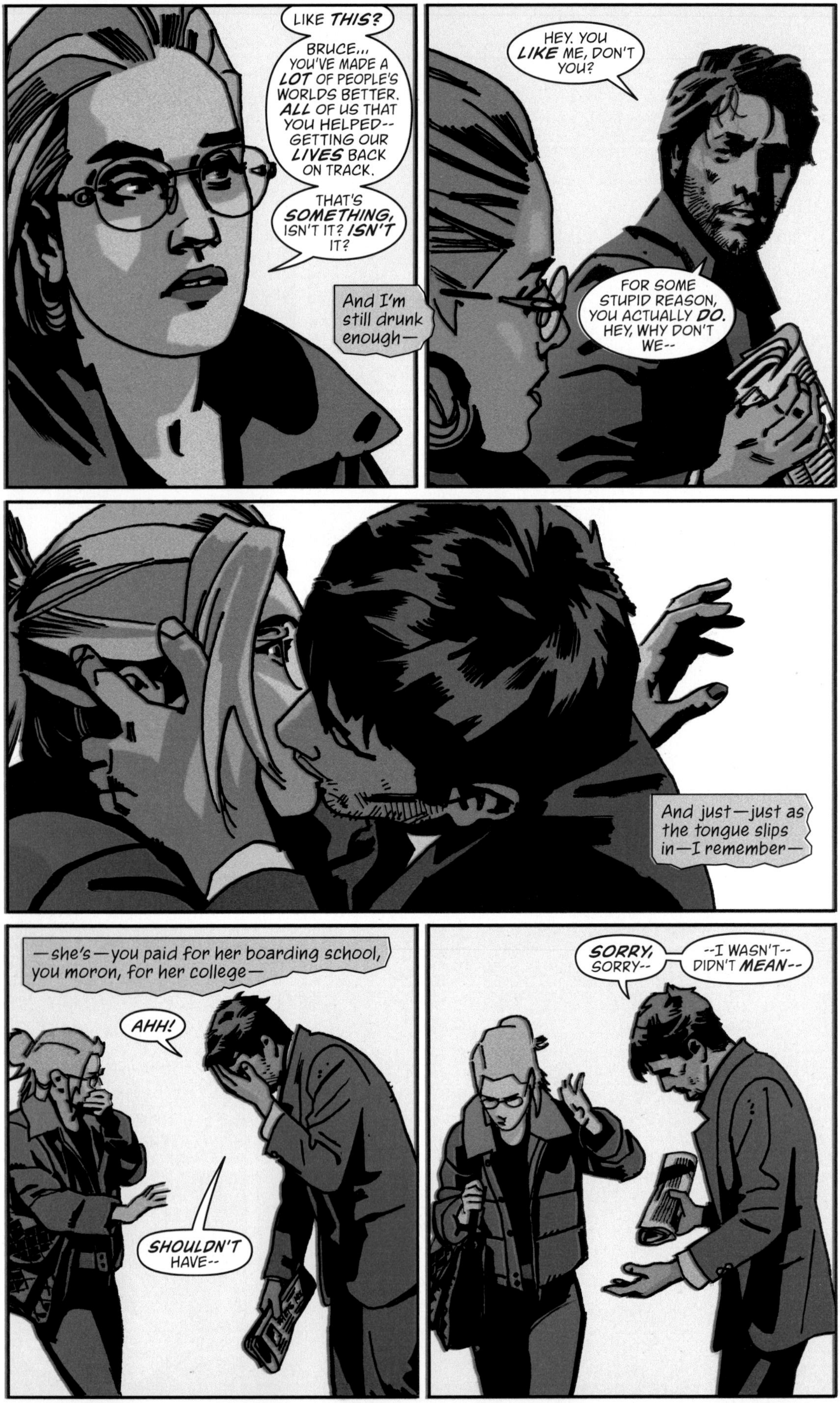

LIKE *THIS?*
BRUCE... YOU'VE MADE A *LOT* OF PEOPLE'S WORLDS BETTER. *ALL* OF US THAT YOU HELPED-- GETTING OUR *LIVES* BACK ON TRACK.
THAT'S *SOMETHING,* ISN'T IT? *ISN'T* IT?
And I'm still drunk enough—
HEY. YOU *LIKE* ME, DON'T YOU?
FOR SOME STUPID REASON, YOU ACTUALLY *DO.* HEY, WHY DON'T WE--
And just—just as the tongue slips in—I remember—
—she's—you paid for her boarding school, you moron, for her college—
AHH!
SHOULDN'T HAVE--
SORRY, SORRY--
--I WASN'T-- DIDN'T *MEAN*--

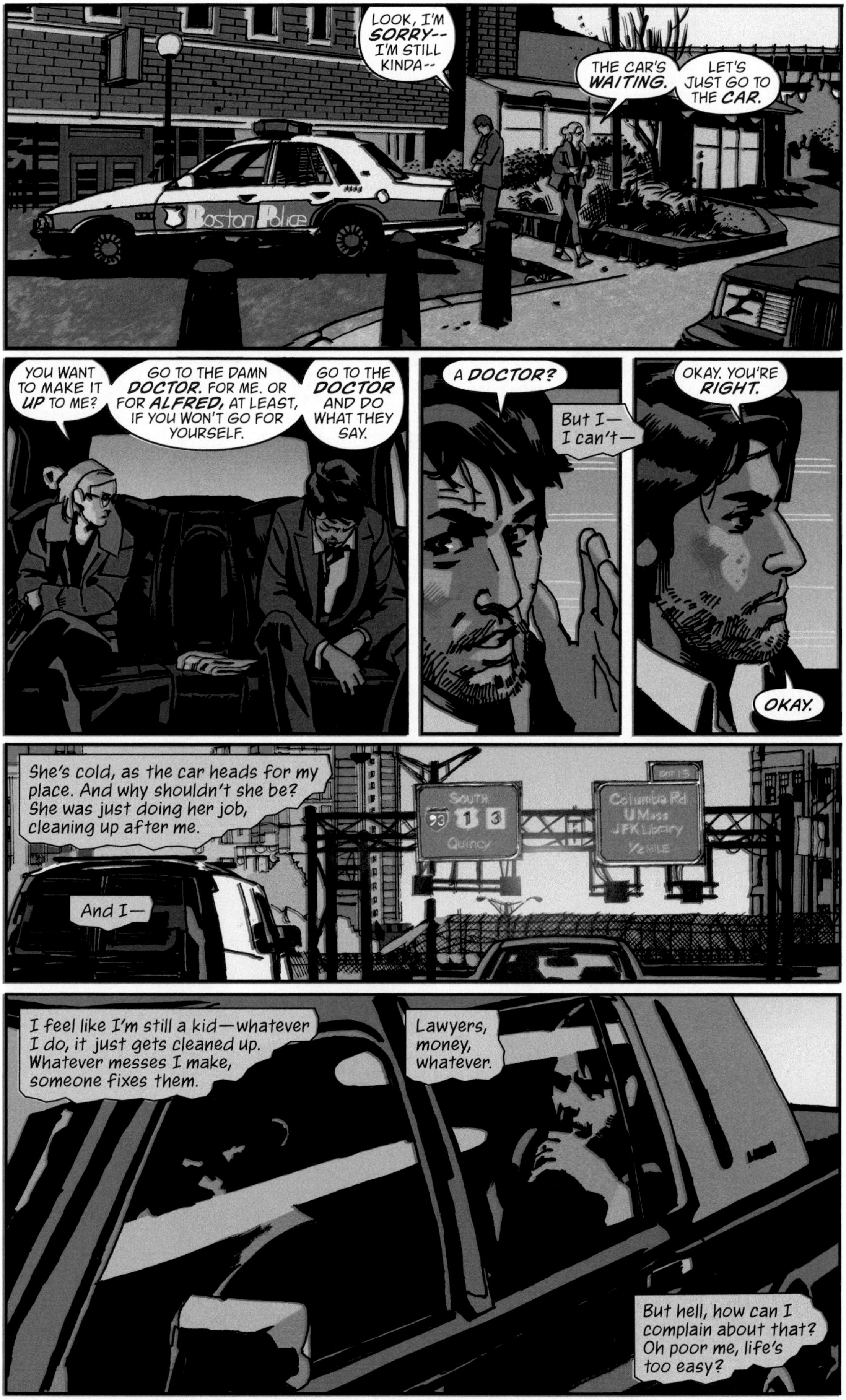
LOOK, I'M SORRY-- I'M STILL KINDA--
THE CAR'S WAITING.
LET'S JUST GO TO THE CAR.
Boston Police
YOU WANT TO MAKE IT UP TO ME?
GO TO THE DAMN DOCTOR. FOR ME. OR FOR ALFRED, AT LEAST, IF YOU WON'T GO FOR YOURSELF.
GO TO THE DOCTOR AND DO WHAT THEY SAY.
A DOCTOR?
But I— I can't—
OKAY. YOU'RE RIGHT.
OKAY.
She's cold, as the car heads for my place. And why shouldn't she be? She was just doing her job, cleaning up after me.
SOUTH
93 1 3
Quincy
Columbia Rd
U Mass
JFK Library
And I—
I feel like I'm still a kid—whatever I do, it just gets cleaned up. Whatever messes I make, someone fixes them.
Lawyers, money, whatever.
But hell, how can I complain about that? Oh poor me, life's too easy?

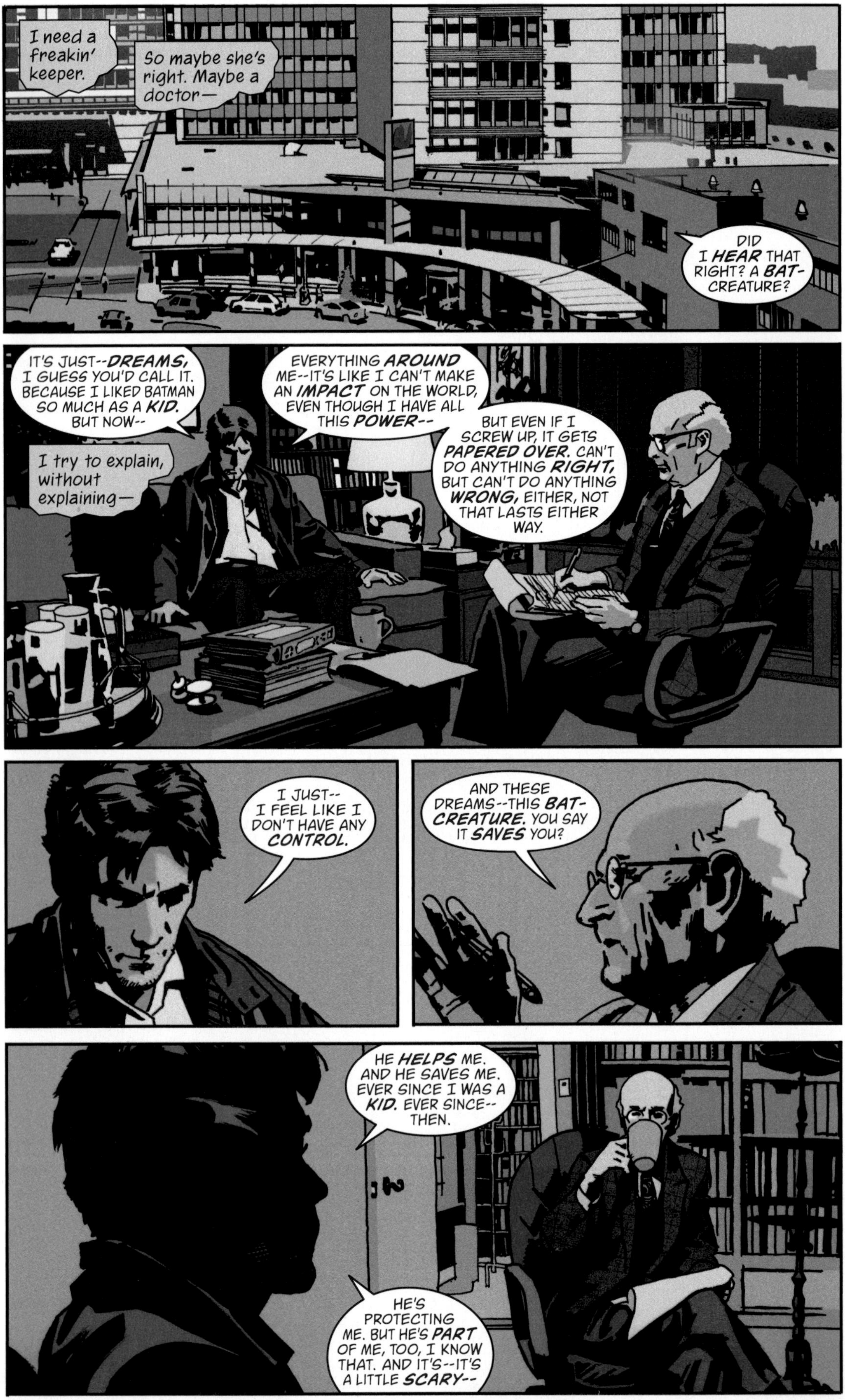
I need a freakin' keeper.
So maybe she's right. Maybe a doctor—
DID I HEAR THAT RIGHT? A BAT-CREATURE?
IT'S JUST--DREAMS, I GUESS YOU'D CALL IT. BECAUSE I LIKED BATMAN SO MUCH AS A KID. BUT NOW--
I try to explain, without explaining—
EVERYTHING AROUND ME--IT'S LIKE I CAN'T MAKE AN IMPACT ON THE WORLD, EVEN THOUGH I HAVE ALL THIS POWER--
BUT EVEN IF I SCREW UP, IT GETS PAPERED OVER. CAN'T DO ANYTHING RIGHT, BUT CAN'T DO ANYTHING WRONG, EITHER, NOT THAT LASTS EITHER WAY.
I JUST-- I FEEL LIKE I DON'T HAVE ANY CONTROL.
AND THESE DREAMS--THIS BAT-CREATURE. YOU SAY IT SAVES YOU?
HE HELPS ME. AND HE SAVES ME. EVER SINCE I WAS A KID. EVER SINCE-- THEN.
HE'S PROTECTING ME. BUT HE'S PART OF ME, TOO, I KNOW THAT. AND IT'S--IT'S A LITTLE SCARY--

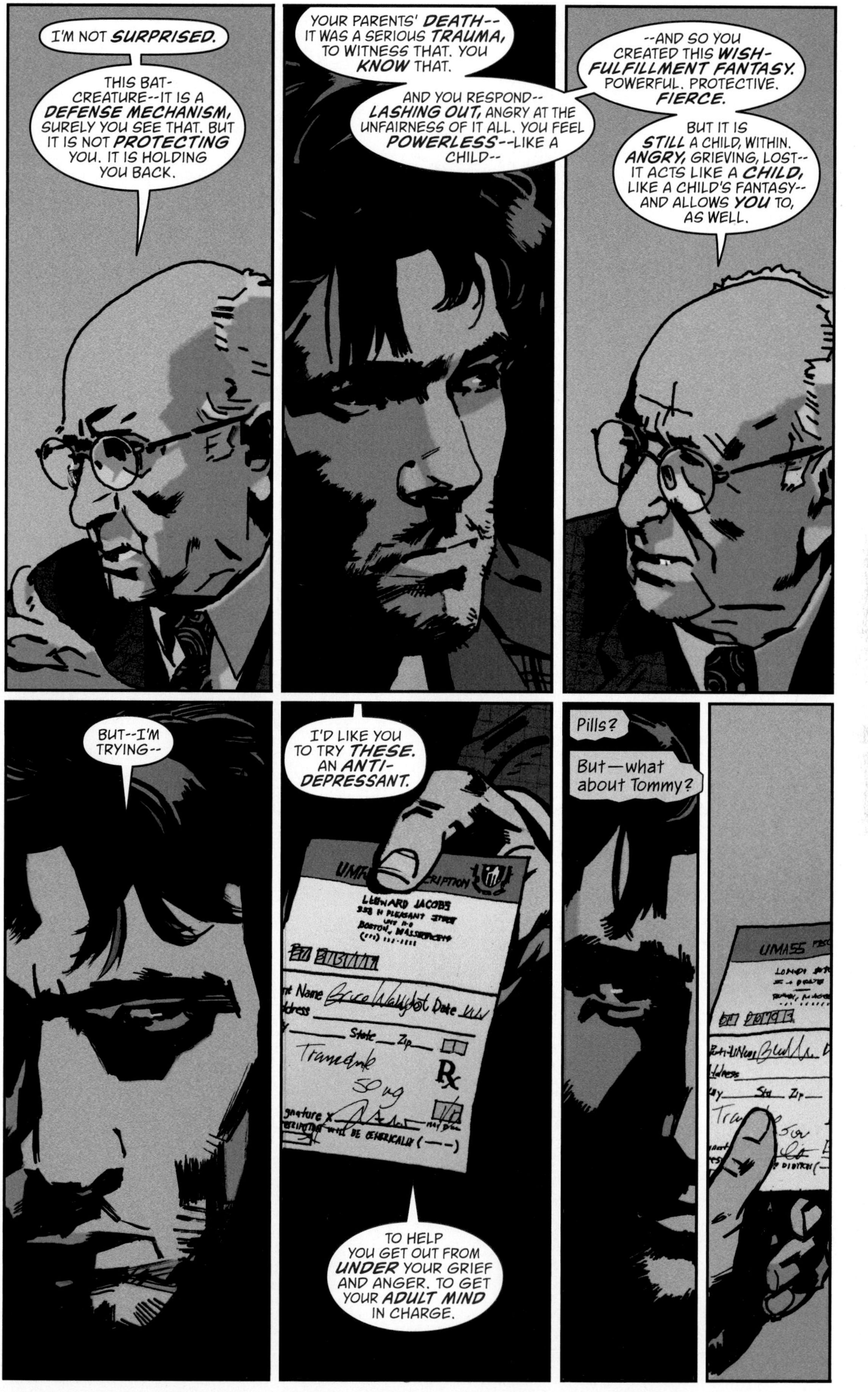
I'M NOT SURPRISED.
THIS BAT-CREATURE--IT IS A DEFENSE MECHANISM, SURELY YOU SEE THAT. BUT IT IS NOT PROTECTING YOU. IT IS HOLDING YOU BACK.
YOUR PARENTS' DEATH--IT WAS A SERIOUS TRAUMA, TO WITNESS THAT. YOU KNOW THAT.
AND YOU RESPOND--LASHING OUT, ANGRY AT THE UNFAIRNESS OF IT ALL. YOU FEEL POWERLESS--LIKE A CHILD--
--AND SO YOU CREATED THIS WISH-FULFILLMENT FANTASY. POWERFUL. PROTECTIVE. FIERCE.
BUT IT IS STILL A CHILD, WITHIN. ANGRY, GRIEVING, LOST--IT ACTS LIKE A CHILD, LIKE A CHILD'S FANTASY--AND ALLOWS YOU TO, AS WELL.
BUT--I'M TRYING--
I'D LIKE YOU TO TRY THESE. AN ANTI-DEPRESSANT.
TO HELP YOU GET OUT FROM UNDER YOUR GRIEF AND ANGER. TO GET YOUR ADULT MIND IN CHARGE.
Pills?
But—what about Tommy?

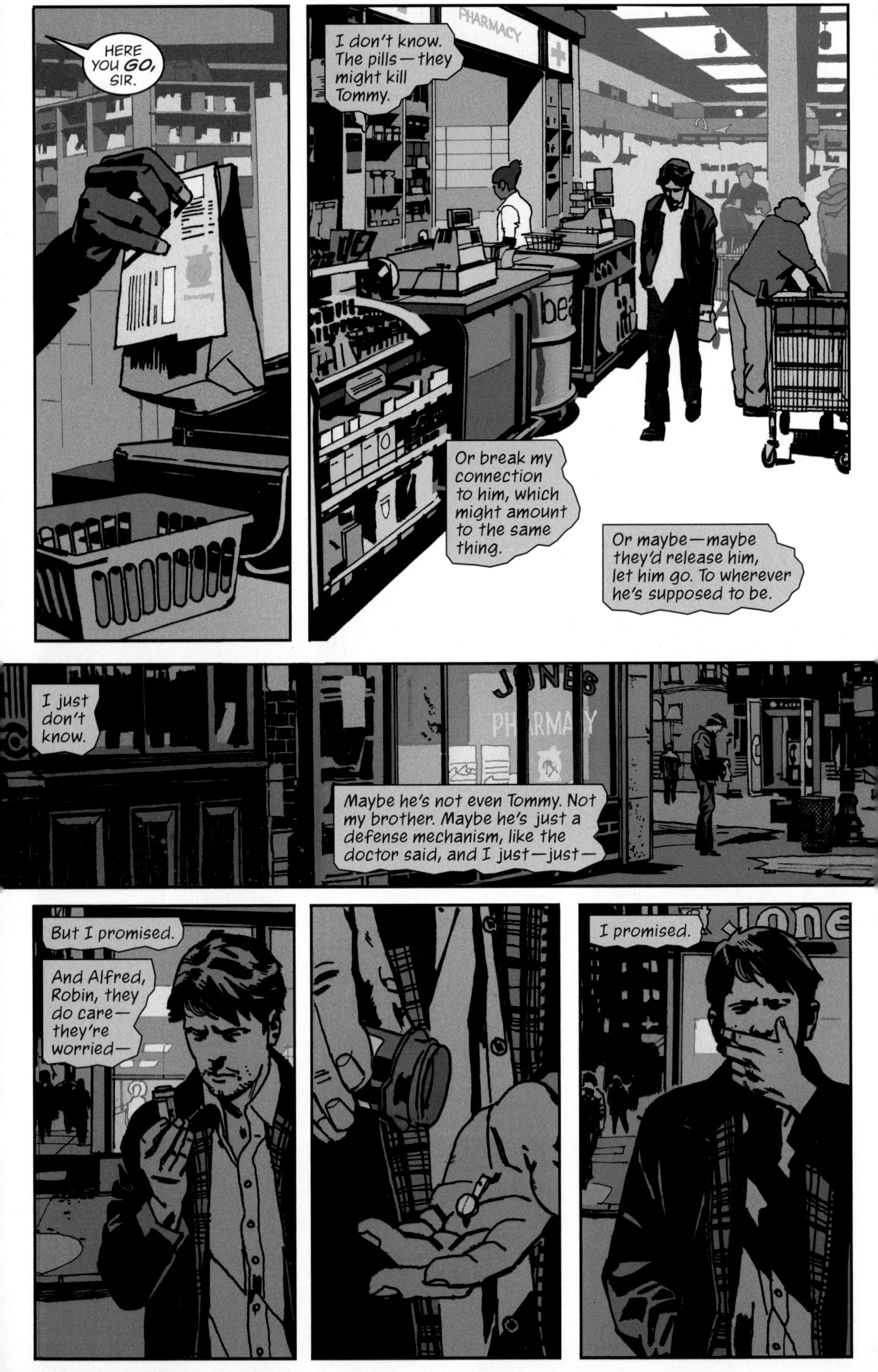
HERE YOU GO, SIR.
PHARMACY
I don't know. The pills—they might kill Tommy.
Or break my connection to him, which might amount to the same thing.
Or maybe—maybe they'd release him, let him go. To wherever he's supposed to be.
I just don't know.
PHARMA
Maybe he's not even Tommy. Not my brother. Maybe he's just a defense mechanism, like the doctor said, and I just—just—
But I promised.
And Alfred, Robin, they do care—they're worried—
I promised.

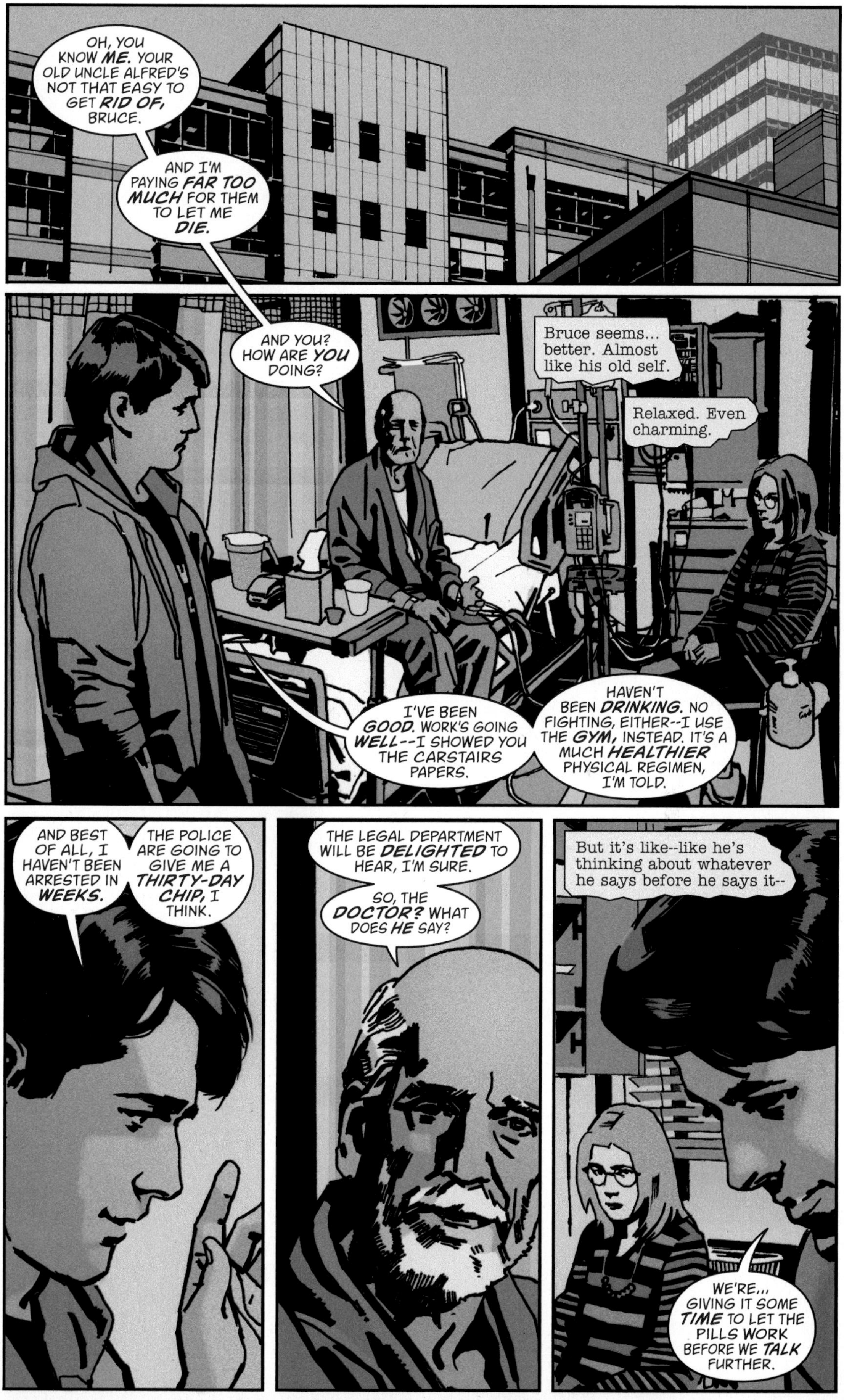
OH, YOU KNOW ME. YOUR OLD UNCLE ALFRED'S NOT THAT EASY TO GET RID OF, BRUCE.
AND I'M PAYING FAR TOO MUCH FOR THEM TO LET ME DIE.
AND YOU? HOW ARE YOU DOING?
Bruce seems... better. Almost like his old self.
Relaxed. Even charming.
I'VE BEEN GOOD. WORK'S GOING WELL--I SHOWED YOU THE CARSTAIRS PAPERS.
HAVEN'T BEEN DRINKING. NO FIGHTING, EITHER--I USE THE GYM, INSTEAD. IT'S A MUCH HEALTHIER PHYSICAL REGIMEN, I'M TOLD.
AND BEST OF ALL, I HAVEN'T BEEN ARRESTED IN WEEKS.
THE POLICE ARE GOING TO GIVE ME A THIRTY-DAY CHIP, I THINK.
THE LEGAL DEPARTMENT WILL BE DELIGHTED TO HEAR, I'M SURE.
SO, THE DOCTOR? WHAT DOES HE SAY?
But it's like--like he's thinking about whatever he says before he says it--
WE'RE... GIVING IT SOME TIME TO LET THE PILLS WORK BEFORE WE TALK FURTHER.

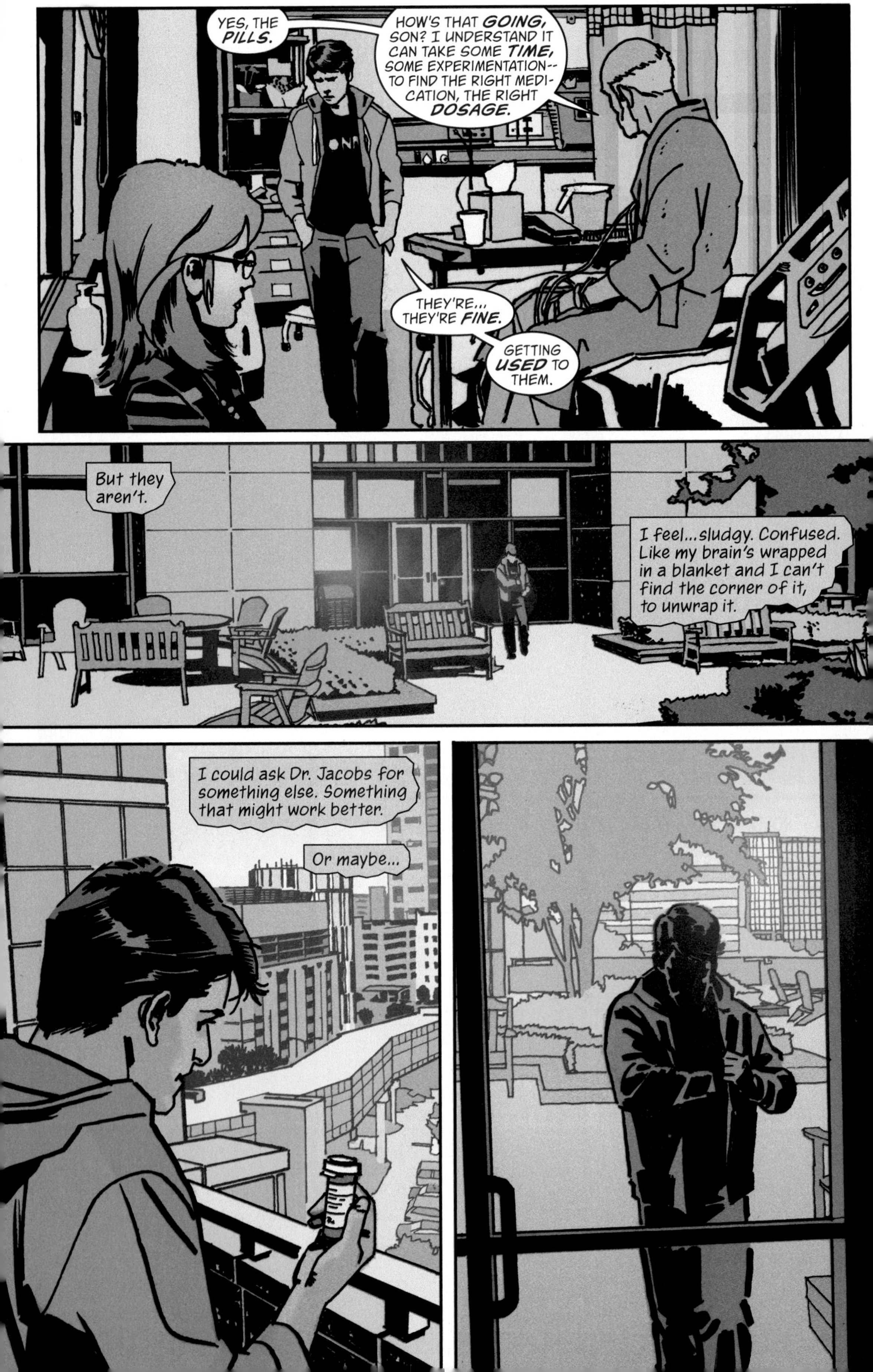

YES, THE PILLS.
HOW'S THAT GOING, SON? I UNDERSTAND IT CAN TAKE SOME TIME, SOME EXPERIMENTATION-- TO FIND THE RIGHT MEDI-CATION, THE RIGHT DOSAGE.
THEY'RE... THEY'RE FINE.
GETTING USED TO THEM.
But they aren't.
I feel...sludgy. Confused. Like my brain's wrapped in a blanket and I can't find the corner of it, to unwrap it.
I could ask Dr. Jacobs for something else. Something that might work better.
Or maybe...

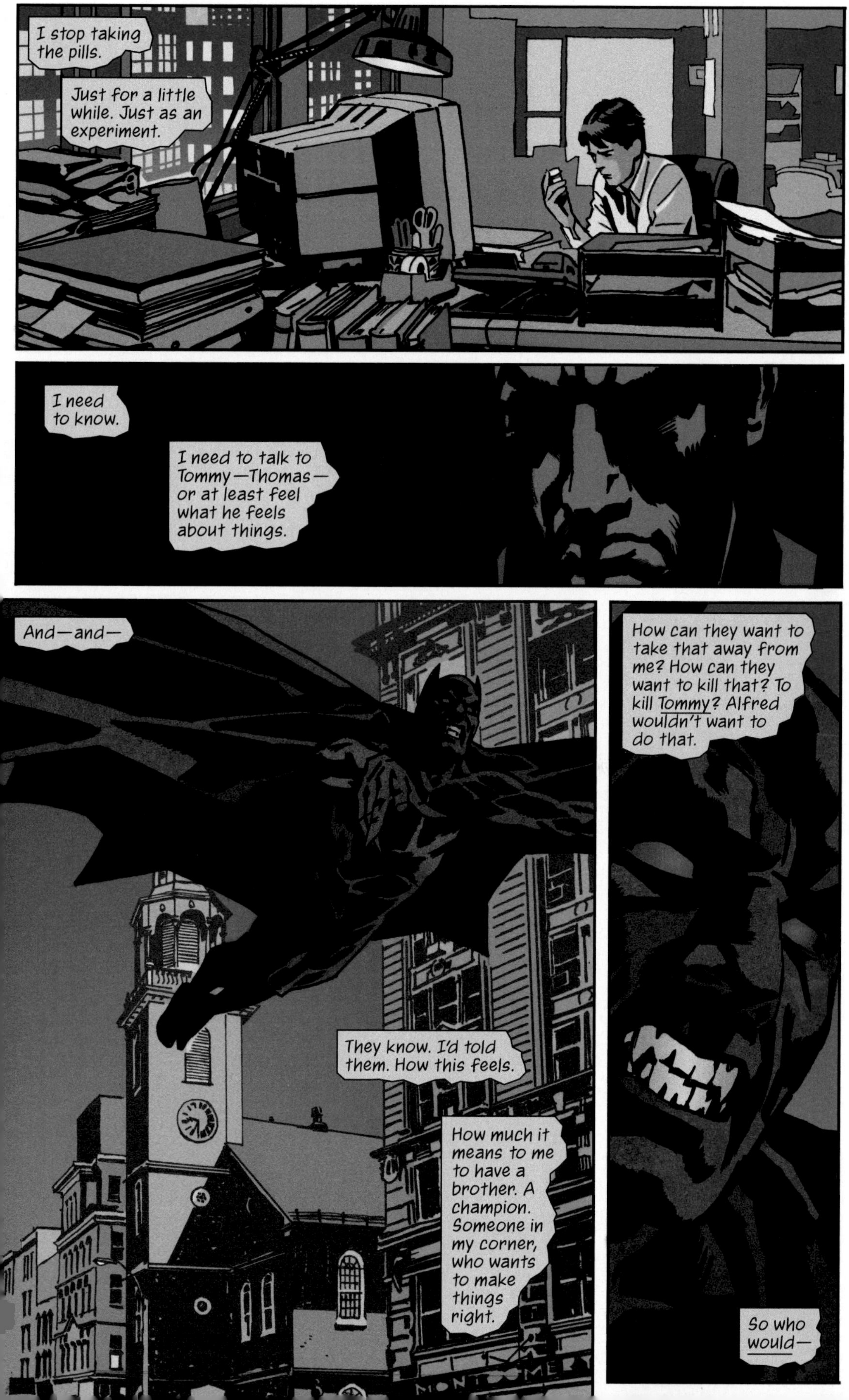
I stop taking the pills.
Just for a little while. Just as an experiment.
I need to know.
I need to talk to Tommy—Thomas—or at least feel what he feels about things.
And—and—
They know. I'd told them. How this feels.
How much it means to me to have a brother. A champion. Someone in my corner, who wants to make things right.
How can they want to take that away from me? How can they want to kill that? To kill Tommy? Alfred wouldn't want to do that.
So who would—

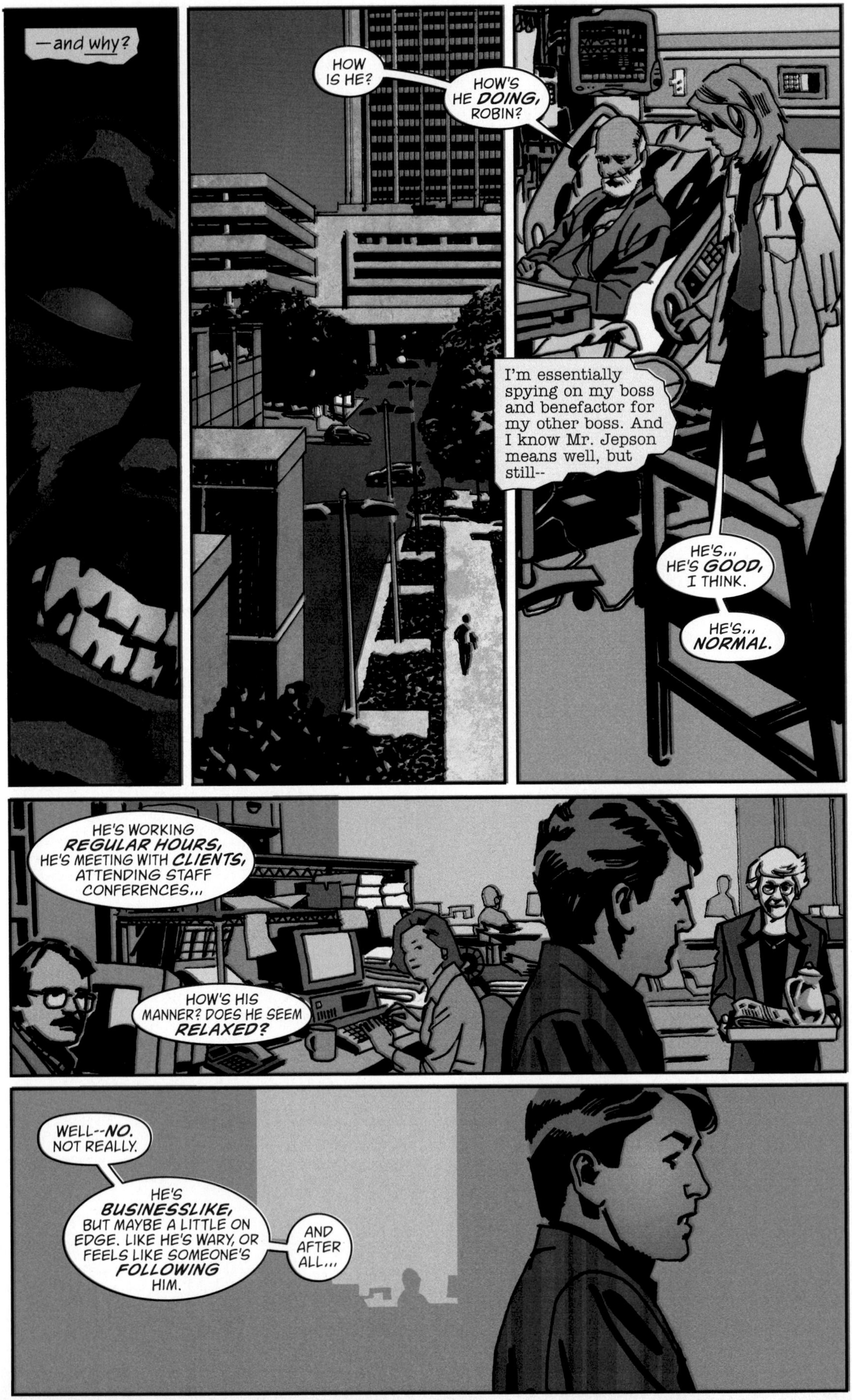
—and why?
HOW IS HE?
HOW'S HE DOING, ROBIN?
I'm essentially spying on my boss and benefactor for my other boss. And I know Mr. Jepson means well, but still--
HE'S... HE'S GOOD, I THINK.
HE'S... NORMAL.
HE'S WORKING REGULAR HOURS, HE'S MEETING WITH CLIENTS, ATTENDING STAFF CONFERENCES...
HOW'S HIS MANNER? DOES HE SEEM RELAXED?
WELL--NO. NOT REALLY.
HE'S BUSINESSLIKE, BUT MAYBE A LITTLE ON EDGE. LIKE HE'S WARY, OR FEELS LIKE SOMEONE'S FOLLOWING HIM.
AND AFTER ALL...

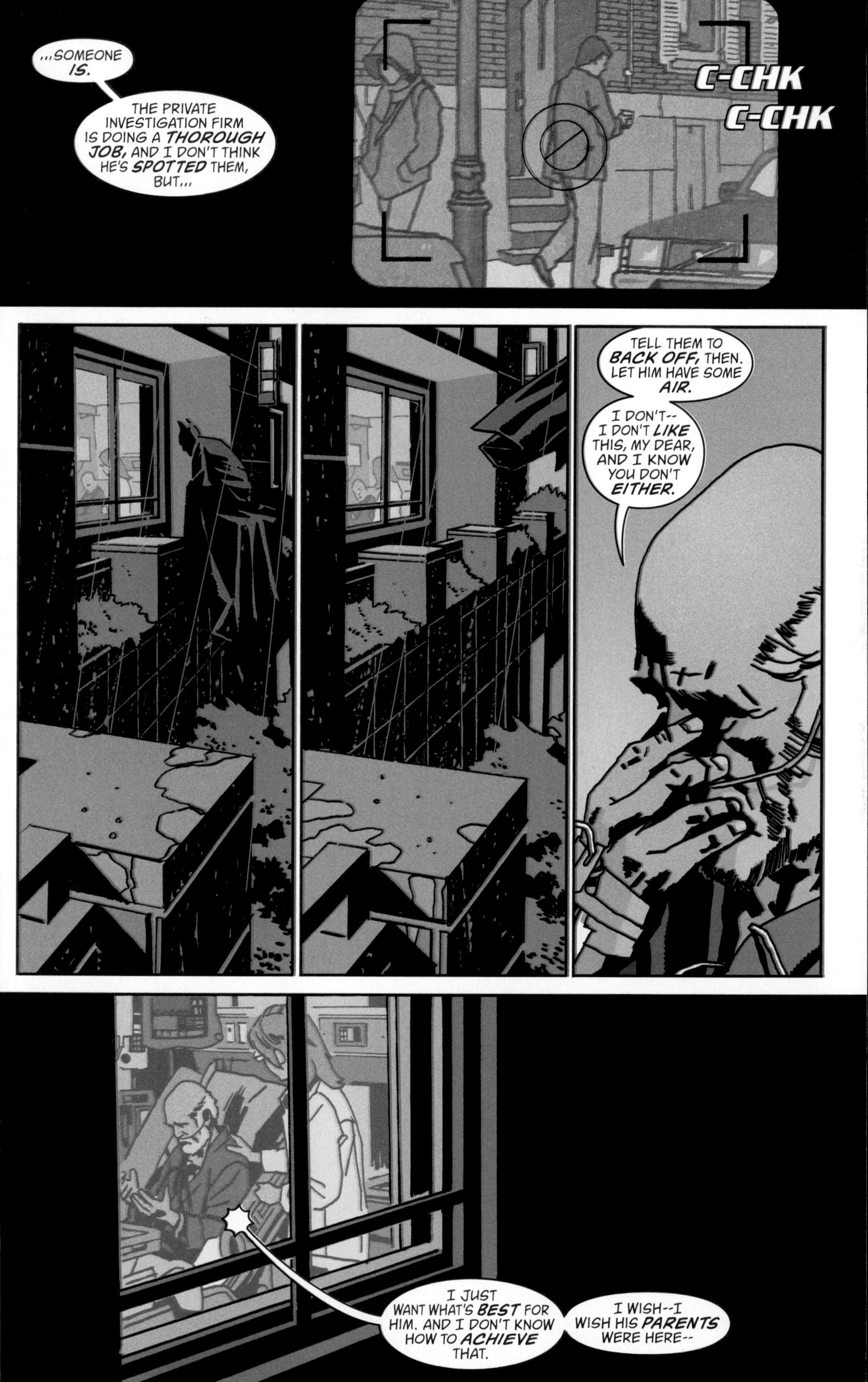
...SOMEONE *IS.*
THE PRIVATE INVESTIGATION FIRM IS DOING A *THOROUGH JOB,* AND I DON'T THINK HE'S *SPOTTED* THEM, BUT...
C-CHK
C-CHK
TELL THEM TO *BACK OFF,* THEN. LET HIM HAVE SOME *AIR.*
I DON'T-- I DON'T *LIKE* THIS, MY DEAR, AND I KNOW YOU DON'T *EITHER.*
I JUST WANT WHAT'S *BEST* FOR HIM. AND I DON'T KNOW HOW TO *ACHIEVE* THAT.
I WISH--I WISH HIS *PARENTS* WERE HERE--

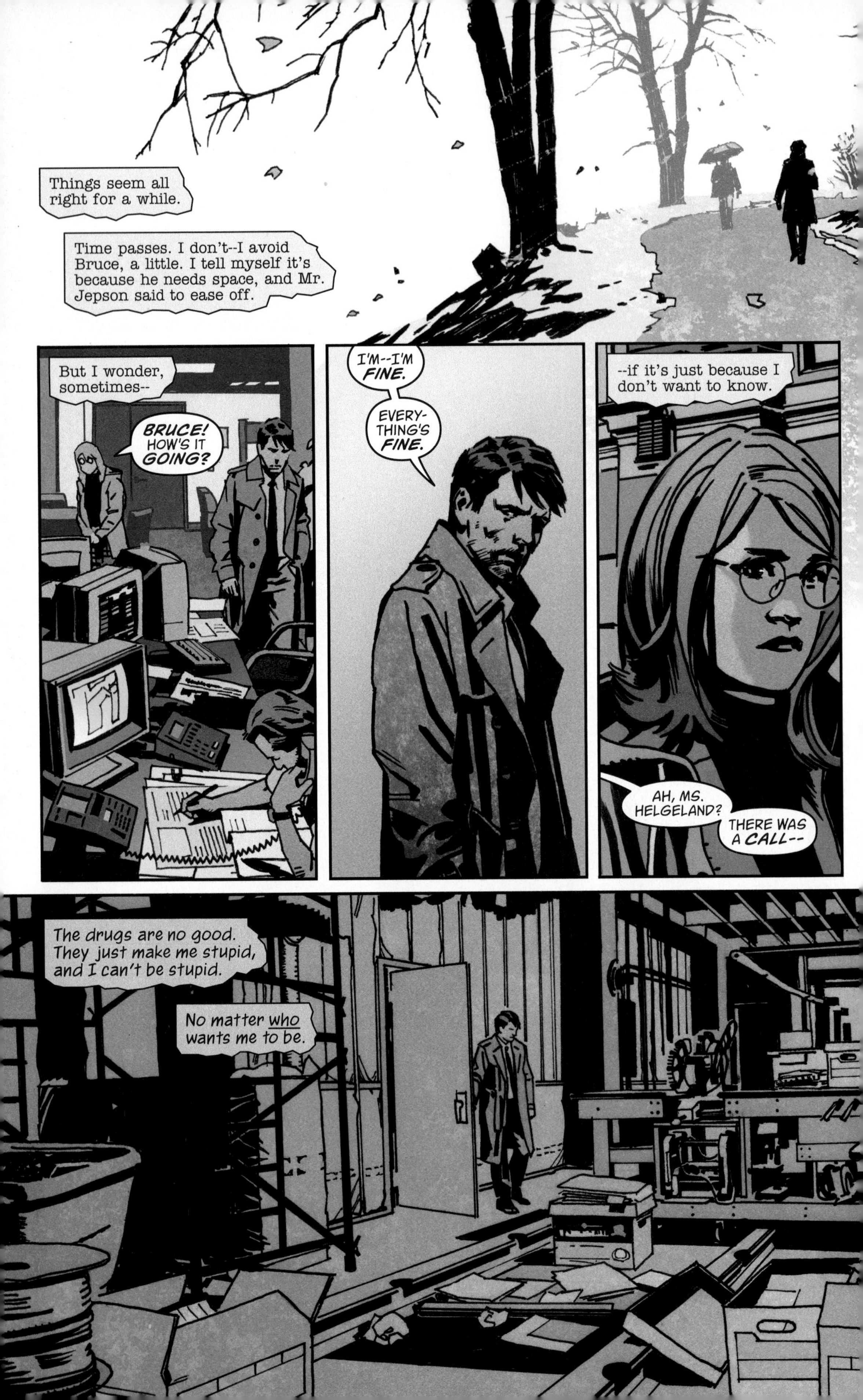

Things seem all right for a while.
Time passes. I don't--I avoid Bruce, a little. I tell myself it's because he needs space, and Mr. Jepson said to ease off.
But I wonder, sometimes--
BRUCE! HOW'S IT GOING?
I'M--I'M FINE.
EVERY-THING'S FINE.
--if it's just because I don't want to know.
AH, MS. HELGELAND?
THERE WAS A CALL--
The drugs are no good. They just make me stupid, and I can't be stupid.
No matter who wants me to be.

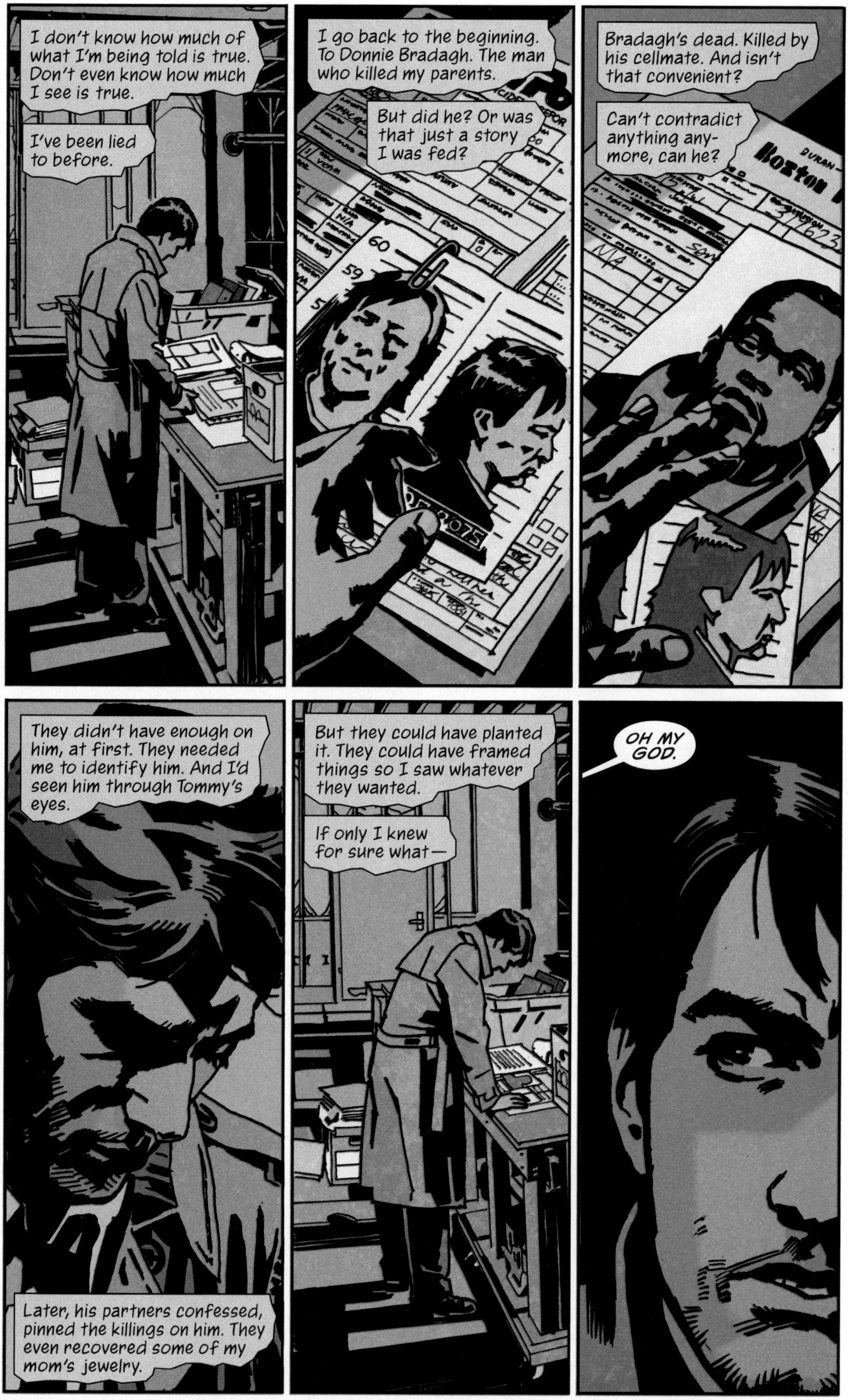
I don't know how much of what I'm being told is true. Don't even know how much I see is true.
I've been lied to before.
I go back to the beginning. To Donnie Bradagh. The man who killed my parents.
But did he? Or was that just a story I was fed?
Bradagh's dead. Killed by his cellmate. And isn't that convenient?
Can't contradict anything any-more, can he?
They didn't have enough on him, at first. They needed me to identify him. And I'd seen him through Tommy's eyes.
Later, his partners confessed, pinned the killings on him. They even recovered some of my mom's jewelry.
But they could have planted it. They could have framed things so I saw whatever they wanted.
If only I knew for sure what—
OH MY GOD.

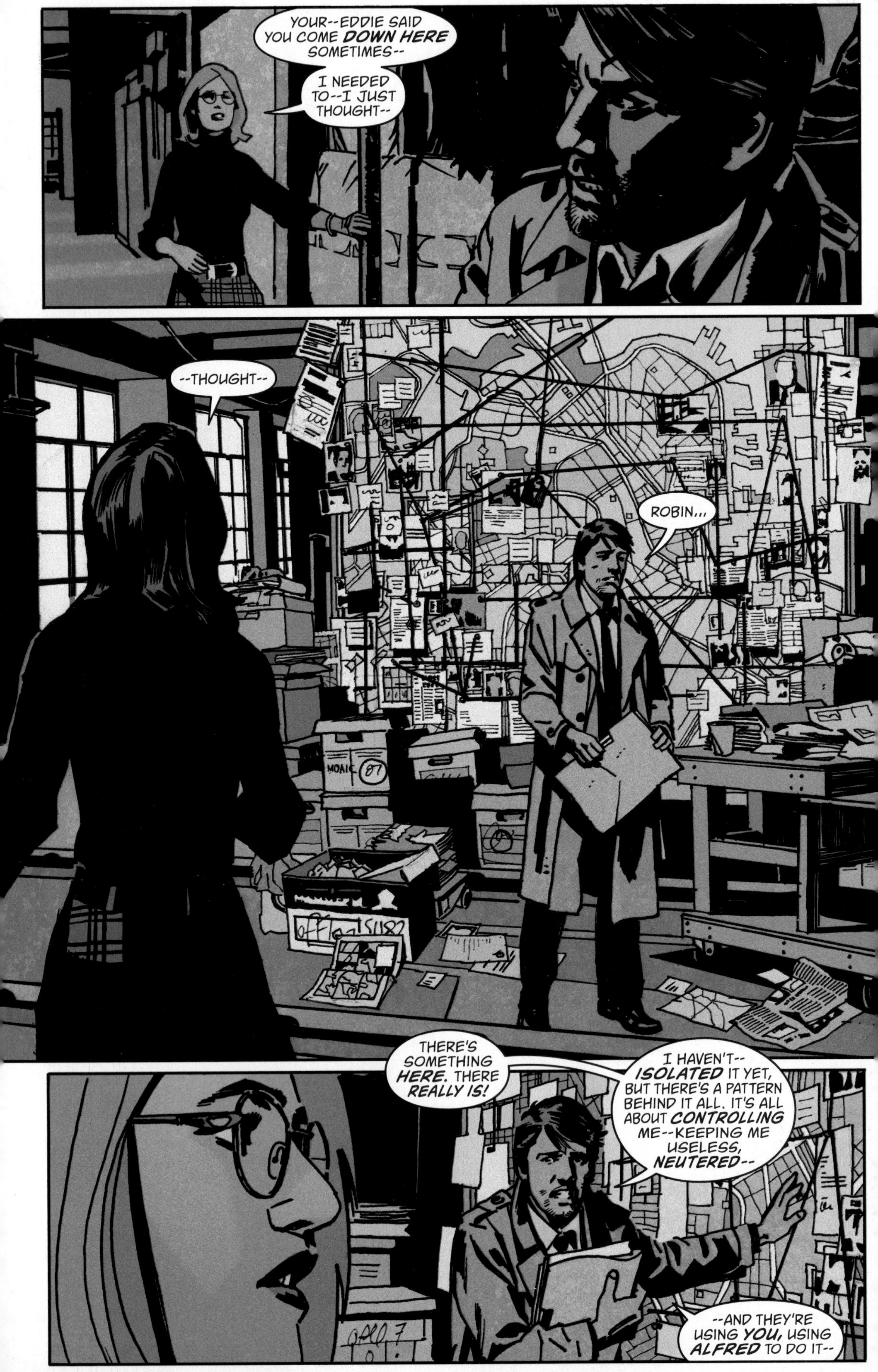
YOUR--EDDIE SAID YOU COME DOWN HERE SOMETIMES--
I NEEDED TO--I JUST THOUGHT--
--THOUGHT--
ROBIN...
THERE'S SOMETHING HERE. THERE REALLY IS!
I HAVEN'T--ISOLATED IT YET, BUT THERE'S A PATTERN BEHIND IT ALL. IT'S ALL ABOUT CONTROLLING ME--KEEPING ME USELESS, NEUTERED--
--AND THEY'RE USING YOU, USING ALFRED TO DO IT--

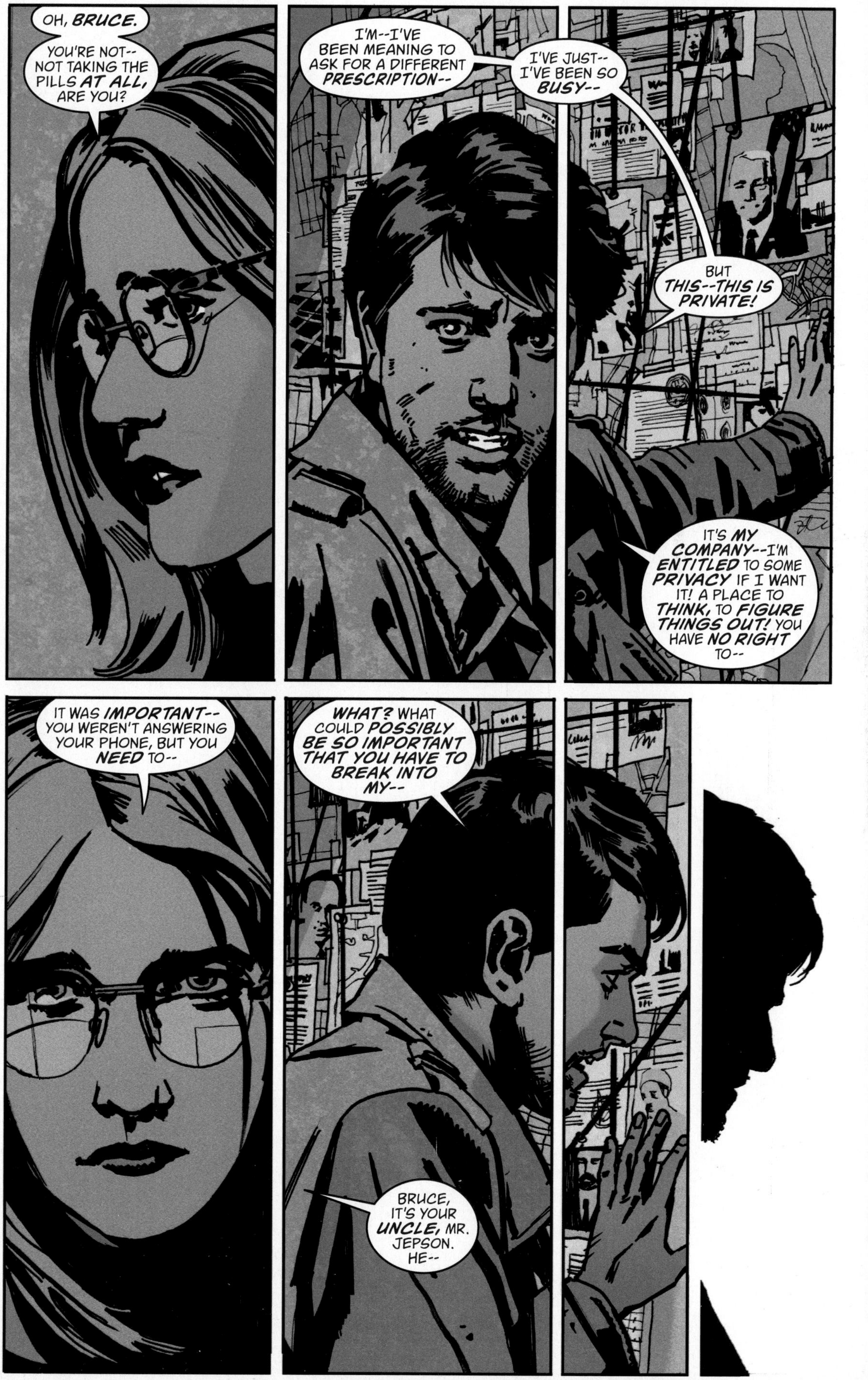
OH, BRUCE.
YOU'RE NOT-- NOT TAKING THE PILLS AT ALL, ARE YOU?
I'M--I'VE BEEN MEANING TO ASK FOR A DIFFERENT PRESCRIPTION--
I'VE JUST-- I'VE BEEN SO BUSY--
BUT THIS--THIS IS PRIVATE!
IT'S MY COMPANY--I'M ENTITLED TO SOME PRIVACY IF I WANT IT! A PLACE TO THINK, TO FIGURE THINGS OUT! YOU HAVE NO RIGHT TO--
IT WAS IMPORTANT-- YOU WEREN'T ANSWERING YOUR PHONE, BUT YOU NEED TO--
WHAT? WHAT COULD POSSIBLY BE SO IMPORTANT THAT YOU HAVE TO BREAK INTO MY--
BRUCE, IT'S YOUR UNCLE, MR. JEPSON. HE--

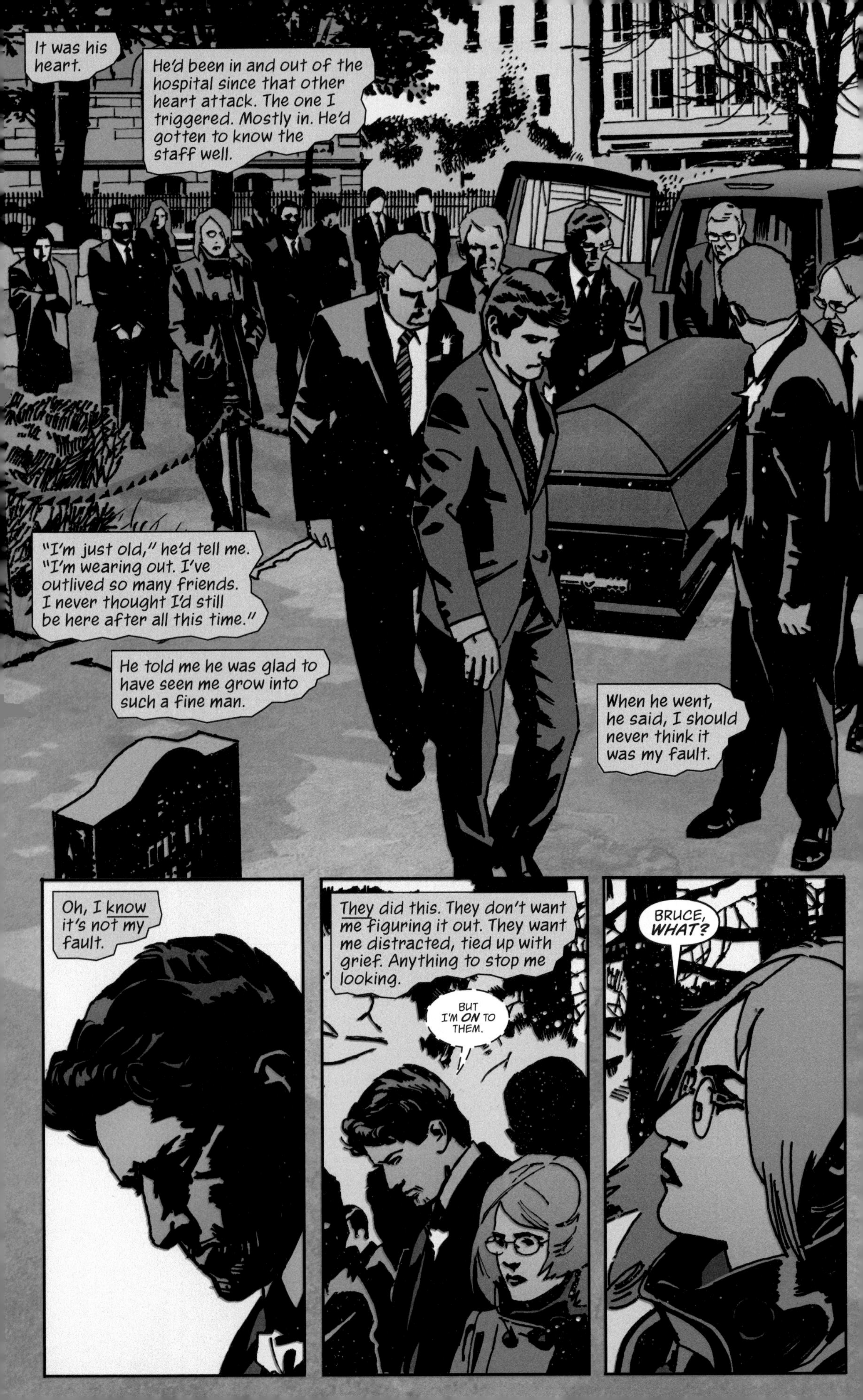

It was his heart.
He'd been in and out of the hospital since that other heart attack. The one I triggered. Mostly in. He'd gotten to know the staff well.
"I'm just old," he'd tell me. "I'm wearing out. I've outlived so many friends. I never thought I'd still be here after all this time."
He told me he was glad to have seen me grow into such a fine man.
When he went, he said, I should never think it was my fault.
Oh, I know it's not my fault.
They did this. They don't want me figuring it out. They want me distracted, tied up with grief. Anything to stop me looking.
BUT I'M ON TO THEM.
BRUCE, WHAT?

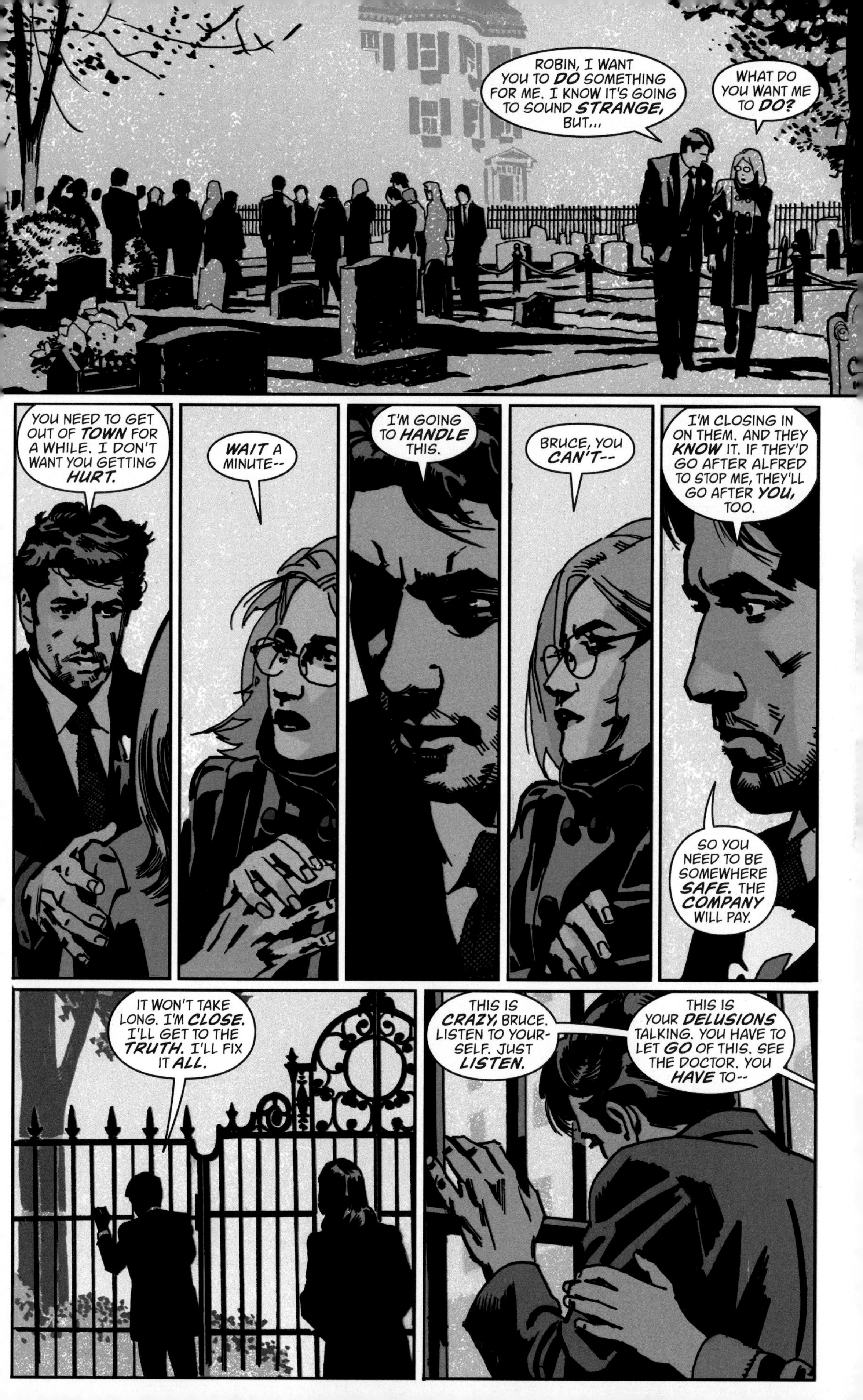
ROBIN, I WANT YOU TO DO SOMETHING FOR ME. I KNOW IT'S GOING TO SOUND STRANGE, BUT...
WHAT DO YOU WANT ME TO DO?
YOU NEED TO GET OUT OF TOWN FOR A WHILE. I DON'T WANT YOU GETTING HURT.
WAIT A MINUTE--
I'M GOING TO HANDLE THIS.
BRUCE, YOU CAN'T--
I'M CLOSING IN ON THEM. AND THEY KNOW IT. IF THEY'D GO AFTER ALFRED TO STOP ME, THEY'LL GO AFTER YOU, TOO.
SO YOU NEED TO BE SOMEWHERE SAFE. THE COMPANY WILL PAY.
IT WON'T TAKE LONG. I'M CLOSE. I'LL GET TO THE TRUTH. I'LL FIX IT ALL.
THIS IS CRAZY, BRUCE. LISTEN TO YOURSELF. JUST LISTEN.
THIS IS YOUR DELUSIONS TALKING. YOU HAVE TO LET GO OF THIS. SEE THE DOCTOR. YOU HAVE TO--

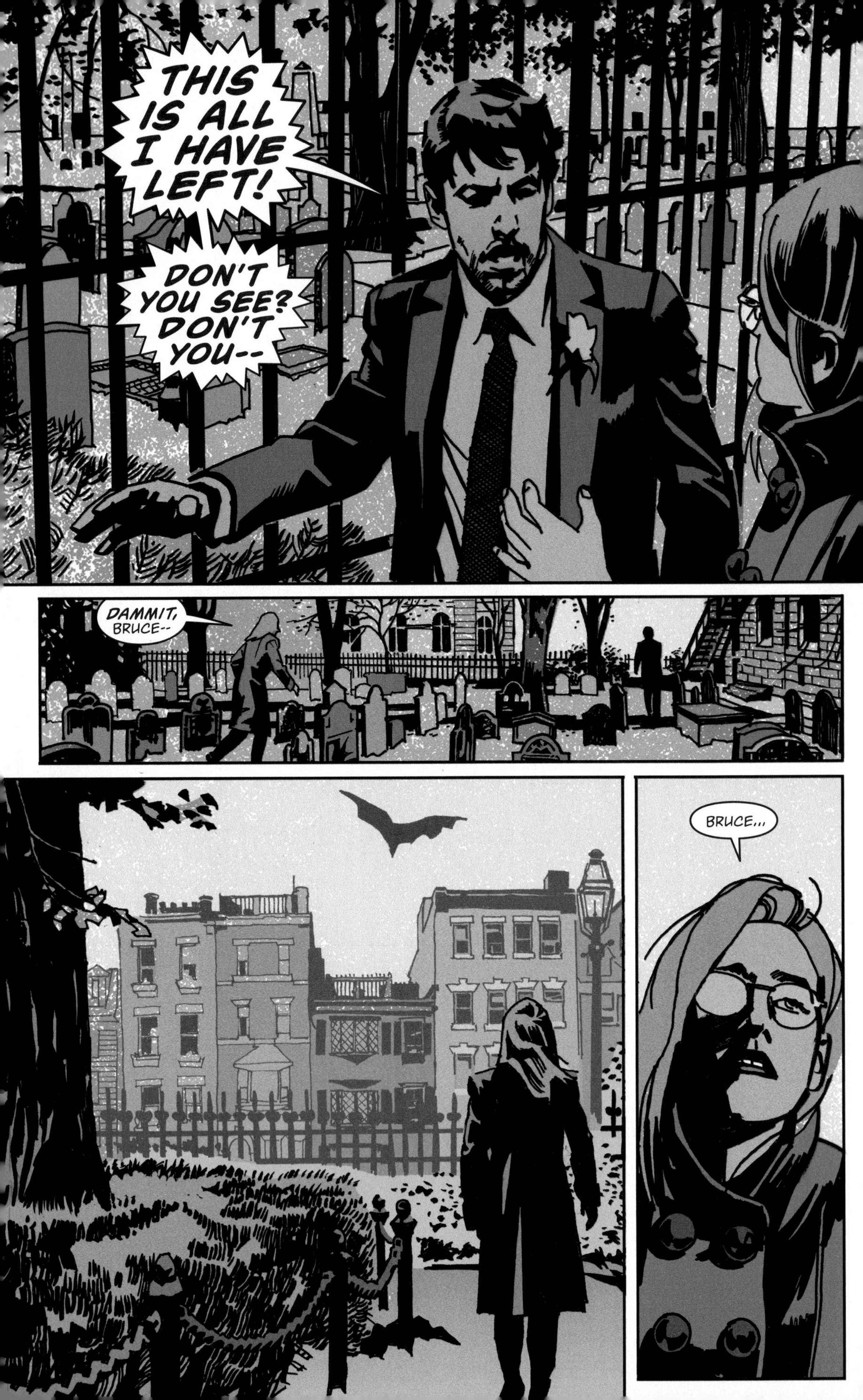
THIS IS ALL I HAVE LEFT!
DON'T YOU SEE? DON'T YOU--
DAMMIT, BRUCE--
BRUCE...

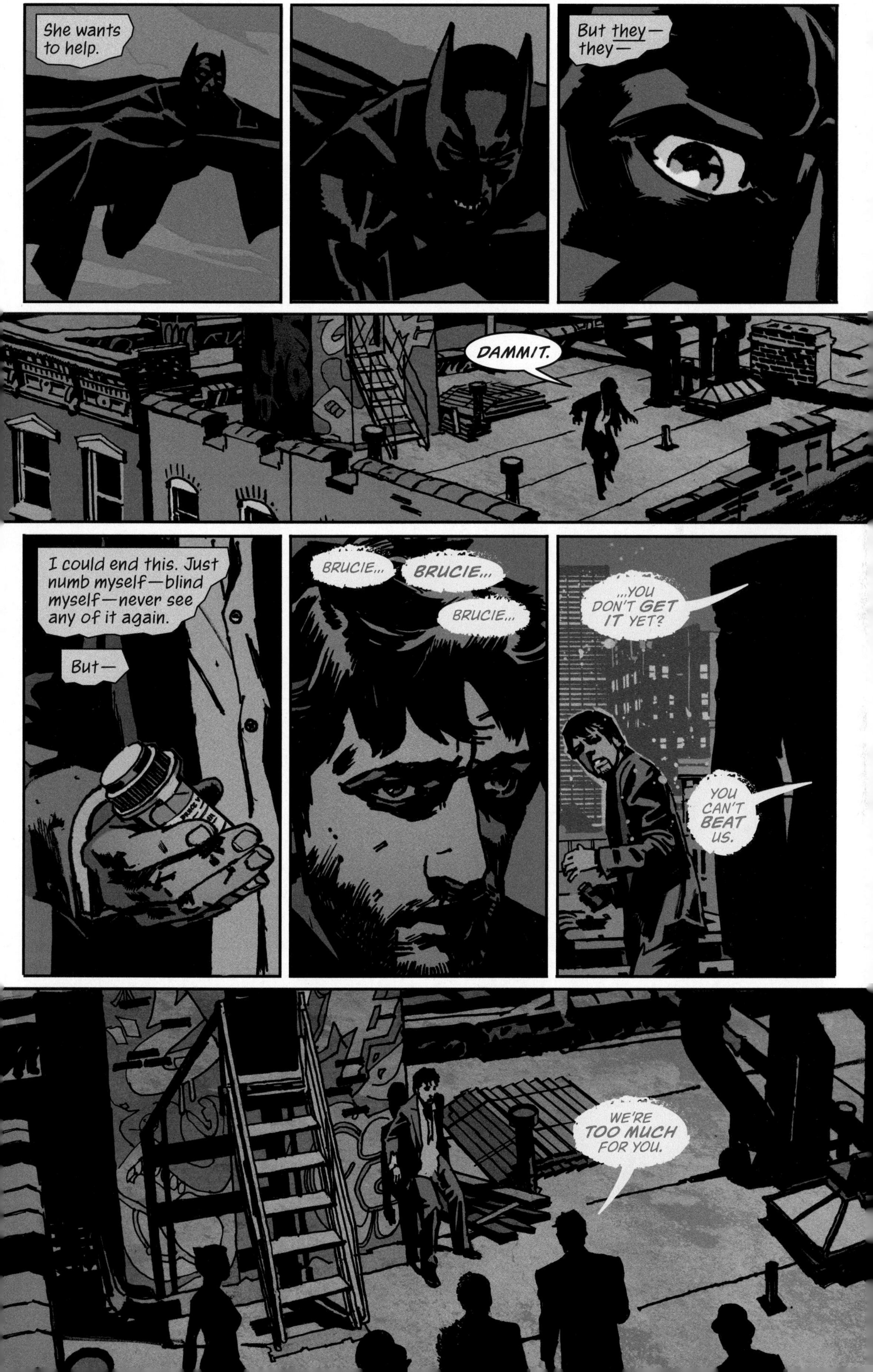

She wants to help.
But they— they—
DAMMIT.
I could end this. Just numb myself—blind myself—never see any of it again.
But—
BRUCIE...
BRUCIE...
BRUCIE...
...YOU DON'T GET IT YET?
YOU CAN'T BEAT US.
WE'RE TOO MUCH FOR YOU.

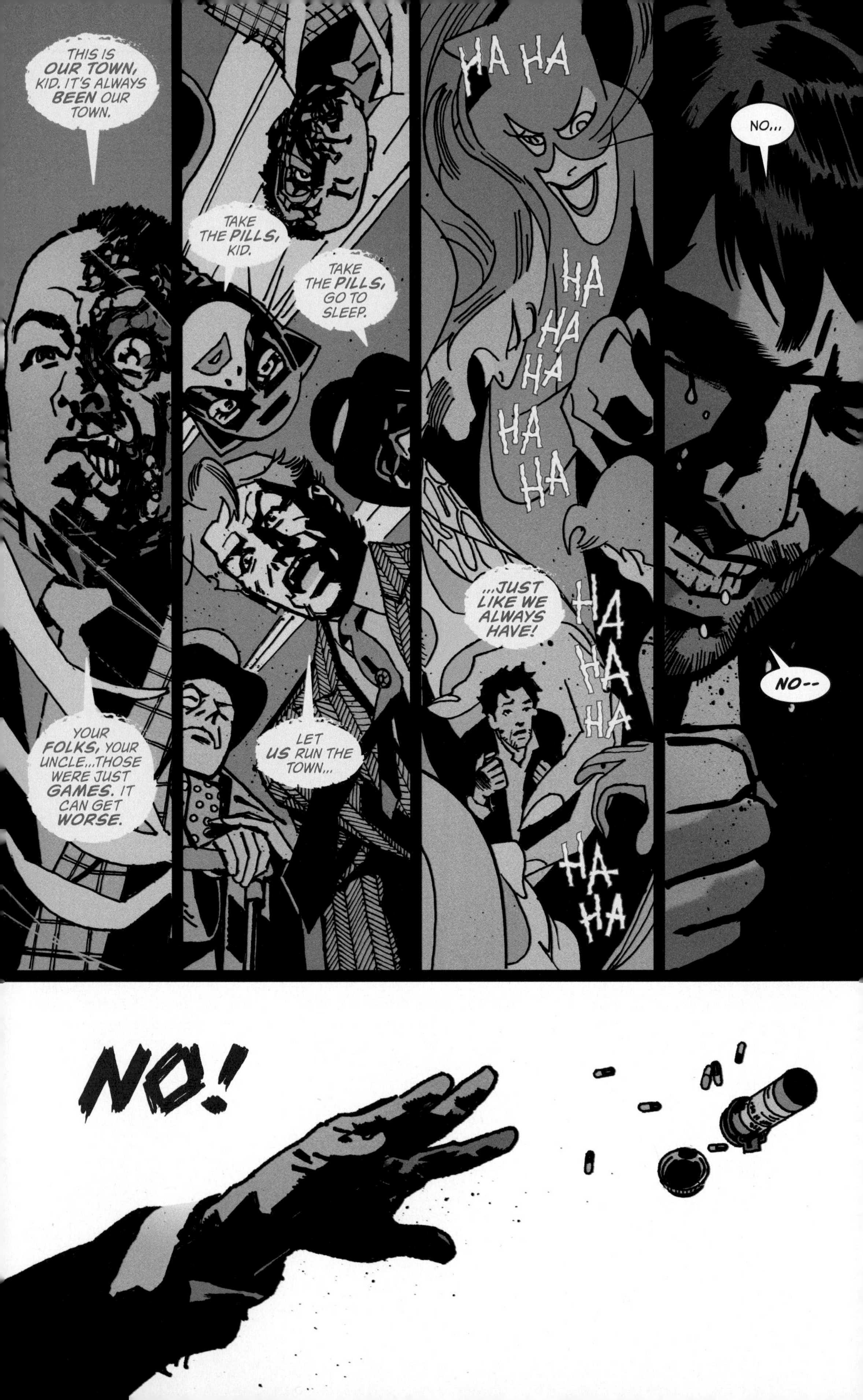
THIS IS OUR TOWN, KID. IT'S ALWAYS BEEN OUR TOWN.
YOUR FOLKS, YOUR UNCLE...THOSE WERE JUST GAMES. IT CAN GET WORSE.
TAKE THE PILLS, KID.
TAKE THE PILLS, GO TO SLEEP.
LET US RUN THE TOWN...
HA HA
HA HA HA HA HA HA
...JUST LIKE WE ALWAYS HAVE!
HA HA HA HA
HA HA
NO...
NO--
NO!

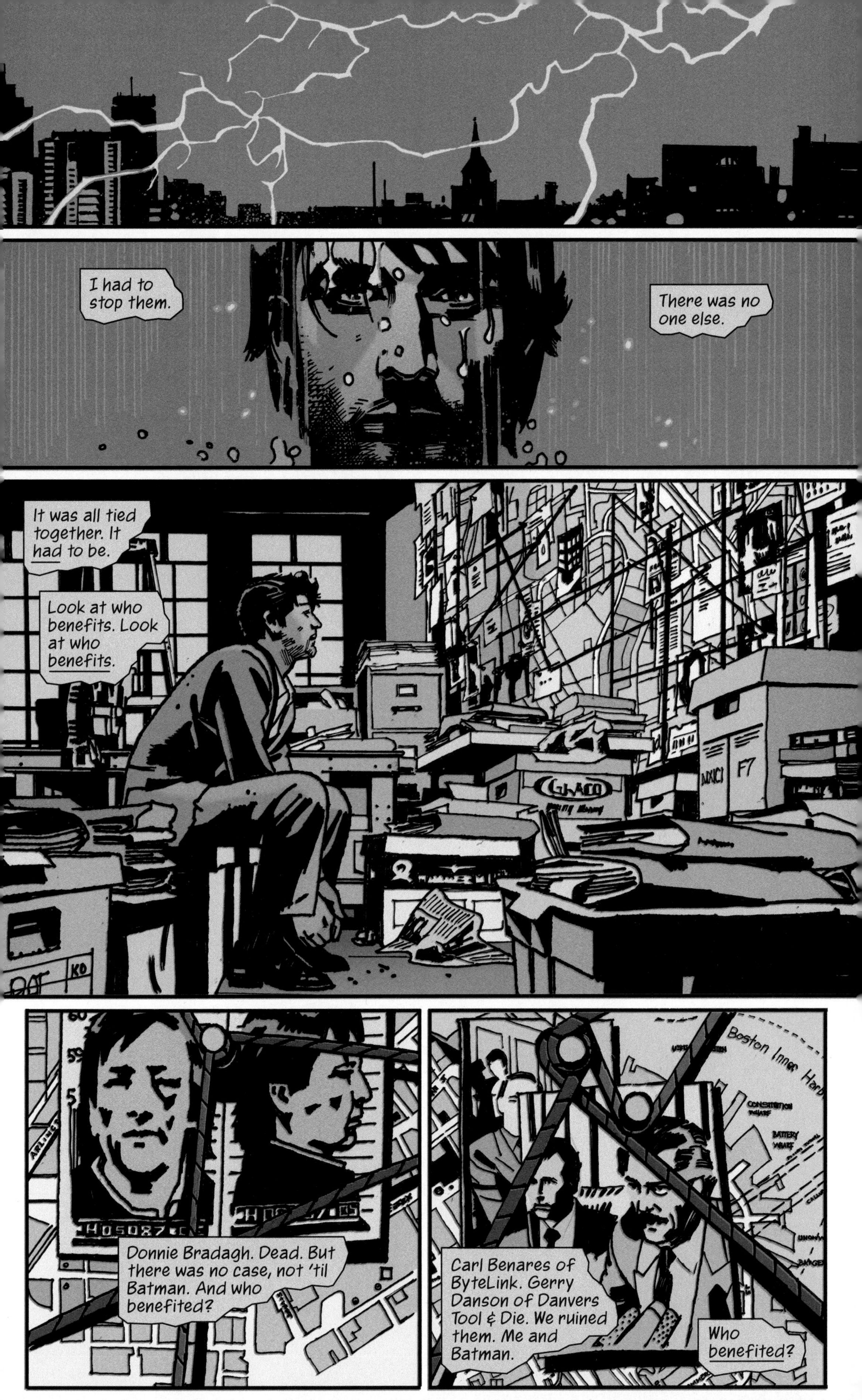
I had to stop them.
There was no one else.
It was all tied together. It had to be.
Look at who benefits. Look at who benefits.
Donnie Bradagh. Dead. But there was no case, not 'til Batman. And who benefited?
Carl Benares of ByteLink. Gerry Danson of Danvers Tool & Die. We ruined them. Me and Batman.
Who benefited?
Boston Inner Harb

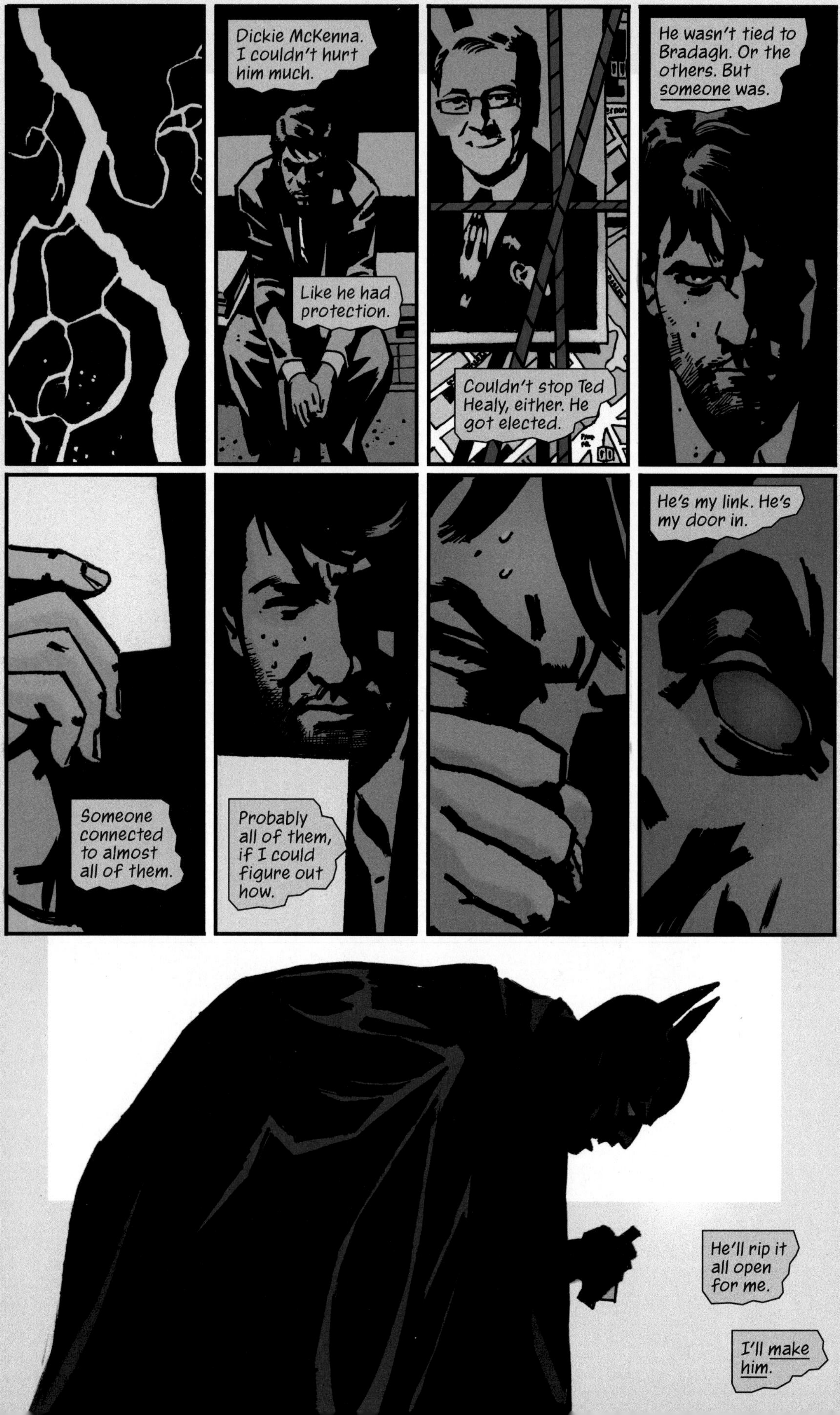
Dickie McKenna. I couldn't hurt him much.
Like he had protection.
Couldn't stop Ted Healy, either. He got elected.
He wasn't tied to Bradagh. Or the others. But someone was.
Someone connected to almost all of them.
Probably all of them, if I could figure out how.
He's my link. He's my door in.
He'll rip it all open for me.
I'll make him.

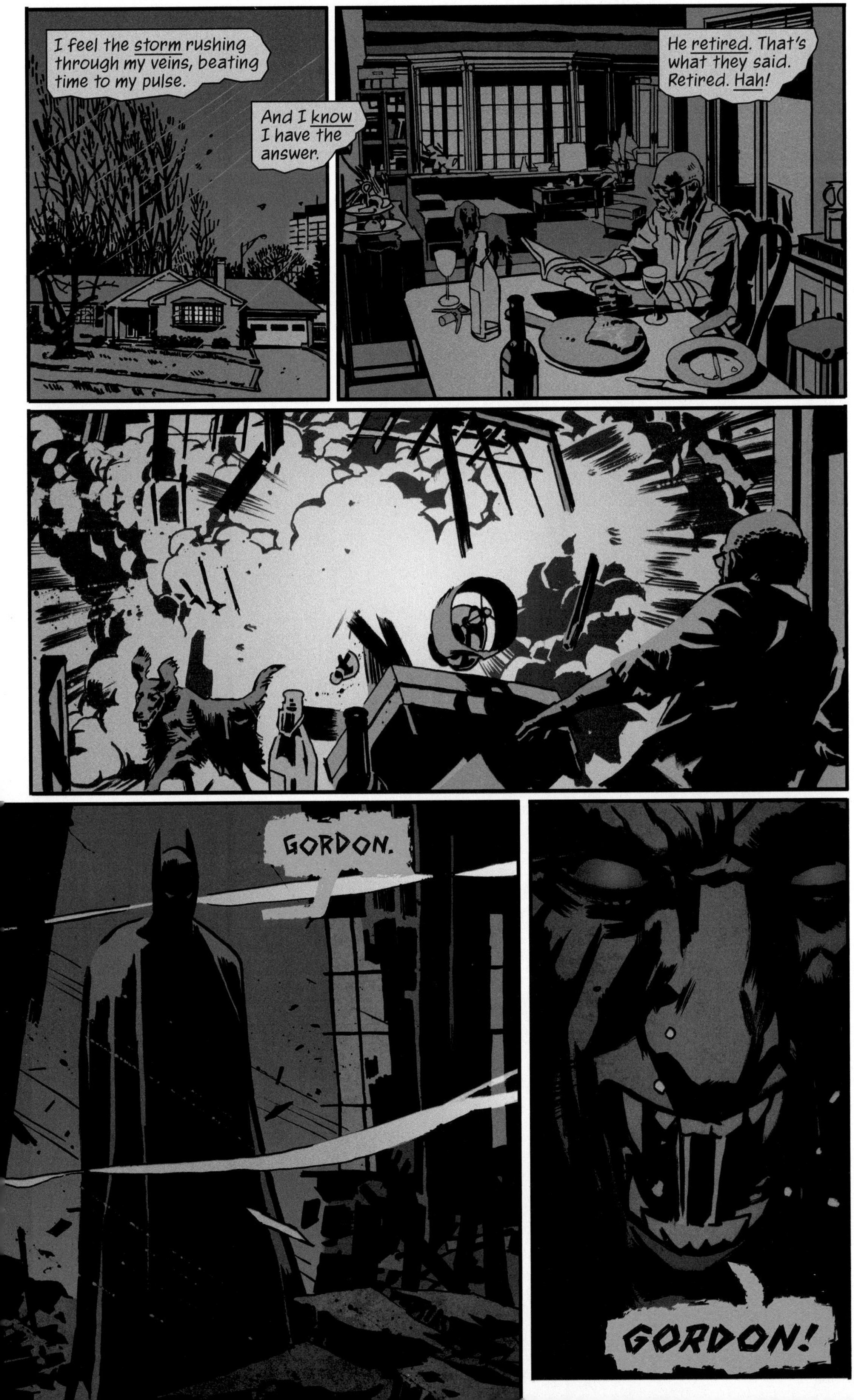
I feel the storm rushing through my veins, beating time to my pulse.
And I know I have the answer.
He retired. That's what they said. Retired. Hah!
GORDON.
GORDON!

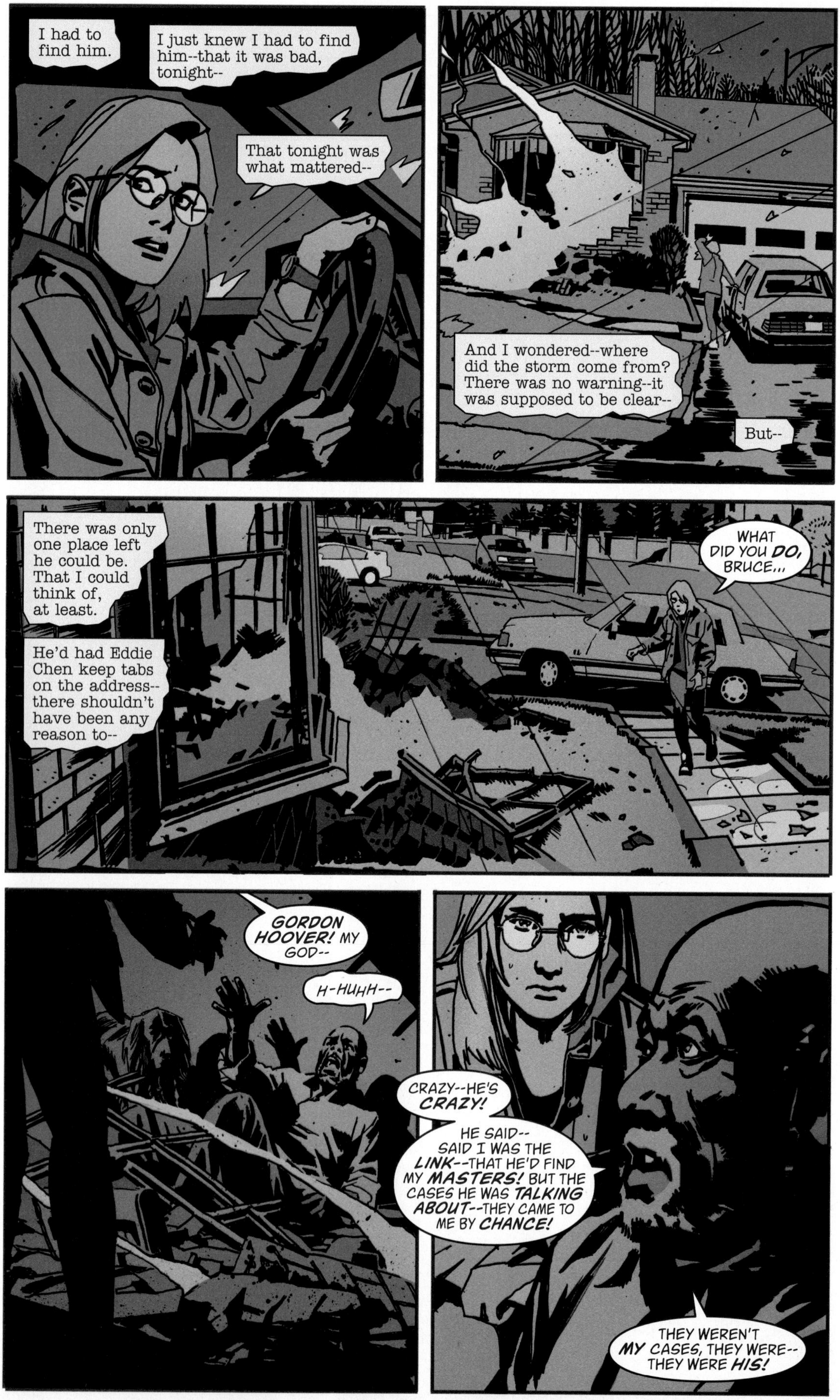

I had to find him.
I just knew I had to find him--that it was bad, tonight--
That tonight was what mattered--
And I wondered--where did the storm come from? There was no warning--it was supposed to be clear--
But--
There was only one place left he could be. That I could think of, at least.
He'd had Eddie Chen keep tabs on the address--there shouldn't have been any reason to--
WHAT DID YOU DO, BRUCE...
GORDON HOOVER! MY GOD--
H-HUHH--
CRAZY--HE'S CRAZY!
HE SAID--SAID I WAS THE LINK--THAT HE'D FIND MY MASTERS! BUT THE CASES HE WAS TALKING ABOUT--THEY CAME TO ME BY CHANCE!
THEY WEREN'T MY CASES, THEY WERE--THEY WERE HIS!

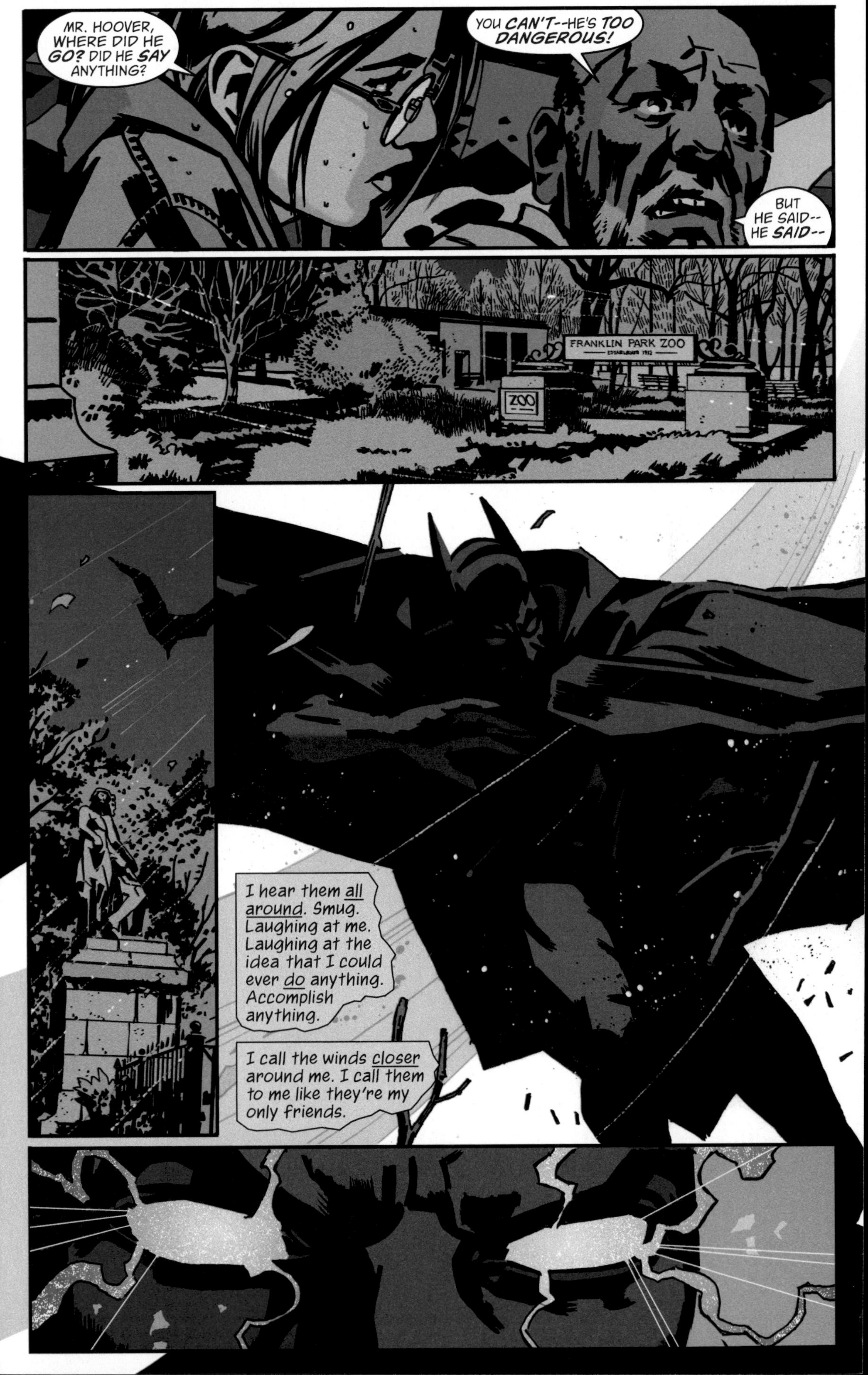
MR. HOOVER, WHERE DID HE GO? DID HE SAY ANYTHING?
YOU CAN'T--HE'S TOO DANGEROUS!
BUT HE SAID-- HE SAID--
FRANKLIN PARK ZOO
ZOO
I hear them all around. Smug. Laughing at me. Laughing at the idea that I could ever do anything. Accomplish anything.
I call the winds closer around me. I call them to me like they're my only friends.

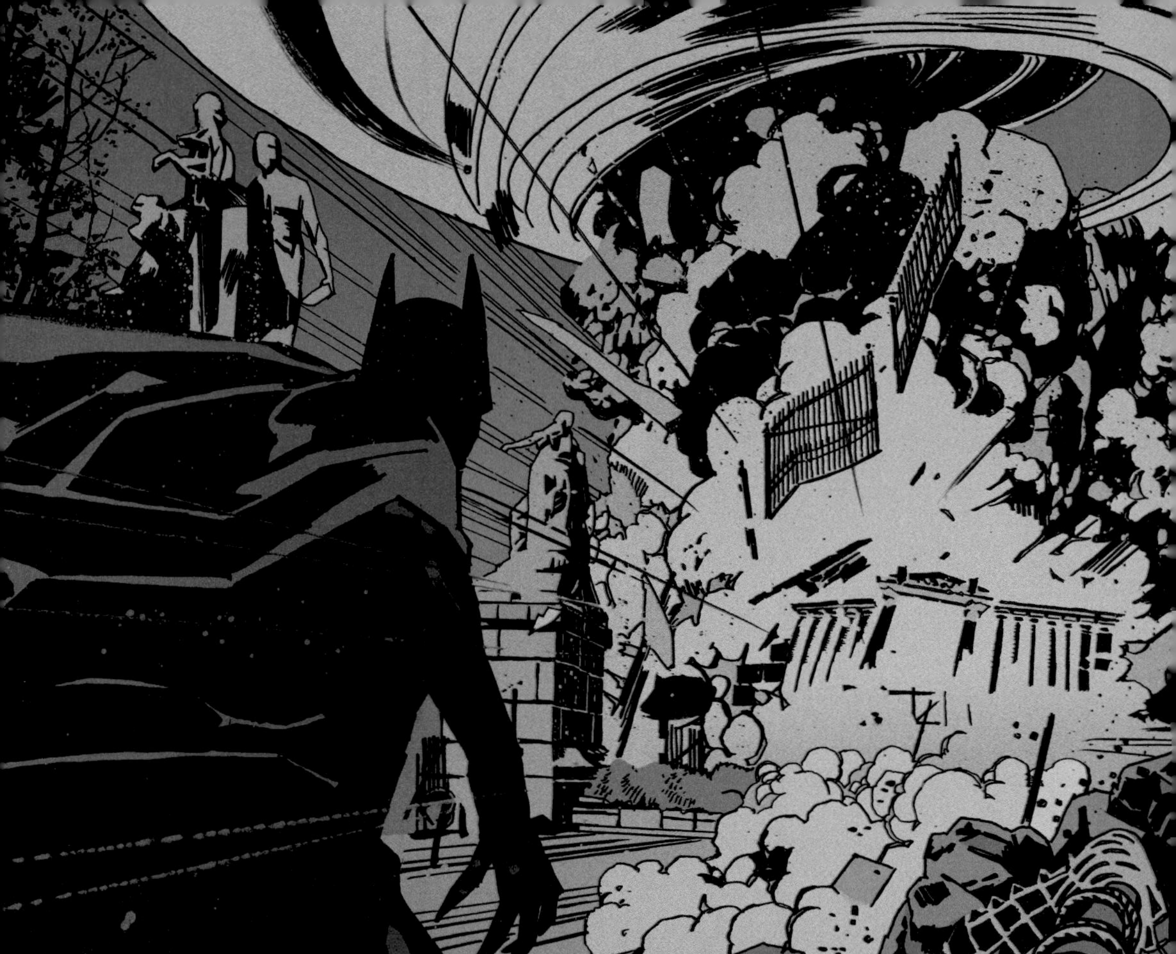

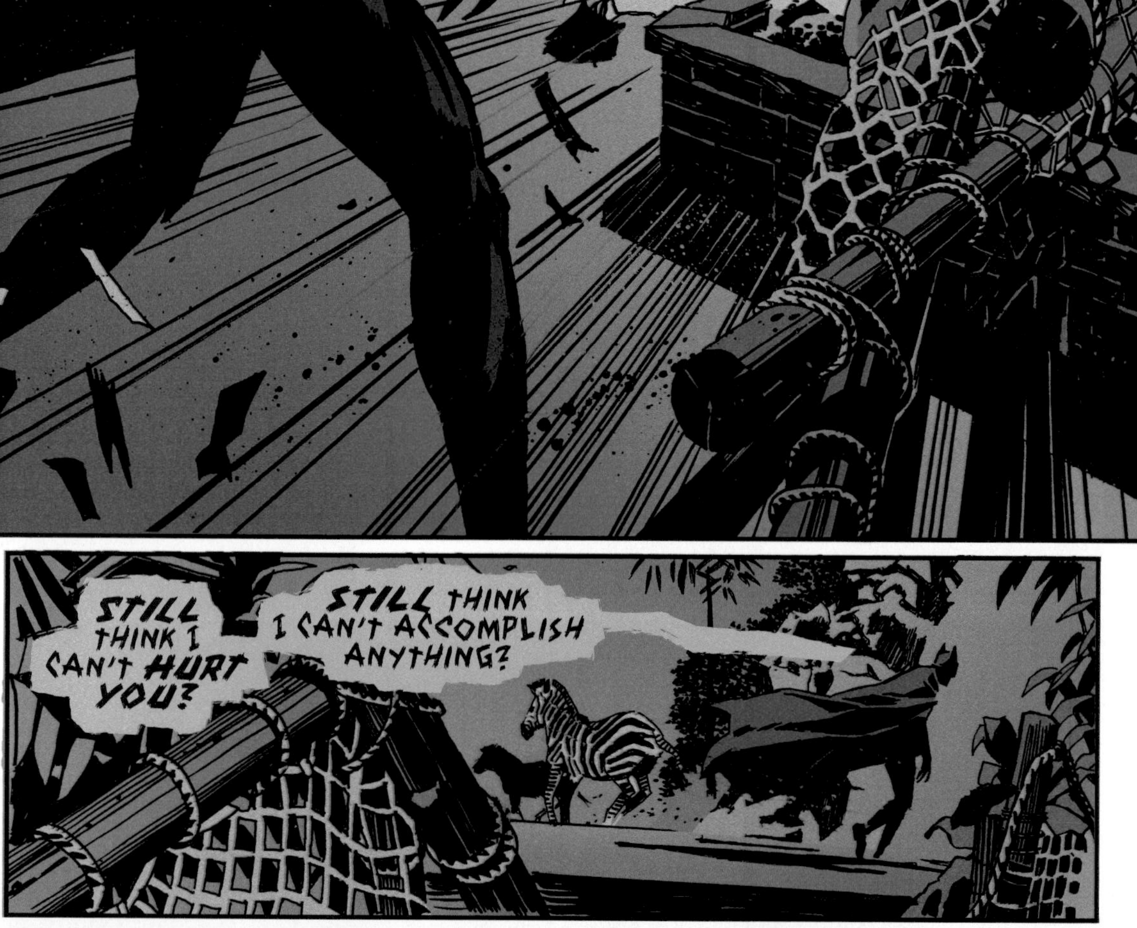
STILL THINK I CAN'T HURT YOU?
STILL THINK I CAN'T ACCOMPLISH ANYTHING?

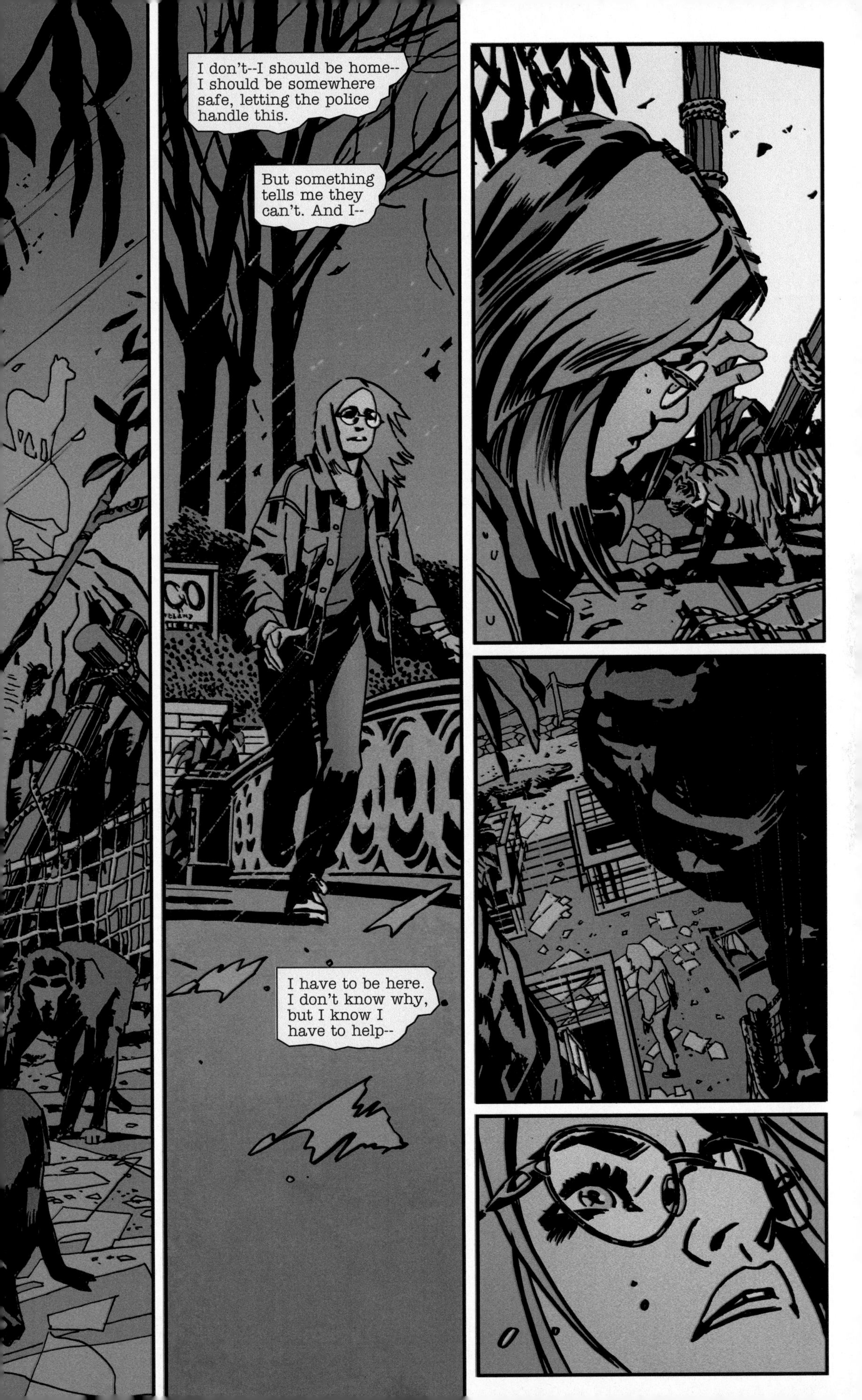
I don't--I should be home--
I should be somewhere safe, letting the police handle this.
But something tells me they can't. And I--
I have to be here. I don't know why, but I know I have to help--

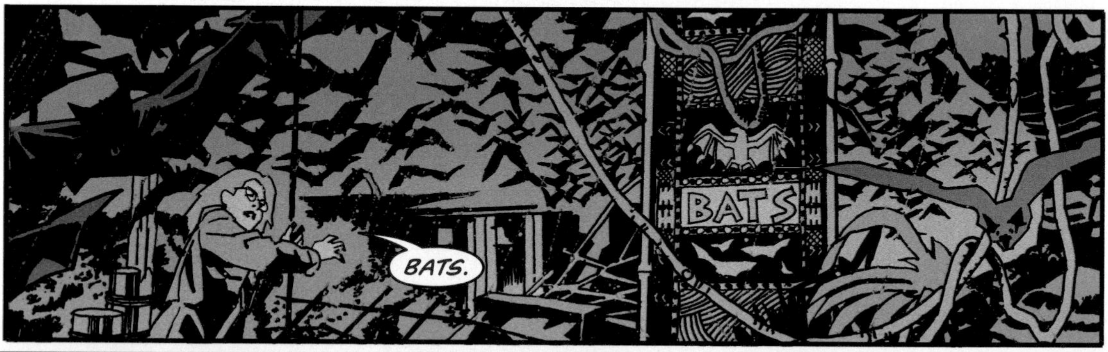
BATS.
BATS

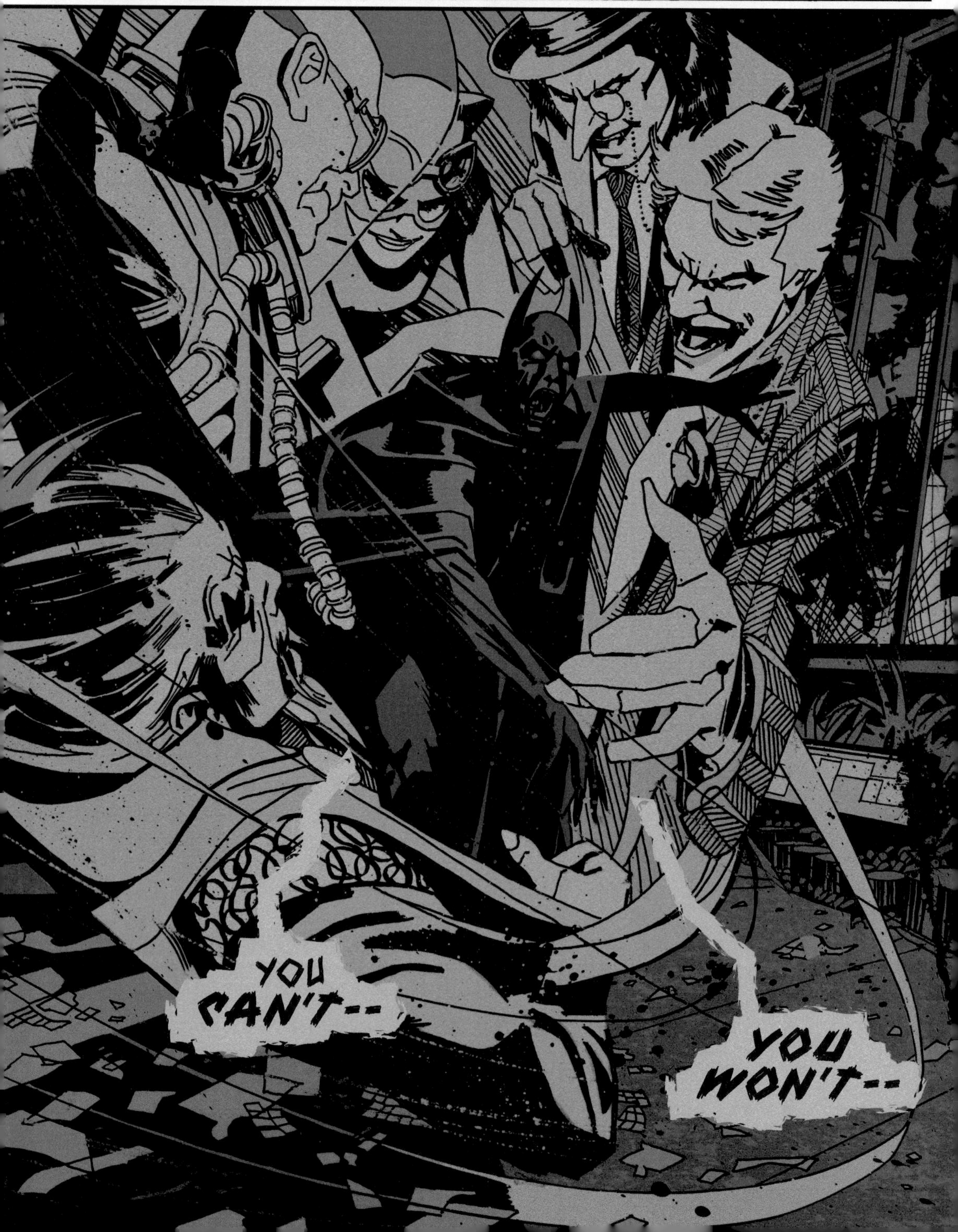
YOU CAN'T--
YOU WON'T--

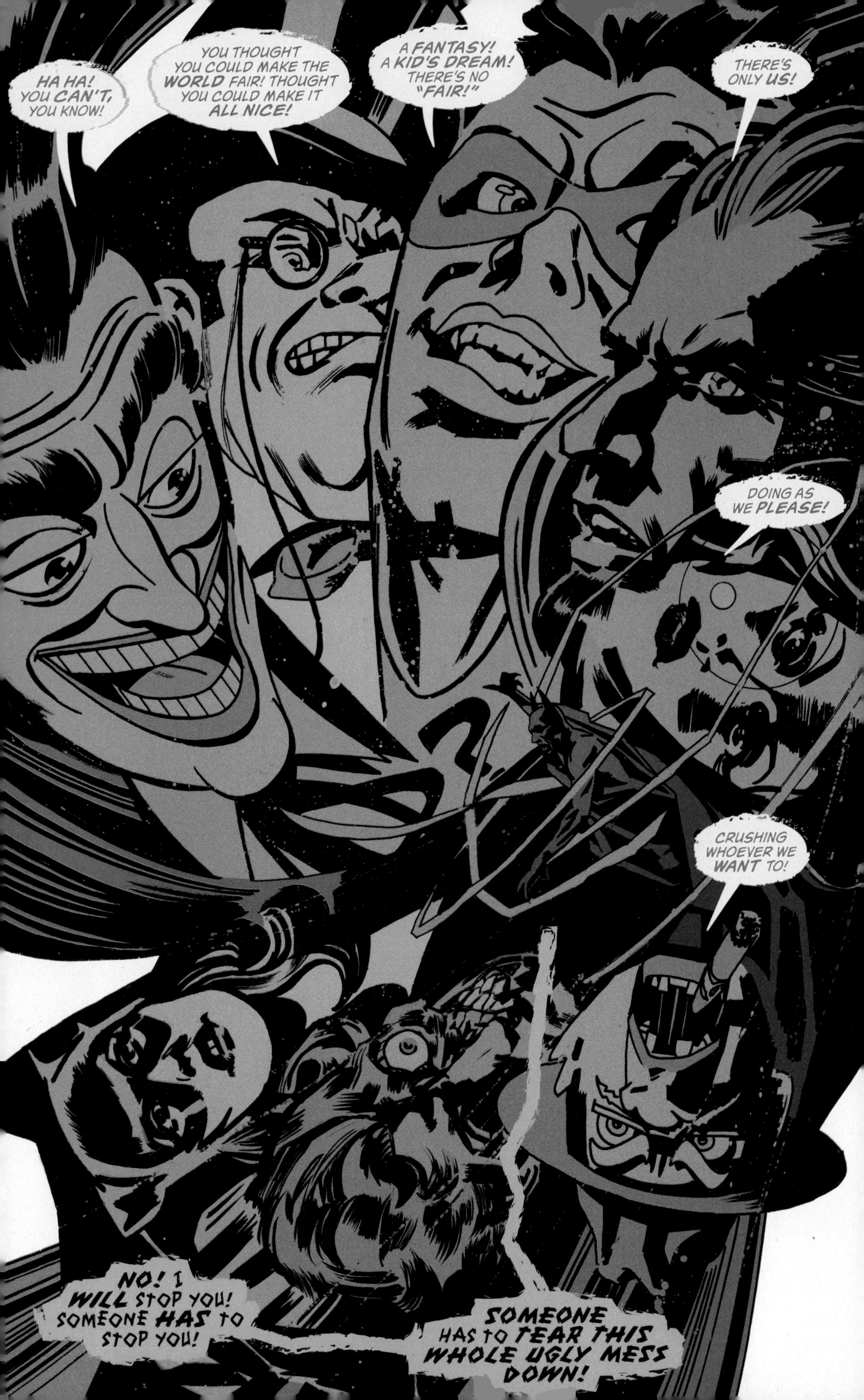
HA HA! YOU CAN'T, YOU KNOW!
YOU THOUGHT YOU COULD MAKE THE WORLD FAIR! THOUGHT YOU COULD MAKE IT ALL NICE!
A FANTASY! A KID'S DREAM! THERE'S NO "FAIR!"
THERE'S ONLY US!
DOING AS WE PLEASE!
CRUSHING WHOEVER WE WANT TO!
NO! I WILL STOP YOU! SOMEONE HAS TO STOP YOU!
SOMEONE HAS TO TEAR THIS WHOLE UGLY MESS DOWN!

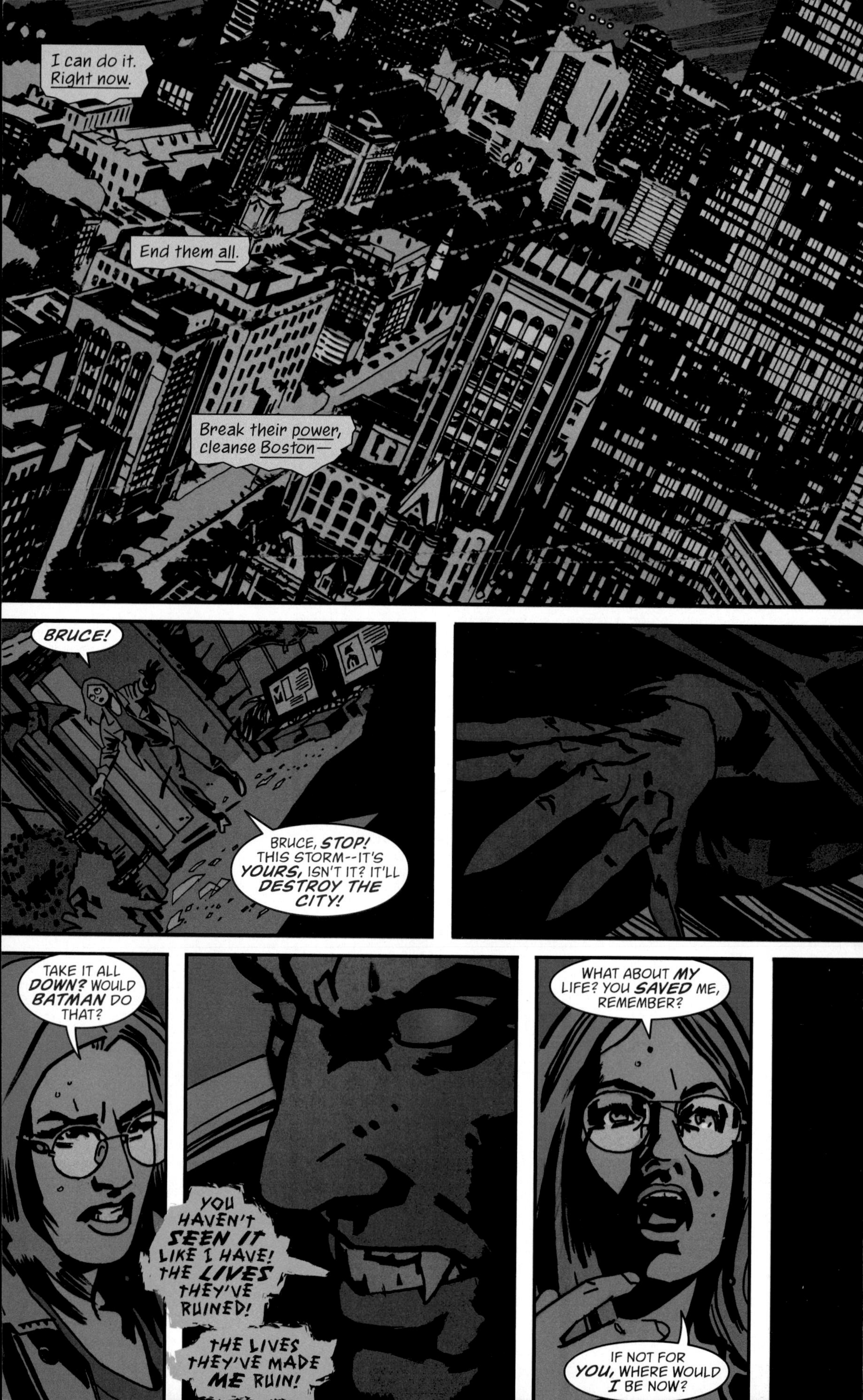

I can do it. Right now.
End them all.
Break their power, cleanse Boston—
BRUCE!
BRUCE, STOP! THIS STORM--IT'S YOURS, ISN'T IT? IT'LL DESTROY THE CITY!
TAKE IT ALL DOWN? WOULD BATMAN DO THAT?
YOU HAVEN'T SEEN IT LIKE I HAVE! THE LIVES THEY'VE RUINED!
THE LIVES THEY'VE MADE ME RUIN!
WHAT ABOUT MY LIFE? YOU SAVED ME, REMEMBER?
IF NOT FOR YOU, WHERE WOULD I BE NOW?

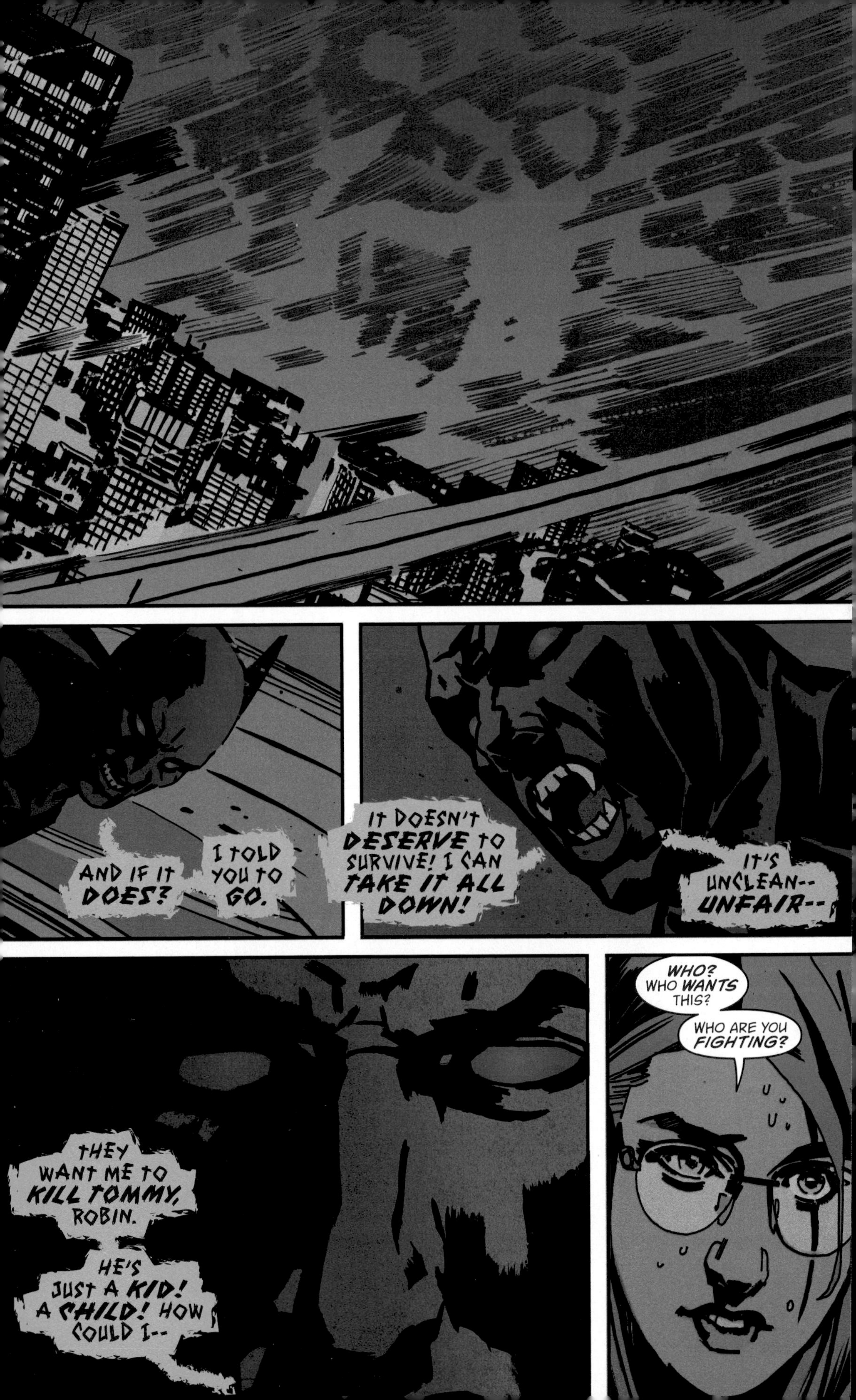

AND IF IT DOES?
I TOLD YOU TO GO.
IT DOESN'T DESERVE TO SURVIVE! I CAN TAKE IT ALL DOWN!
IT'S UNCLEAN-- UNFAIR--
THEY WANT ME TO KILL TOMMY, ROBIN.
HE'S JUST A KID! A CHILD! HOW COULD I--
WHO? WHO WANTS THIS?
WHO ARE YOU FIGHTING?

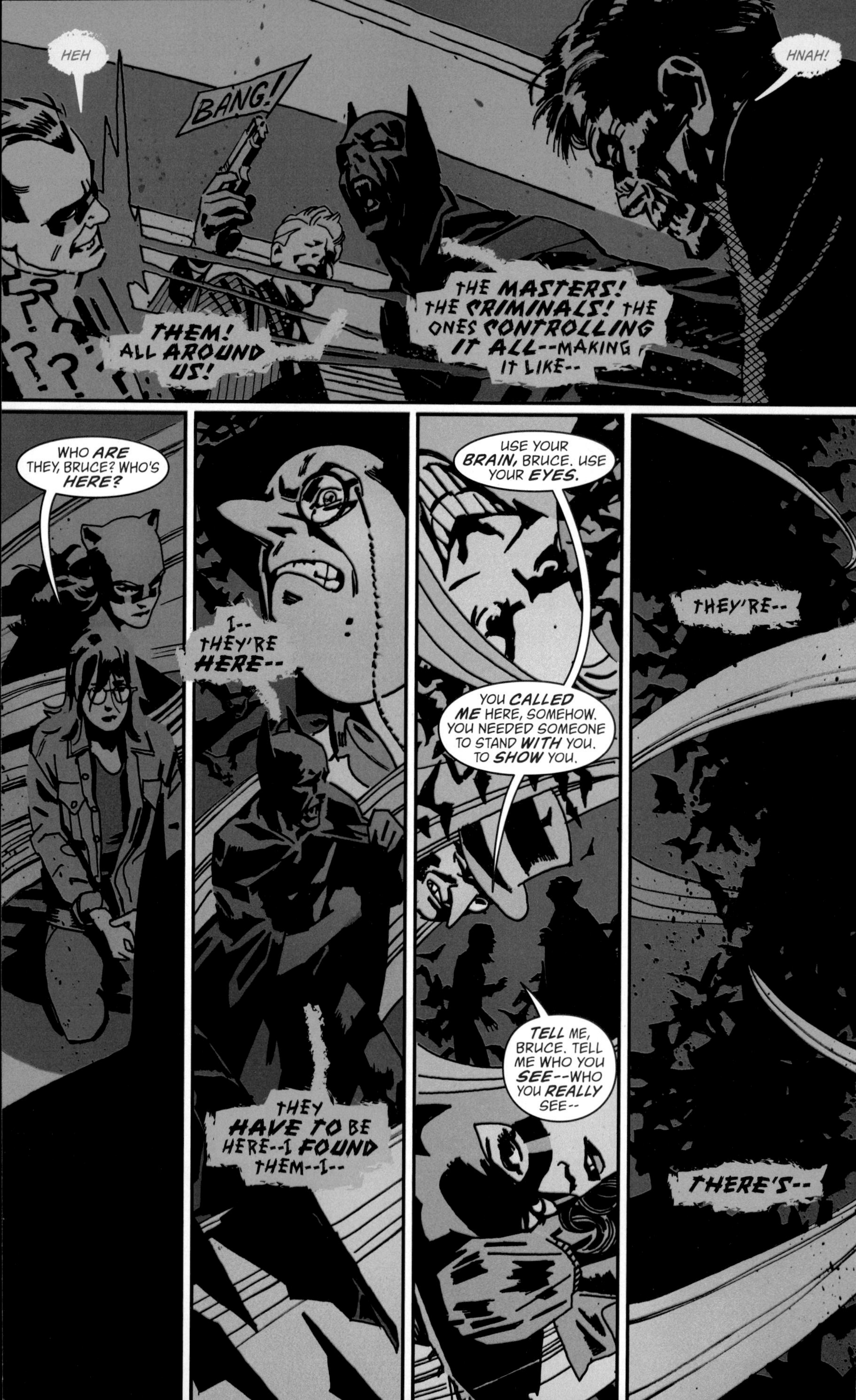
HEH
BANG!
HNAH!
THEM! ALL AROUND US!
THE MASTERS! THE CRIMINALS! THE ONES CONTROLLING IT ALL--MAKING IT LIKE--
WHO ARE THEY, BRUCE? WHO'S HERE?
I-- THEY'RE HERE--
THEY HAVE TO BE HERE--I FOUND THEM--I--
USE YOUR BRAIN, BRUCE. USE YOUR EYES.
YOU CALLED ME HERE, SOMEHOW. YOU NEEDED SOMEONE TO STAND WITH YOU. TO SHOW YOU.
TELL ME, BRUCE. TELL ME WHO YOU SEE--WHO YOU REALLY SEE--
THEY'RE--
THERE'S--

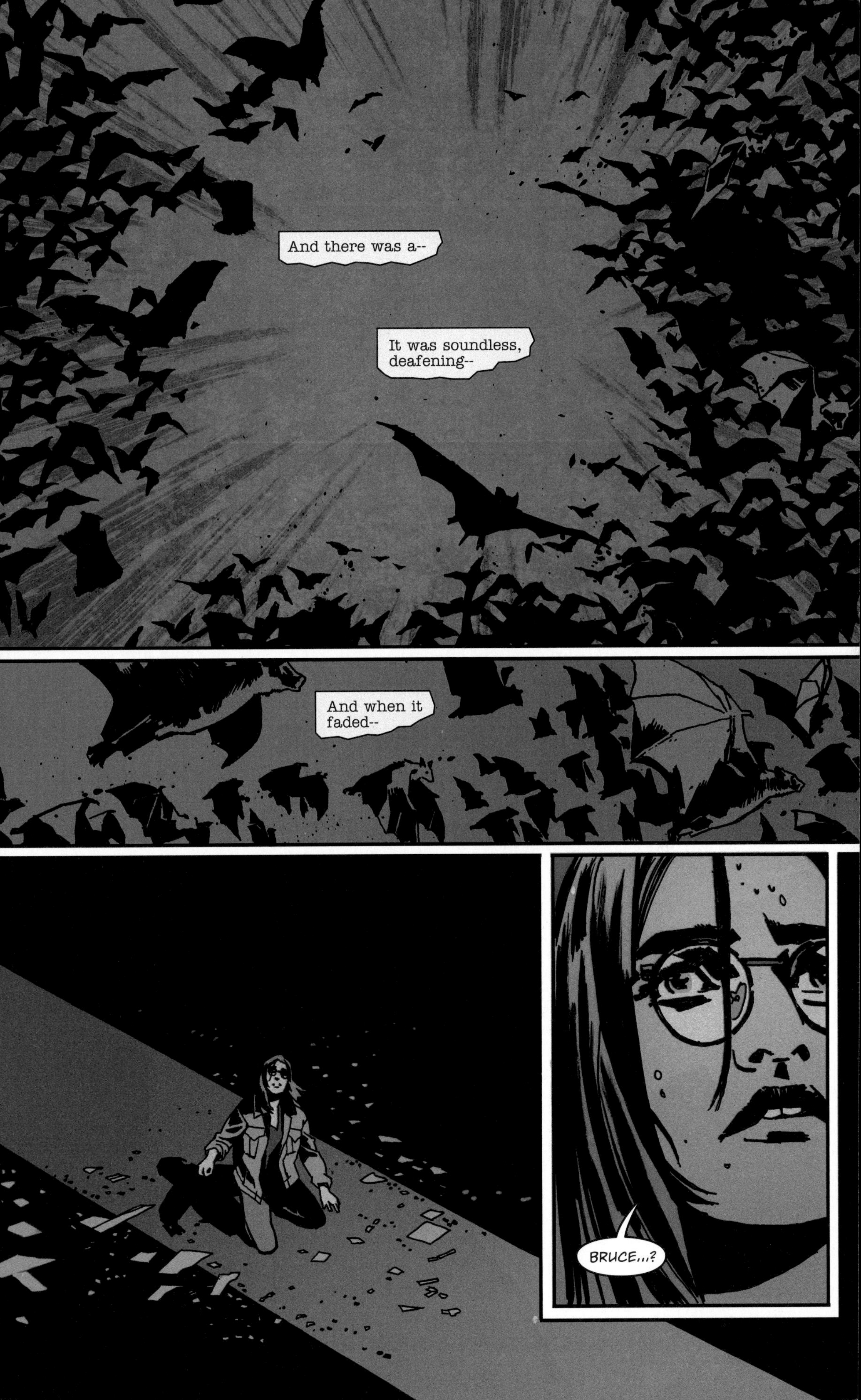
And there was a--
It was soundless, deafening--
And when it faded--
BRUCE...?

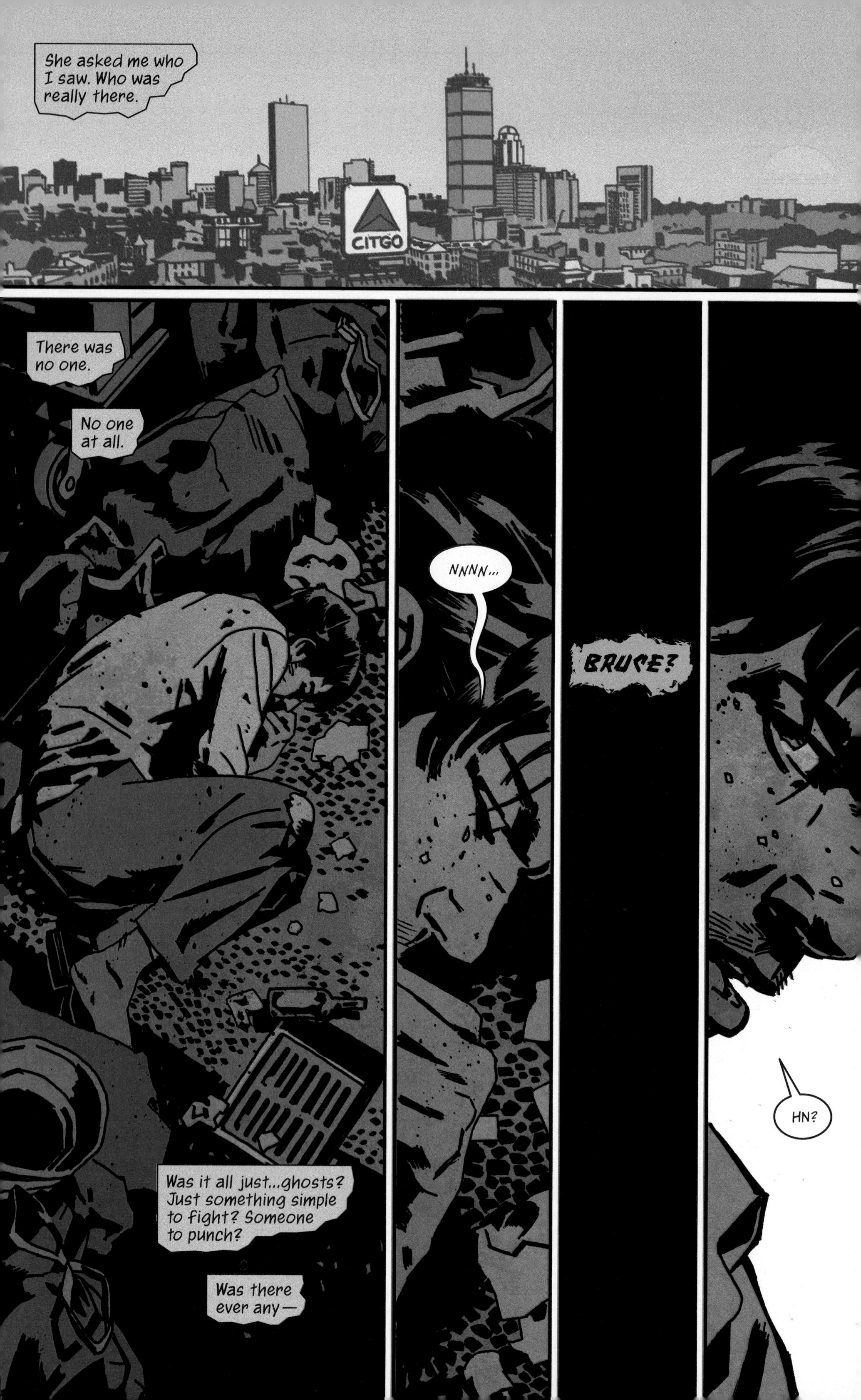
She asked me who I saw. Who was really there.
CITGO
There was no one.
No one at all.
Was it all just...ghosts? Just something simple to fight? Someone to punch?
Was there ever any—
NNNN...
BRUCE?
HN?

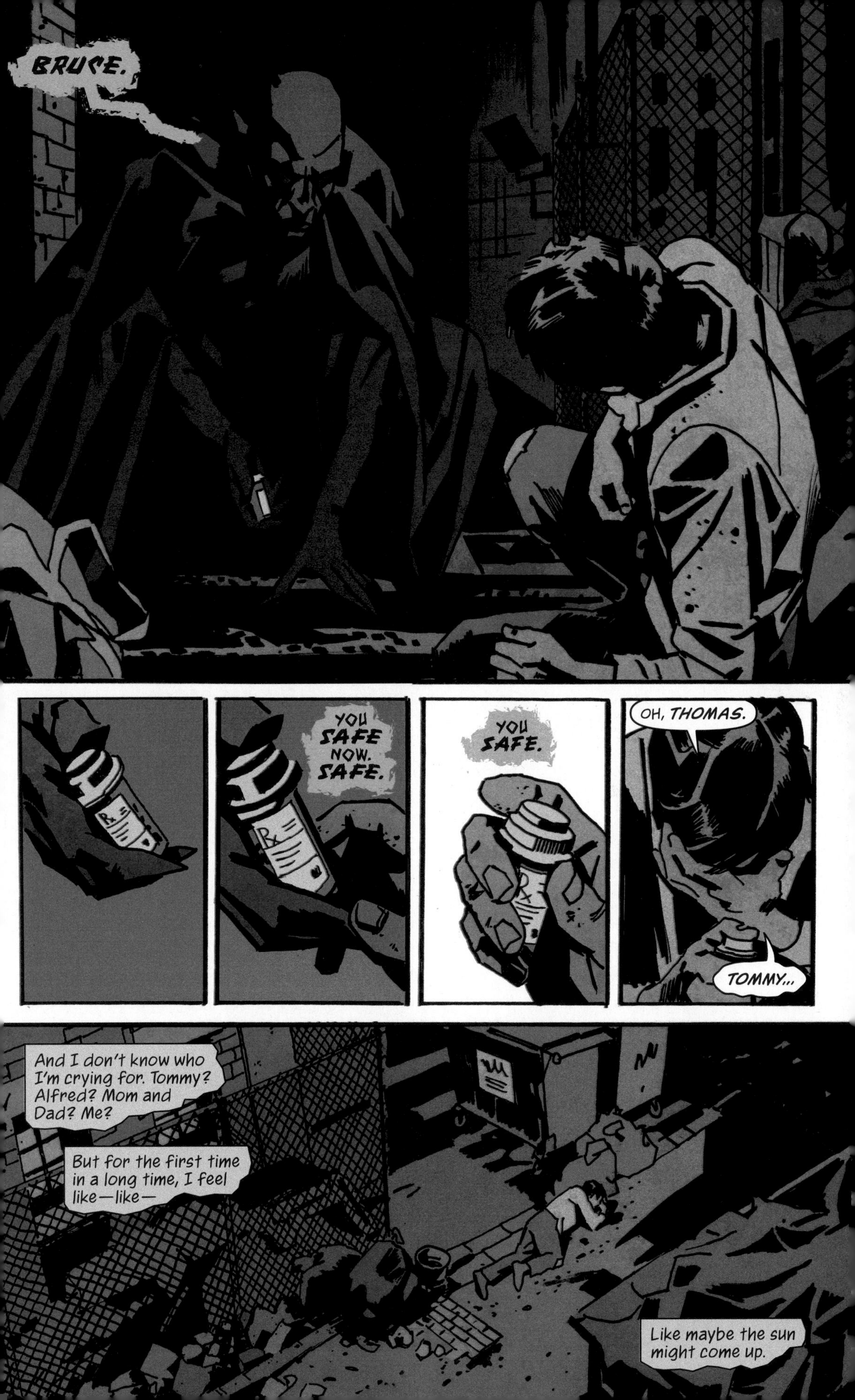
BRUCE.
YOU SAFE NOW. SAFE.
YOU SAFE.
OH, THOMAS.
TOMMY...
And I don't know who I'm crying for. Tommy? Alfred? Mom and Dad? Me?
But for the first time in a long time, I feel like—like—
Like maybe the sun might come up.

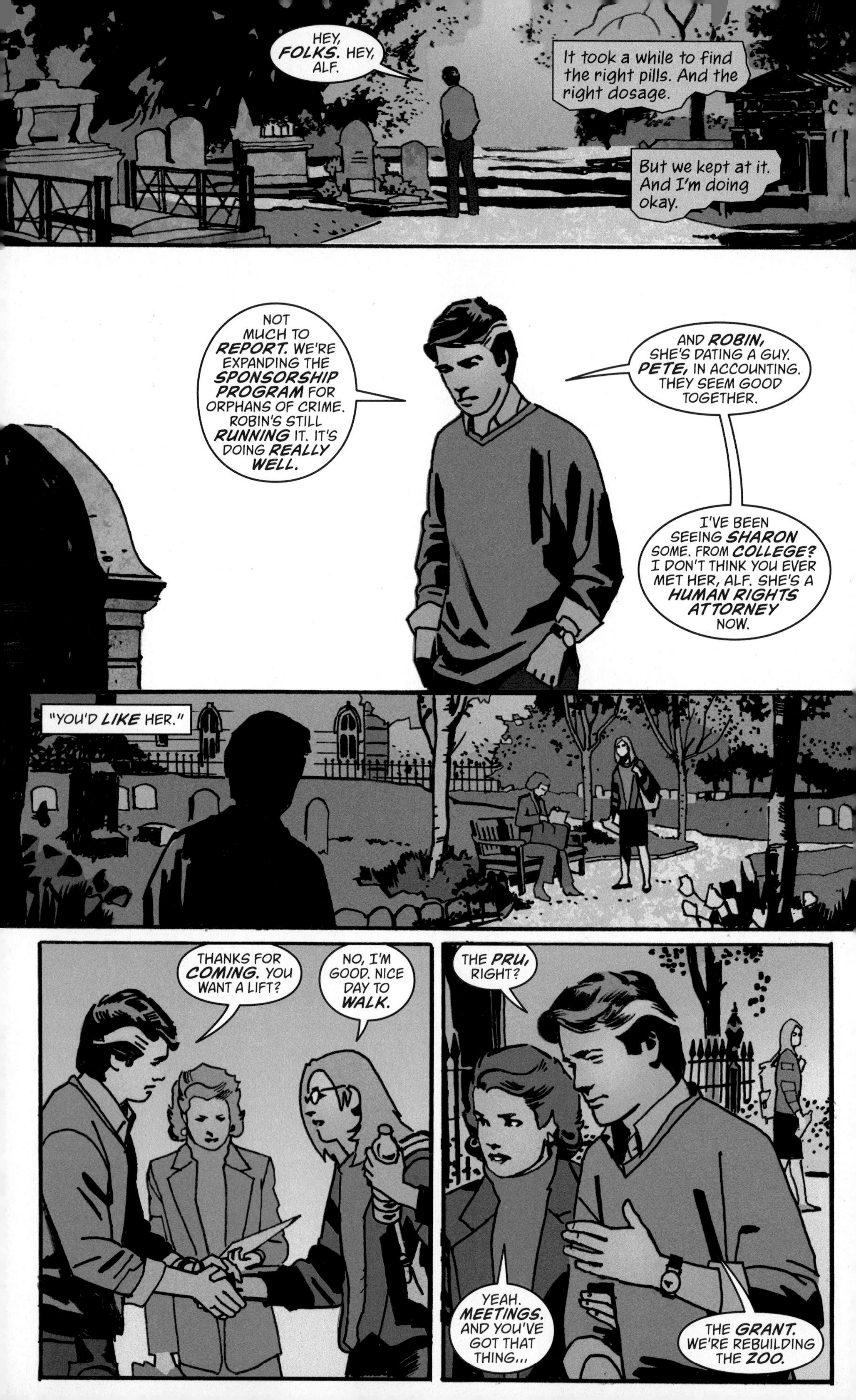
HEY, FOLKS. HEY, ALF.
It took a while to find the right pills. And the right dosage.
But we kept at it. And I'm doing okay.
NOT MUCH TO REPORT. WE'RE EXPANDING THE SPONSORSHIP PROGRAM FOR ORPHANS OF CRIME. ROBIN'S STILL RUNNING IT. IT'S DOING REALLY WELL.
AND ROBIN, SHE'S DATING A GUY. PETE, IN ACCOUNTING. THEY SEEM GOOD TOGETHER.
I'VE BEEN SEEING SHARON SOME. FROM COLLEGE? I DON'T THINK YOU EVER MET HER, ALF. SHE'S A HUMAN RIGHTS ATTORNEY NOW.
"YOU'D LIKE HER."
THANKS FOR COMING. YOU WANT A LIFT?
NO, I'M GOOD. NICE DAY TO WALK.
THE PRU, RIGHT?
YEAH. MEETINGS. AND YOU'VE GOT THAT THING...
THE GRANT. WE'RE REBUILDING THE ZOO.

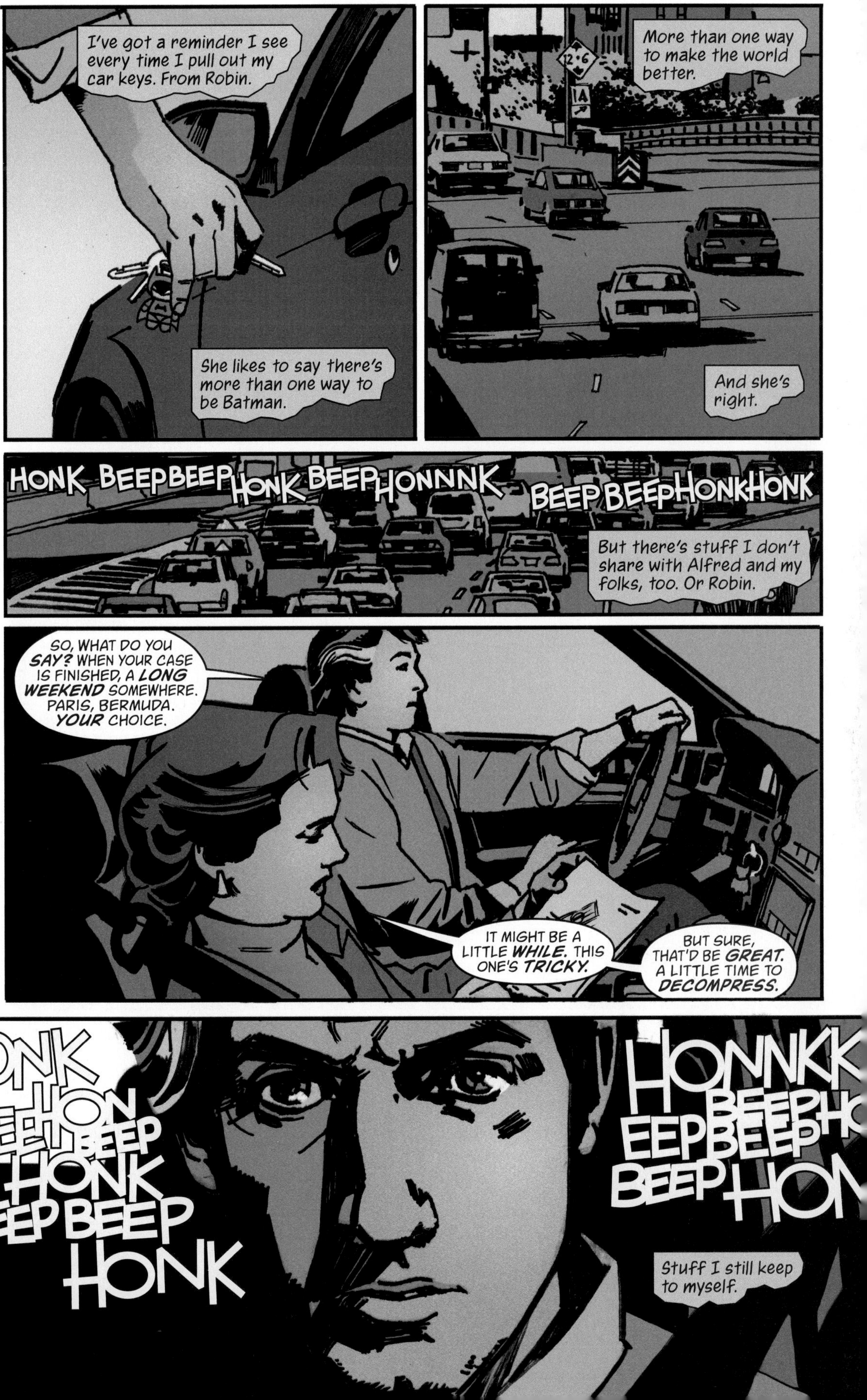

I've got a reminder I see every time I pull out my car keys. From Robin.
She likes to say there's more than one way to be Batman.
More than one way to make the world better.
And she's right.
HONK BEEPBEEP HONK BEEP HONNNK
BEEP BEEP HONK HONK
But there's stuff I don't share with Alfred and my folks, too. Or Robin.
SO, WHAT DO YOU SAY? WHEN YOUR CASE IS FINISHED, A LONG WEEKEND SOMEWHERE. PARIS, BERMUDA. YOUR CHOICE.
IT MIGHT BE A LITTLE WHILE. THIS ONE'S TRICKY.
BUT SURE, THAT'D BE GREAT. A LITTLE TIME TO DECOMPRESS.
HON
BEEP
HONK
BEEP
HONK
HONNKK
BEEP
BEEP
BEEP
Stuff I still keep to myself.

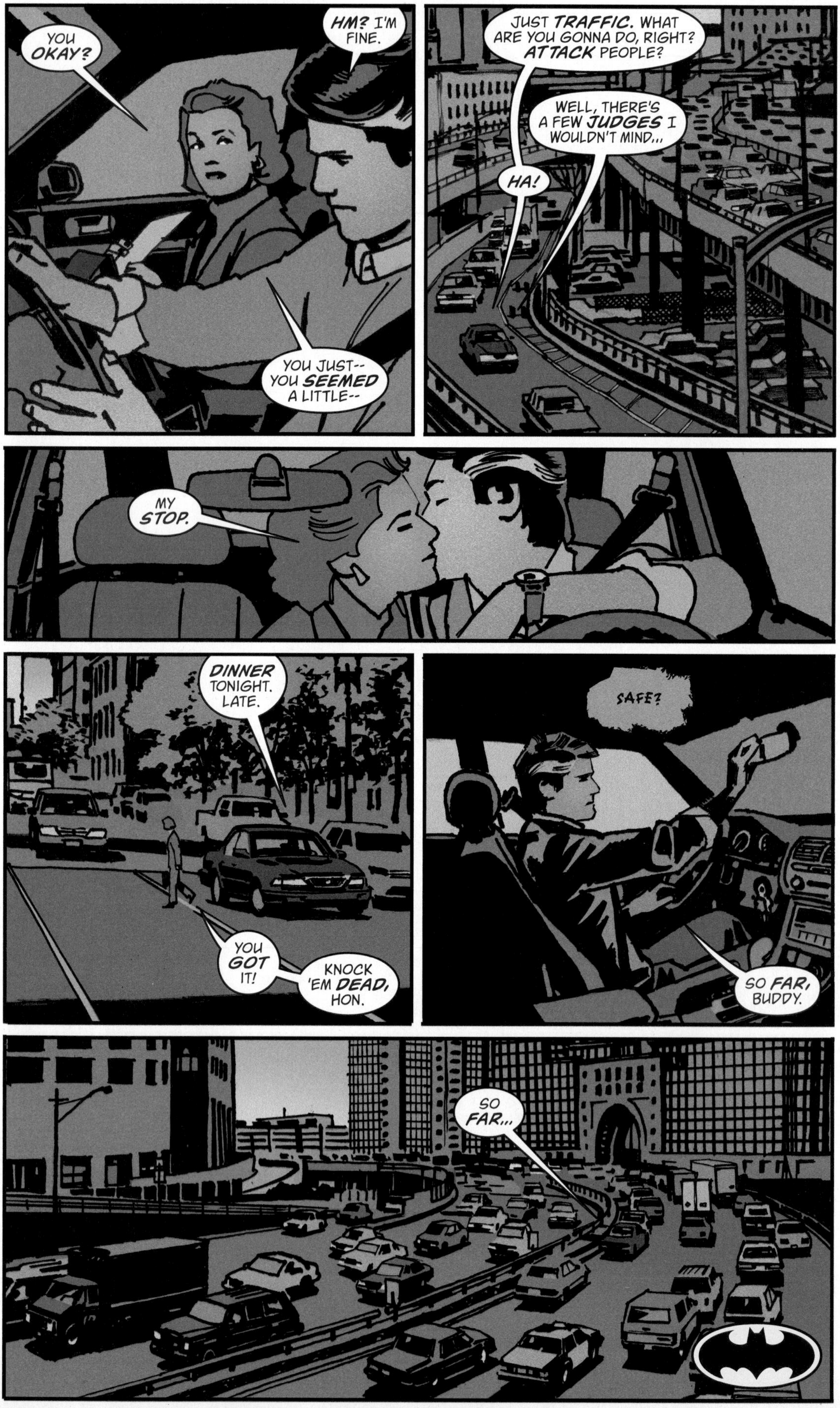
YOU OKAY?
HM? I'M FINE.
YOU JUST-- YOU SEEMED A LITTLE--
JUST TRAFFIC. WHAT ARE YOU GONNA DO, RIGHT? ATTACK PEOPLE?
WELL, THERE'S A FEW JUDGES I WOULDN'T MIND...
HA!
MY STOP.
DINNER TONIGHT. LATE.
YOU GOT IT!
KNOCK 'EM DEAD, HON.
SAFE?
SO FAR, BUDDY.
SO FAR...

And for all that you've waited patiently for two years (!) between the first and final issue of this series—and we humbly thank you for that patience and hope you think it was worth it—it's been longer than you know. We wanted to make up for that wait a little with an extra-length finale, and with a little something extra—in this case, the original pitch for the series, written in the wake of the success of *Superman: Secret Identity*, fifteen years ago. Fifteen?! My kids weren't even in first grade yet! It's been a long road indeed. We went through two different artists and a period when I thought the book was dead (and the guy who revived it—thanks, Bob!—has been retired from DC for five years now himself), before bringing the great John Paul Leon on board. And then we had all kinds of difficulties, but here we are, reaching the finale at last. So here's the very beginning...

BATMAN: CREATURE OF THE NIGHT

Four 48-Page Issues

Like *Superman: Secret Identity*, *Batman: Creature of the Night* is an extended look at one of DC's superhero icons from a different perspective, examining the emotional core of the character by translating it into a more realistic setting, removing the trappings of the DCU and exploring beyond the bounds that the action-adventure context usually demands.

Like *Superman: Secret Identity*, it concerns a young man with surface similarities to a DC icon, aware of the character as a comic book character, and how his life is shaped after those similarities become something deeper. Each issue will open with a different stage of the icon's history, and examine a different stage in the lead's development, and the series will have a similar character- and emotion-focused approach, grounded in realistic human drama in order to make the fantasy aspects that much more unearthly and impressive.

Unlike *Superman: Secret Identity*, this is not the story of a man's struggle with identity across the course of his life. Superman is, at heart, about identity, about the hero beneath Clark Kent's surface, about the adolescent ideal of the boy becoming the man. Batman, at heart, taps into something younger and simpler -- it's a child's rage at the world for being unfair, and that child's inarticulate desire to control the world, to make it fair by force of will.

Superman: Secret Identity was an examination of adulthood in a science-fiction setting, a biography of Clark Kent's sense of identity at different stages of his life. *Batman: Creature of the Night*, on the other hand, is a horror story.

It's an examination of obsession at different stages, as a child's rage is set loose on the world, and has to be dealt with by a man who does not stay a child.

🦇 🦇 🦇

Batman: Creature of the Night is the story of Bruce Wainwright, the son of a wealthy couple in a large and old American city (New York, most likely, but maybe Boston). Young Bruce is a comics fan, and has always been fascinated by Batman, in great part because of the similarity of their names. Unlike Clark in *Secret Identity,* he likes the connection, and likes Batman...

...right up until his parents are killed by unknown assailants, and he's left an orphan at age 9.

In anguish and in anger at the world for being so unfair, Bruce wishes there really was a Batman, who could stop things like this. And within a short time ... there is. Unlike the DCU Batman, though, this is not Bruce after years of training and study. This is a supernatural, spectral figure, not fully human, who does all the things Batman does by illusion -- comes and goes like a ghost, vanishes into the shadows and more. This is a scary, unkillable Batman who exists for one reason and one reason only: To make the world fair, by Bruce's nine-year-old standards.

Again, as with *Secret Identity*, we'll offer an explanation as to what happened but never really confirm it: Bruce would have been a twin, except that during gestation, as occasionally happens, one fetus absorbs the other, taking it back into itself. This has possibly left Bruce with a "psychic twin," a bodiless brother who had no real existence until Bruce's grief and rage gave him form.

Bruce's need to deal with this obsession-driven side of himself is what will shape the story.

The only other major characters I'm sure of so far are:

• Alfred, who in this story is not a butler, but a longtime employee of Bruce's father and the trustee of the Wainwright Estate. He acts in loco parentis to Bruce, and while his job is to safeguard Bruce's financial future, he comes to see himself as responsible for Bruce on a wider scale, to see him grow up well-balanced and happy.

• A police detective (not named Gordon) who investigates the Wainwrights' murder and becomes a friend to Bruce and an odd sort of ally to Batman. He's not sure whether he believes there's a supernatural being out there preying on criminals, but he likes the results -- particularly since Batman doesn't kill.

There will be women, probably one who Bruce winds up with in the end, but his obsession prevents him from letting anyone in and his wealth allows him to live a shallow life, so he won't be making any deep connections quickly.

The story will roughly break down like this:

#1: The birth of the obsession. The story of Bruce's childhood and the murder, and the debut of Batman. The turning point at the end is Bruce coming face-to-face with Batman and realizing that they're linked, that Batman is born of him.

#2. Living with the obsession, kidding yourself that it's not a problem. Bruce thinks he's doing a good thing, making his city safe. Batman is doing good, making the streets safe. Bruce is a young man by now, starting to get involved in business, and it's as if he's got the Midas touch. Everything goes right, everything works. The turning point at the end is Bruce realizing that Batman is still protecting him, still making the world "fair" by making Bruce's wishes come true -- Batman is ruining his competitors to ensure Bruce's business success.

#3: Wrestling with the obsession; can it be overcome. Bruce has to try to put the genie back in the bottle. But can he? Should he? How many people are alive today, how many criminals are off the streets, thanks to Batman? Bruce starts to find out more about Batman as he looks for ways to control him, learns about his never-born twin. Can he kill off his own brother, after killing him in the womb? Bruce's feelings of guilt and responsibility start tearing his life apart. By the end of the issue, Bruce takes Batman into himself, seemingly conquering him. But shortly thereafter, Bruce disappears, leaving a note telling Alfred not to look for him.

#4: Bruce is living on the streets, a physical and emotional wreck. All his efforts go into hold Batman in, and he's not entirely successful. But when Batman gets out, he's more savage than ever. He's fighting to survive, just as Bruce is fighting to kill him. Bruce has to come to terms with the reason for his obsession before he can truly deal with it -- with the idea that adults take care of themselves, that it's by accepting the risk of failure and taking responsibility for ourselves that we become adults, that the world is what we, individually and collectively, make it, not something that's made safe for us, like a terrarium. Only then can he truly let his obsession go, and start to apply some of the lessons he's learned -- using his fortune to help people make the world better, doing

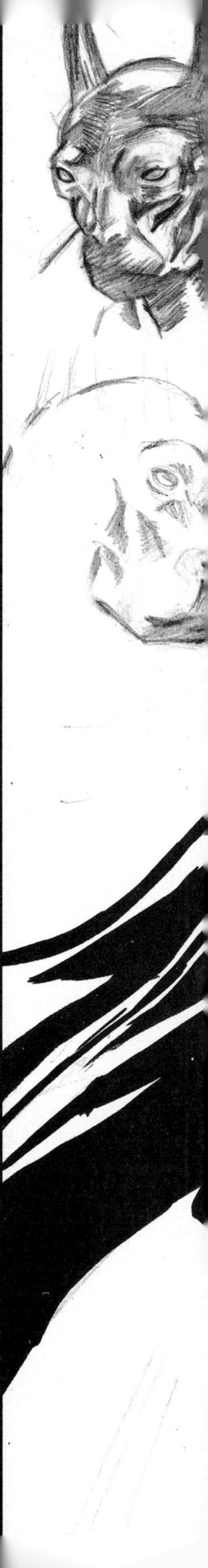

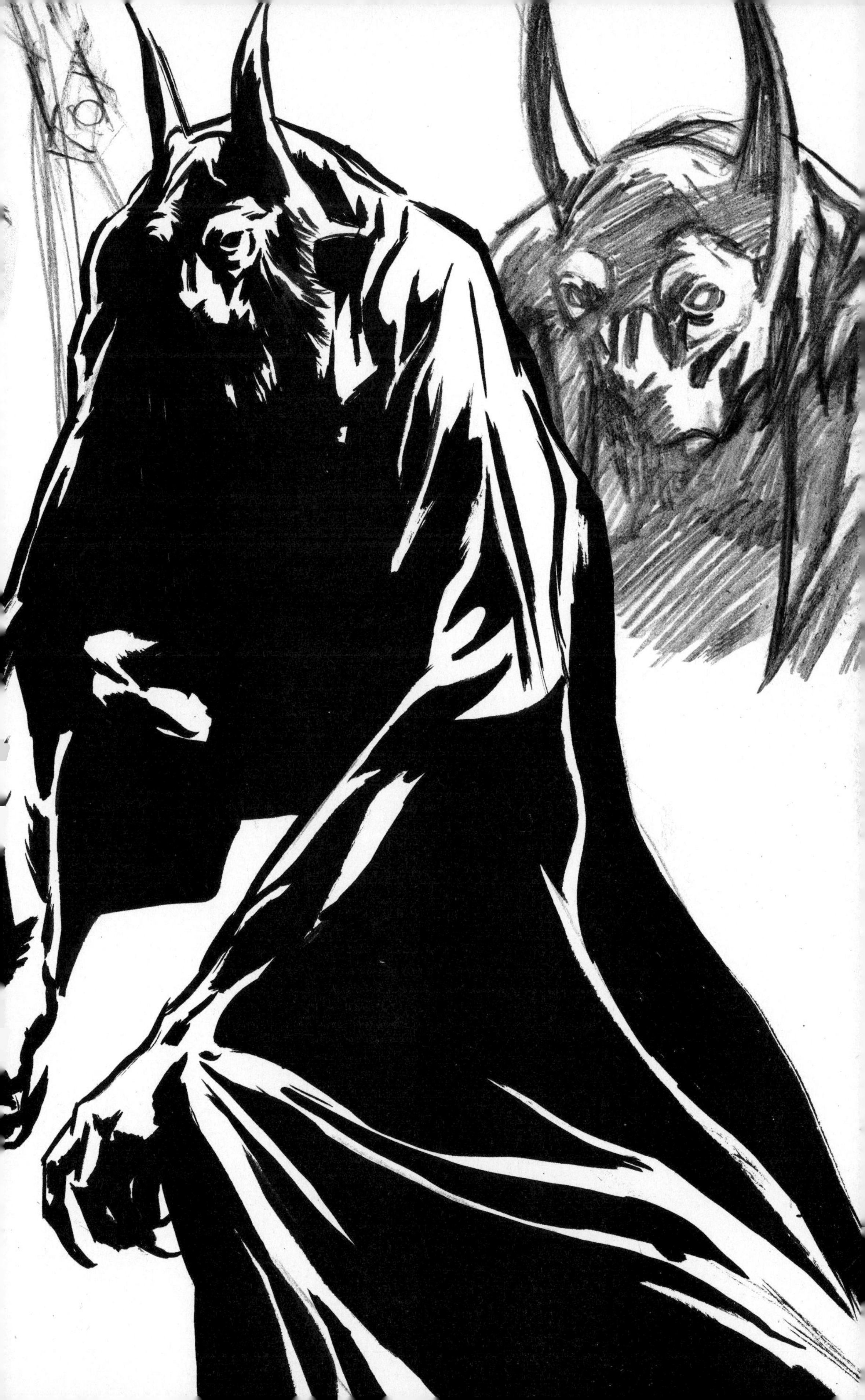

n the end, Bruce has gone from a traumatized child wishing the world could be forced into fairness to an adult making his own best efforts to improve things. Alfred would most likely have died by this point, leaving Bruce with a grave to stand over, to react to as an adult. And the police detective may be a captain by now (or even commissioner), and is still going to make use of whatever tools are available to him to do the job. He may not have Batman as a dark angel of vengeance, but he's got Bruce as a benefactor to the city.

A few general thoughts:

Bruce and his parents may be major benefactors to the local zoo, both to give Bruce a reason to hang around the bat exhibits and to make the distinction later in the series that animals in the zoo are taken care of like children, but adults take care of themselves.

I'm tempted to have the whole thing narrated by Alfred, up until he dies, whereupon Bruce finishes it off after reading Alfred's journals. That's partially because I've always liked the way most of Nevil Shute's novels are narrated by an older man who witnesses the drama but is at a remove from it, and partially because it allows us to see Bruce as traumatized and shallow and defensive from the outside as well as the inside. But it may be that won't work.

There will also be a revelation in #3 -- a false one -- that it was Bruce who caused the Wainwrights' death himself, as a means of letting Batman be born. Batman doesn't kill, but there's a third face to this obsession, the face of the Joker, who symbolizes the madness that makes Batman necessary. This would all be devastating to Bruce, and would be what drives him to disappear at the end of #3, but it's not true, it's Bruce's obsession warping his view of reality as a means of preserving itself.

Aside from that being a cool revelation and an emotional bombshell, it solves one of the problems of the series, which is that if there really is this creepy force out there doing good, why not just lock Bruce up somewhere and let him do it? Is Bruce's sanity more important than the lives of those who'll die without Batman? If Batman grows more warped over time as he fights to stay "alive," then yes, he's demonstrably dangerous. And it'll make for a nice emotional moment as Bruce stands up to Batman in #4, not letting his obsession control him any longer.

As you can see, this isn't all worked out yet, but the basics of it are there, at least.

🦇 🦇 🦇

Not all worked out at all! I didn't even have Robin yet!

And we changed quite a bit along the way–it was John Paul's suggestion that our Officer Gordon (who we wound up naming Gordon after all) not be the helpful ally I'd originally intended, which turned out to be a very fruitful decision that gave the story a lot more shadowy texture and intriguing tangles. And my original "Joker" plans fell by the wayside as the story got more nuanced and realistic, not quite so overtly symbolic. (Or at least, I think that's what happened; I no longer remember what I'd had in mind for that Joker reference, other than what's there in the pitch.)

I hope you like the result, and I have to give huge thanks to John Paul Leon, who not only immersed himself in this world–making the story dramatic, emotional, and utterly beautiful–but transformed it by asking the right questions and making great suggestions. (When I didn't know where to put the finale, for instance, he's the guy who said: "How about bringing it back full circle? End it at the zoo.") And to Joey Cavalieri, for starting it all up, Chris Conroy for seeing it through, Bob Wayne for asking me "Whatever happened to that Batman thing? Can we get that going again?", Todd Klein for masterful lettering and great design suggestions, and everyone at DC for being incredibly patient and believing in the book.

And all of you, too. Thanks very much for being here. It's been a pleasure telling our tale of wishes come

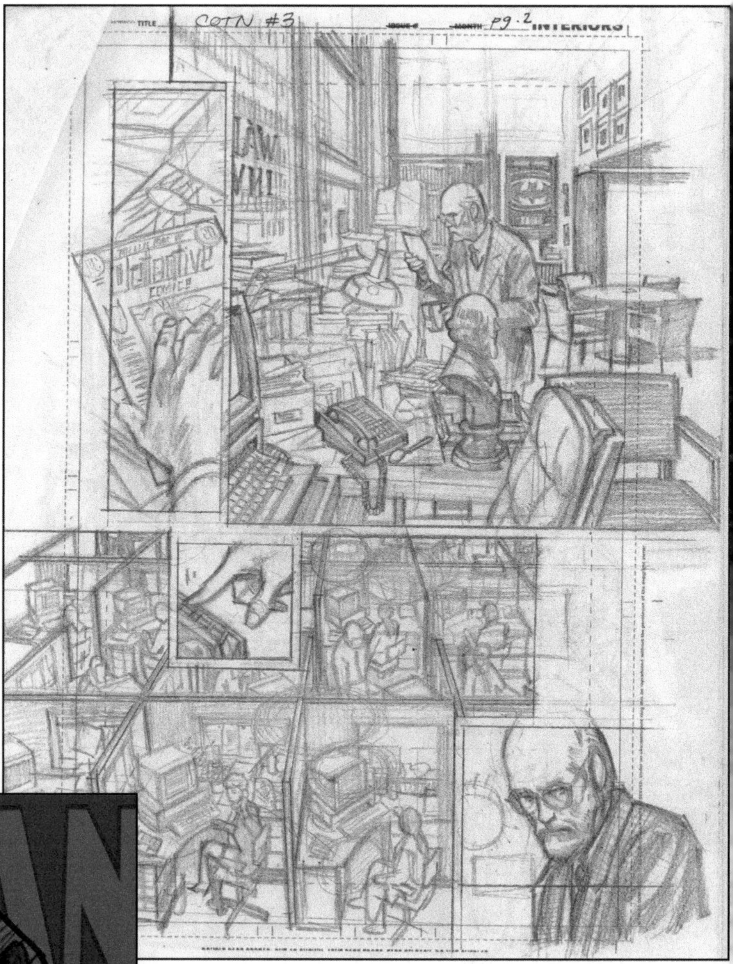
TITLE COTN #3
pg. 2
INTERIORS
Detective Comics

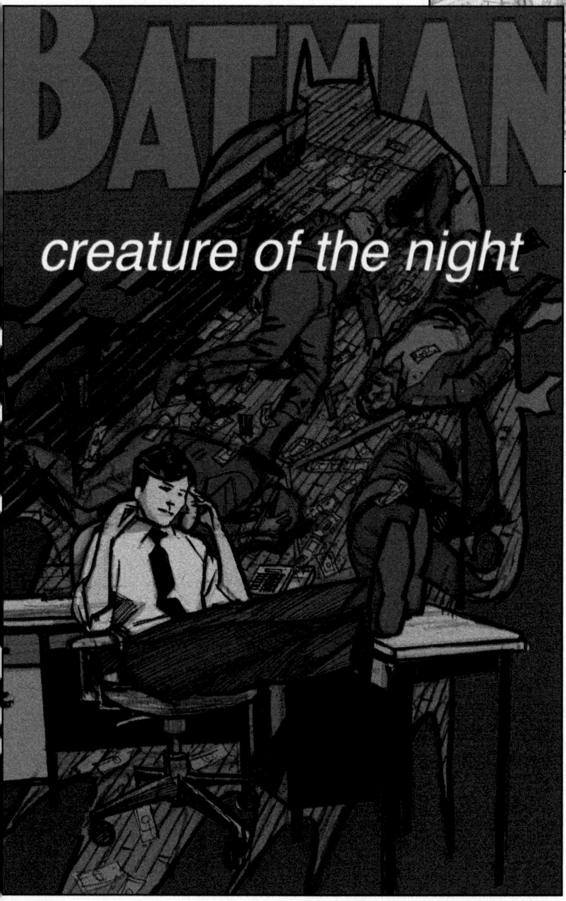
BATMAN
creature of the night

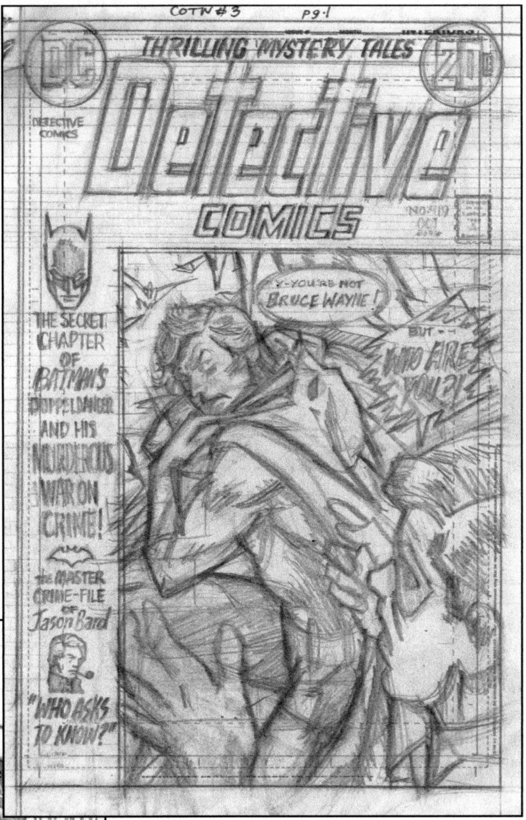
COTN #3
pg. 1
THRILLING MYSTERY TALES
DC
DETECTIVE COMICS
Detective
COMICS
Y-YOU'RE NOT BRUCE WAYNE!
BUT--
WHO ARE YOU?!
THE SECRET CHAPTER OF BATMAN'S DOPPELGANGER AND HIS MURDEROUS WAR ON CRIME!
the MASTER CRIME-FILE of Jason Bard
"WHO ASKS TO KNOW?"

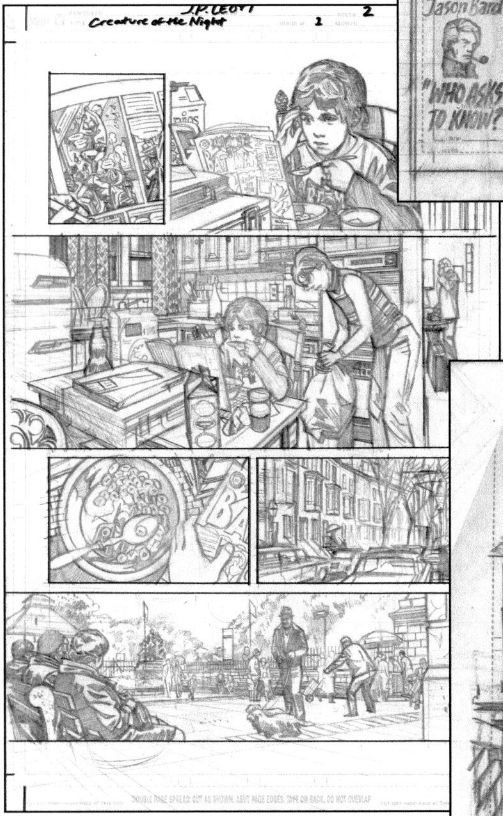
J.P. LEON
Creature of the Night
2
DOUBLE PAGE SPREAD: CUT AS SHOWN, ABUT PAGE EDGES, TAPE ON BACK, DO NOT OVERLAP

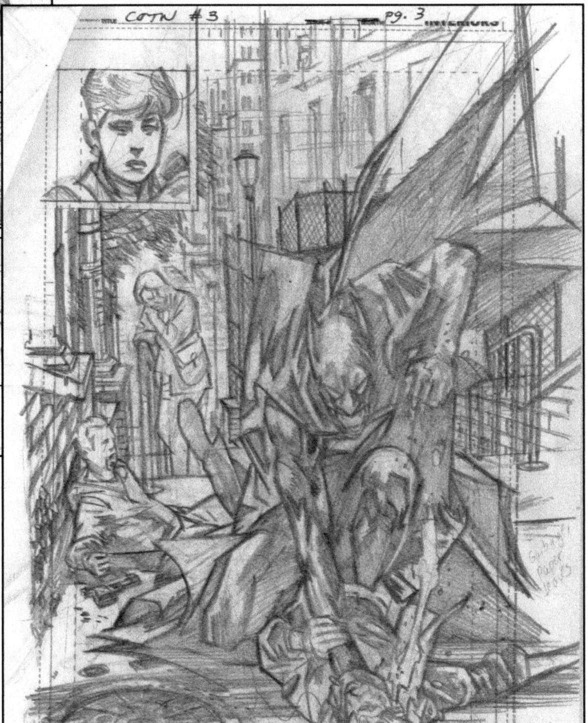
COTN #3
pg. 3

Batman: Creature of the Night pencils by **John Paul Leon**

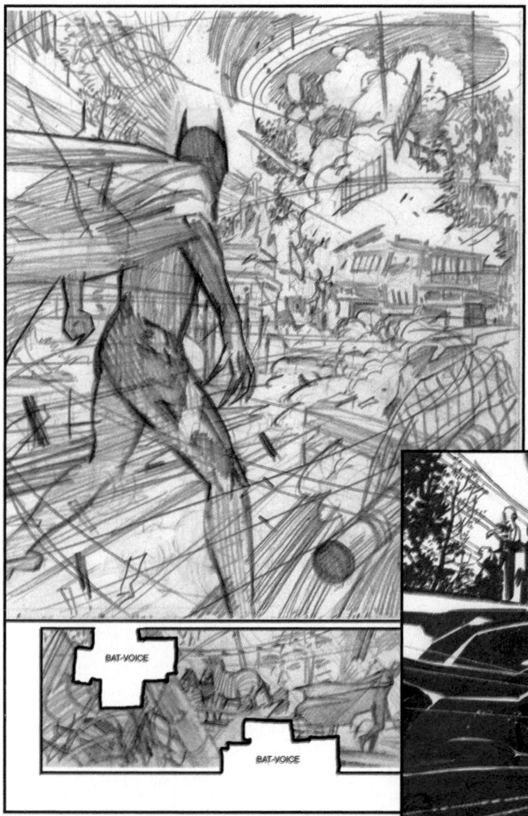
BAT-VOICE
BAT-VOICE

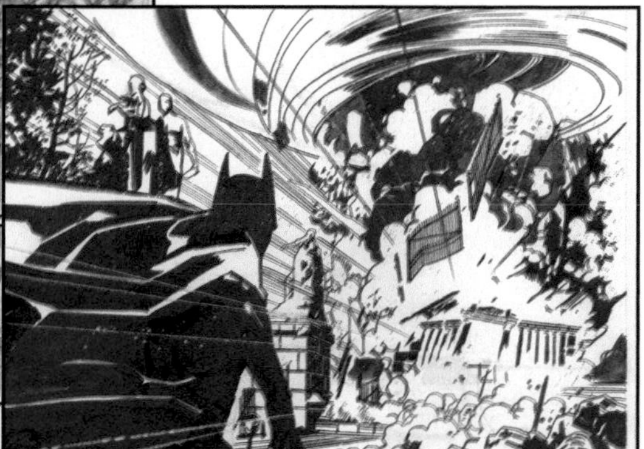

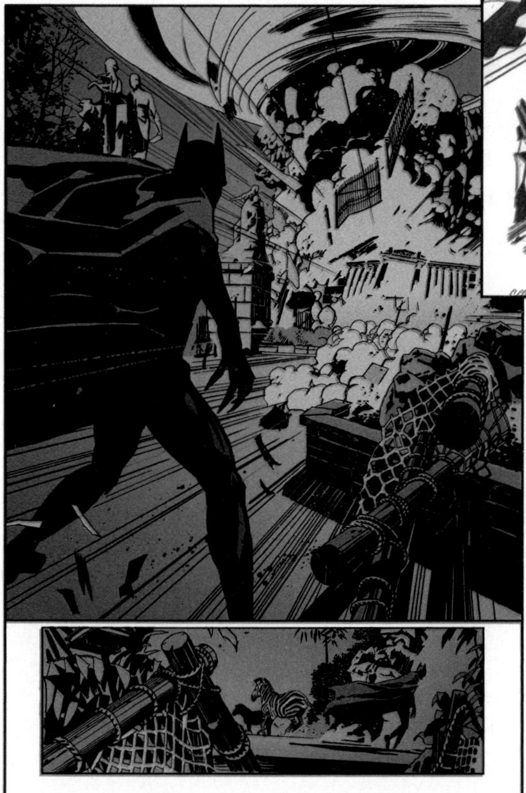

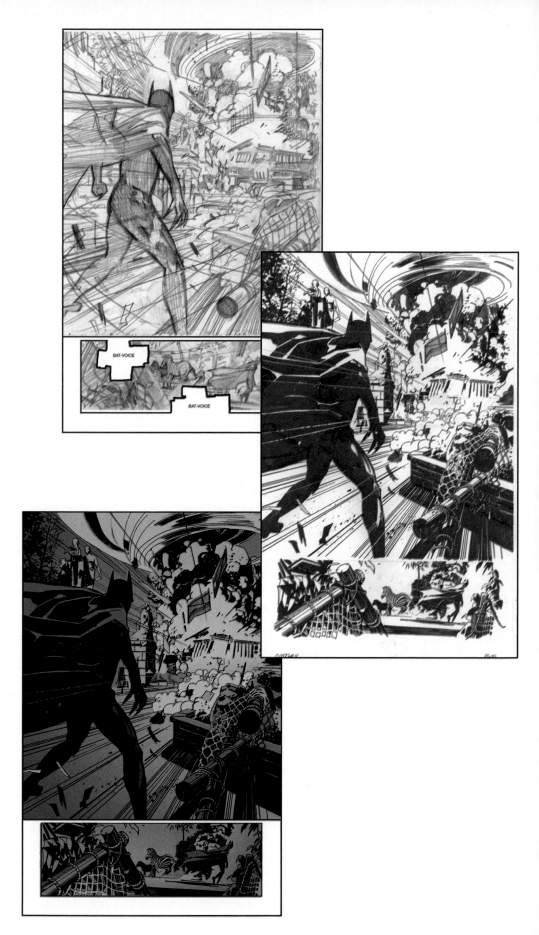

Batman: Creature of the Night #4 page 40 art progression by **John Paul Leon**

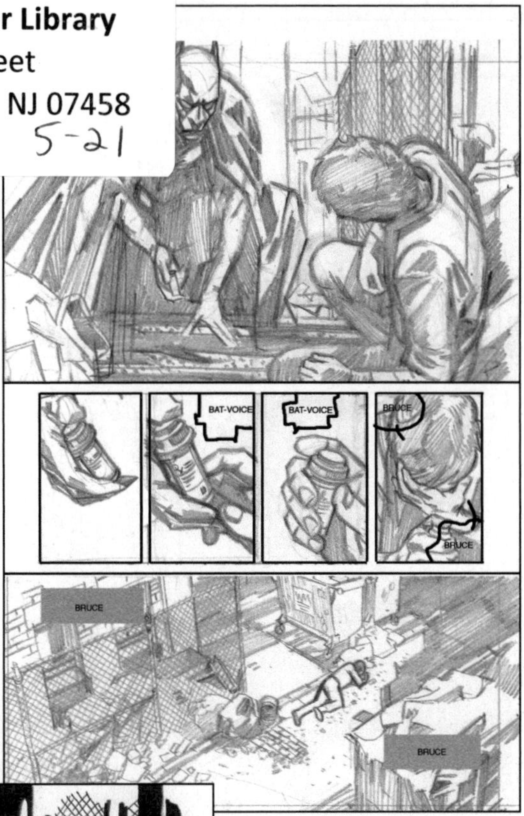
BAT-VOICE
BAT-VOICE
BRUCE
BRUCE
BRUCE
BRUCE

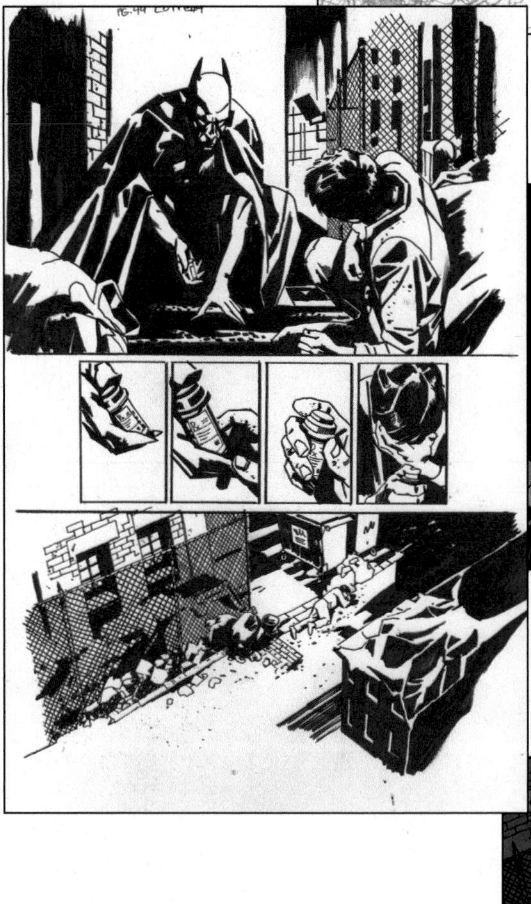

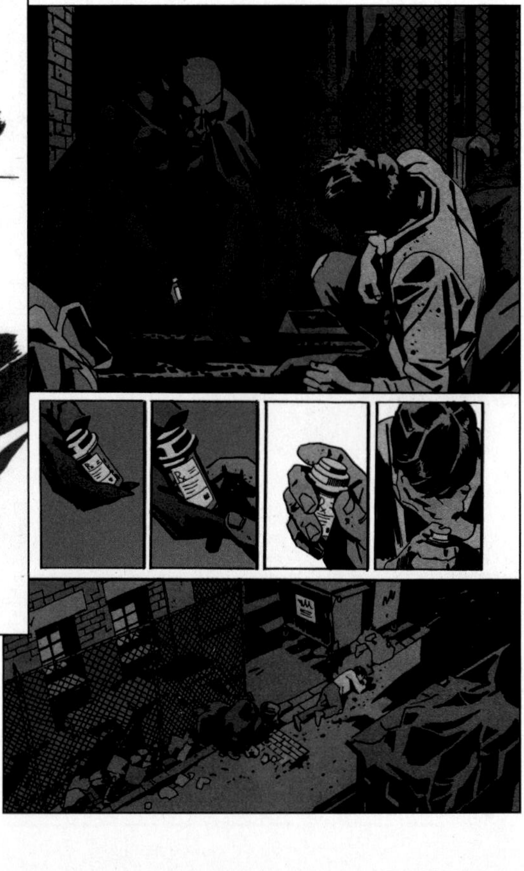

Batman: Creature of the Night **#4 page 49 art progression by John Paul Leon**